T0408903

THE COTTAGE
IN INTERWAR ENGLAND

ARCHITECTURAL HISTORY OF THE BRITISH ISLES

Series Editor: Dr Timothy Brittain-Catlin, University of Cambridge

British architectural history has a very prominent reputation internationally and sets the standard for publishing and for the development of new ideas and narratives in the field. Covering all periods of architectural history, the series consists of accessible and authoritative studies of specific periods, styles, architects and types of building, and provides fresh insights into fascinating subjects with perpetual appeal. The series is not comprehensive in terms of its selection, but offers the best scholarship in this field, reflecting the richness and quality of British architecture.

THE COTTAGE
IN INTERWAR ENGLAND

CLASS AND THE PICTURESQUE

George Entwistle

LUND
HUMPHRIES

First published in 2024 by Lund Humphries

Lund Humphries
Huckletree Shoreditch
Alphabeta Building
18 Finsbury Square
London EC2A 1AH
UK

www.lundhumphries.com

ISBN: 978-1-84822-698-2

A Cataloguing-in-Publication record for this book is available from the British Library.

Cover: *Metro-land* guidebook cover (1921), illustration by C.A. Wilkinson for the Metropolitan Railway, London Transport Museum. Photograph: © TFL from the London Transport Museum (2004/2504).

Copy edited by Pamela Bertram
Designed by Jacqui Cornish
Proofread by Patrick Cole
Cover design by Adrian Hunt
Set in Arnhem Pro and Quasimoda
Printed in Bosnia and Herzegovina

The publisher and the author gratefully acknowledge the generous support of the following organisations: Palma Pictures; Marc Fitch Fund; Scouloudi Foundation/Institute of Historical Research; The Voysey Society; Wates Group; and the Society of Architectural Historians of Great Britain.

This book is printed on sustainably sourced FSC paper

CONTENTS

INTRODUCTION

1   Card No. 19, 'Amberley, Sussex', Player's Cigarettes, *Picturesque Cottages* (1929)

I knew by the smoke that so gracefully curl'd
Above the green elms, that a cottage was near;
And I said, 'If there's peace to be found in the world,
A heart that was humble might hope for it here'.[1]

This book is about the cottage in England between the First and Second World Wars – what it looked like, what it meant, and the part it played in shaping domestic architecture. It was the focus of so much attention at the time that the novelist Evelyn Waugh would write in 1930 of a 'craze for cottages'.[2] Osbert Lancaster, the satirist, was of like mind: 'The Englishman's home need no longer be his castle, but it must at all costs (even when it is within

easy reach of the City) be his country cottage'.[3] Not everyone thought the craze a good thing. At a public meeting in 1938, the respected professor of architecture Albert Richardson expressed dismay in biblical terms: 'As a nation, we have sold our birthright for a mess of cottages!'[4]

So many homes were built between 1919 and 1939 – four million local authority and owner-occupied dwellings[5] – that the period's domestic architecture today comprises large tracts of the suburban English landscape. It was an era of dramatic change. In a letter to *The Times* published on 1 July 1919, Henry Hare, outgoing President of the Royal Institute of British Architects (RIBA), foresaw 'The face of the country from Land's End to John O'Groats . . . permanently stamped with the impress of the present age'.[6] Karl Silex, the London correspondent for the German newspaper *Deutsche Allgemeine Zeitung* in the 1920s, called house building the 'only great achievement of the English people since the War'.[7]

Observations like these explain why the period's home building has been of such interest to historians. Their studies come, for the most part, in three categories – the genesis of state-funded council housing (Burnett, Merrett, Swenarton, Ravetz, Boughton); the visual culture of private sector suburbia (Oliver, Davis and Bentley, Edwards, Stamp, Sugg Ryan); and the arrival and influence of modernism (F.R.S. Yorke, Gibberd and Pevsner from the 1930s, Powers, Benton, Darling). This book foregrounds instead the idea of the cottage – as an architectural and social concept; as a problematic continuity with class and cultural dimensions; and

GEORGE **REED** & SONS LTD

BUILDERS & ESTATE DEVELOPERS
ESTATES AT
WINCHMORE HILL,
ENFIELD WEST & SOUTHGATE

2   Brochure from the North London builder George Reed & Sons Ltd, 1930s,
Museum of Domestic Design and Architecture, Middlesex University

3 Today, the idea of the cottage has found a kind of equilibrium, denoting 'a better, safer, quieter life'. The Old Bakery tea-room, Branscombe, Devon (National Trust)

in its relationship with the aesthetic theory and tradition of the Picturesque, which shaped domestic architecture in England long after its inception in the late eighteenth century.

Today, the idea of the cottage has found a kind of equilibrium, denoting 'a better, safer, quieter life away from the city' (fig.3).[8] Between the wars, things were more complicated. Analysis by the *Oxford English Dictionary* shows the word itself in much wider circulation then than now. At a frequency of 14.5 instances per million printed words, between 1920 and 1930, 'cottage' cropped up, on average,

more than twice as often as it does today.[9] This was in part because the government was planning, from 1916–17, to build hundreds of thousands of 'cottages' – their word – for the nation's poorly housed working classes. Prime Minister Lloyd George's manifesto for the 1918 General Election pledged 'to acquire land . . . for men who have served in the war . . . for cottages with gardens, allotments or smallholdings'.[10] It was an ambitious scheme; and it revitalised one identity the cottage had embodied throughout the nineteenth century – an ideologically loaded domestic architectural type at the heart of housing debate.

Interwar cottages were important not only to politicians, planners, and working-class council tenants. They were of interest to other members of the middle and upper classes too – those wanting to acquire them as weekend retreats; those campaigning to protect and preserve them; and those seeking to buy a new suburban home with aesthetics that were 'not so much a style as an idiom . . . borrowed from many previous centuries to produce the general effect of a country cottage'.[11]

What people meant when they used the term is pivotal. In 1922, Arthur Wakerley, the Liberal Party chairman of the council housing committee in Leicester, one of many English cities wrestling with overcrowding and slum dwelling after the war, described the 'generally conceived idea [of] successful cottage design' with reference to a best-selling Victorian illustrator – 'small panes, a touch of the gamekeeper's lodge, with a dash or flavour of Miss Greenaway's drawings'.[12] Charged with the creation of new social housing for his city, here was a man entranced by picturesqueness. Yet Wakerley's was a broadly shared vision of how the ideal cottage was supposed to look. It stemmed from the deep-rooted influence of the Picturesque – an English aesthetic philosophy, in circulation since it was set out in the late eighteenth century, that would inflect domestic architecture for close to 150 years.

5   Card No. 7, 'Winterbourne Stickland, Dorset', Player's Cigarettes, *Picturesque Cottages* (1929)

Few historians today contest its significance. Rosemary Hill calls the Picturesque 'the single most important theme in English architecture until modernism'.[13] Even modernists would dream of ways it might be made to serve them. But its impact between the Victorian Gothic Revival and the 1930s was more lasting than is sometimes supposed – particularly so its influence, positive and negative, in shaping the story of interwar domestic architecture.

In 1796, one of the first theorists of the Picturesque had written:

> A cottage of a quiet colour, half-concealed among trees . . . is one of the most tranquil and soothing of all rural objects; and when the sun strikes upon it, and discovers a number of lively picturesque circumstances, one of the most cheerful.[14]

4   Card No. 25, 'Ombersley, Worcestershire', Player's Cigarettes, *Picturesque Cottages* (1929). The text on the reverse describes the cottage as 'the type of Elizabethan cottage . . . so extensively copied by the modern builder'

An interpretation also advanced by the historian John Macarthur and the theorist Lars Spuybroek,[15] this identification of the cottage as a key manifestation of the Picturesque illustrates a connection between the two that was just as strong – and even more controversial – between 1910 and 1939.

The government's plan to build hundreds of thousands of cottages for the nation's ill-housed working classes broke down in 1921–22 amid public recriminations over the aesthetic character such dwellings were supposed to have and whether the state could afford to build them. When it came to council estates, the upshot was a determination in Whitehall that the visuality of picturesque cottages was too expensive for the public purse. The collapse of England's first state-funded social housing programme came, then, just as the interwar period's great private housing boom began. And the aesthetic that emerged as predominant for house builders and mortgage-holders – summed up by Christopher Hussey in 1927 with his memorable image, the 'terra-cotta dragon on the gable'[16] – was none other than the Picturesque. Private homebuyers' aesthetic preferences, it transpired, were part of an historical continuum, congruent with the model cottages described in many of the Picturesque's early nineteenth-century pattern books. As Terence Conran puts it: 'Many detached and semi-detached houses built between the wars pretend to be cottages'.[17]

The image of the cottage picturesque was everywhere in those days – from Mrs Evershed's Embroidered Cottage Tea Cosy (£2 10s), to jigsaw puzzles, postcards, and biscuit tins.[18] One architect talked in 1918 of 'the attraction of the Picturesque' as 'nearly universal amongst the general public'.[19] No wonder Player's Cigarettes, in 1929, chose *Picturesque Cottages* for one of their new sets of cards – 25 in total, each printed on the front with a colour illustration of a traditional English cottage; on the reverse with texts drawing appreciatively on the poetry of the Picturesque. In a country which smoked over 45.5 million cigarettes that year, emotive imagery linking the two ideas at the heart

6 Card No. 5, 'Marnhull, Dorset', Player's Cigarettes, *Picturesque Cottages* (1929). According to the text on the reverse, 'Thomas Hardy is said to have chosen this cottage for the home of Tess, the heroine of his novel *Tess of the d'Urbervilles*'

of this book found itself in hundreds of thousands of pockets, reflecting the extraordinary affection in which this time-honoured vision of home was held.

In the 1920s, however, cottage picturesque also started to function architecturally as a class shibboleth. Its visuality was celebrated across popular culture, but – when it came to people's homes – was effectively off-limits to most council tenants after 1922 while purchased in millions by the private-sector mortgage-holder from 1923. Here are to be found the beginnings of what Lynsey Hanley today describes as building 'class . . . into our landscape in the form of housing';[20] what government housing supremo Raymond Unwin warned against in 1918 when he called for small

7   Plan No. 2, non-parlour Class A cottage – one of the designs recommended in the Local Government Board *Manual*, April 1919, Museum of Domestic Design and Architecture, Middlesex University. Modelled in clay for the 'Model Homes Exhibition', May 1919

8   Mrs Asquith outside her 'country retreat' at Sutton Courtenay, Berkshire, *The Ideal Home*, vol.2, no.6, December 1920, p.202, The Bodleian Libraries, University of Oxford

No. 2.   CLASS A—URBAN—SOUTHERLY ASPECT.

council dwellings attractive enough to 'afford no justification, by their lack of comeliness, for the well-to-do to live out of sight of them'.[21]

Professional architectural discourse in the years before and after the First World War dealt in the Picturesque to a greater degree than is often acknowledged. A range of the period's most influential voices – Charles Reilly, the militantly pro-classical Professor of Architecture at Liverpool University;[22] the art historian Geoffrey Scott in his celebrated 1914 book *The Architecture of Humanism*; Royal Institute of British Architects grandee Reginald Blomfield;[23] vorticist provocateur Wyndham Lewis;[24] even the Arts and Crafts hierarch

11

9 Reginald Grenville Eves, *Stanley Baldwin*, c.1933, oil on canvas, 781 × 660 mm, National Portrait Gallery, London. Baldwin was Conservative Prime Minister three times between 1923 and 1937

W.R. Lethaby[25] – wanted to purge the Picturesque from the nation's domestic architectural repertoire. Most of them argued at first for a 'return' to the discipline of what Scott called formal architecture – restrained, rules-based, classically inspired. After 1925, some shifted their advocacy from neo-Georgian to modernism. But these two styles were linked by an elite professional mindset that abjured the Picturesque and favoured an epistocratic interpretation of the role of architects over any real appetite to cater for the tastes of the public.

The cottage made a journey of its own over the same period. Council cottages built after 1922 rarely came close to resembling the image of home captured on the Player's cigarette cards. They started being referred to as 'council houses' – a term not generally used with this meaning prior to 1920. The reality of the cottage, meanwhile, was appropriated by tribes in the middle and upper classes: those who sought to elevate the dwelling to the status of heritage asset within a national picturesque; those who longed to acquire picturesque cottages for exclusive weekend boltholes; and the Conservative politicians who recognised the cottage as a rhetorical emblem of tradition and stability, useful in helping tranquillise a divided nation after the General Strike of 1926. As effectively as the state denied picturesque social housing to largely working-class council tenants after the early 1920s, the working classes saw their historical title to the *cottage idea* challenged too.

'You may attempt to explain these twenty years,' Stanley Baldwin told a rally at the Royal Albert Hall in May 1937, 'in terms of economics or in terms of politics; some see only the one, some see only the other.'[26] The interwar period certainly witnessed 'a particularly exciting and intense form' – in Alison Light's words – of the 'dialectic between old and new . . . holding on and letting go'.[27] Cultural historian Stuart Sillars calls for a recognition that English society after 1918 was traumatised by a 'massive collective bereavement', the horror of whose human losses forged a space in which 'ideas and ideals of English identity [were] repeatedly addressed and reconstructed'.[28] But the novelist D.H. Lawrence presaged Light's idea of 'holding on' in architectural terms: 'The Englishman,' he wrote in 1929, 'still likes to think of himself as a "cottager"'.[29] Implicit in that intuition was a third factor for Prime Minister Baldwin to consider – one he made a career of obfuscating – the 'continuing centrality of class in British history'.[30]

Immediately after the First World War, the link between class and housing was explicit in public conversation. In the 1920 first edition of a new magazine, *The Ideal Home*, the editor set out his manifesto in wholly class-conscious terms:

> The Government and Local Authorities . . . in every case . . . are only dealing with what might be termed 'Working or Artisan class houses'. The policy of *The Ideal Home* is to cater for the wide circle of the middle class . . .[31]

This casual employment of the language of class distinction was prefigured by decades of housing legislation that reflected and actuated public understanding of socio-economic differences. Between 1851 and 1867, housing acts focused on the 'Labouring Classes' or 'Artisans'. After the Royal Commission on Housing, 1884–85, a turn in statutory language informed the Housing of the Working Classes Acts, 1885 and 1890.[32] Thus the law made class a government tool and an agent in people's understanding of themselves. Charged with building postwar council cottages, Minister of Reconstruction Christopher Addison asked one of his committees whether a precise class definition could be attempted. Reporting in October 1918, they concluded none of '(a) occupation, (b) income, (c) rent; or (d) type of house' was good enough to pin down the working classes. It would, therefore, be 'undesirable to have a general statutory definition'.[33] This left Addison legislating to provide new housing for a class of people without official guidance as to who they actually were.

One of the period's pre-eminent theorists of social organisation, Leonard Trelawny Hobhouse, referred throughout the 1920s to 'class' and 'classes' as if they were generally understood.[34] Though many agreed, interwar statisticians Carr-Saunders and Caradog Jones were prepared to define only the working class: 'characterized by . . . a greater degree of uncertainty about future employment than faces other members of the community'.[35] Hobhouse's student and, later, colleague Morris Ginsberg, Professor of Sociology at University College London after 1929, articulated the general understanding – a 'working class . . . who depend exclusively on the sale of their labour for their living'; an 'upper class', which maintained 'a relatively high standard of life, largely on incomes from accumulated wealth'; and a 'middle class', which comprised 'numerous marginal groups whose classification is doubtful'.[36] Cannadine calls this the 'triadic' model.[37] Ginsberg's contemporary, the Christian socialist academic R.H. Tawney, glossed it as 'a system of social groups with varying standards of expenditure and habits of life'.[38] The Communist Party-affiliated thinker Allen Hutt, writing in 1933, was prepared to quantify the three tiers: the middle class at 15 per cent of the population; the 'capitalist class' at 5 per cent; the working class at 80 per cent.[39]

THE VICTIM.

10   Leonard Raven-Hill, 'The Victim', *Punch*, vol.156, 12 February 1919, p.115, Punch Cartoon Library/TopFoto

Versions of the triad underpinned housing commentary in the period's newspapers and specialist architectural press. Faced with the cottages promised to the working classes, a 1919 *Daily Mirror* article cried: 'We are filled with envy, we of the Middle Class!'[40] Weeks later, *Punch* magazine's cartoonist Leonard Raven-Hill contrived a revealing amalgam of the working/middle/upper and Marxian class models (fig.10), in which Labour resorted to fisticuffs with Capital. The 'victim' of their class struggle was the 'long-suffering public'.[41]

Something similar, theoretically, was floated by the right-wing Conservative MP for Finchley John Pretyman Newman – co-founder, in 1919, of the Middle Class Union, one of whose main grievances was government willingness to fund dwellings for the working but not the middle classes. Pretyman Newman saw the people he represented squeezed between 'organised Labour and federated Capital, standing in ordered ranks on his right hand and on his left'.[42]

After Rex and Moore in 1967, most sociologists would acknowledge the vital connection between class and habitation: 'there is a class struggle over the use of houses and . . . this class struggle is the central process of the city as a social unit'.[43] More recent thinking, influenced by the French sociologist Pierre Bourdieu, expands on this: 'One's residence is a crucial, possibly *the* crucial identifier of who you are'.[44] These approaches direct us towards a theoretical framework that redefines social mobility, implies agency for the location and aesthetics of domestic architecture, and endues architects with moral responsibility in creating them. Charles Voysey understood this in 1919: 'All classes of the community are blessed with the same emotions and moral feelings . . . we have no right to assume a want of taste or feeling when providing homes for the relatively poor. Beauty is essential to all'.[45]

In the re-ordered domestic architectural landscape that resulted both from local authority building and explosive growth in private sector provision between the wars, where one lived and what it looked like were crucial determinants of England's new class settlement. The meaning of

11   Card No. 24, 'West Tarring, Sussex', Player's Cigarettes, *Picturesque Cottages* (1929)

that for cottages – 'there is something lovable about that term'[46] – was the subject of social contest across the period. Were they individualistic and picturesque or could they be reimagined as tidy formal expressions of civic order? Was Midge Carne, the teenage heiress to Maythorpe Hall in Holtby's 1936 *South Riding*, right when she said cottages were for 'poor people' – or were they for weekenders too?[47] Was their protection a primary concern as a preservation spectacle in the picturesque landscape or were they places the agricultural poor should continue to live? And how did it change things that the Conservative government, after the General Strike, embraced cottage picturesque mythology to help persuade the English to reject class antagonisms and return to the quietude of a largely imaginary past?

'Cottage' in the 1920s was the sort of word for which Raymond Williams sees 'the problems of its meanings . . . inextricably bound up with the problems it [is] being used to discuss'.[48] Its history in culture, language, class formation, the built environment – and its visuality – made it a dynamic concept, infiltrating aesthetic, moral, social, and mythological content into every aspect of its place in argument or landscape. Karen Sayer, in her study of the meaning of the rural cottage,[49] and Daniel Maudlin in *The Idea of the Cottage in English Architecture, 1760–1860*, interpret the word with similar force. Anthony King's *The Bungalow* recognises building type as a vector for the social and economic forces inevitably sublimated in domestic architecture.

This book uses 'sources which illuminate everyday practices as well as emphasising the effect on everyday life of changes in fundamental concepts'[50] to assess how competing factions – the architects and builders who fêted it, and those who sought to purge its romantic influence – made cottage-picturesque visuality an essential factor in shaping the aesthetics of the interwar dwelling. The building type visualised so colourfully by Player's Cigarettes in 1929 is used here as a tool to investigate how the rise and fall of the radical social-housing policy of 1919–21, class and political contests over cottage meaning in the 1920s, and the emergence of a mass-market of privately built single-family homes after 1923, were all shaped simultaneously by the same deep continuities in English domestic architectural history and its class significations. Between the wars, who was permitted the aesthetics of the cottage picturesque, who was not – and why – are questions that reward closer examination.

1

THE COTTAGE PICTURESQUE

Between 1915 and 1917, the British government recognised that it was facing a housing crisis that war had made unignorable. Its solution was to build exchequer-funded 'cottages' for the nation's poorly housed working classes – a policy that reinvigorated the term's standing as something more than a neutral denotation for a certain size or type of dwelling. In the world of interwar housing, 'cottage' would function as a concept laden with social and political content.[1] This chapter aims to explore how cottages and the way they looked became so deeply acculturated as aesthetic, political, and class phenomena – and what that meant when they were affirmed at the heart of state housing policy from 1918.

In 1885, the Royal Commission on the Housing of the Working Classes had found 'the evils of overcrowding, especially in London, [were] still a public scandal, and [were] becoming in certain localities more serious than they ever were'.[2] Housing and planning acts between 1890 and 1909 brought scant improvement: 'thirty years have passed and . . . comparatively little has been done', complained a 1919 editorial in *The Times*.[3] Dismay about the standards of much working-class housing expressed by the Liberal MP for Cleveland, President of the Local Government Board Herbert Samuel, speaking in the House of Commons in 1914, was widely shared:

> If only the whole of our population were housed in such conditions as already happily prevail in the Garden City at Letchworth . . . the Garden Suburbs at Hampstead, Bournville, Port Sunlight . . . [4]

A few months later, the First World War began, and the optimism of the Edwardian garden city and garden suburb builders, whose work Samuel had publicly admired, seemed a long way away.

Competing demands for labour and materials during the war brought house building in Britain to a near-standstill. In Birmingham, figures for dwellings completed fell from 1,785 in 1910 to 341 in 1917, a decline of over 80 per cent.[5] The National Housing and Town Planning Conference in April 1915 expressed fears that 'at the close of the War all the worst features of a house famine would exist'.[6] By 1917, reports from the *Commission of Enquiry into Industrial Unrest* concluded that shortages of acceptable housing had been one of the main causes of working-class discontent and industrial agitation from 1916 onwards.[7]

By October 1917, the housing situation had deteriorated further, now an 'Emergency Problem' in the words of the Ministry of Reconstruction's Advisory Housing Panel[8] – a committee chaired by the fourth Marquess of Salisbury, son of the Victorian Prime Minister, and a past-President of the Garden Cities and Town Planning Association.[9] Other panel members included the Fabian leader Beatrice Webb and the sociologist Seebohm Rowntree. Raymond Unwin, Chief Inspector of Planning for the Local Government Board (LGB),[10] who had been seconded to the Ministry of Munitions in 1915, acted as adviser.

Unwin was an architect and planner who had helped design a housing estate for Rowntree's father at New Earswick outside York in 1902; he did

12 'A pair of cottages: to be built in Norfolk after the war', designed by George Skipper, FRIBA, *The Builder*, vol.114, no.3931, 7 June 1918, p.346 (vii), The Bodleian Libraries, University of Oxford

much of the panel's underlying research. But his colleagues also relied on the 1911 Census, which showed over three million people living at two or more to the room; and a 1912 estimate that rural districts were short of 120,000 dwellings.[11] The conclusion was that England and Wales would need 300,000 new dwellings by the end of 1917, with an additional 75,000 per annum for every further year of war. The panel's final memorandum laid the foundations for the 1919 Housing Act by recommending that the state, via local authorities, should take financial responsibility for building new homes for the working classes. In the initiative that has become known as the Addison Scheme, the 1919 Act would put into statute a central government

13 Cottages in the Rowntree-funded garden suburb at New Earswick, near York, illustration 3 in Richard Reiss, *The Home I Want* (London: Hodder & Stoughton, 1919), The Bodleian Libraries, University of Oxford

commitment to meet the costs (above the proceeds of one penny from the local rates) of 500,000 cottages – a number that LGB President William Hayes Fisher quoted to a deputation of MPs in August 1918.[12] Local authorities across England and Wales would be placed under statutory obligation to build. It was the country's most ambitious social housing scheme to date.

Government plans were theoretically under the direction, in 1917, of the Local Government Board, whose then-new President Hayes Fisher was *laissez faire* by instinct and keen not to disincentivise house building by the private sector. Waiting in the wings, though, was Dr Christopher Addison, a Liberal MP, confidant of Lloyd George, and Minister of Reconstruction after July 1917. Addison was a medic by training. Appointed to the Chair of Anatomy at Sheffield Medical School as a 28-year-old in 1897, he moved later to Charing Cross Hospital in London, where he developed 'a lifelong concern with health and social deprivation in London's East End'.[13]

His brief as wartime Reconstruction supremo allowed him to intervene in the work of other departments whenever necessary;[14] and he was not impressed by Hayes Fisher, noting in his diary after an early meeting: 'It is pitiful after . . . Rhondda [a Hayes Fisher predecessor] to have a man with his parochial attitude at the LGB'.[15] Addison was convinced that only large-scale state intervention could fix the housing problems he had witnessed.

Work with Salisbury's housing panel helped lay the ground. In August 1917, two months before they submitted their final report, Salisbury's committee produced a private paper – 'Answers to the Questions Submitted by Dr Addison to the Housing Panel' – that addressed issues such as whether housing provision should be made the statutory duty of local authorities; and whether any state assistance might be given to the private builder to encourage them to take part in the forthcoming housing scheme. At the top of the list of questions that Addison submitted was one that goes to the heart of this book: 'What steps,' he asked, 'should be taken to settle design?'[16]

Addison would have known that Hayes Fisher, the previous month, had asked Sir John Tudor

14 Christopher Addison MP, President of the Local Government Board (1919), then the UK's first Minister for Health (1919–21), photographed by Walter Stoneman (1917), National Portait Gallery, London

Walters (supported by Addison's *de facto* adviser Unwin) to lead a committee considering new standards for home planning, room sizes, number of bedrooms, provision of bathrooms, and site layout. So, Addison's question to Salisbury must have been intended at least in part to address the question of what Britain's hundreds of thousands of new state-aided dwellings were going to look like. To furnish an answer, the panel suggested a familiar architectural expedient:

if a competition, open to all recognised architects, were held, and the plans sent in were judged by assessors of high repute, the selected plans would be regarded generally as representing the best available ideas in cottage building.[17]

Architectural competitions were an established part of Victorian and Edwardian culture: Roberts records a Royal Agricultural Society cottage competition in 1849;[18] the Garden City at Letchworth was the setting for a high-profile Cheap Cottage Exhibition in 1905; contests were a feature of the early *Daily Mail* Ideal Home Exhibitions from 1908 onwards; and other publications – *The Spectator* in 1913 was one – joined in. But the National Cottage Competition in 1917–18, organised in response to Salisbury's committee, was potentially the most significant to date.

THE IDEA OF THE COTTAGE AFTER THE FIRST WORLD WAR

That the government was searching, as the First World War came to an end, for 'the best available ideas in cottage building' emphasises the paradox at the heart of their otherwise radical commitment to state-funded working-class housing. The project started out yoked rhetorically to an antique architectural type. But this was no eccentricity: practically every architect or commentator at the time used the term 'cottage' when discussing working-class dwellings. Marriner records it as 'normal practice . . . to refer to all working-class houses as "cottages"'.[19] Most of the period's key government documents did so: a 1913 Board of Agriculture report distinguished in plain class terms between smallholders' houses and rural labourers' cottages;[20] the seminal Tudor Walters Report (1918) declared 'the two-storey cottage is the type which should generally be adopted';[21] as did the LGB *Manual* of Spring 1919.[22] Even the Garden City guru Ebenezer Howard, in a March 1919 letter to *The Times*, distinguished 'good cottages' for the workers from 'houses of a larger type'.[23] The Ministry of Health's advice magazine, *Housing* – distributed every two weeks to local authorities from July 1919 – observed the same distinction. There, government architect Manning Robertson

would write: 'It is impossible to overestimate the tremendous importance of cottage architecture. It permeates the whole country, it affects every individual, and is the basis of social life, health and development'.[24]

Yet to use the word 'cottage' in connection with dwellings in England after the First World War was to invoke an artefact with roots deep in the English national imagination. Sydney Jones's 1912 book *The Village Homes of England* showed how deep. Cottages were nothing less than

> records of lives well spent; [telling] of contented possession, of love of home, and country and memory . . . ideas of order, of security and comfort, that result from the observance of long-established custom and usage; they bear witness to well settled beliefs transmitted from father to son.[25]

The Arts and Crafts architect Baillie Scott credited the dwelling with qualities almost magical: 'The cottage should be the dream come true . . . should have a soul of its own. The art . . . should be so intimate to the structure that, without it, it would not exist at all'.[26] Giving rise to what some in England called the cottage style (translated in Germany as *der 'Cottage' Stil*; celebrated in Belgium from 1903–5 by the journal *Le Cottage*), the word's numerous shades of meaning and interpretation had a normative impact on every discourse it was used to facilitate.[27] By 1919, when the British government legislated to build cottages for its ill-housed working classes, the concept was already overdetermined – as Sayer describes the rural cottage: a 'contested sign built on the shifting sands of nostalgia, time, sex, sexuality, gender, class and race'.[28]

Debate about the accommodation required of a labourer's dwelling had been underway since at least 1775 when Nathaniel Kent questioned the need for separate boys' and girls' bedrooms in the model cottage, on the grounds that boys would leave home early to work on farms.[29] A paper given to the RIBA in 1850 by Henry Roberts, architect to the Society for Improving the Condition of the Labouring Classes, disagreed: 'the principle of separating the sexes' was, he said, 'essential to morality and decency'.[30] No fewer than three bedrooms were required. He also stipulated that labourers' dwellings be 'dry and well-ventilated', with minimum room sizes. The government legislated in 1861 to ensure that landowners proposing to build or improve cottages on their estates met these standards, specifying construction 'in a substantial and proper Manner', with cottages 'properly and sufficiently supplied with Windows and Chimneys, and properly and sufficiently ventilated and drained'.[31] But the regulations had nothing to say about overcrowding. And the Royal Commission on the Housing of the Working Classes heard evidence in 1884 concerning the moral danger of parents and children sharing the same bedroom: 'the one-room system always leads . . . to the one-bed system'.[32]

Unwin's pamphlet for the Fabians, *Cottage Plans and Common Sense* (published in 1902; reprinted in 1908 and 1919), was the twentieth century's best early attempt at cottage plan codification – discussing, alongside plans with three bedrooms and an upstairs bathroom, the need for sunlight, low-density suburban estate layout (six dwellings per acre), and the virtues of a larger living room in preference to the seldom-used parlour (an early rejection, incidentally, of working-class preferences).[33] William Alexander Harvey (the main architect on the Cadbury estate at Bournville) and Raymond Unwin (with his partner Barry Parker) published designs for this 'most economical form of cottage' in the Garden City Association's journal in June 1906 – plain, rectangular dwellings, with three first floor bedrooms, and baths provided downstairs in the scullery. Yet even in cottages 'designed primarily for economy', one of Parker and Unwin's designs included decorative gables on front and rear elevations; another, a two-storey canted bay on the gable end.[34] The plans and elevations supplied with the Board of Agriculture's 1913 *Report as to Buildings for Smallholdings*, to which Raymond Unwin again contributed, featured designs still more austere.[35]

Having proposed a cottage architecture competition to Hayes Fisher's Local Government

15 Raymond Unwin, photographed by Bassano Ltd (1932), National Portrait Gallery, London. Unwin was one of the two most senior architects at the Local Government Board (which became the Ministry of Health) during the Addison Scheme and is thought to have done much of the research and writing for the Tudor Walters Report in 1918

Board, Lord Salisbury's Advisory Housing Panel completed its wider memorandum prior to the competition's launch in November 1917. Their final draft stated: 'we are convinced that it would be a policy . . . criminal in its effects on posterity . . . to accept in future the accretion to our great towns of mean street on mean street'.[36] And the coalition's 1918 manifesto duly included the commitment to build state-funded cottages for returning servicemen and their families – 'to acquire land . . . for men who have served in the war . . . for cottages with gardens, allotments or smallholdings'[37] – evoking a tradition of dwelling construction centuries old and instinct with aesthetic, cultural, practical, and social class dimensions.

'Is the term cottage definable?' picturesque architect James Malton had asked in 1798.[38] Samuel Johnson's dictionary of 1755 had tried, noting that *cottage* derived from the Saxon *cot*: 'A hut; a mean habitation; a cot; a little house'. Of *cottager*, Johnson wrote: 'in law, . . . one that lives on the common, without paying rent and without any land of his own'.[39]

The state-of-the-art in 1918 was provided in the *Oxford English Dictionary*'s precursor, *A New English Dictionary on Historical Principles*. Part VII of Volume II dated from 1893 and contained the following cottage definition:

> A dwelling-house of small size and humble character, such as is occupied by farm labourers, villagers, miners, etc. Historically the term is found first applied to the dwelling-places or holdings which under the feudal system were occupied by the cottars, cottiers, cotsets or cotterels . . . when under a certain rental [they] were exempted from paying church rate, poor-rate, etc; with the disappearance of legal regulations and exemptions . . . the term has become more vague in its application.[40]

The dictionary editor in 1893, J.A.H. Murray, singled out 'cottage' as a term 'of historical interest'.[41] One important difference between his definition and Samuel Johnson's – separated by nearly 150 years – lies in the way the cottage, a rural phenomenon for Johnson, had acquired a wider industrial setting in the *New English Dictionary* ('miners etc'). This raises a major background theme that will not be examined at length here, but which is inescapable nonetheless – English culture's preoccupation with the countryside.[42]

Wherever the cottage was valorised, it functioned in part as proxy for an ideological vision of the wider virtues of countryside existence – 'a Utopian, dreamlike . . . ideal of a rural paradise that never existed', according to Curl;[43] 'decent living and good neighbourhood – honesty, truth and purity

16 Best-selling author H.V. Morton, photographed by Howard Coster (1930s), National Portrait Gallery, London

of word and life' for the Conservative historian Arthur Bryant.[44] Virginia Woolf's father Leslie Stephen reflected: 'A love of the country is taken, I know not why, to indicate the presence of all the cardinal virtues'.[45] Interwar writers paid even less attention to the wherefores. In his 1927 best-seller *In Search of England*, H.V. Morton claimed: 'The average townsman of no matter what class feels a deep love for the country . . . finds there the answer to an ancient instinct'.[46] Myth for Morton became politics for Stanley Baldwin a year later: 'the country represents the eternal values and the eternal traditions from which we must never allow ourselves to be separated'.[47]

The ways this rural belief system has fired and replenished the English imagination have been thoroughly analysed – by Bermingham, Kumar, Mandler, Matless, and Readman, to name a handful.

And ruralism's intersection with the interwar politics of antisemitism and the far-right – tackled by Griffiths, Webber, and Wright[48] – should not be overlooked. But Alun Howkins articulates the consensus: 'the ideology of England and Englishness is to a remarkable degree rural. Most importantly, a large part of the English *ideal* is rural'.[49]

For the architectural historian, the study of buildings rather than of the landscape as a whole takes centre stage. And the cottage stands as the architectural talisman of benign rural ideology – a credo exalted by Bryant in 1940:

> If the apex of the agricultural community . . . was the country house, its basis was the cottage. It was here that those who reaped and sowed were born and bred. Their homely virtues were as vital to their country's splendid achievement as the genius and assurance of the hereditary aristocrats who led them.[50]

On the cusp of the nineteenth and twentieth centuries, scientific enthusiasm for sunlight and fresh air had merged with sentiments like Bryant's and Morton's to make the dwelling an eloquent shorthand for healthy, moral living. Activists of every stripe – Charles Dickens and Angela Burdett-Coutts at Urania Cottage in 1847;[51] the developers of

the Cottage Home idea for pauper children in the 1870s;[52] and Octavia Hill with her housing-reform followers – helped reimagine and reimport the dwelling into city and suburb, determined to see it work its magic there. The result was one at which conservationist Thomas Sharp, in 1932, was aghast: 'The town was no longer to be a town, but a loose collection of country cottages; and the looser and more countrified the better'.[53]

These cottages, rural and urban, and the strains of meaning they transmitted in 1919, are the subject for this chapter – first, their class-structural significance; secondly, their cultural back-story; and, thirdly, the origins and still vital meaning of their dominant architectural context, the Picturesque. A cabinet of educated men committed themselves publicly in 1919 to a huge programme of cottage building – binding themselves to work in the shadow of all three.

THE COTTAGE AND SOCIAL CLASS

Cottages had long been rhetorical catnip to the statesman. William Pitt (the Elder) used them to emphasise notions of the Englishman's proud independence: 'The poorest man may in his cottage bid defiance to all the forces of the Crown';[54] Disraeli, to illustrate his 'One Nation' philosophy: 'The Palace is not safe, when the cottage is not happy'.[55] Lloyd George's 1918 coalition manifesto also drew from the well, trying to resuscitate the collective spirit of the early days of war: 'Well and truly have rich and poor, castle and cottage, stood the ordeal of fire'.[56] Even after history's most industrialised conflict, the Prime Minister could not resist invoking England's class structure in this traditional language of dwelling-type, juxtaposing the simplicities of Macaulay – 'And tower and town and cottage /Have heard the trumpet's blast' – with the Victorian hymnal's vision of a settled class dispensation: 'rich man' in castle, 'poor man' at gate.[57]

Choosing the term 'unarchitectural' to convey the un-self-conscious nature of the earliest cottages, Charles Innocent, in 1916, cited evidence for the

17   Card No. 16, 'Weobley, Herefordshire', Player's Cigarettes, *Picturesque Cottages* (1929)

18   Lloyd George MP, Prime Minister 1916–22, photographed by Olive Edis (1917), National Portrait Gallery, London

Cottages like this symbolised the English labourer's independence of spirit and action. The rights and lifestyles of their poor occupants were protected in law until the end of Edward VI's reign.[62] Dwellings that often started life in an entirely makeshift manner were patched up, buttressed, extended, or reconstructed – some surviving for centuries, as Flora Thompson records in *Lark Rise to Candleford* (1939).[63]

By the late sixteenth century, the proliferation of the commoner's self-raised cottage had become socially contentious. With a view to inhibiting rural migration – which had implications for the parish poor-rate, and the consumption of local resources – Elizabethan law sought to control spread of the dwelling.[64] Fines of £10 or 40s per month for the construction or maintenance of illegal cottages were in statute from the 1589 'Act against the Erecting and Maintaining of Cottages' onwards, confirming cottages as disputed territory.[65] Though it is sometimes seen as sheltering or promoting the cottage way of life, this statute's sharp regulatory intent is clear to Wrightson and Tankard.[66] According to Hindle, Charles II's Poor Relief Act (1662) would later unambiguously identify cottages as part of the unwelcome economic migrant's bag of tricks:

existence of small, oblong, gabled dwellings in eighth-century Saxon England.[58] Published in 1911, and reprinted during the interwar years, the Hammonds' book *The Village Labourer* informed their early twentieth-century readership that, throughout the middle ages, the peasant's cottage subsisted in a tradition – part myth, part reality[59] – of the rough dwelling raised by a poor family on the common or waste, sometimes in a single night.[60] William Gilpin, apostle of the Picturesque, had written in his *Remarks on Forest Scenery*:

I have known all the materials of one of these habitations brought together – the house built – covered in – the goods removed – a fire kindled – and the family in possession, during the course of a moonlight night.[61]

poor people are not restrained from going from one Parish to another and therefore doe endeavour to settle themselves . . . where there is the best Stocke, the largest Commons or wastes to build cottages.[67]

By the late eighteenth century, after decades of enclosure and revisions to the law, understandings of cottage meaning had split firmly along class lines. For current or former occupants, the idea might communicate homeliness – as in John Clare's nostalgic poem 'To My Cottage'. Beyond independence and autarky, the cottage had also begun to connote loss, as for Oliver Goldsmith in 'The Deserted Village'.[68] Another Clare poem, 'The Fallen Elm', married that loss to the commoner's wider experience of displacement:

Thus came enclosure – ruin was its guide
But freedom's clapping hands enjoyed the sight
Though comfort's cottage soon was thrust aside
And workhouse prisons raised upon the site.[69]

Conversely, for many landowners and poor-rate payers, cottages had become a nuisance – 'nurseries of idleness'[70] – objectionable for incubating a vexatiously unbiddable workforce. Landowners' attitudes to cottages and their inhabitants at the time are encapsulated by E.P. Thompson in the language of class distinction: 'It became a matter of public-spirited policy for the gentleman to remove cottagers from the commons'.[71] Disraeli's Young England novel *Sybil*, a favourite of Lloyd George, levelled graver charges: 'the proprietors of the neighbourhood . . . destroying the cottages on their estates in order to become exempted from the maintenance of the population'.[72] This simplified narrative of enclosure and its consequences survived well into the twentieth century. Clough Williams-Ellis's propaganda tract *Britain and the Beast* (1937) invited H.J. Massingham to give it an interwar lease on life: 'the voteless and evicted villager was neither consulted in the appropriation of his glebe and demolition of his cottage, nor compensated for being suddenly transformed into an exile and a vagabond'.[73]

Barrell sees the cottage on the cusp of the eighteenth and nineteenth centuries as a battleground between radicals (who agitated, like the Reverend Crabbe, on behalf of its poverty-stricken occupants)[74] and loyalists, whose rehabilitated image of the dwelling – as homely and pure-spirited – was needed for transmission, through pamphlets, poetry, and cottage prints, back to the labourers who lived there in an effort to guide them away from imported revolutionary sentiment.[75] Bainbridge identifies an inversion of the same imagery at work in the early nineteenth

19   Avon Street, Vickerstown, designed by the Barrow-in-Furness architect W. Moss Settle (1902), Cumbria Archives – with perhaps a little Port Sunlight picturesque in mind

century, the 'ruined cottage' an emblem of the price that would inevitably be paid by the English and their lost menfolk in the righteous war against Napoleon.[76] During these years, the idea of the cottage was repeatedly politicised from multiple class standpoints.

Champions of the poor sought to retain control of its traditional meaning. Cobbett's 50,000-selling *Cottage-Economy* presented the dwelling as the site of labouring families' self-sufficiency.[77] Joyce finds the idea doing similar work for the Chartists;[78] and it was present too in the rhetoric of the factory reformer and anti-Poor Law campaigner Richard Oastler, whose paternalist maxim was 'The Altar, the Throne and the Cottage'.[79] The dwelling's enduring social significance as home to the labourer materialised in the actual cottages built under the Chartists' Land Plan, which sought to enfranchise freeholding workers by meeting the property qualification of the 1832 Reform Act. But throughout the previous century, the cottage as labourer's dwelling was shifting in character from expression-of-independence to proof-of-dependence – no longer self-built, but either 'tied' by landowner to the provision of labour or let by rural landlord at the market rate.[80]

Over two and a half centuries, the class polarity of cottage building in England was reversed. Where once the labourer built the cottage for themselves, now it was provided more often by the land- or factory-owner, for mostly self-interested reasons: 'cottages are as much agricultural plant as machinery is . . . a minimum supply of them is indispensable to the proper working of a farm'.[81] Purpose-built dwellings – at Lowther in Westmoreland (1766–73), Milton Abbas in Dorset (1774 onwards), and Blaise Hamlet near Bristol (1811) – architecturalised interpretations of the class-structural obligations understood to exist between landowner and labourer (active or retired), leading to an industrial version at Saltaire (1851 onwards) where workforce housing was created at the mill-owner's expense to ensure a supply of labour both grateful and propinquitous.[82] Relationships of dependence such as this bore fruit until the cusp of the nineteenth

and twentieth centuries – in the cottages Lord Lever built for his workers at Port Sunlight (from 1888); those erected by the Cadburys at Bournville (from 1893); at Vickerstown in Cumbria (from 1901); and in the cottages put up by the Rowntree family at New Earswick, near York (from 1902).

By then, rhetoric expressing the balance of power between landlord and tenant had grown sophisticated. Lever did not see himself as a philanthropist; high-quality housing was, for him, part of a bargain between employer and employees – 'prosperity sharing'[83] – in which everyone did better. But, as Nicholas Taylor says, there is 'an undeniably almshousey atmosphere about Port Sunlight';[84] cottages there and elsewhere were materially expressive of the dominant class paradigm – dwellings that those with money and influence built for tenants with little or none of either.

As 1918 turned to 1919, where in class terms had the cottage come to rest? We have seen how Prime Minister Lloyd George used the concept in his election manifesto as a metonym for the lower classes. It was his new government, peppered with Liberal and Tory knights, that planned to build 500,000 cottages as the centrepiece of a dramatic new turn in the emergence of the welfare state.

The newly ensconced Labour opposition, with many MPs from less traditional House of Commons backgrounds, were just as taken with the cottage's redemptive promise. In January 1918, the party conference at Nottingham heard a paper entitled *Labour and the New Social Order*, which called for 'The rehousing of the population to the extent, possibly, of a million new cottages'.[85] During the election campaign at the end of the year, *The Times* sent a special correspondent to cover Labour's approach to the housing question in London's Deptford, where their incumbent candidate, C.W. Bowerman, published a leaflet demanding 'fair cottages set in fair streets, green with the shade of trees, and the grass of playing grounds'.[86] In late 1918, even though the heart of British democratic politics was in flux, all sides seemed to agree that state-funded cottages were the answer to the working-class housing crisis.

But the older class dynamics of cottage building survived the war too. Philanthropic individual cottage-builders, from society's upper reaches, were still to be found. One took the shape of the MP Noel Pemberton Billing – 'aviator and self-publicist'[87] – who celebrated his re-election as the independent member for Hertford by promising to build his constituents a row of ferro-concrete cottages, costing £400 each, on a meadow opposite his home.[88] The more clubbable Sir Martin Conway MP (alpinist, art historian, elected in December 1918 as coalition member for the Combined English Universities)[89] confessed to the Commons, during the Addison Housing Bill's passage in April 1919, that he too had recently gone in for a bit of cottage building. He had, however, found a budget of £750 apiece only half what was needed. 'The trouble,' he told the House, 'was that I attempted too considerable an artistic invention.'[90]

Charged with winding up the Addison Bill's April 1919 second reading in the Commons was Major Waldorf Astor – Conservative MP for Plymouth Sutton; parliamentary secretary for housing at the Local Government Board;[91] heir to one of the world's great fortunes; and owner of Cliveden in Buckinghamshire, whose grounds boasted five picturesque cottages designed by George Devey.[92] That a man of such wealth should devote himself to understanding the finer detail of English working-class cottage provision bespeaks the consensus that existed on the need for housing reform. But these responsibilities also inducted the US-born Astor into a long-standing tradition of aristocratic and upper-middle-class English cottage builders.

An exchange of letters published by *The Spectator* in the autumn of 1919 encapsulates how, for the wealthy, cottage building remained a vital concern. Writing from Woburn Abbey to the newspaper proprietor Lord Northcliffe, the 11th Duke of Bedford took exception to criticism in the *Daily Mail* of his pre-war estate cottages.[93] He challenged Northcliffe to a comparison,

between the plan, cost of construction, and rent of my cottages, which you have held up to public

20 Noel Pemberton Billing MP, 'aviator and self-publicist', photographed by Elliott & Fry (1920s), National Portrait Gallery, London

execration, and the type of dwelling which has been selected for housing labour on your Lordship's estate. The contrast between cottages built as a result of the practical experience of several generations, all interested in cottage building, and those on a new and up-to-date estate, unblighted by tradition, and by the heirloom taint . . . cannot fail to be a useful contribution to the discussion which is now taking place . . .[94]

The *Daily Mail* had crossed swords with the wrong duke; Bedford's family had been building highly regarded labourers' cottages for generations.[95] Wisely, the press mogul apologised. He paid

21 (left) Alfred Harmsworth, 1st Viscount Northcliffe (c.1908) posing with one of his cherished cars, Heritage Image Partnership Ltd/Alamy; (above) Herbrand Arthur Russell, 11th Duke of Bedford, photographed by Walter Stoneman (1921), National Portrait Gallery, London. New money Northcliffe retreated from his cottage confrontation with old money Bedford

epistolary tribute to 'the national reputation of the Woburn Estate' and invited the duke, by way of a peace offering, to visit the Northcliffe estate. The fact that two such powerful figures found so much at stake in the matter of cottage building shows how close to feudal the surrounding atmospherics remained.

Radical though the 1919 Addison Scheme was in obliging and funding local authorities all over the country to join the nation's traditional stock of cottage landlords, the underlying class relationships in English cottage-building had been top-down for well over a century. Ravetz calls Lloyd George's plan, 'a culture transfer amounting to a cultural colonization: a vision forged by one section of society for application to another'.[96] In planning to build 'cottages' for the working classes, the coalition government blended its radical vision for the provision of social housing with still-potent historical convention, casting a potentially new relationship between state-funded architecture and class not as revolution, but as problematic continuity.

CULTURE AND THE COTTAGE

Accompanying the play of class-structural forces in determining the meaning of the cottage over these many years, a profound acculturation had also taken place, relating particularly to cottage visuality and its connection with the idea of home. When Ruskin apostrophised 'cottage scenery and . . . the inexhaustible imagery of literature which is founded upon it',[97] he referred to an inheritance with roots in the passion of the eighteenth-century English gentleman for the pastoral writing of the classical poets – 'when shall I see my native land again? . . . the turf-dressed roof of my simple cottage'[98] – fruit of a classical education specifically designed to distinguish its participants from *hoi polloi*, and part of the process through which English idealisation of the cottage began.[99]

Hall and Stead discuss how *class* and the idea of the *classical* grew from the same root – both in Latin as a language and in Ancient Roman society. The Roman king Servius Tullius's 'legendary first census', around 550–535 BCE, divided Romans into six social tiers, the men at the top – the *classici* – being those with the most money and property. Thereafter, to be at the apex of anything, was to be 'classical'. And this gave rise at the beginning of the eighteenth century to an educational curriculum tailor-made to lend distinction to 'the newly defined British "gentleman" . . . whether his fees were paid by landed estates or commerce'.[100] An educational imperative grew, under the influence of Addison and *The Spectator*, into a broader

22   Thomas Gainsborough, *Wooded Landscape, Cottage, Figures, and Boat on a Lake*, 1783–85, oil and wash on paper, 404 × 557 mm, Birmingham Museums Trust. The cottage picturesque almost invariably features a steeply pitched roof and prominent gables

code of gentlemanly taste and culture – which was how the passion of classical writers for what English translators termed the 'cottage' came to be inculcated in people whose forebears had rarely been obliged to live in one.[101]

Milton made idealising classical allusions to the cottage in his poem 'L'Allegro' as early as 1631–32.[102] Sarah Lloyd finds 'influential cottage scenes' in James Thomson's *Seasons* from 1726.[103] The cultural connection between 'our immortal bard'[104] and the cottage, meanwhile, proved stronger as a function of the life than of the work. Shakespeare's supposed cottage birthplace in Stratford-upon-Avon was the subject of commemoration as early as David Garrick's Jubilee in 1769 (five years after the bicentenary of Shakespeare's birth), then famously enshrined as one of the country's foremost tourist attractions after the Shakespeare Birthplace Committee bought the former butcher's shop and horse-letting business in 1847.[105]

The other key Shakespearean cottage was, theoretically, Anne Hathaway's, in the village of Shottery outside Stratford. 'Discovered' in 1793 by the engraver Samuel Ireland's *Picturesque Views on the Upper or Warwickshire Avon*, the cottage helped feed the Picturesque's hunger for imagery, later becoming a tourist attraction itself. Longfellow, Tennyson, Dickens, and the art historian Kenneth Clarke all visited.[106]

With 'Fears in Solitude', Coleridge had in 1798 embraced the existential consolations of home and family by forsaking the city for a damp cottage in Somerset: 'hidden from my view /Is my own lovely cottage, where my babe /And my babe's mother dwell in peace!'[107] And, perhaps the most cottage-loving of all the Romantics, Wordsworth extolled the dwelling's virtues in 'Michael' – inducing politicians to fear the poet might be in danger of stirring dissent among small farmers.[108] At greater length in 'The Excursion', its first part also known as 'The Ruined Cottage', Wordsworth's narrator explored anxieties shared with Goldsmith and Clare about abandonment and loss; his melancholy staunched only by an intuition that Margaret's ruined cottage sheltered the 'secret spirit of humanity'.[109]

23 Samuel Ireland, 'House at Shotery in which Anne Hathaway the wife of Shakespere resided', from *Picturesque Views on the Upper or Warwickshire Avon* (1795), The Bodleian Libraries, University of Oxford

The Romantics' determination to find virtue and beauty in England's cottages – despite their being, in many cases, rotting hovels – gave rise to what Ford calls the 'Cottage Controversy':[110] a row between Southey and Macaulay around 1830 about the 'scandal' of Romantic indifference to the plight of the rural poor.[111] But nothing could tarnish the fast-becoming-mythical dwelling. The society poet Samuel Rogers had sold over 23,000 copies of his poem 'The Pleasures of Memory' (1792), which celebrated 'The dear abode of peace and privacy/. . . the thatch among the trees'. And in 'A Wish', later, Rogers repeated the trick – 'Mine be a cot beside the hill' – hymning the universal dwelling's swallow-thronged thatch and 'ivied porch'.[112] A summit of

still higher popular enthusiasm was then scaled by the pen of Felicia Hemans, the 'most widely read woman poet in the English-speaking world'.[113] In her 1820s *Blackwood's Magazine* masterpiece 'The Homes of England', she helped seal a potent bond between ideas of home and cottage: 'The Cottage homes of England! /By thousands on her plains, / They are smiling o'er the silvery brooks, /And round the hamlet fanes'.[114]

Irresistible as a vector for Romantic-domestic imagery, the cottage pullulated in the margins of Sir Walter Scott: glimpsed from horseback by a passing knight; sought in refuge of a stormy evening; a symbol of purity – 'Who envies now the shepherd's lot /His healthy fare, his rural cot?'[115] For Mandler,

Scott was *fons et origo* of this popular vision of the fifteenth- and sixteenth-century golden age in English and Scottish history – a vision propagated widely thanks to the revolution in print technologies in the early decades of the nineteenth century.[116] Cheap periodicals such as *The Mirror of Literature, Amusement and Instruction* (from 1823) and *The Penny Magazine* (from 1832) – the latter with a circulation of over 200,000 – leant heavily on Scott's Olden Times to scripturalise a past in which cottage idealisation was a fundamental pillar. *The Penny Magazine* expounded it canonically (quoting Moore's 'Ballad Stanzas' in the process):

> when we observe rich men unhappy, in large mansions . . . we then think of the contrast which the simplicity and content of the "peasant's nest"

offers. Who has not looked upon [its] whitened walls, half covered with roses and jessamine, and the neat garden where ornament is blended with utility,

> *And said, if there's peace to be found in the world*
> *A heart that is humble may hope for it here.*[117]

Dickens, an author whose career was built on the reach and appeal of the affordable literary periodical, betrayed exactly this sentimentality regarding Mrs Maylie's country cottage in *Oliver Twist*.[118] He shifted to satirising such enthusiasms in *Little Dorrit*;[119] but his eldest son Charley, in describing a real-world visit to Anne Hathaway's Cottage, published in *All the Year Round* in 1892, rediscovered old-time cottage religion: 'a substantial

24   Thomas Gainsborough, *Wooded Landscape with Figures and Pigs Outside Cottage*, 1775–80, pencil, pen and ink, chalk and watercolour, 214 × 313 mm, Eton College, Windsor. A typical 'cottage door' – the contented family gathering outside the half-timbered, lattice-dormered cottage picturesque

25 John Constable, *A Cottage in a Cornfield*, 1815–17, oil on canvas, 315 × 263 mm, Amgueddfa Cymru – Museum Wales. An original rectangular-plan gabled cottage rendered asymmetrical by the catslide-roof extension to the right

the journals – *The Literary Souvenir*, *The Keepsake*, *Bentley's Miscellany* – or, as Rose sets out, via second-hand bookstalls, Palgrave's Golden Treasury, and, later, J.M. Dent's Everyman's Library, working men's colleges, and the Workers' Educational Association.[124]

Cottages were a painterly obsession too. Uvedale Price's riding companion Thomas Gainsborough[125] helped catalyse the first flush of the Picturesque by painting 'cottage doors' in the 1770s and 1780s – landscapes featuring prominent cottages, outside which attractive mothers and children played[126] – 'possibly the most potent visual representations of innocence and health created in the eighteenth century'.[127] George Morland joined Gainsborough, together with John Constable and Samuel Palmer, in expanding a landscape tradition inherited from seventeenth-century Europe in which cottages often commanded the scene.[128] Frances Spalding finds Palmer's etching *The Herdsman's Cottage* catching the attention of Goldsmith's students in the mid-1920s;[129] while Dixon Hunt sees in the same artist's *Gleaning Field* of 1833 (fig.26), with its thatched cottage in the background, complete with dormer window and gabled outshot, 'associations of visionary plenitude, of Golden Age fecundity'.[130] The home-loving labourer's family waiting perpetually at the cottage door became a staple – and was translated to a wider market throughout the later nineteenth century via the prints, watercolours, and anthologies of Myles Birket Foster, Kate Greenaway, and Helen Allingham.[131]

An artistic career that saw Greenaway's name become a 'household word'[132] was shaped in no small measure by the cottages she visited and drew in the village of Rolleston in Nottinghamshire, where she spent time as a child. As Greenaway developed influential friendships later in life with her fellow artist Helen Allingham, and with John Ruskin, affection for cottages functioned as a bond between the trio. An early Ruskin letter to Greenaway enthused: 'I never dreamed you were one of my readers . . . I am so delighted . . . with your really liking blue sky – and those actual cottages'.[133] In what became an extended correspondence,

timbered . . . building of the Elizabethan period with roof of thick thatch . . . diamond-paned casements that gleam and glimmer in the sunshine, and plaster coated walls to which the ivy clings lovingly'.[120] George Eliot's *Middlemarch* had brought keener social understanding to the cottage,[121] but a folkloric reverence became the norm, exemplified in *Under the Greenwood Tree* and *Tess of the D'Urbervilles*[122] by the Victorian architect-turned-novelist Thomas Hardy – who won the RIBA's silver medal in 1863 for an essay on bricks and terracotta,[123] and returns to this study, still marching under the cottage banner, in the 1920s.

Literary cottages were not just middle-class perquisites. As the nineteenth century advanced, working-class readers could have encountered the writers considered here, either in the pages of

26 Samuel Palmer, *The Gleaning Field*, 1833, tempera on mahogany, 305 × 454 mm, Tate.
Bequeathed by Mrs Mary Louisa Garrett, 1936, NO4842

Greenaway wrote to Ruskin a few years later about meeting Allingham, who had 'often wished to give you a little drawing [and] asked me what subject I thought you would like best – I said I fancied a pretty little girl with a little cottage'.[134] Though they had been students together at the Slade in the early 1870s, Greenaway and Allingham grew closer from 1888 when they started to accompany one another on painting trips. Allingham recalled her friend to be 'delighted with the beauty of the country and the picturesque old towns . . . always scrupulously thoughtful for the convenience and feelings of the owners of the farm or cottage we wished to paint'.[135]

Greenaway's art and illustration focused principally on children, but even when she did not paint cottages for their own sake, there they were in the background – gabled, lattice-windowed, picturesque (figs 27 and 28). Between 1878 and 1898, she sold over 932,000 copies of children's books, almanacks, and anthologies, helping lodge in the minds of her readership an eidetic impression of the cottage picturesque. 'It has been said,' wrote an architect in *The Builder* in 1923, 'that Kate Greenaway first inspired architects to take an interest in Old English cottage life.'[136] George Gissing's semi-autobiographical *The Private Papers of Henry Ryecroft* spelled out how the cycle of acculturation – in which Greenaway played her part – worked its magic: 'Let me but come upon the poorest little woodcut, the cheapest "process" illustration, representing a thatched cottage, a lane, a field, and I hear that music begin to murmur'.[137]

Ruskin was intoxicated by Greenaway's art, and by Allingham's. He gave a lecture in May 1883, in his Slade series 'The Art of England', about the pair of them,[138] connecting their pictures with fairy tales – another of his passions – whose publication in England he had championed in the second half of the nineteenth century, and which made their own generic contribution to the consolidation of cottage mythology.[139] When, in 1886, the Fine Art Society staged the first exhibition in London of Allingham's paintings, cottages were the only subject.

Later, another selection of her work was reproduced in a best-selling book written by Fine Art Society managing director Marcus Huish. Published in 1903, reprinted in 1909, *Happy England* was still being bruited evangelically by *The Times* in November 1917: 'That is the art we have lost. That is the England we are destroying'.[140] And Allingham furnished the

pictures for another publishing success in 1909 – *The Cottage Homes of England*. This time the introduction was written by Stewart Dick, who achieved near-rapture in the union of cottage and home:

> If you wish to find the typical English home, you must leave the cities . . . go out into the country . . . pass by the mansions of the great and the prosperous homes of the middle classes, and you will find it in the humble cottage.[141]

Helmreich sees the cottage in Allingham's hands as 'a form of national patrimony'.[142] Evidence from witnesses at the 1884 hearings for the Royal Commission on housing suggests that even the most miserably lodged inner-city labourers' families shared this outlook. Thomas Bird, a Visitor with the London Schools Board, told the commissioners

left

27   Kate Greenaway, 'A Surrey Cottage', in M.H. Spielmann and G.S. Layard, *Kate Greenaway* (London: A.&C. Black Ltd, 1905), pp 198–9, The Bodleian Libraries, University of Oxford

right

28   Kate Greenaway, 'Street Show', from *Marigold Garden* (London: George Routledge and Sons, 1885), The Bodleian Libraries, University of Oxford. Note the picturesque architectural backdrop

about a 'house' at 8 Stephen Street, off Tottenham Court Road in Central London, where 97 people lived in just 25 rooms. 'They are crowded,' said Mr Bird, 'and the back rooms are very dark, because where the yard should be, what they term a cottage, three storeys high, is built, within two yards of the back windows of the front house.'[143] In 1909, Masterman had acknowledged 'the desperate efforts made by a race reared in village communities to maintain in the urban aggregation some semblance of a home'.[144] Was it a recognition of these origins that led to England's first-ever council housing – two tenement blocks of four storeys, built in Liverpool's Ashfield Street in 1869 – being designated 'St Martin's Cottages'?[145]

By the end of the nineteenth century the domestic attractions of the cottage confounded social stratification. In 1845, the *Penny Cyclopaedia Supplement* defined a version of the home freed from its less fortunate connotations: 'The term *cottage* has for some time been in vogue . . . for small country residences and detached suburban houses . . . in this sense of it, the name is divested of all associations with poverty'.[146] Fifty years later, the dwelling's cultural resonance ran the gamut from high to popular; and despite (or because of) the manipulative ideological uses to which it had been put, its associations were benign. In popular literature, the cottage home wove a powerful spell. Kenneth Grahame's *The Wind in the Willows* saw Rat and Mole approach a village after a day's hunting:

> where the firelight or lamplight of each cottage overflowed through the casements into the dark world without. Most of the low, latticed windows were innocent of blinds . . . the inmates, gathered round the tea-table, absorbed in handiwork, or talking with laughter and gesture.[147]

A widespread sense of entitlement to these verities of cottage life was firmly rooted by the start of the twentieth century. In *Folk of the Furrow*, Christopher Holdenby regretted 'the cottage coveted of those who live on exteriors and journey past with the artistic eye',[148] but cottage enthusiasm was by no means the preserve of the day-tripper. *Punch*'s cartoonists satirised the emerging passion among the Edwardian middle classes for spending their holidays in cottages, getting back to basics. In one cartoon (fig.29), a richly dressed woman complains: 'No more simple life for *me*, my dear. I've been roughing it in a tiny cottage for two months, and my second footman away ill nearly the whole

time!'[149] Thus could the moneyed Edwardian strive to recuperate what Voysey called 'the honest homely instincts of the cottager'[150] – just as the well-to-do Georgian had sought to recover theirs through the enjoyment of *cottages ornés*.[151]

After a decade of scrutinising the Edwardian era's crisis for the rural poor in country cottage availability and maintenance, *Country Life* magazine in 1913 published *The 'Country Life' Book of Cottages*, written by Lawrence Weaver. Enthusiastically reviewed,[152] it summed up, for the beginning of the twentieth century, the class

THE STOICS OF MAYFAIR.

"No more simple life for *me*, my dear. I've been roughing it in a tiny cottage for two months, and my second footman away ill nearly the whole time!"

29   V.L.C. Booth, 'The Stoics of Mayfair', *Punch*, vol.133, no.3490, 30 October 1907, p.319, Punch Cartoon Library/TopFoto

breadth of the dwelling's appeal. In build-cost per unit ranging from £150 to £600:

> every type has been shown, whether built for the rural labourer, the smallholder, the estate servant, the clerk who lives outside the town, the "week ender", or the people of moderate means . . . whose permanent home must be built with severe regard to economy.[153]

The architect Gordon Allen described the nation's attitude to cottages during this time as a 'craze' and a 'cult'.[154] From soot-clad council blocks in industrial Liverpool to *Punch*'s 'Stoics of Mayfair', the cultural appeal of the cottage had become, in class terms, as good as universal. If a government's mission were to build any dwelling-type *en masse*, what choice could have better associations?

THE COTTAGE AND THE PICTURESQUE

It remains then to investigate how, from the late eighteenth century, the cottage became emblematic of the Picturesque – what Christopher Hussey calls 'the accepted aesthetic of most cultivated people throughout the nineteenth century',[155] and Rebecca Tropp 'arguably Britain's most distinctive and enduring contribution to global visual culture'.[156] Macarthur and Spuybroek endorse the key connection at the heart of this book between the Picturesque and the idea of the cottage. As Macarthur puts it: 'if we wish to understand the picturesque in its pure character we should resort to the cottage'.[157]

The same coupling is remarked in theoretical writing as early as Robert Kerr's *The Gentleman's House* in 1864, published soon after his appointment as Professor of the Arts of Construction at King's College, London, in 1861.[158] He situated 'the Cottage style' on the picturesque side of his 'great primary division of all architectural art . . . into the Classical and the Picturesque';[159] and, even in the early decades of the twentieth century, the idiom's most consistent critics still acknowledged the

30 Landscape, in the manner of John Constable, Amgueddfa Cymru – Museum Wales. A picturesque cottage with blue smoke rising from the chimney

strength of the connection. In 1911, the Liverpool University formalist Stanley Adshead was disturbed by the 'abnormally picturesque' arrangement of the new dwellings at Gidea Park, in Essex, most of which modelled 'the English cottage style'.[160] His critique suggests Macarthur's formula could also be reversed: to understand fully the appearance and meanings of the cottage, one must fathom the Picturesque.

As a coherent architectural theory that addresses plan and elevation – set out by Gilpin, Price, and Knight on the cusp of the eighteenth and nineteenth centuries[161] – the Picturesque has been neglected in academic analysis of the 1919–39 dwelling. Ballantyne and Law, alert to its importance, borrow its '-esque' for their 'Tudoresque',[162] but that was a word used rarely between the wars[163] and makes a debatable substitute for an idea – the Picturesque itself – widely discussed at the time.

31   Christopher Hussey, who rediscovered the Picturesque for interwar readers, photographed by Elliott & Fry (1942), National Portrait Gallery, London

The Picturesque has not lacked attention in art and architectural history more generally. The historian Oliver Cox cites a 1950 letter to Christopher Hussey from Ivor de Wolfe (the *nom de plume* of Hubert de Cronin Hastings, Chairman of the Architectural Press) describing the Picturesque, grandiloquently, as 'the aesthetic principle of Romanticism (the differentiative principle)' that 'happens to explain . . . the perennial basis of the English aesthetic impulse'.[164] Goodhart-Rendel, Hitchcock, Banham, Saint, Watkin, Bermingham, Mordaunt Crook, Robinson, Ballantyne, Hill, Macarthur, de Jong, and Spuybroek all recognise its theoretical power and the durability of its influence on architecture.

Some have tried to corral it. In striving to emphasise the importance of the Picturesque as primarily a landscape theory – 'a planning idea'[165] – while de-emphasising its engagement with the architecture of buildings themselves, Pevsner errs in this direction. He sees indications of Price and Knight's writing on picturesque architecture as 'rare and faint'. Further, 'The search for evidence in eighteenth century literature of an appreciation of picturesque architecture has brought us but a meagre harvest'.[166] He was in error here. Price and Knight both examined picturesque architecture in considerable detail; the latter in *An Analytical Inquiry into the Principles of Taste* (1805); the former in his *Essay on the Picturesque*, Vol. II (1798) and *Dialogue* (1801).[167]

Pevsner's student Banham takes the Picturesque seriously, but also approaches it as an insight principally into architecture's relationship with site and the grouping of buildings.[168] Mordaunt Crook compasses its full architectural significance, but is inclined to periodise it (1790–1834), interpreting the Picturesque diachronically as giving way to Puginian rationalism.[169] Hill by contrast concurs with Hitchcock in construing Pugin as the Victorian period's first crucial re-inventor of the Picturesque[170] – and Saint with Hussey in regarding it, reinvented thus, as the enduring inspiration for Ruskin and his disciples.[171]

In addressing the subject, most recognise the importance of Hussey's pioneering 1927 book *The Picturesque*, which functions here as both primary and secondary source. As the latter, it remains valuable in tracing the roots of the Picturesque in the English grand tourist's love for the landscape painting of seventeenth- and eighteenth-century masters from France, Spain, Italy, and the Low Countries.[172] As a primary source, it symbolises the interwar resurgence of interest in the Picturesque and provides a contemporary insight into interwar domestic architecture that rewards greater attention.

'Blenheim is picturesque,' wrote Hussey in 1927, but 'so is the modern speculating builder's six-roomed house, with its sham half-timbering, unbalanced fenestration, bay window, and terracotta dragon on the gable'.[173] This is one of interwar domestic architectural history's clearest insights, demonstrating Hussey's understanding of the Picturesque as a theory of abstract aesthetics and associations, 'a method of using and combining styles'.[174] Banham usefully describes it as 'unstylistic aesthetic practice'[175] – an aesthetic philosophy that provides insight into textures and tectonics that please the human eye and connect the mind with the past.

There is not space here to set out a comprehensive genesis of the Picturesque as architectural theory. After writing by Hogarth about beauty, and Burke on the sublime, Reynolds began exploring its application to architecture;[176] Gilpin broached the theoretical Picturesque and popularised its description;[177] Knight and Price, often in dialogue, established its theoretical coherence;[178] Repton dug it into the landscape as a commercial business.[179] As a landscape philosophy, the Picturesque had roots older than the eighteenth century, Pevsner dating it back to Sir William Temple's *Gardens of Epicurus* in the late seventeenth.[180] But by the time Gilpin, Price, and Knight had done their work, it had also become a fully fledged theory of architectural aesthetics – explicating abstract visual qualities in such a way that it could (and still can[181]) be applied to the analysis of real-world plan and elevation: 'a design method, but also . . . a way of observing and experiencing architecture'.[182] Thomas Frederick Hunt, expanding on Gilpin, spelled this out in his 1825 book *Half a Dozen Hints on Picturesque Domestic Architecture* – 'the Picturesque in Architecture does not belong exclusively to ruinous and useless hovels, but . . . it may be produced in newly erected and comfortable Houses'.[183]

Price came closest to a concise exposition in his *Essay*: 'the two opposite qualities of roughness and of sudden variation, joined to that of irregularity, are the most efficient causes of the Picturesque'.[184] Between them, Price and Knight went on to apply other vital perceptual characteristics specifically to architecture: asymmetry, surface richness, detail and intricacy, partial concealment, depth and range of colour, irregular masses of light and shadow, sharp angles, and broken lines. They generated a canonical list of desirable visual effects, in short;

32 'A Gate Lodge', plate 1, from T.F. Hunt, *Half a Dozen Hints on Picturesque Domestic Architecture* (London: Henry G. Bohn, 1841), The Bodleian Libraries, University of Oxford

but, unlike the theorists of classical architecture, they deliberately did not provide guidance as to how those effects should be achieved or used together.

The Picturesque's founding fathers had a common enthusiasm for one architectural type in particular – the cottage. Price and Knight both had cottages on their estates. Programmes for the improvement of their demesnes should be understood as motivated by agrarian efficiency as well as by the Picturesque.[185] But Gilpin was not a landowner and bore no responsibility for cottages or their tenants. His perspective was the most purely aesthetic; a feeling, according to Michasiw, for *haecceity* – 'any more or less fortunate assemblage of light and mass, colour and form'.[186]

The late eighteenth-century artist John Thomas Smith illustrated the emerging conjunction of cottage and Picturesque when he published *Remarks on Rural Scenery* in 1797. Smith believed the English cottage merited 'particular notice' due to its being among 'the richest treasures of pictoresque [sic] Nature'.[187] His book offered advice on where to look for such subjects and how to treat them – complete 'with twenty etchings of cottages' of his own (fig.34). Francis Stevens followed him in 1815 with more etchings in *Views of Cottages and Farm-Houses in England and Wales*.[188]

33 Thomas Gainsborough, *Landscape with a Cottage and Cart*, 1786, oil on canvas, 394 × 495 mm, Birmingham Museums Trust

The major theorists of the Picturesque were similarly enchanted. Viewing the cottage from a distance with a painter's eye, and encountering it more closely while roaming the forest, Gilpin romanticised 'a dwelling where happiness may reside, unsupported by wealth . . . where we may still continue to enjoy peace, though we should be deprived of all the favours of fortune'.[189] Uvedale Price enthused, in his exposition of picturesque theory, about the aesthetic attractions of peasant buildings of every kind – huts, barns, and mills – but about one in particular:

A cottage of a quiet colour, half-concealed among trees . . . is one of the most tranquil and soothing of all rural objects; and when the sun strikes upon it, and discovers a number of lively picturesque circumstances, one of the most cheerful.[190]

Richard Payne Knight had dedicated *The Landscape: A Didactic Poem* to Price, using it to express his affection for the cottage: 'Nor yet unenvy'd, to whose humbler lot /Falls the retir'd and antiquated cot; / Its roof with weeds and mosses cover'd oe'r /And honeysuckles climbing round the door'.[191] And in his

34 John Thomas Smith, 'On Scotland Green, Ponder's End', from *Remarks on Rural Scenery* (London: Nathaniel Smith, 1797), The Bodleian Libraries, University of Oxford. Smith liked his cottages 'fast-ruinating' (an approach to the Picturesque later deplored by Ruskin). Beneath the decay, note the gabled main block, prominent chimney, latticed casements, and the cross-wing gable (left) articulating the broken plan

Red Book for John Scandrett Harford's new landscape at Blaise Castle (1795–96), Humphry Repton put picturesque ideas into practice by proposing the cottage as a perfect eye-catcher (fig.35):

> The form of this cottage must partake of the wildness of the scenery without meanness . . . its simplicity should be the effect of Art and not accident . . . I think a covered seat at the gable end of a neat, thatched cottage will be the best mode of producing the object here required.[192]

Repton's perspective reveals much of what the Picturesque's theorists loved about the cottage. Gables, dormers, prominent chimneystacks, latticed windows, pent-roofed shelters – what P.F. Robinson called the 'Leanto'[193] – in standalone cottages like this, all contributed to picturesque irregularity and texture as a function of plan and elevation.

Beyond the purely visual, the Picturesque is accounted a philosophy of broader consequence by Bermingham, Robinson, Michasiw, Everett, Macarthur, and Spuybroek.[194] It can be seen as a metaphor for the politics of the age (seeking a compassionate middle-ground, in liberty, between

licence and despotism).[195] It is cherished for the fundamental motility of its intellectual method and outcomes – resisting the *diktats* of any rule-based aesthetic system. Its plurality of 'gazes' is acknowledged as surprisingly modern – improving landowner or sensitised tourist; constantly shifting ground to find a new viewpoint or navigate a middle way via the dynamics of naturally placed or deliberately interpolated irregularities.[196] But the individualism of the Picturesque's aesthetic code should not be allowed to obscure, in the eighteenth century, the enduring formality of class relations that it was in many ways intended to disguise – 'the basis', as Copley and Garside write, 'on which the Picturesque translates the political and the social into the decorative'.[197]

Knight and Price rejected contemporary political and aesthetic ideology. The Picturesque was their countermeasure. They celebrated the aesthetics of change wrought by the slow distress of time but understood that a key challenge they faced was 'to counterfeit the effects of time in an intentional compositional act'.[198] Says Spuybroek: 'the Picturesque did not remain a way of looking at existing landscapes and rural buildings but instead

35   Humphry Repton, 'The Cottage', in *The Red Book of Blaise Castle* (1795–96), Bristol Museums. Note the two main gables, prominent chimney, gabled dormer window, and pentice at the near end

36   'A Double Cottage', plate 6, from T.F. Hunt, *Half a Dozen Hints on Picturesque Domestic Architecture* (London: Henry G. Bohn, 1841), The Bodleian Libraries, University of Oxford

developed into a way of designing new ones'.[199] In correspondence with Repton, Price acknowledged that his advocacy of picturesque irregularity and aesthetic nonconformism was period-specific – a reflection of his distaste for the fashionable symmetries of Palladianism – but he, Gilpin, and Knight were so successful in proselytising their alternative perspective that it was turned, not least by their followers, into an enduring practice.

COTTAGE PATTERN BOOKS

The crucial element in that evolution, and one that did still more to marry the Picturesque to the idea of the cottage, was the flood of cottage pattern books published between 1785 and 1835[200] – filled, in Macarthur's words, 'with designs that mimic the additive unclosed forms and the mixed materials of vernacular buildings'.[201] James Malton's *An Essay on British Cottage Architecture* (1798) is perhaps the most important. It dedicated itself to 'the peculiar beauty of the British picturesque'[202] and included a detailed description of the ideal cottage exterior:

> of odd, irregular form, with various, harmonious colouring . . . a porch at entrance; irregular breaks in the direction of the walls; one part higher than another; various roofing of different materials, thatch particularly, boldly projecting; fronts partly built of . . . brick, partly weatherboarded and partly brick-noggin dashed; casement window lights.[203]

Other key examples include Atkinson's *Views of Picturesque Cottages* (1805), Pocock's *Architectural Designs for Rustic Cottages* (1807), Robinson's *Rural and Village Architecture* (1823), Hunt's *Half a Dozen Hints on Picturesque Domestic Architecture* (1825), and J.C. Loudon's *Encyclopaedia of Cottage, Farm and Villa Architecture* (1833).

These publications, and many others like them, collated the raw material for a commoditised cottage picturesque – a dwelling whose inspiration their 'architect'-authors (touting sedulously for business) found, theoretically, in the writings of Price and Knight; and, experientially, in the peasants' cottages and small yeoman's houses in which 'the forms and decorations of the old Rural Architecture [were] scattered widely abroad'.[204]

Some of this inspiration was Elizabethan in origin, a style whose 'great glory' was 'that it produced beautifully simple, yet perfectly architectural, cottages for the poor'.[205] Some was older. But the interpretation

37   John Thomas Smith, 'In Bury Street, Edmonton', from *Remarks on Rural Scenery* (London: Nathaniel Smith, 1797), The Bodleian Libraries, University of Oxford. Smith's eye was particularly taken by 'the antient, feeble, roof-oppressed hovel' – the kind of observation that gave the Picturesque a bad name for privileging pictoriality over the conditions in which people lived (*Remarks on Rural Scenery*, p.12)

SUGGESTIONS FOR THE GROUPING OF DOUBLE COTTAGES

Nᵒ 2 or 5

Nᵒ 2 or 5

Nᵒ 2 or 5

Nᵒ 6

Nᵒ 2 or 5

Nᵒ 4

Nᵒ 2 or 5

Nᵒ 2 or 5

Nᵒ 4

Nᵒ 2 or 5

Nᵒ 4

Nᵒ 6

Nᵒ 4

Nᵒ 2 or 5

Nᵒˢ 1.3 or 8 may be substituted for Nᵒ 6 and Nᵒ 7 for Nᵒ 4.

Day & Son, lith. to the Queen.

left

38 Cottage designs by Henry Roberts, presented as a guide to the way different elevations could be grouped for variety in large estates, in Roberts, *The Dwellings of the Labouring Classes: Their Arrangement and Construction* (London: The Society for Improving the Condition of the Labouring Classes, 1850), p.48, The Bodleian Libraries, University of Oxford

below

39 'A Gamekeeper's House', plate 3, from T.F. Hunt, *Half a Dozen Hints on Picturesque Domestic Architecture* (London: Henry G. Bohn, 1841), The Bodleian Libraries, University of Oxford

of the Picturesque as an English phenomenon – as the implicitly revivalist architectural movement that Kenneth Clarke acknowledges[206] – is grounded in this confluence of theory and inspiration from the preceding centuries' architectural survivals.

The apogee of the Picturesque in cottage design came from John Nash, the architect who invented the picturesque suburb at Regent's Park,[207] and created the paradigmatic picturesque village Blaise Hamlet in 1811. Nash was 'masterly in his ability to contrive a simple vocabulary of traditional cottage ingredients and to assemble and reassemble them'.[208] In achieving this, Blaise Hamlet perfected the tradition of *cottage orné* (explored in depth by Roger White) that evolved in tandem with the theoretical exposition of the Picturesque, beginning with the garden buildings of the earlier eighteenth century and reaching adult form with Queen Charlotte's cottage at Kew around 1771.[209] The scenographic purpose of such buildings inspired the pattern-book architects of the early nineteenth century to design cottages aesthetically a world away from the plain, low, hip-roofed Georgian boxes that Walpole had built to rehouse his tenants at Houghton in Norfolk, around 1730, and that Kent and Wood espoused in their late neo-classical cottage pattern books.[210]

An evolution of the new aesthetic can then be detected in Henry Roberts's 1850 book *The Dwellings of the Labouring Classes*, where the author specifically emphasised the importance of 'picturesque effect'[211] in the cottages he designed

40   The National Trust's eighteenth-century Hop Kiln Farmhouse near Bromyard in Herefordshire. The kitchen (in the lower left-hand wing) has two outshots, on either side of the main range's external chimneystack. The larger pentice-roofed outshot houses the bread oven; the smaller, nearer one, the washing copper. The external aesthetic effect – the broken rectangle of the wing itself, the asymmetry of the outshots, the non-matching angles of their two roofs, in combination with the external chimneystacks' volume and verticality – exemplifies the unconscious irregularity that inspired the self-conscious Picturesque

for the Society for Improving the Condition of the Labouring Classes (fig.38). Roberts's models are remarkable for the way they prefigure – with gabled main blocks, cross-wing gables articulating ornamental plan breaks, and dormer windows – what would become the attenuated picturesqueness of the best 1919–21 local authority Addison Scheme cottages.

The Picturesque's theoreticians and pattern-book architects introduced into the English cottage's self-conscious architectural vocabulary a set of aesthetic tropes: the front- or street-facing gable (inspired by the medieval cross-wing),[212] steep roofs and broken eaves lines, half-timbering, roughcast, brick- or flint-nogging, the gabled dormer, gabled or pent-roofed porches and other outshots, intricate bargeboards, latticed casement windows, and the complex, prominent, usually external chimneystack. With their capacity for wide circulation, the pattern books of the early 1800s – and later examples like

Roberts's – helped de-localise traditional architecture and spread visualities as widely as the printed page would carry them. Hence Mercer's judgement that, by the early nineteenth century, there was a 'national theme with regional variations' in cottage architecture, rather than a 'bundle of independent themes'.[213]

What the Picturesque became after the pattern-book architects had commoditised it fell short in sophistication of the aesthetic philosophy iterated in colloquy by Price and Knight. But even in this etiolated version – as a guide on how to achieve certain appealing visual effects through architecture – it was attractive, accessible, and patriotic; in Hunt's words, 'a style which may be said to be indigenous to this soil'.[214]

The powerful bond created between picturesque architecture and the idea of the cottage helps establish the context for Saint, Watkin, and Tinniswood[215] when they discuss the enduring influence of the Picturesque throughout the nineteenth century. Goodhart-Rendel, in his 1953 *English Architecture since the Regency*, writes: 'if any governing character has unified the English architecture we have reviewed already, that character was due, unquestionably, to the Picturesque's former dominion'.[216] And this is how, from the beginning of the nineteenth century, the cottage came to embody the English national domestic-architectural idiom – imbricating class history with Romantic cultural expression in painting, literature, and popular print; and synthesising them with the visuality of the Picturesque to produce an idea of, and an aesthetic for, the autochthonous English home that was very much still alive after the First World War.

RUSKIN AND THE COTTAGE PICTURESQUE

The flowering of the Picturesque in the early decades of the nineteenth century might have represented the high-water mark for the cottage in English architectural thought, had it not been for Ruskin. Numerous cottage passages span the *Poetry of Architecture* at the start and *Praeterita* at the end

of his career. Echoing Samuel Rogers – as well as his beloved Wordsworth at Tintern Abbey: 'These plots of cottage-ground . . . and wreaths of smoke / Sent up in silence, from among the trees!'[217] – the young Ruskin found the little home

> beautiful always and everywhere . . . looking out of the woody dingle with its eye-like window and sending up the motion of azure smoke between the silver trunks of aged trees . . . the cottage always gives the idea of a thing to be beloved . . . as peaceful as silence itself.[218]

Middle period Ruskin lost none of this affection: 'you must over and over again have paused at the wicket gate of some cottage garden, delighted by the simple beauty of the honeysuckle porch and latticed window'.[219] And years after that, in 1872, not only was the cottage lovely, it should nearly always suffice: 'a cottage all of our own, with its little garden . . . Less than this, no man should be content with for his nest; more than this, few should seek'.[220]

This combination of picturesque aesthetics and moral sufficiency could not flow from a cottage's being decayed or collapsing. Just as he cherished the cottage, Ruskin was determined to make serviceable its companion, the Picturesque. He famously observed: 'probably no word in the language (exclusive of theological expressions) has

41   John Ruskin, photographed by Frederick Hollyer (1894), National Portrait Gallery, London

been the subject of so frequent or so prolonged dispute'. Yet he also considered the Picturesque, 'occultly', to have 'been the ground of much that is true and just in our judgement of art . . . that idea which all feel and (to appearance) with respect to similar things'.[221] To effect its recuperation, he 'sublimated picturesque theory to his own ideals',[222] re-conceptualising it as 'parasitical sublimity', adduced from the geomorphology of the sheltering earth: 'An architect should live as little in cities as a painter. Send him to our hills, and let him study there what nature understands by a buttress, and what by a dome'.[223]

At the heart of Ruskin's appreciation of the Picturesque was the cottage roof[224] – 'the roof should be visible, so the best and most natural form of roof in the north is . . . the steep gable'. Ruskin expanded:

> you actually do owe . . . a great part of your pleasure in all cottage scenery, and in all the inexhaustible imagery of literature which is founded upon it, to the conspicuousness of the cottage roof . . . The very soul of the cottage – the essence and meaning of it – are in its roof.[225]

This from the Edinburgh Lectures (1853), where Ruskin described the key architectural features of a properly handled exterior. He further disclosed that his search for picturesque inspiration was not restricted to English vernacular models:

> In Picardy, and Normandy, again, and many towns in Germany . . . the effect of the whole street depends on the prominence of the gables; not only of the fronts . . . but of the sides also, set with small garret or dormer windows, each of the most fantastic and beautiful form, and crowned with a little spire or pinnacle.[226]

Traditional English architecture was undoubtedly the model for the Picturesque's early theoreticians – in Taylor's words: 'There was . . . an instinctive rightness in the landscape of the English cottage long before anyone thought of calling it "picturesque"'.[227] And Knight's interest in associationism betrayed the fundamentally revivalist character of early exercises in picturesque design. But as the movement developed, it started to understand better its own abstract aesthetic content – asymmetries, irregularities, sharp and contrasting edges, contrapuntal massing, and decorative variety. Articulated in the Ruskin passage above is the importance of the architectural feature that delivers so many of those effects – the gable. And whereas the architectural tectonics that Ruskin described could easily have been inferred from Price and Knight (as they were by the early nineteenth-century picturesque pattern-book 'architects'), here they were set out in detail by the most famous art and architectural thinker of his day. Ruskin, furthermore, was not simply describing architecture; he was interweaving tectonics with the dignity of the moral home: 'all good architecture rises out of good and simple domestic work . . . before you attempt to build great churches and palaces, you must build good house doors and garret windows'.[228]

There were additional implications for the builder in the Edinburgh Lectures. Ruskin emphasised the importance of the gable-roofed Gothic porch, under which 'you can put down your umbrella at your leisure'; and extolled the 'delightfulness of a bow window. I can hardly fancy a room can be perfect without one'.[229] Picturesque in their potential for aesthetic irregularity, such suggestions were adopted enthusiastically by English house builders in the decades that followed, as was Ruskin's broader stipulation that Gothic was the style everyone should use. Whatever an architect's motivation for revisiting it – from Wyatt's scenography to Pugin's revived fourteenth-century functionalism – Gothic's visuality was intrinsically picturesque.[230] Pugin himself called it the 'true Picturesque'.[231] And the great Goth made the connection plainer in one of his most often quoted sentences: 'An architect should exhibit his skill by turning the difficulties which occur in raising an elevation from a convenient plan into so many picturesque beauties'.[232]

Ruskin's writing leaves little doubt as to his standing as the great inheritor of Gilpin, Price, and Knight's philosophy.[233] His *Seven Lamps*, says Hill, was a 'reinvention of the Picturesque . . . essentially the same aesthetic philosophy, recast for the High Victorians'.[234] Inheriting both picturesque theory and its practitioners' love of the cottage, Ruskin did the Picturesque a service by cleaning up its 'facile preoccupation with visual qualities which blind the weak minded to human suffering'.[235] He believed the cottage could embody great architecture and great moral value – 'I know what it is to live in a cottage with a deal floor and roof . . . I know it to be in many respects healthier and happier than living between a Turkey carpet and gilded ceiling'.[236]

In effect, an architecture commoditised in the early 1800s, as a collection of tectonic and associational techniques to create picturesque cottage elevations intended largely for scenic consumption, was alchemised by Ruskin through the admixture of moral and aesthetic gravity. As Saint puts it, 'a moral vocabulary of the house . . . emerged'.[237] And after this transformation, cottage picturesque was taken upmarket in domestic architecture by Shaw, Nesfield, Devey, et al., to consolidate what Hunt had designated 'Old English', for middle- and upper-class clients – a development that had been consolidated at the tail-end of the Picturesque's theoretical exposition by Gilbert Laing Meason in 1828: 'as we had no other model of domestic architecture than the gable-end cottage, by the duplication of this simple form . . . was constructed what has been called the Old English Manor-house style'.[238] It was this, rather than the picturesque Italianate that Nash ventured at Regent's Park, that would come to dominate quotidian domestic architecture.

George Devey's Ruskin-inspired accomplishment in building Old English with local materials is well documented. His estate cottages at Penshurst in Kent were to the Picturesque's continuing traditional revival what Pugin's work was, in some senses, to the mature Gothic – a more archaeological phase, fascinated by original sources, more rigorous in their application, but still essentially picturesque.[239] Spatially at the other end of the scale, the mansions that Shaw built at Cragside and Leys Wood positively broadcast their roots in the cottage picturesque. Both were gabled, timbered, tiled, and jettied. Each boasted a baronial tower, topped with a 'hutch'[240] – tile-hung at Leys Wood, timbered at Cragside. Saint sees the influence of Nesfield's stable tower at Cloverley, and 'a hint back to the city gateways of Nuremberg'.[241] One might also observe that both houses ended up with something looking strikingly similar to an A-frame picturesque cottage mounted, like a warship's battle ensign, in pride of place at the buildings' uppermost point. 'The origin of Victorian eclecticism,' says Mordaunt Crook, 'has to be looked for among the historicist aspects of the Picturesque.'[242]

Shaw's was a domestic picturesque that sustained the moral intensity of the Ruskinian cottage even as homes grew in size. He invoked the cottage sampler with his carved inscription 'East or West, Hame's Best' in the stone of Armstrong's dining-room fireplace at Cragside.[243] The Harvard philosopher George Santayana, in Oxford for the duration of the First World War, solved the puzzle: 'An English country house, which is a cottage in appearance, may turn out on examination to be almost a palace in extent'.[244] Yet the pattern-book architect Robinson had beaten him to this conclusion in 1823. His 'Design XX' was for a house of 'some extent', yet which 'in some points of view . . . scarcely assumes more than the appearance of a cottage'.[245] Devey's work for the Rothschilds at Ascott conformed – the rambling finished result seen by Mary Gladstone as 'a palace-like cottage'.[246] And it is this picturesque enthusiasm for aesthetically articulated plan/ functional addition that gives rise to Spuybroek's concept of the 'megacottage'.[247]

Shaw's 'influence on all matters cognate to his profession was supreme', *The Builder* declared in autumn 1918.[248] John Betjeman, poet and interwar architectural historian, concurred. In his 1973 BBC film *Metro-Land*, he specified two dwellings as central to templating the early twentieth century's domestic architecture. Charles Voysey's cottage 'The Orchard', at Chorleywood (1900–1901), was one: 'the parent of thousands of simple English houses'. The other was 'Grim's Dyke', the 1870–72 house that Norman Shaw built for the artist Frederick Goodall in Harrow Weald – the 'prototype', mused Betjeman, 'of all suburban homes in Southern England'.[249] Indeed, the prototype's onward transmission was witnessed at first hand by the illustrator Kate Greenaway in 1885, who spotted 'a horrid man' sketching the outside of her new Shaw house in Hampstead: 'I suppose he is cribbing Mr Shaw's design, and going to put my house up somewhere else, who knows where'.[250]

The late-nineteenth-century synthesis of 'home' and the Picturesque, contrived by Shaw for Greenaway, and many others besides, took a step away from Ruskin when it was stylistically modulated from Old English to Queen Anne – 'dilettante picturesque', as Philip Webb called it.[251] But William Burges had seen through the new fashion as early as 1875 – its 'great object being to get the picturesque by any and every means'.[252]

English architecture was not the sole source for these Victorian experiments. Picturesque exteriors demand an objectively definable core of aesthetic abstractions. Their inspiration could be English building from the fourteenth to seventeenth centuries, as it had been for most of the cottage pattern-books between 1800 and 1830.[253] But from the mid-nineteenth century, it did not have to be English at all. The *Architect* magazine in the 1870s and 1880s groaned with accounts of architectural tourism in continental Europe in search of the Picturesque. Shaw had followed Ruskin to study architecture in northern France, sketching raw material for his designs there and in Strasbourg, Assisi, Naples, Erfurt, Nuremberg, Prague, and Bruges. 'We have recently commenced,' he wrote on his return, 'to engraft on our national style many beauties and peculiarities hitherto confined to the Continent.'[254] Girouard contextualises:

Shaw needed half-timbering for the particular romantic effects he wanted . . . in his earlier days it did not worry him (though it has worried his critics since) that he used it with complete disregard of the vernacular traditions of the neighbourhood.[255]

The tradition Shaw mined instead was, at root, Ruskinian.[256] And even in 1919, though Ruskin had died at the turn of the century, his influence persisted – in the picturesque appearance of most English houses from the late nineteenth century into the Edwardian period (Geoffrey Scott's architecture with 'so firm a hold in England'),[257] and in his sheer cultural prominence. Around the centenary of his birth, a *Daily Mail* column on 8 February 1919, 'The Letters of an Englishman', allowed Charles Whibley – for many years a contributor to the reactionary *Blackwood's Magazine* – to lament the way 'an easily persuaded public was led to confuse the moral and the picturesque until it accepted as a new gospel whatever time-worn commonplaces Ruskin chose to give it'.[258] Prominent among those commonplaces was the nostalgic vision of the cottage.

From Saxon cottars, via Milton, Wordsworth, Clare and Cobbett, Gainsborough, Constable, Price, and Knight, to Allingham and Greenaway – much of their aesthetic exemplified at one time or another by Ruskin, Webb, Nesfield, Shaw, Devey, Voysey, and Baillie Scott – such was the kinetic energy of the English cottage tradition at the end of the First World War. Had Lloyd George, Christopher Addison, and the organisers of the RIBA/LGB National Cottage Competition in 1917–18 apprehended the weight of class, cultural, and architectural precedent that their cottage-building ambitions might invoke, perhaps they would have been less surprised by the traditional bent of most of the entries. England's architectural power-brokers were drawn collectively to formalism in the post-1900 period, as we shall see. But they experienced an abrupt awakening when they came face to face, in 1918, with the picturesque visuality still entertained by architects across the country for the idea of the cottage.

2

THE COTTAGE CONTESTED

The First World War had come to an end with the British state promising its working classes 500,000 new cottages – but without having worked out what they should look like. Although we have seen how dominant in cultural reception the picturesque vision of the cottage was, there was no question of canvassing what the architect Beresford Pite called 'the unqualified tastes of the inhabitant class'.[1] The government's plan instead was to devolve new cottage aesthetics to the architectural profession.

Julienne Hanson observes: 'architects are rarely "of the culture" for which they design'.[2] Here an almost exclusively middle-class profession[3] was to

be asked to act as agents for a government with a similar or more elevated class profile. Historical continuity in the class dynamics of cottage provision was thus guaranteed: working-class tenants would have to live with domestic aesthetics chosen for them, as they mostly had done since the eighteenth century. What level of aesthetic continuity this process should imply was to be left to the architects. 'The face of the country [. . .] is to be permanently stamped with the impress of the present age', RIBA President Henry Hare would remark.[4] The government resolved architects should be responsible for the stamping.

42   A prize-winner in the RIBA/LGB National Cottage Competition (1918). The group of six non-parlour cottages by Harry Heathman from Bristol took the Class A Second Premium in the South-West Area. RIBA Collections

The Local Government Board-sponsored 1918 National Cottage Competition was the solution initially reached to determine how the state-funded dwelling of the future should look. As we shall see, the majority view of the architects who entered was that a traditional picturesque cottage visuality remained appropriate. Competitors so inclined were swimming with the historical tide; their designs would harmonise with a wealth of then relatively recent cottage literature, from Ralph Nevill's *The Old Cottage and Domestic Architecture of South-West Surrey* in 1889 to Basil Oliver's *Old Houses and Village Buildings in East Anglia* in 1912 – books that valorised the traditional cottage while making liberal and approving use of the term 'picturesque'. Guy Dawber's *Old Cottages and Farm-houses in Kent and Sussex* (1900) stood for all when he wrote of the cottage's 'picturesqueness', its 'beauty and subtle charm', and 'the wonderful feeling of homeliness that pervades every feature'.[5] Who would not want to live in such a dwelling?

Despite this consensus, one faction of architects had something different in mind. Holder and McKellar, Burton, and Curl all shed useful light on the origins of the formal or neo-Georgian turn in English architecture from the late nineteenth century. An influential group including Reginald Blomfield, Professor Albert Richardson, Professor Charles Reilly at Liverpool University, and some of his colleagues and students – most of them enthusiasts for the American City Beautiful movement, founded in Chicago and led by Daniel Burnham – carried this enthusiasm into the 1900s. Reilly and his supporters also sought to extend their imprimatur to cottage building. They were critical of the Picturesque and would attempt to shape the aesthetics of state housing to ensure their taste for formal civic architecture prevailed.

THE NATIONAL COTTAGE COMPETITION

Organisationally split between the RIBA and the Society of Architects, agitated still by the 1890s' arguments of Art versus Profession,[6] architects in England and Wales after 1900 were also divided by a fundamental aesthetic polarity. The argument between Robert Kerr's 'Classical and the Picturesque' had never gone away.[7] As the First World War came to an end, although the architectural *apparat* at the RIBA, the leading architectural schools, and key sections of the specialist press were increasingly agreed on the desirability of a formal approach to civic architecture,[8] when it came to cottages architects more broadly seemed to retain an atavistic affection for the Picturesque.

The war had put cottages at the forefront of professionals' minds.[9] Architecture's leaders at the RIBA recognised the government's housing scheme would be an opportunity to remobilise a profession diverted by military service or just plain starved of work. But, as Stanley Adshead pointed out in March 1918, the opportunity would not just fall into their laps: 'I feel our profession must bestir itself if it is to qualify [for] the great work that undoubtedly lies ahead'.[10]

An early step towards winning that work had come in August 1917, when the Ministry of Reconstruction's Advisory Housing Panel suggested to Addison that the project 'should be in the charge of an architect, otherwise the high standard of design and layout . . . will not be secured'.[11] Then came the agreement the Local Government Board (LGB) reached with the RIBA to stage a competition in search of 'the best available ideas in cottage building'[12] – a political coup on which Adshead publicly congratulated RIBA President Hare in June 1918.[13] The breakthrough was also celebrated by *The Builder*: 'the RIBA, at last getting some sort of recognition after being ignored for so long'.[14] Hare later accounted the competition's principal value as having been 'to identify architects more fully than has hitherto been the case with this class of building'.[15]

What became the National Cottage Competition[16] was seen at the time as crucial to the realisation of the Lloyd George government's housing scheme. Theories about how postwar working-class cottages should be planned, and what they might look like, were to be tested against specification and cost constraints in a government-mandated forum. The contest's parameters were agreed between the LGB and the RIBA in the autumn of 1917; a sum of £5,000 was allotted for its administration; and the competition was formally launched in the Institute's November journal.[17] 'When the National Cottage Competition was announced,' reported *The Builder*, 'architects all over the country hoped that the RIBA . . . would rise to the occasion.'[18]

The National Cottage Competition was in fact six regionally based competitions, co-ordinated by the RIBA in London. Organisers divided England and Wales into geographical areas reflecting the RIBA's Allied Societies, then invited entries in four classes of cottage: Class A – living room, scullery and three bedrooms; Class B – adding a parlour to A's specification; Class C – parlour, living room, scullery and *two* bedrooms; and Class D – variations of A, B or C, but planned mainly as a single storey. The First and Second Premiums would be £100 and £50 for the best designs in Classes A–C in each region, with premiums of £50 and £30 for the best Class D designs. The RIBA planned to appoint six separate panels of judges centrally, one for each area, whose identity would be revealed once the results were published.

Competitors were encouraged to design 'without regard to any existing by-laws . . . the object being to show the best types possible if any existing restrictions are removed'. Other guidance included the desirability of avoiding 'back additions'; the need for a fixed bath and water supply; and room height of not less than eight feet.[19] The regulations gave no guidance about exterior style. A further document, 'Supplementary Particulars in Response to Questions by Competitors', extended the closing date to 31 January 1918 and provided an important clarification: 'Bedrooms may be partly in the roofs'.[20] This ruled in dormer windows, which had a significance beyond their capacity to light attics. Another tangentially aesthetic determinant was also specified: 'It is essential that strict economy be exercised throughout the design'.[21]

Even before the results were published, the competition provoked controversy. Late in 1917, the *Evening Standard* worried that the nationwide initiative might lead to the architectural 'Prussianisation' of the country.[22] *The Builder* recorded dissatisfaction with the 'poor and inadequate conditions' of the RIBA's competition

specification.[23] But from mid-February 1918, across the participating regions, the results were revealed and must at least have allayed fears of uniformity. In April 1918, the RIBA staged a London exhibition of the winning plans and elevations, and published the full results in the June 1918 edition of their journal.[24]

Over 800 architects entered: 1700 separate designs were submitted,[25] and the competition momentarily became – for the world of planning and architecture – the centre of attention. There were 48 first and second premiated cottage designs to unveil, worth £3,180 in prize money (over £182,000 at today's values).[26] To help sort wheat from chaff, the RIBA's Committee of Selection adopted a set of criteria among which one point stands out: 'satisfactory architectural treatment having regard to the English tradition of cottage building'.[27]

The phrase hints at the disagreements to come. Publication of the premium winners in book form came in June 1918 – a 'well got-up and well-illustrated booklet',[28] packed with high-quality perspective drawings by some of the doyens of interwar architectural draughtsmanship, notably Cyril Farey and Raffles Davison.[29] The entries were accompanied by a RIBA commentary which articulated how the traditional class-structural dimension of cottage meaning (discussed in Chapter 1) remained alive and well. As the government's agent, the RIBA adopted the perspective of the 'improving landowner', prescribing both the character and destiny of their dependants:

> We may look upon a cottage as the home of a working-class family of limited means and sufficient self-respect to be desirous of paying its rent without either undue encroachment on income or undue reliance on subsidy.[30]

This outlook implicitly consolidated the idea that council cottages would be for people who could afford to pay at least some rent, not the poorest of the poor.

The competition's class dynamics were those of historical continuity. Sadly for the RIBA contingent in London at least, the architectural outcome also looked discouragingly traditional. A clear majority of the cottage designs was picturesque in

43   Courtenay Crickmer's Class A First Premium winner in the Home Counties Area. A non-parlour, three-bedroom house (a prototypical council house type), formal in essence, as attested to by the symmetry of the block ends and setbacks. RIBA Collections

44   Alfred Cox won the Class B First Premium in the Home Counties Area for his formal row of three-bedroom parlour cottages. There are sash windows and flat-roofed dormers, except at both ends where the dormers have neo-classical pediments. The Home Counties area was dominated by formally designed winners. RIBA Collections

character – in the description Temple gives to Nash's Blaise Hamlet cottages: 'casemented dormers, bay windows with neatly tiled roofs . . . skilfully handled to create asymmetrical profiles'.[31] Only a minority even of the successful entries reflected the formalism of RIBA HQ's emergent orthodoxy. Yet the winners' undeniably high levels of 'regard to the English tradition of cottage building' should not have been a surprise. An article in *The Times* late in November 1917 had insisted: 'if our architects will condescend to study the old cottages in our ancient villages, they will find more to be learnt from them for our present needs than from all the temples of Greece and Rome'.[32] Many British architects, it transpired, thought the same way.

The RIBA had staffed its competition judging panels with some of the most influential practitioners in the country. Home Counties Area assessors included: the President, Henry Hare; the President-elect, E. Guy Dawber, Cotswold enthusiast and previously a judge for the 1911 Gidea Park housing exhibition; Sir Aston Webb, designer of Admiralty Arch and cottages in the Home Counties; and H.V. Lanchester, architect

for Cardiff City Hall and Westminster's Methodist Central Hall. These luminaries were joined by Stanley Adshead, Professor of Town Planning at University College, London – a 'great exponent' of the classical tradition,[33] and thoroughly primed, after years with Charles Reilly at Liverpool University, to evangelise for the formal in design, not for what he called 'the picturesque village of the past'.[34]

The Home Counties judges' civic architectural enthusiasms leaned towards the neo-classical and – in contrast to prize-winners in many of the other competition regions – the designs they rewarded were more formal in appearance. Habitual competition winner Courtenay Crickmer's Class A First Premium design (fig.43) was one, recalling the slightly dour cottages he had worked on at Gretna.[35] Alfred Cox, a RIBA Fellow with a track record of public libraries, a picture gallery at Kingston, and Barnet Infirmary,[36] won the First Premium in Class B with a similarly regimented block (fig.44). Yet even among the Home Counties winners, Crickmer's Class C First Premium design (fig.45) broke with economy of roofline by deploying

45   Courtenay Crickmer's Home Counties Class C First Premium entry. Fundamentally formal, but picturesque indiscipline detectable in the broken eaves, roof lines and gabled dormers. RIBA Collections

46 Cyril Wontner Smith was honourably mentioned for his Home Counties Area Class A entry. The apotheosis of cottage picturesque: decorated street-facing gables, plan breaks, bay windows, prominent chimneystacks, articulated quoining, dormers breaking the roof slope, and mullioned lattice casements. RIBA Collections

multiple individually gabled dormers and a complex roofscape.

Still more surprising from the Home Counties jury (though he had worked in the office of panel member Sir Aston Webb) was Cyril Wontner Smith's Honourable Mention for his Class A rhapsody in decorated Cotswold gabling, broken roofscape, dormer windows, and latticed casements (fig.46). 'Beautiful designs', of 'very marked aesthetic quality',[37] reported *The Builder* – showing the Picturesque could still raise a cheer.

Across the rest of the competition's territories, the Picturesque was more dominant. In the North, the First Premium for Class A went to the York-based

RIBA licentiate J. Hervey Rutherford, whose block (fig.47) boasted two large street-facing gables (each with a tile motif at the apex) on a broken plan, with a complex roofscape and an eaves line punctuated by dormer windows with individual hipped roofs. Alex T. Scott took the First Premium in North Class B and the Second Premium in North Class C for designs characterised by street-facing gables and the broken plans they articulated (fig.48) – the mood again evoking the avowedly picturesque cottages of Henry Roberts (1850).

The competition's South Wales Area saw honours evenly shared in Class A, between a First Premium-winning formal design and the Second Premium

47   Northern Area Class A First Premium winner, by J. Hervey Rutherford. More Picturesque than Palladian, with its large street-facing gables, hipped dormer windows, broken plan and complex roof. Perspective by Raffles Davison, RIBA Collections

left, top

48   Northern Area Class B First Premium winner, by Alex T. Scott, modelled a gabled main block, with two street-facing gables on a broken plan. Materials of the locality featured too, in the stone ground storey, divided from the roughcast first floor by a string course. RIBA Collections

middle

49   An Honourable Mention for Thomas Bevan's Class A three-bedroom non-parlour cottages in the South Wales Area. Again, essentially Picturesque – broken plan, swept cross-wing gables decorated at the apex and bracketed pentice porch roofs. RIBA Collections

bottom

50   William Ravenscroft took the South-West Area Class C Second Premium with this strongly picturesque deployment of street-facing gables, dormer windows, complex roofscape, and even some shallow jettying. RIBA Collections

for something more picturesque. But the balance in Class A was tipped towards picturesqueness by Thomas Bevan's Honourable Mention (fig.49) with its four giant, swept, cross-wing gables – each articulating a broken plan, and again decorated at the apex.

Stanley Adshead did double duty by serving on the London jury and with the South-West Area assessors, where perhaps as a result formal winners were in greater evidence. But even in the South-West, Adshead did not entirely staunch the picturesque flood. William Ravenscroft's Class C Second Premium-winning block makes this plain (fig.50) with its gabled main block, huge, arrow-looped, street-facing gable pair at the centre, dormer windows, and subsidiary swept gables at each end.

The Midland Area assessors included William Alexander Harvey, principal architect for the Cadburys at Bournville, who had preached simplicity for cottage design in his 1906 book, but whose *penchant* for the Picturesque was a matter of built record in Birmingham.[38] This enthusiasm was to be discerned among the premiums awarded in

the competition – notably, the design by Frederick William Charles Gregory, a RIBA Silver Medal Winner for Measured Drawing in 1902, who took the Class C First Premium with a gabled main block, on a broken plan, with a complex roof, multiple casement dormers, and asymmetric handling of window sizes.

Perhaps the most perfect symbol of the competition's failure to produce the results that the modernising formalists hoped for came on their home turf – the Manchester, Liverpool, and North Wales Area. Here, the First Premium for a Class A cottage block (fig.51) was awarded to the 47-year-old Welshman Herbert Luck North, who had worked as an assistant with Lutyens and William Alfred Pite. Unusually, North had been both architect *and* developer for the gabled and roughcast picturesque houses at The Close in Llanfairfechan, North Wales, built on his family's land after 1901.[39] He was also responsible for a highly regarded antiquarian book, *The Old Cottages of Snowdonia*, co-authored with Harold Hughes,[40] which rejected the Renaissance as a model – for 'its foreign pride and pedantry'[41] – and expressed little affection for the neo-Georgian: 'flatter roofs and symmetrical fronts are not very inspiring'.[42] North's prize-winner was a six-dwelling block in true cottage picturesque, with a complex, thatch-style roofscape, curved in 'eyebrows' over the first-floor casements, and bracketed pent-roof porches throwing deep shadows over the front doors. In the perspective sketch, evidence of cosily banked fireplaces rises from one among the massy, elaborated chimneystacks.

Shortly before the competition closed, *The Builder* had effectively previewed the impending debate with its review of Frank Baines's new Office of Works air industry workers' scheme at Roe Green, Kingsbury, built in 1917–18.[43] Just as he had on the Well Hall Estate in Eltham, south-east London, Baines designed an estate of fundamentally picturesque dwellings. *The Builder* recognised this – and its potential to provoke argument:

There will always be a difference of opinion as to whether this type, or one based on Georgian

51 The First Premium for a Class A, three-bedroom, non-parlour cottage in the Manchester, Liverpool, and North Wales Area was won by Herbert Luck North's exercise in true cottage picturesque. Note the broken plan, complex thatch-style roof pattern, prominent chimneystacks, bracketed pentice porches, and casement windows. RIBA Collections

traditions, in which the roofs are uniformly of low pitch . . . is the preferable type to adopt; but as far as we can judge, the advocates of what we may term the picturesque traditional type are at present in the ascendant.[44]

The binary in this critique is Kerr's and Geoffrey Scott's – the formal Georgian contrasted with the Picturesque. No mention is made of the Arts and Crafts, the vernacular, the Tudor or Elizabethan, and the article in *The Builder* came only a couple of months before everyone would discover just how greatly in the ascendant 'the picturesque traditional type' remained.

Prominently gabled, with high roofs and dormer windows, many of the RIBA competition entries satisfied the key criteria of the Picturesque restated by Ruskin in 1880 – 'angular and broken

lines, vigorous oppositions of light and shadow'[45] – itself a formula applied to domestic architecture decades earlier in Uvedale Price's description of the parsonage house encountered by his wandering trio in the *Dialogue* of 1801:

a singular mixture of neatness and irregularity. . . . there were all kinds of projections – of differently shaped windows and chimneys – of rooms in odd corners – of roofs crossing each other in different directions.[46]

The competition's rules asked for cottage designs in six-unit blocks, which left little scope for true picturesque irregularity or asymmetry of plan. But many entries still modelled complex roofscapes and large cross-wing gables, usually motivated by only the slightest of plan breaks. In addition, strict formal rectangles were disrupted repeatedly by pent-roofed porches, gabled dormers, and other encrustations. The winners went on show from mid-February around the country. As early as 13 March 1918, a disapproving Stanley Adshead pronounced judgement: 'A general inspection of the designs submitted shows . . . as a profession we have not yet realised that the cottage of the future cannot be the cottage of the past'.[47] Adshead feared that the opportunity provided by the government's new housing scheme to strike out in bold new architectural and social directions was being squandered. Indeed, the competition results came as a disappointment to both the Liverpool tendency and to the ruling group at the top of the RIBA, largely converts to the formalist tenor of the time.

The Builder seemed wrong-footed by the winning designs. The magazine's individual reviews were positive at times about the influence of the Picturesque on competitors' architecture: 'Mr North's exterior treatment has more of the character and flavour of our typical old cottage design than most . . . the general effect being picturesque and pleasantly proportioned';[48] 'Messrs Johnson and Richards' elevations are picturesque';[49] 'Mr Robinson has a picturesque group'.[50] The magazine's leader-writer, though, was contrastingly sceptical, echoing disgruntlement at the RIBA. In the 5 April 1918 edition, the magazine complained:

> We had intended to review the designs submitted in the Government Housing Competition, now on view at the RIBA, but on reflection we can see no useful purpose in doing so . . . It may be that as a nation we are so inherently conservative and prejudiced that we are unwilling to accept anything better for several generations to come, and, if this be so, we may industriously produce small and picturesque modifications of what we have seen in the past.

The editorial linked the competition's failure to embrace modernity with the mythologised history of the cottage discussed in Chapter 1, pleading antiphrastically: 'leave us our dreams about the picturesque cottage framed with honeysuckle and roses, and gilded by the rays of the setting sun'.[51]

Over the previous year, *The Builder* had anticipated the costliness of state-funded dwellings, and worried repeatedly about where the money for the government's cottages was to be found. The magazine linked government plans for state-funded cottages directly to the tensions of the English class system:

> Each one of us is to be called upon to take his share in paying for these 300,000 cottages . . . We are to invert the order of things, and the favoured classes are to be the poorest, to whose wants everyone else will have to contribute.[52]

They were wrong, in fact, about the very poorest being the intended beneficiaries. But the kernel of *their* horror lay in the phrase 'invert the order of things'. These closest observers of the government's housing plans recognised their potential for class disruption. If the RIBA/LGB competition results were conclusive, the symbol of an inversion in the established order would be taxpayer-funded Picturesque for the working classes.

In June 1918, when the RIBA published the outcome of the competition in book form, it damned its own proceedings with faint praise: 'although many able designs have been submitted, nothing very original or revolutionary has resulted'.[53] Almost a year later, the competition was still under attack. Writing in the *Architects' and Builders' Journal* in February 1919, Harry Goodhart-Rendel, a young architect with a career ahead of him as educator and theorist, agreed:

> We are spared the delicate task of estimating the value of the designs rewarded in the recent RIBA competition by quoting the words of the promoters – 'it may even be complained that the premiated schemes exhibit on the whole the dullness of mediocrity rather than the sparkle of genius'. It may.[54]

This is how the competition has gone down in history. What could have been seen as a comprehensive national snapshot of the architectural profession's interpretation of one crucial building type was discounted. The competition's domination by the Picturesque meant it would not become Whitehall's template for Dr Addison's forthcoming national housing scheme. But the Liberal-Tory coalition and the Labour Party had both promised cottages in their campaigns for the general election at the end of 1918. The Tudor Walters committee's November 1918 report had fixed on the word *cottage* to designate the dwellings it hoped to see built. If not picturesque, what were they going to look like?

POST-FIRST WORLD WAR COTTAGE AESTHETICS – THE ORIGINS OF THE ARGUMENT

At the massive Town Planning Conference organised by the RIBA in October 1910, the herald extraordinary of 'civic design', Liverpool University's Professor Charles Reilly, opened fire on the Picturesque. Whyte sees the conference defined by a fissure between Edwardian representatives of Kerr's 'primary division'.[55] In one address, the President of the Local Government Board and progenitor of the 1909 Town Planning Act, the Rt Hon John Burns MP, appeared to link social progress directly with picturesque architecture:

> the artisan is now clamouring, and securing in Bournville, Port Sunlight, Hampstead, Earswick, Tooting, Tottenham, Ealing . . . houses at rents and of a character and beauty that were not within the reach of the average artisan twenty-five or thirty years ago.[56]

On the other side of the divide, Reilly gave a talk titled 'The Immediate Future in England', which moved beyond his increasingly familiar advocacy of formal architecture to deliver a direct indictment of the Picturesque and its cottages.

Of those that represented domestic architecture in the places conference delegates had been invited to visit – Bedford Park, Port Sunlight, Bournville,

52   Professor Charles Reilly, Liverpool University, photographed by Howard Coster (1943), National Portrait Gallery, London

Hampstead Garden Suburb, Letchworth, even the London County Council's new cottage estate at White Hart Lane in London's Tottenham – Reilly asked his audience:

> is it entirely appropriate that they should in the main be based upon the early medieval type of cottage, with high pitched roofs and gables, with wood mullion windows . . . rather than on the later Georgian types with flatter roofs and sash windows?[57]

In a critique he would sustain into the 1930s,[58] Reilly brought his argument round to the Picturesque: 'our Gothic inheritance of picturesqueness has prevented our desire for simplicity from taking the

53   140–142 Hampstead Way, early Unwin and Parker cottages at Hampstead Garden Suburb (1907). They featured elements scorned by Charles Reilly, 'tempted . . . to angular shapes and bay windows'

form of simple rooms simply put together. It has instead tempted us to all sorts of angular shapes and bay windows'.[59]

Reilly did not name him, but one man represented much that Liverpool thought wrong. Ruskin abhorred the classical: 'pediments, and stylobates, and architraves never excited a single pleasurable feeling in you – never will'.[60] Reilly and his circle disagreed. Sir Reginald Blomfield – a neo-classical architect and scholar of the Renaissance, who served as both Visitor and External Examiner at Liverpool University[61] – dismissed the sage of Brantwood's 'cant of nature' and the 'many other fancies which make admirable reading but have very little relevance to architecture'.[62] Years later, Liverpool alumnus Trystan Edwards would talk of 'crooked self-righteous little teeth – the Ruskinian rats . . . gnawing, nibbling and picking away at masterpiece after masterpiece of our national civic art'.[63]

Having focused their attack on picturesque cottages, the Liverpool School had little choice but to challenge also Ruskin's moral proprietorship of the cottage idea, its connection with the Picturesque, and social orthodoxy concerning working-class housing. Ruskin's cottage credo had been turned into practical policy in the late nineteenth century by the social housing pioneer Octavia Hill, who borrowed money from him to renovate some of the country's earliest philanthropic cottages.[64] Hill shared Ruskin's willingness to look beyond autocthonous England for architectural inspiration. She wrote to her disciples about the picturesque homes of the Italian Alps and the Tyrol in 1879: 'the home-like oriel windows . . . pretty little separate conical roofs . . . this home-like irregularity, this prominence of roof, this simplicity of brick ornament, could be at once applied to our people's houses'.[65] Hill also shared Ruskin's view of the cottage as a repository of moral energy,[66] contrasting it with the block dwellings she had inspected in London:

where numerous families reside, and the staircases, laundries and yards are used in common . . . if anything goes wrong, the quiet steady tenants have no redress, they therefore leave . . . Compare it with the quiet, separate little home in the cottage. . . . The place has the capacity of being a home, not a couple of barrack-like rooms.[67]

Restoring worn-out cottages in London as social housing, and building anew, Hill helped import the Picturesque into the aesthetics of inner-city working-class dwellings.[68] Her architect Elijah Hoole utilised a widely shared cottage palette – cross-wing gables, timbering, bay windows, roughcast and tile-hanging – in Southwark's Redcross Cottages (1887), Gable Cottages (1889), and in Marylebone's St Botolph Cottages in Ranston Street (1895).[69]

Throughout the early years of the twentieth century, key instances of the cottage architecture that Reilly and his supporters disliked could be traced back to Ruskin and Hill, and were linked by the Garden City Movement. Picturesque cottages at New Earswick near York (1902–), Letchworth Garden City (1903–), and Hampstead Garden Suburb (1907–) connected government housing tsar Raymond Unwin to Hill. A cottage dweller herself – living since 1884 at 'Larksfield', Crockham Hill, in Kent, an Hoole-designed exercise in picturesque brick, tile-hung gables, and extravagant chimneystacks[70] – Hill was Henrietta Barnett's inspiration at Hampstead Garden Suburb, two of whose trustees were W.H. Lever of Port Sunlight and George Cadbury of Bournville.[71] One of Hill's later acts as a housing reformer was to judge the cottage exhibition in 1905 at the Garden City Movement's first great experiment, Letchworth (alongside Arts and Crafts intellectual W.R. Lethaby).[72] Meanwhile, the supervising architects for the cottages at Letchworth, New Earswick, and Hampstead – most of them picturesque in inspiration – were partners Barry Parker and Raymond Unwin.

This was the tightly bound network that Reilly and his followers needed to disrupt. It remained a good part of the reason, on the eve of the First World War, that the appearance of the ideal home

54   John Singer Sargent, *Octavia Hill*, 1898, oil on canvas, 1020 × 822 mm, National Portrait Gallery, London

in many public minds was still picturesque. But after their leader fired the starting gun in 1910, Liverpool's assault on the Picturesque grew in intensity. Peter Richmond notes the concerted nature of the attacks, many of them hosted by the Lever-funded *Town Planning Review*.[73] In 1911, Stanley Adshead used the journal to criticise street pictures at the new, privately built garden suburb at Gidea Park, in Romford, as 'abnormally picturesque' – a mistaken effort, in his view, to 'make our suburbs so extra suburban as to be merely wild rural retreats, better suited for woodmen and peasants than for ordinary city men'.[74] Only the single 'row of Georgian houses' facing Heath Drive gave Adshead any real satisfaction, and they had been built specifically in response to Reilly's advocacy at the Town Planning Conference the year before.[75] In April 1913, Patrick Abercrombie called for architectural change 'from the picturesque irregularities of rusticity to the severer refinement of a more highly civilized art'.[76] And in a critique of the Garden City movement as a whole, Trystan Edwards complained: 'In adopting a picturesque style, some of the worst and most insanitary features of medieval building have been incorporated'.[77] The villain in the rhetoric of the time was almost invariably the Picturesque.[78] That non-expert audiences loved it, an article in *The British Architect* in March 1918 held to be self-evident: 'The attraction of the picturesque in buildings is . . . nearly universal amongst the general public'.[79] Its persistence at the heart of early twentieth-century English architectural discourse has been under-reported.

By the beginning of 1914, the Liverpool tendency believed they were gaining the upper hand in their ideological battle against it. Reginald Blomfield – who described his own approach to education as a mission 'to divert students from the fashion for the picturesque'[80] – gave the address at the RIBA's General Meeting of 9 February, in which he arrogated to his cause that picturesque master Richard Norman Shaw, whose move 'to the Neo-Classic of his later days' Blomfield claimed as a victory for the new order: 'a feeling that was in the air . . . daily gathering force and giving stability to the architecture of this country'.[81]

In August 1914, the Liverpool-inspired campaign was strengthened by the publication of Geoffrey Scott's book *The Architecture of Humanism*.[82] This celebrated critique of architectural history's four great 'fallacies' – Romantic, Mechanical, Ethical, and Biological – laid its guns squarely on the Picturesque:

> the picturesque *ideal* is at variance with tradition and repugnant to design. . . . as an ideal, the picturesque renders taste obtuse . . . Like a coarse weed, not unbeautiful in itself, it tends to stifle every opportunity of growth. . . . the aesthetic content of the picturesque is not constructive and cannot be extended. Nevertheless it is on this quality, so low in the scale, so unhopeful for future creation, and so unhelpful for an understanding of the formal past, that modern taste has been concentrated.[83]

And Scott did not stop at debunking the Picturesque on aesthetic grounds. To weaken its hold on people's imaginations, he saw its connection with morality had to be broken too.[84] This was attempted via his exposition of 'The Ethical Fallacy' which he found in the writing of Ruskin.[85] Scott's view was that 'the psychological basis which Ruskin sought to establish for architecture was exclusively moral . . . in the narrowest sense. . . . the history of architecture was made a pledge of social justice'.[86] Scott sought, in 'the most influential single publication since Ruskin's Stones of Venice',[87] to dethrone the master.

Honoured in Liverpool, the book provoked strong reactions. One contemporary reader was

55 Geoffrey Scott, author of *The Architecture of Humanism* (1914), unknown photographer (early 1910s), National Portrait Gallery, London

brought to rapture by 'the vigour and grace of its prose'.[88] Another, the young Kenneth Clarke, found himself 'hoping to apply Scott's theories'[89] as he started work on *The Gothic Revival* (1928). Scott's book resounded still, 20 years after first publication, when Blomfield devoted a chapter of *Modernismus* to agreeing with the author over his fallacies, but disputing his understanding of both humanism and the Baroque.[90]

What Scott argued *for* must have delighted the formalists as much as that which he disapprobated. Like the Bloomsbury Group artist and critic Roger Fry, whom he may have encountered at the Berenson villa in Settignano in 1907,[91] Scott had a passion for 'the aesthetic interest of form'. He wanted architectural discourse returned to 'Mass, Space, Line and Coherence . . . the irreducible elements of its aesthetic method'. In pursuing this, he re-expressed Kerr's great primary division of 50 years before – but this time, as between the Picturesque on the one hand and 'formal architecture' on the other. The latter, he insisted, 'is to the picturesque as the whole body of musical art to the lazy hum and vaguely occupying murmur of the summer fields'.[92]

For Scott, love of the traditionally picturesque was central to the sorry condition of England's contemporary built-aesthetics: 'an architecture which . . . relies on a miscellany of sloping roofs and jutting chimneys . . . it looks to the old farm-buildings, long lived in, patched, adapted, overgrown'.[93] He conceded its popularity, but he and his supporters in Liverpool were bent upon disestablishing a visuality that had, since the early nineteenth century, reified 'home' – swimming hard against a tide of collective picturesque achievement from Romantics, Goths, Ruskin, masters of Old English such as Nesfield, Devey, and Shaw, and – more recently – Voysey and the Arts and Crafts movement.

During the First World War, with discussions already underway about the country's housing problems, the Liverpool School's formalists made their strongest attack to date on the dominance of the Picturesque in cottage architecture. In

56   Stanley Davenport Adshead, photographed by Bassano Ltd (1927), National Portrait Gallery, London. Advocate of the Standard Cottage – 'not . . . the home of an individual . . . but the home of a member of a certain class of the community'

1916, Stanley Adshead wrote an article titled 'The Standard Cottage', which advanced the argument from theoretical criticism of the Picturesque – or 'the English Cottage style', as Adshead sometimes called it[94] – to detailed prescription (architectural and social) for the working-class dwellings that most acknowledged would soon be needed.

Adshead had joined Liverpool University's architecture school in 1909 as associate professor in the newly created Department of Civic Design.[95] He burnished his reputation by designing (with colleague Stanley Ramsey) formally styled artisan's dwellings on the Duchy of Cornwall's estate in Kennington, London, in 1911.[96] But his vision for the Standard Cottage made the ornamentations of Kennington's Gothick window-glazing and trellised porches look fey. This time, there would be no concessions to the decorative. Ruskin's cottage formula – 'beautiful always, and everywhere'[97] – was not for the Standard Cottage:

> there is no room for corners, no room for features . . . no room for detail of peculiar interest: detail which might be a pleasure to look at once, but which continually repeated would be like the constant repetition of an irritating catchphrase.[98]

The 'detail of peculiar interest' that picturesque architecture viewed as so important, Adshead found exceptionable. And he seemed to entertain little doubt that his point of view ought to prevail over those of the potential occupants of standard cottages.

Adshead's essay represents the Liverpool tendency jumping at the opportunity presented by state-funded cottage building to reinforce their arguments in favour of more formal domestic aesthetics. There is no reason to think that their interest in improving housing standards for the working classes was less genuine than anyone else's – Adshead's patron Reilly had been a member of the Fabian Society while at Cambridge University; his autobiography recalls talks by Keir Hardie, Ramsay MacDonald, and George Lansbury.[99] But his ideological commitment to the neo-classical – complex in origin and effect – was all-encompassing. The Edwardian surge in enthusiasm for the Georgian was not limited to architecture. Mandler sees it as 'a generational rebellion against the Arts and Crafts aesthetic',[100] but it was an elite affair, never really reflecting wider public taste. Architects got there early, and for them it had a specialist application – represented by Reilly's project at Liverpool University to professionalise disciplinary training using 'the methods of the *École des Beaux-Arts* at Paris and . . . the American Schools of Architecture'.[101] As Reilly wrote to the architect Wilfrid Travers around 1908: 'The foundation

necessary is best sought – where French students have always sought it – in the Classic forms'.[102]

Inherent in the attacks on the Picturesque from Reilly, Adshead, and other contributors to Liverpool University's *Town Planning Review* – implicit in their rejection of its individualism, and central to their new approach to civic provision of working-class housing – were considerations that went beyond aesthetics and at which Reilly had begun to hint in his speech of 1910:

> If . . . the house of the future suburb is on the one hand to express something of the new submission of the individual to the community, and on the other hand to answer to a more exacting and refined if less sentimental taste, it is obvious . . . a new type of small house . . . is indeed the most pressing architectural problem.

This is the less remarked-upon aspect of Reilly's address that day. He moved beyond architecture to connect his proposals with an implicitly class-based vision for who should be accommodated and what would be required of them. As well as rejecting the Picturesque, Reilly prescribed the social mindset he expected from beneficiaries of his civic vision: willingness to accept the 'suppression of individual idiosyncrasies for the general good'; 'supression of rampant individualism for certain general amenities'; and even 'a further suppression of the individual taste for the good of the common whole'.[103]

Shasore contends that progressive politics were at the root of Liverpool's search for 'a unified civic consciousness'[104] – and for the formal architecture that would reify it. But it is difficult not to detect epistocracy at work too in Reilly's 1910 address: a readiness to impose a theory of architectural civics on others, echoed more recently by Roger Scruton's assertion that 'ordinary people' would come to appreciate the elements of classical architecture, 'as soon as they learn to think of them as not chosen for their personal benefit, but for the common good'.[105] Reilly believed in what D.H. Lawrence called 'the bigger gesture of the citizen, not the cottager'.[106] But in its Liverpool iteration, this vision – an architecture defined by formal rule-taking – suggested the working classes might have to trade individuality of cottage and temperament in return for the privilege of social housing.

Six years later, in his exposition of the Standard Cottage, Adshead instrumentalised architectural aesthetics still further to make points about the organisation and class structure of society. His call was for a new dwelling that

> will depend for any attraction that it may possess, not upon . . . its peculiarity or idiosyncrasy, nor in a word upon its individuality, but upon . . . suitability to purpose and excellence of design. It will not be the home of an individual, of an anarchist; but the home of a member of a certain class of the community, of a communist.[107]

The Liverpool School's commitment to formal architecture is here for sure[108] – in Reilly's words, the return to 'balanced palace shapes rather than . . . the mere picturesqueness of farmhouse and cottage'[109] – but Adshead's philosophy was aesthetic only in part. It amplified also the social-class implications of Reilly's appetite for 'suppression'. Liverpool's longed-for new civics was to be built on the foundations of working-class uniformity and acquiescence.

The Standard Cottage essay can be read in at least two ways: as architectural hypothesis, and as contemporary gloss on middle- and upper-class preconceptions about the supposedly homogeneous working classes. John Carey records Thomas Hardy (in his 1880s notebooks) scaring himself with the 'Four Millions' he imagined pullulating around him in Tooting. E.M. Forster's Margaret Schlegel baulked at 'odours from the abyss' in 1910.[110] To T.S. Eliot in the 1920s, Scruton's 'ordinary people' were 'cheese mites'; to Ezra Pound, 'a mass of dolts'; to Virginia Woolf, 'a vast . . . shapeless jelly of human stuff'.[111] Adshead is nowhere near so misanthropic, but he was prepared to identify 'a certain class' of people who could be housed in an architecture free from 'individuality' – an architecture that visualised the way he and his peers saw them, not

one that need pay much attention to how they saw themselves. This class consciousness suggests an appetite for social engineering by architecture that is hard to interpret as democratic.[112] And although Adshead would go on to think more carefully about the impact of class on housing and *vice versa* in his 1923 book *Town Planning and Town Development*, he remained fatalistic: 'you may try as you like to mingle the occupants of a suburb, but certain sections will not mix'.[113]

Social engineering was not on the minds of everyone going back to first principles in domestic architecture in the years before 1918. Roger Fry had built his own house in 1909 – 'Durbins', in Guildford, Surrey.[114] He wrote about it in *Vogue* in 1918: 'the secret of economy was concentration on plan . . . I arranged the rooms to form as nearly as possible a solid block and placed a number of [them] in a . . . Mansard roof'.[115] A non-architect, hobbled by shortage of funds, he ended up building a house that Nairn describes as 'severely classical . . . a blunt, four-square block'.[116] Fry had not been looking for Kerr's 'great primary division', but it found him anyway:

> My own house is neighboured by houses of the most gentlemanly picturesqueness, houses from which tiny gables with window slits jut out at any unexpected angle, and naturally it is regarded as a monstrous eyesore by their inhabitants.[117]

57 'Durbins', the house in Guildford that Roger Fry designed for himself in 1909, photographed by Ray and Oliver Strachey (1916), National Portrait Gallery, London

Pursuing economy led Fry to build an aesthetically formal house. His contemporaries could have told him he had ended up with 'forms – often used politically – [which] had always been symbols of authority and privilege',[118] because the idea that formal architecture had its own *locus* in the class system was well understood at the time.[119] In *Where the Great City Stands*, the designer C.R. Ashbee regretted post-1900 neo-Georgianism's 'easy semblance of wealth and taste', and explained how it fitted into a wider picture of exhibitionism by the wealthy.[120] 'Neo-Georgianism and genuine Democracy,' Ashbee wrote, 'are, and always will be, incompatible.'[121] Lethaby, son of a gilder and woodworker, agreed; classicism was the architectural argot of the rich and powerful. He wrote, in November 1919, that the English aristocracy's fascination with Italian Renaissance architecture 'was imposed as part of a general movement to divide off the aristocracy from mere English folk'.[122]

In early twentieth-century England, whether the pilgrimage that led you to formal domestic architecture was ideological and academically focused (like Reilly's and Adshead's) or empirical (like Fry's), on arrival you would inevitably be confronted by the apartness of your destination. While that might have been serendipitous for an elite tastemaker such as Fry, both Ashbee and Lethaby recognised its anti-democratic downsides. Formal architecture was not obviously the most suitable aesthetic for housing the working classes, who had been subject in the past – in the first generation of officially recommended prison and workhouse architecture, for example[123] – to the state's affection for authoritarian neo-classicism.[124]

'How often,' W.G. Newton (editor of *The Architectural Review*) asked in 1924, 'are plainness and severity condemned as recalling a prison or workhouse?' What he called public man's 'natural taste' for prettiness was, however, not to be indulged.[125] The success of the Liverpool faction's arguments in official circles would eventually help to detach post-First World War municipal dwellings from the nation's picturesque domestic tradition –

ending up with state-aided cottage tenants housed in an identifiably different domestic style, and one with some unappealing associations.

In 1919, the Arts and Crafts architect Baillie Scott, would hear an unattractive echo of early nineteenth-century institutional thinking in suggestions of the new conformity some expected from tenants in social housing:

> we have invented a new horror in building. It is the colony of "dwellings for the working classes". The phrase itself carries with it condemnation of our social system, implying . . . a broad division of the community into those who work, and live in duplicated little dwellings imposed upon them by the State, and those who don't work, and live where they like or can.[126]

These were the dangers of architecturalised class distinction – in Lynsey Hanley's words, 'class . . . built into our landscape in the form of housing'.[127] Baillie Scott echoed the arguments of Henrietta Barnett – who had conceived Hampstead Garden Suburb as an experiment where 'the intermingling of the classes' would be a positive benefit of the suburb's layout and architecture[128] – and the one-time sentiments of Unwin, too: 'it is in every way most desirable . . . that all classes of the community should live together . . . to produce a healthy, interesting and open-minded society'.[129] It was not clear that the formal side of the argument shared Unwin and Barnett's sentiments.

THE ADDISON SCHEME

With the new Housing Bill (the official launch of the Addison Scheme) expected in the spring of 1919, a crucial paper – dating from November the previous year and commissioned to assist Local Government Board (LGB) and local authority planning – was already on its way to becoming one of the most influential studies in the history of British social housing. Published in November 1918, the Tudor Walters Report (TWR),[130] was produced by a committee chaired by Sir John Tudor Walters, Liberal MP for Sheffield Brightside, who remembered it as 'the best work I have ever done in public life'.[131] Its purpose was to specify a new standard for the state-funded cottages that everyone expected after the war.

Disinclined to offer a clear description of the external style of cottages it favoured, the TWR adopted a tone of didactic discouragement to express its architectural vision. The report ruled out flats, official suspicion of which had been consensual in discussions of social housing since at least the Royal Commission on the Housing of the Working Classes in 1884–85, where Octavia Hill attested to tenement blocks being hated for their 'dreary monotony . . . terrible sameness . . . hopeless ugliness'.[132] The research done in the first half of 1918 by Miss Maud Bell for the Ministry of Reconstruction's Women's Housing Sub-Committee[133] – a group of expert women set up to advise the government on the internal layout and equipment of the state's planned new cottages – had provided the Tudor Walters committee with up-to-date evidence that working-class preference clearly made 'the two-storey cottage . . . the type which should generally be adopted'.[134]

Just as the 1913 Board of Agriculture report had conformed with Ruskinian precedent by architecturally typologising the nation's class structure – 'houses' for smallholders; 'cottages' for rural labourers, their social inferiors[135] – the TWR linked the working classes to the idea of the cottage. But this could never have been a sociologically disinterested association for, as Midge Carne had declared, 'Poor people lived in cottages'.[136] Nunn expands on this perception of cottage as social concept: 'The term cottage . . . implies taxonomy of class. . . . the hierarchy in which the term for your home (cottage, hall or chateau) is essential to social identity'.[137]

As we have seen, the idea of the cottage also communicated a widely acculturated visuality. 'To the Englishman,' writes Taylor, 'the cosy pitched roof' was a 'psychological necessity . . . a sacrament of family love.'[138] As a whole, however,

the TWR discouraged, for individual cottage plan and elevation, use of the techniques intrinsic to the Picturesque.[139] Even though the report recognised that use of 'standardised designs' ran risks,[140] a preference for the plainness of Adshead's 1916 Standard Cottage was unmistakeable. The fashion among the noisiest architectural lobbyists of the time was for variants of formal architecture, so perhaps this is no surprise. But the fact that a report specifically recommending cottages should have gone out of its way to repudiate the picturesqueness that many of the National Cottage Competition's entrants – and all Batsford's pre-1918 cottage writers – seemed to expect from the term was an augury.

Immediately after the war, the national preoccupation was not with official reports or cottage visuality but with the stark challenge of finding shelter. Throughout 1919, *Punch* magazine shared one concern with England's working classes: the difficulty of finding somewhere to live. Sixpence every Wednesday bought a selection of housing jokes: 'Concerning the statement that the Kaiser is to be supplied with a house in London while awaiting his trial, might it not be sufficient punishment to make him find it himself?'[141] *The Times* first covered dwelling shortages early in January: 'demand for houses and flats . . . as well as for workmen's dwellings and tenements, is probably unprecedented, and the supply seems to be smaller than ever'.[142] A soldier told *The Daily Mirror* in February: 'I have spent practically the whole of my leave in tramping around the suburbs to get a house. . . . It was the same story everywhere – none to be had for love or money'.[143]

Greatly though they enjoyed complaining, the newspapers knew the government had building plans in hand. At a meeting of supporters in Downing Street on 12 November 1918, the Prime Minister had pledged 'habitations fit for the heroes who have won the war'.[144] A building campaign was promised in the coalition's December 1918 election manifesto, and preparations begun for a Housing Bill, to be introduced by the new President of the Local Government Board (soon to lead the UK's first Health

THE MAN WHO ASKED A HOUSE-AGENT IF HE HAD A HOUSE TO LET.

58   H.M. Bateman, *Punch*, vol.157, 16 July 1919, p.69, H.M. Bateman Designs

Ministry) Dr Christopher Addison. Government-sponsored papers and booklets were expected imminently that would reveal what the government believed its new cottages should look like.

Four days into 1919, *The Daily Mirror* headlined a story '£100,000,000 Housing Plan', the article continuing: 'Big Scheme for Brighter Homes – No More "Brick Boxes"'.[145] Another of the Harmsworth family's newspapers, Northcliffe's *Daily Mail*, was equally fascinated:

In conjunction with the London County Council, the Local Government Board is arranging for building in London a village of model houses

59   Three-bedroom, non-
parlour, semi-detached cottage
pair. Perspective by Raffles
Davison from the government
booklet by Raymond Unwin,
ed., *The Nation's New Houses:
Pictures and Plans* (London:
The Daily News, 1919), p.20,
University of Manchester

. . . for the guidance of local authorities, both
as regards architectural style and internal
arrangements.[146]

This 'village of model houses' was one of several
measures intended to communicate government
guidance to the local authorities responsible for
building Addison Scheme cottages – and to the
public. The *Daily Mail* story provided a clue as to the
fate of the predominantly picturesque cottage designs
(discussed earlier in this chapter) produced for the
LGB/RIBA National Cottage Competition in 1918.

Despite the contest's unfavourable reception,
RIBA President Henry Hare had announced plans
on 4 November 1918 to erect 'a small number of
these cottages in a readily accessible position near
London'.[147] The project's progress can then be traced
in the pages of *The Builder*. Model cottages were
eagerly awaited in the 17 January 1919 edition;[148] by
February, the magazine believed they were to be
built on the LCC's Tabard Street site;[149] in early May
1919, an agreement between the architects and the

LGB was reported that eighteen cottages 'should be
erected from the premiated designs in the Cottage
Competitions . . . A suitable site has recently been
provided on the London County Council's Old Oak
Lane Housing Estate at Hammersmith'.[150] But the
model village never quite arrived. With Addison's
Housing Bill proceeding through parliament, there
was a danger it would be overtaken by events.

The government had other irons in the fire. One
was a collaboration between the Local Government
Board and the *Daily News* (a rare left-of-centre
newspaper, historically connected with the Cadbury
family) to produce a paperback booklet, *The Nation's
New Houses*. Edited by Raymond Unwin with a
foreword by Christopher Addison, it went on sale
on 7 April 1919,[151] containing, in the view of *The
Common Cause* magazine, 'the greatest quantity of
valuable . . . knowledge ever offered to the public
for sixpence'.[152] Whereas Board publications were
usually aimed at local authorities, *The Nation's
New Houses* was intended for public consumption
and was advertised in local newspapers across the

60 Semi-detached pairs of three-bedroom parlour cottages, formal in style, with two-storey rectangular bays and gabled main blocks. Perspective by Raffles Davison, in Raymond Unwin, ed., *The Nation's New Houses: Pictures and Plans* (London: The Daily News, 1919), University of Manchester

61 Semi-detached, three-bedroom, parlour cottage pair. More picturesque in character than fig.60, the main block is gabled, with four front-facing gables above the bedroom windows. Perspective by Raffles Davison, in Raymond Unwin, ed., *The Nation's New Houses: Pictures and Plans* (London: The Daily News, 1919), p.12, University of Manchester

country.[153] Its contents were 'brief and popular', in Addison's words, giving 'information on the planning of cottages which is up-to-date and authoritative'.[154]

The booklet's cover used the word 'houses' rather than 'cottages'; but in the main text, the first thing the reader saw was a rhetorical question – 'What are the essentials of a good cottage?'

> In the past . . . architects have devoted their knowledge and skill to the building of large mansions, while the houses of the people have been left to the mercies of the speculative builder. . . . The result has been the production of houses that . . . offend our eyes by their ugly and sordid appearance.[155]

Those days were over; architects would henceforward be tasked to work for the people – designing cottages and the landscapes in which they would stand. 'Second only in importance to the plan of the individual cottage is its environment,' the booklet explained. Grouped 'round greens and quadrangles', cottages of genuine beauty would be funded by the coalition government:

> the New England, of which all housing reformers dream, is to be a fair land. The homes we build, therefore, must be beautiful as well as convenient . . . they will strike no discordant note, but harmonise with their surroundings.[156]

The tone of the booklet suggested the austerity of the Tudor Walters Report may have been misleading. Once they had finished the text, readers were left to enjoy the drawings of Raffles Davison, an artist whose experience of creating perspectives for architects across the profession made him pre-eminent.

Raffles Davison was born in 1853 in Stockton-on-Tees and worked as the editor of *The British Architect* in Manchester between 1878 and 1919. In addition to practice as an architect,[157] he turned a hobby of country sketching into a pipeline of illustrations for his own magazine where his appetite for the

62   Sketch by Raffles Davison in *Raffles Davison: A Record of his Life and Work from 1870 to 1926* (London: B.T. Batsford, 1927), frontispiece

'picturesque beauty' of Old English architecture was given free rein.[158]

Catching the eye of architects, Davison was hired to work up perspectives of their designs for competitions (until the RIBA dispensed with competition perspectives in 1900) and to help clients visualise finished products. Among the architect's kit of drawings (plan, section, elevation), 'Perspective is the only one which represents his contemplated building as it would appear to a spectator'.[159] At the Liverpool School of Architecture, Professor Reilly forbade his twentieth-century students use of perspectives, believing they 'led to distortion and false picturesqueness'.[160]

Davison was not an innovator in the form; Stamp traces its origins back to the 1770s.[161] But his work was good. 'To architects he has been known for nearly half a century,' wrote Aston Webb, 'for his peculiar power in . . . truthfully portraying the design of the architect.'[162]

Providing perspectives for several of the RIBA/ LGB's National Cottage Competition winners in 1918 (figs 47, 49 and 50) made Davison an obvious choice to illustrate the government's designs in *The Nation's*

63 Thomas Raffles Davison, photograph by 'Swaine', from *Raffles Davison: A Record of his Life and Work from 1870 to 1926* (London: B.T. Batsford, 1927), p.iv

New Houses. Add the inherently pictorial nature of the process to his decades-long passion for Old English subjects,[163] and the decision to have Davison help market the Addison Scheme's new cottages always had the potential to infuse the exercise with one particular aesthetic. 'Davison's style was best with [the] picturesque', says Stamp.[164]

The Nation's New Houses illustrated an architectural mix of formal and picturesque cottage exteriors. But Davison visualised all his cottage subjects with an artist's eye – sequestering them among mature trees (just as Uvedale Price liked them[165]), often with a welcoming plume of woodsmoke rising from the chimneys. In one, the artist undermined the formality of the underlying architecture with his depiction of pent-roofed porches, each sided with rose-festooned latticework

(fig.64). Tectonically, this was formal architecture, but in Davison's hands the atmosphere became decidedly picturesque. Indeed, his images feel like a tribute to Gainsborough and Morland's late eighteenth-century 'cottage doors' – where attractive mothers and children can be seen waiting outside the front for the *pater familias* to return. In Gainsborough's paintings the woodcutter, laden with branches, is sometimes discernible at a distance.[166] In Davison's, the returning father – out of frame – is probably on his way back from the station.

The Raffles Davison vision – in its costly combination of gables, porches, and prominent chimneystacks – confounded the insistence upon economy in the Tudor Walters text. Viewed *in toto*, the effect of *The Nation's New Houses* was to put Davison's practised pencil at the service of a cottage vision closer in character to the rejected picturesque designs of the 1918 National Cottage Competition than to the formality championed in Liverpool.

As well as Davison's drawings, there was – unlikely though it sounds – a showbusiness component to the Addison Scheme launch, which reinforced the picturesque interpretation. In front of an audience of 1,350 people, the Garden Cities and Town Planning Association staged an event – at Sir Oswald Stoll's Alhambra Theatre in Leicester Square, London – on the afternoon of 22 May 1919. 'Tickets are now almost unobtainable,' reported the *Westminster Gazette* the day before. Lucky attendees, including the Prince of Wales, Christopher Addison, and 'many Members of Parliament, and bureaucrats',[167] were treated to the premiere of the LGB-approved 'Cinematograph Exhibition of Housing Schemes' – a curious *mélange* of an entertainment comprising an introductory talk by the government's planning supremo Raymond Unwin, music from the Alhambra Orchestra, and a series of short films about exemplary housing developments.

The promotional films concentrated almost exclusively on the cottage picturesque – Port Sunlight (fig.67), Bournville, Letchworth, and Hampstead Garden Suburb, all of them

64 A four-unit block of three-bedroom parlour cottages. The underlying architecture was formal, but the artist added pent-roofed porches, latticework, and prominent chimneys to lend picturesque texture to the image. Perspective by Raffles Davison, in Raymond Unwin, ed., *The Nation's New Houses: Pictures and Plans* (London: The Daily News, 1919), p.10, University of Manchester

developments where most of the cottage architecture would not have been out of place in the Picturesque movement's pattern books. Only one film flew the formal banner, featuring the neo-Georgian regiment from Unwin's munitions village, Gretna. Overall, it was 'an interesting series of pictures,' reported *The Daily Telegraph*, 'with instructive details' from Unwin.[168] The Prince was said to have shown 'great interest in the films'.[169] The next step was for the production to go on tour around the country, probably without the Alhambra musicians. A casual viewer might fairly have concluded that the cottages chosen for the films – from the Wirral, from Letchworth, from the suburbs of Birmingham and London – were indicative of the sort of cottage appearance they might expect from the government's new scheme.

But the next government publication contradicted this public-facing picturesque. In April – the day after retailing Davison's smoke-smudged cottage perspectives – the Local Government Board unveiled its Addison Scheme *Manual* of specimen cottage plans. This was intended for planning departments in English and Welsh local authorities, reiterated the government's typological commitment to the 'self-contained two-storey cottage' in the Tudor Walters Report,[170] and included an appendix of 12 plans and elevations 'illustrating generally the requirements of the Board'.[171] Picturesque they were not.

The *Manual* called for 'simple lines and good proportion', 'the avoidance of back projections', and 'simple planning and design . . . avoiding

65 (left) detail from fig.24, Thomas Gainsborough, *Wooded Landscape with Figures and Pigs Outside Cottage*, 1775–80, Eton College, Windsor; (right) detail from fig.64, Raffles Davison, in Raymond Unwin, ed., *The Nation's New Houses: Pictures and Plans* (London: The Daily News, 1919), p.10, University of Manchester. It is hard to believe Davison was not alluding to the tradition of 'cottage door' painting

66 Three-bedroom, non-parlour, semi-detached cottages, drawing again on the Picturesque for their gabled main blocks, huge street-facing cross-wing gables (shared between the dwellings but not articulating anything in the plan), and a shared penticed porch. Perspective by Raffles Davison, in Raymond Unwin, ed., *The Nation's New Houses: Pictures and Plans* (London: The Daily News, 1919), p.18, University of Manchester

67 Postcard of cottages on Greendale Road, Port Sunlight (1909). Printed by Lever Brothers Limited, Author's collection

needless exterior works requiring periodical painting such as bargeboards, fascias and imitation timber'.[172] Plans No. 7 and No. 8 (figs 68 and 69) capture this spirit. They hark back to the aesthetic of economical cottages proposed by Parker and Unwin in *The Garden City* magazine in 1906[173] – and are almost identical to the most basic agricultural labourer's cottage, Plan No. 1, illustrated in the appendix of the 1913 Board of Agriculture Report.[174]

It is striking how different *Manual* Plans No. 7 (Urban) and No. 8 (Rural) are from the majority of the National Cottage Competition entries.[175] If the argument outside government about how state-sponsored cottages should look had been going on inside too, it had apparently resulted in confusion – giving rise simultaneously to the picturesque perspectives of *The Nation's New Houses* and to the austerity of the *Manual*, the latter a close relation of

the Liverpool formalism characterising Adshead's Standard Cottage.

LGB *Manual* Design No. 7 (Urban) is a pure rectangle, with no plan breaks even for bay windows. Design No. 8 (Rural) differs only in permitting a small outshot (for coal storage and an earth closet) to break the plan at the rear. As far as Whitehall was concerned, there need be little substantive difference between rural and urban cottage design. Models of the Manual's cottages were commissioned for Express Newspapers' May 1919 'Model Homes Exhibition', but three-dimensionality did little to enhance their appeal. Attending the exhibition, Dr Addison put on a brave face: 'I am very glad to have seen these models. They mean so much more to me than the plans'.[176]

Diverging from the strictly rectangular in offering hipped cross-wings at each end, Plan No. 4 (fig.71) featured a slightly stepped plan to accommodate four

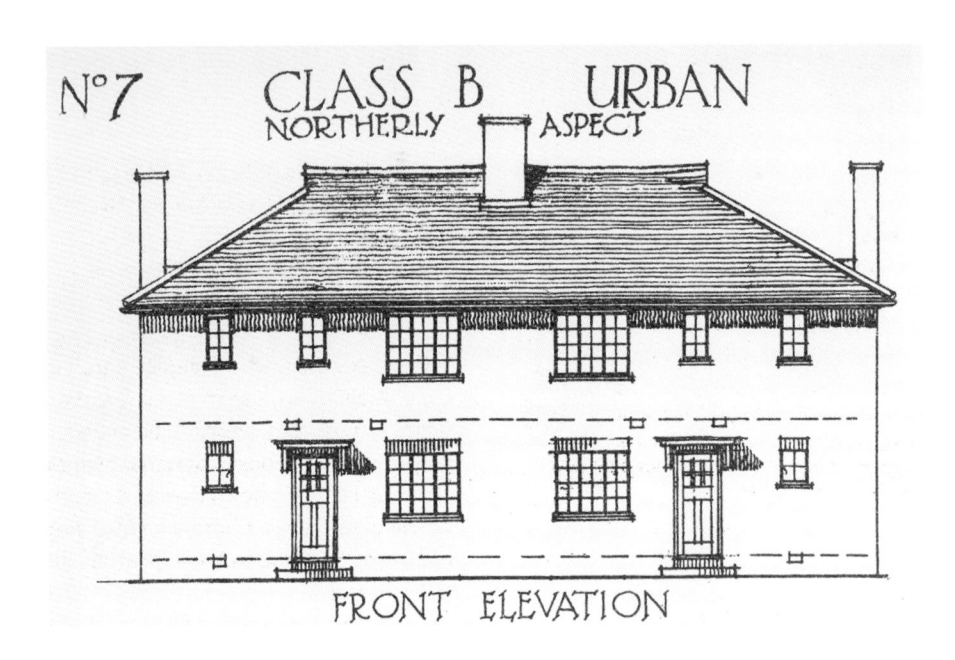

N° 7 CLASS B URBAN
NORTHERLY ASPECT

FRONT ELEVATION

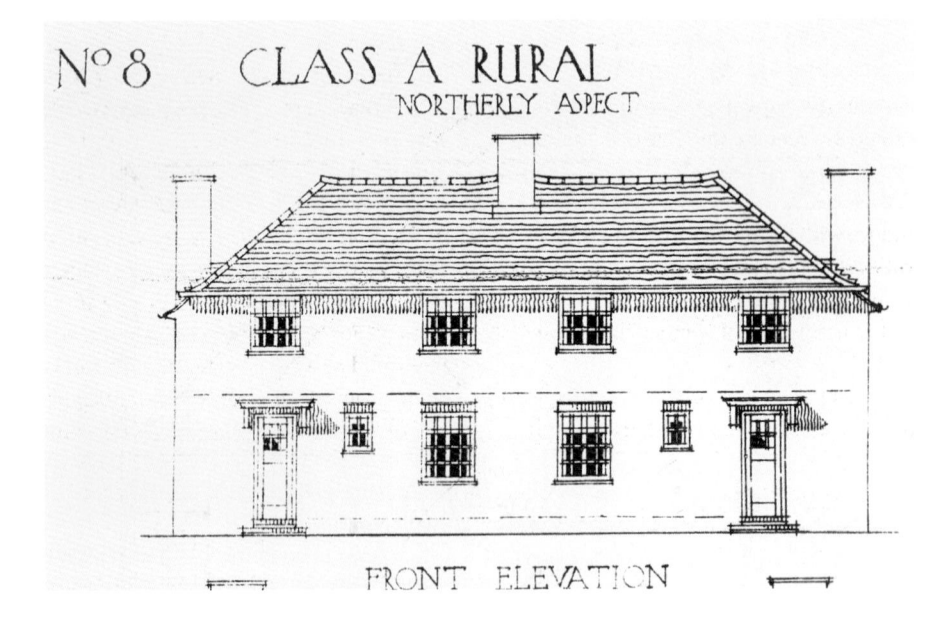

N° 8 CLASS A RURAL
NORTHERLY ASPECT

FRONT ELEVATION

bedrooms. Like Ruskin, Unwin approved of bays – 'Windows facing the street are much less depressing if slightly bayed to invite a peep up and down, as well as across'[177] – so Plan No. 5 allowed for canted ground-floor bay windows, with a flat roof, in the parlour on the front elevation. Apart from the casements and the slightly prominent chimneystacks, however, the designs presented architectural aesthetics stripped of every lineament of the Picturesque.

Their historical antecedent could have been the estate cottages (fig.72) built for Sir Robert Walpole at Houghton, Norfolk, around 1730[178] – the form both had in common being one Uvedale Price had excoriated: 'The ugliest buildings are those which have no feature, no character; those, in short, which most nearly approach to the shape . . . of a clamp of brick, the ugliness of which no-one will dispute'.[179] Trystan Edwards, who occupied a junior position in the architectural team at the Local Government Board in 1919, may well have been delighted with the government's proposed designs. Plan No. 7 and the similarly stripped-down Nos. 2, 3, 6 and 8 were the purest distillation of formal architecture – as close to rectangular as possible in plan; in elevation, as plain as could be.

Country Life magazine celebrated the designs – 'they show us, in fact, how admirably the new houses can be fashioned'[180] – but, eagle-eyed, they spotted evidence of the formalism that shaped them, noting the way Bedroom 1 in Plan No. 7's rear elevation (as in Plan 4; fig.71) was given 'two windows instead of one . . . simply to repeat the fenestration of the ground floor'.[181] And the 1919 *Manual*'s designs did not go down badly in the press more widely. The *Daily Mail* interpreted the government's aesthetic agenda as determination to 'put an end to the system of building in long rows'.[182] For *The Builder*, the *Manual* was to be 'regarded as a very essential addition to the library of the housing expert'.[183] But the frugal designs might not have impressed any remaining staff at

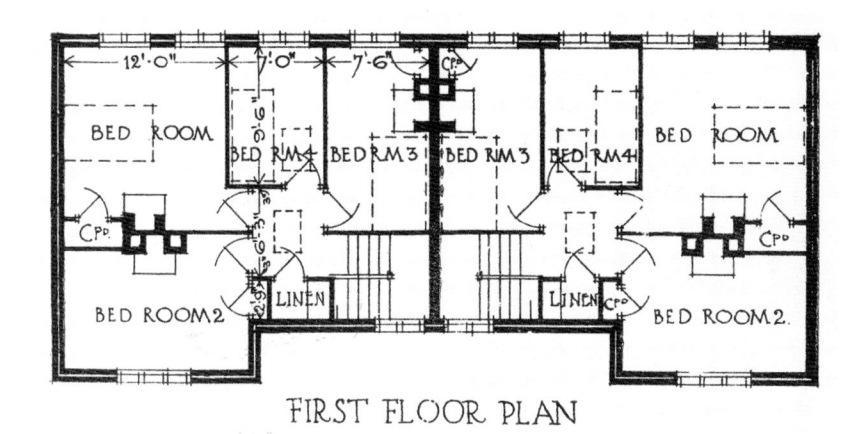

FIRST FLOOR PLAN

71 Plan No. 4, LGB *Manual* (London, 1919), The Bodleian Libraries, University of Oxford. Four-bedroom parlour semis with broken rectangle plans to accommodate the extra bedroom. Like Plan No. 7, criticised by *Country Life*, one bedroom at the back has two windows when, arguably, it needs only one

72 New Houghton Village, Norfolk, built for Sir Robert Walpole, c.1730. Photograph by John Piper, Tate Archive

The British Architect magazine. In September 1917, they had editorialised: 'The high-pitched roof is so associated in our thoughts with ideals of cottage design that it is not easy to feel thrilled by rows of square boxes'.[184] Neither had Board architects paid much apparent attention to the cottage literature back-catalogue – which endlessly valorised the steeply pitched roof.[185]

The *Manual*'s designs were difficult even to reconcile with a talk Raymond Unwin gave to the RIBA on 16 December 1918, when he had invoked dwellings built in England 'before the industrial revolution', their 'exteriors, graced by some feature of special beauty, or distinguished by some mark of individuality, maybe a great porch, a sunny

arbour, or merely a pent-roof shelter giving a sense of homeliness'. Unwin's rhetoric celebrated the traditional irregularities of picturesque cottage architecture. The *Manual* that his department produced did not.

Acknowledging the scale of the government's call 'to build half a million new houses', Unwin had asked:

May it not be the architect's contribution to see that every one of these houses has at least enough . . . of individuality and comeliness without, to inspire in those who shall dwell therein something of the affection which we associate with the word "home"?[186]

This entreaty bore no obvious fruit in the LGB *Manual*. Despite Unwin's personal apprenticeship in the Picturesque, formalism – indistinguishable from economising in this case – seemed to have won the battle to determine government-recommended aesthetics. And this had its perils. Timothy Mowl observes: 'Any cult of simplicity in buildings is automatically vulnerable to capitalist economics and cost-cutting'.[187] Howsoever it transpired, the nation had been promised 500,000 *cottages* by politicians who must have been at least vaguely alive to the cultural and aesthetic tradition that the cottage represented. In the economical line drawings of the LGB *Manual*, nothing of that Picturesque remained.

RUSSELL AND UNWIN – THE ADDISON SCHEME'S ARCHITECTS

The stories of the two key government architects behind the *Manual* that turned the Tudor Walters Report into recommended elevations shed some light on this. In the Housing Department of the LGB in March 1919, two men had been appointed to key posts – Chief Architect, House Planning and Chief Architect, Site Planning[188] – the first going to Samuel Bridgman (S.B.) Russell,[189] who had been an assistant to Raymond Unwin on 1917's neo-Georgian Munitions Ministry estate at Gretna,[190] the second to Unwin himself.

Russell was taught at the Royal Academy Schools in the 1880s by the *École des Beaux-Arts*-trained Richard Phené Spiers (a key instigator of British interest in the *École*'s principles).[191] After articles with Henry Hewitt Bridgman, he enjoyed an early career in the company of eminent architects. He was nominated for his Associateship at the RIBA in 1890 by Spiers and Thomas Collcutt. By 1914, he had two partnerships to his credit, producing the West Riding of Yorkshire's County Hall, in Wakefield, with James Sivewright Gibson in 1898; and later – with Sir Edwin Cooper, designer of the Port of London Authority building – a new town hall in Burslem (1910). These were expensive projects, delivered

in varieties of the neo-classical. Russell liked his buildings in the Grand Manner.

Unwin was a different kettle of fish. His belief in the cottage's potency as a moral vector came from Ruskin.[192] He strove for Ruskinian cadence when describing the cottage's

> simple dignity and beauty . . . which assuredly is necessary, not only to the proper growth of the gentler and finer instincts of men, but to the producing of the indefinable something which makes the difference between a mere shelter and a home.[193]

Early in his career, Unwin had written a definition of the cottage: 'a simple shelter for a simple form of life . . . I propose to regard as a cottage any house in which separate accommodation is not provided for servants'.[194] And when it came to cottage dwellers, Unwin did not share Adshead's determinism about cottage-dwelling labourers' status or obligations: 'it is not our function to prescribe the mode of life [to] suit the kind of houses we should like to build . . . it is our duty rather to understand the modes of life and the ideas which inspire the people'.[195]

What 'the people' might think about the appearance of working-class cottages mattered to Unwin: 'The right of the public to be considered is much clearer than many seem to realize'.[196] By 1918, he had come to regard shared experience in war as an opportunity to put aside 'the rank of life to which we belong':

> men of all sorts and conditions had messed and slept and suffered together. Let [us] do nothing to check this beginning of union. Every scheme of any size . . . should at least reach such a standard of amenity that the smallest types of houses would afford no justification, by their lack of comeliness, for the well-to-do to live out of sight of them.[197]

In his early twentieth-century work with partner Barry Parker at Church Stretton, Shropshire, and Starbeck near Harrogate, we see Unwin's cottage designs achieve 'comeliness' through unabashed implementation of the Picturesque. Early cottages designed for Joseph Rowntree at New Earswick (1902–3) were also economically picturesque in treatment.

Yet there is evidence to the contrary too: the vast Gretna munitions workers' estate in Scotland (1916–17), where, working with Russell and Crickmer, Unwin had again been the supervising architect. The dominant style here was a barracks-like neo-Georgian – 'depressing', said Mrs Alwyn Lloyd, sent to review the estate.[198] She was shown around by Crickmer who drew her attention to the atypical managers' houses he had designed there based on his picturesque, prize-winning cottage at Gidea Park in 1911.[199] 'These,' she reported, were 'a most popular type.' The Staff Club (fig.74) – also designed by Crickmer; 'the most elegant building' on the site[200] – was also picturesque in character, as was the rectory.[201] At Gretna, and not for the last time, picturesque architecture seems to have been reserved for the middle classes.

There was a tension in Unwin's pre-1919 career between the evidence of what he built and the burden of his writing.[202] In the latter, he treated the Picturesque as an aesthetic theory about landscape or architectural grouping[203] while rejecting the idea that picturesqueness should be striven for in individual dwellings:

an attempt is now mostly made to introduce some special features into each individual house, and so to create an artificial picturesqueness . . . turrets from which there is no outlook, or gables which serve no purpose except to provide an excuse for a little black and white half-timber work.[204]

Enthusiasm for aspects of the Picturesque on Unwin's part was unmistakable, but his appreciation seems to have been catalysed less by the original English texts than by the nineteenth-century Viennese city-planning theorist Camillo Sitte,[205] who concentrated on picturesque street layout more than on the architectural qualities of the individual European buildings that so inspired Ruskin, Norman Shaw, and Octavia Hill. This philosophy was brought by Unwin to the Tudor Walters Report, where picturesque street layouts, as distinct from picturesque dwellings, were *de rigueur*:

by so planning the lines of the roads and disposing the spaces and the buildings as to develop the beauty of vista, arrangement and proportion, an attractiveness may be added to the dwellings at little or no extra cost.[206]

When it came to picturesque architecture, however – as the Tudor Walters Report and Local Government

73   Unwin, Russell and Crickmer's munitions worker housing at Gretna in Scotland. 'Simple yet pleasing' was the verdict of Unwin's booklet *The Nation's New Houses: Pictures and Plans* (London: The Daily News, 1919), p.22, University of Manchester. Mrs Alwyn Lloyd, visiting for the Women's Housing Sub-Committee, thought them 'depressing'

74   Staff Club building on the Gretna Village munitions estate, 1917, designed by Courtenay Crickmer. RIBA Collections

Board *Manual* had both made clear – its official consideration for individual cottage design was emphatically ruled out.

COTTAGE AESTHETICS IN 1919 –
THE PUBLIC DEBATE

Whatever arguments were going on behind closed government doors, from January 1919 architects believed that the state had reached a fork in the road – Picturesque in one direction, formal architecture in the other. With 500,000 new cottages in prospect, the architectural commentariat began to ventilate their opinions. At the RIBA on 20 January 1919, one confessed to looking 'forward with some dread to the forthcoming influx of workmen's dwellings'.[207] He quoted Tennyson's picturesque evocation of 'labourers' homes' as evidence for a better age: 'huts /At random scatter'd, each a nest in bloom./ . . . The warm-blue breathings of a hidden hearth / Broke from a bower of vine and honeysuckle'.[208] The Arts and Crafts hierarch Baillie Scott added: 'All that we should now sweep away at the smallest excuse in favour of a cottage with a sanitary dustbin at the back door'.[209]

Throughout 1919, a broadly based public debate about Addison Scheme cottage aesthetics unfolded. Much was at stake. *Country Life* foresaw 'the greatest era of house building ever known in this country'.[210]

Opinions differed as to what that should mean. In February 1919, the novelist Arnold Bennett, writing in *The Evening News*, satirised those 'excellent persons bursting with a sense of beauty, whose one fear is that the cottages of the future will be monotonously all alike'. Bennett was convinced that the terrace was a perfectly respectable option, and – fancifully – cited London's Eaton Square as his proof.[211]

Goodhart-Rendel produced for the *Architects' and Builders' Journal* 'as far as we are aware, the first attempt to deal with the housing problem analytically', in which he provided plans for three-bedroomed cottages, and a variety of elevations to use with them. Of the 12 illustrated, nine were basically picturesque in character. Goodhart-Rendel declared himself animated by the nation's need for architectural inspiration: 'the dullness of mediocrity will soon be exhibited, on rather a large

scale, in bricks and mortar, if genius does not begin to sparkle'.[212]

As the *Architects' and Builders' Journal* went through its moment of transformation into *The Architects' Journal*, in the 5 March 1919 edition, an editorial signed by Arthur Stratton positioned the magazine proudly in the vanguard of formalism:

> The importance of pure form needs to be recognised above all else in the coming years . . . resources no longer permitting . . . meaningless features and ornament which in the past have engendered a false criterion of public taste.[213]

But Stratton's call for formality was not welcome to the whole profession; certainly not to Charles Voysey – 'the cottage is his ideal', wrote Muthesius[214] – who had been a regular exhibitor with the Arts and Crafts Exhibition Society, and a member, then Master, of the Art Workers' Guild.[215]

Voysey carried his anti-classical conviction – 'we ought no more to teach the five orders to students than train them in Chinese' – and his 'hatred of miles of formal building'[216] into the postwar years, persisting in the opinion that 'an ever-varying personal note produces the richest interest and charm' when it came to cottage design. His greatest fear was of government 'forcing us to ugliness by Act of Parliament'.[217]

RIBA President Henry Hare continued to do his collegial duty by lobbying to ensure that architects (and their fees) would remain part of the equation. He told *The Times*: 'The popular idea that a pleasing building necessarily costs more money is ridiculous . . . The feeling is fairly general that houses under the national scheme should be built from designs of artistic merit'.[218] Adshead, however, sustained his ideological battle against the picturesque interpretation of 'artistic' – as his paper presented to the 42nd AGM of the Society for the Protection of Ancient Buildings (SPAB), in Autumn 1919, bore witness: 'perhaps there will be a brick bay . . . a hunchback half-timbered gable, and a sham timbered porch to the door'.[219]

The most Olympian contribution to the cottage aesthetics debate – and at the same time one of the

75   C.F.A. Voysey – 'the cottage is his ideal', wrote Hermann Muthesius in 1904. Photographed by Frank Arthur Swaine (1934), National Portrait Gallery, London

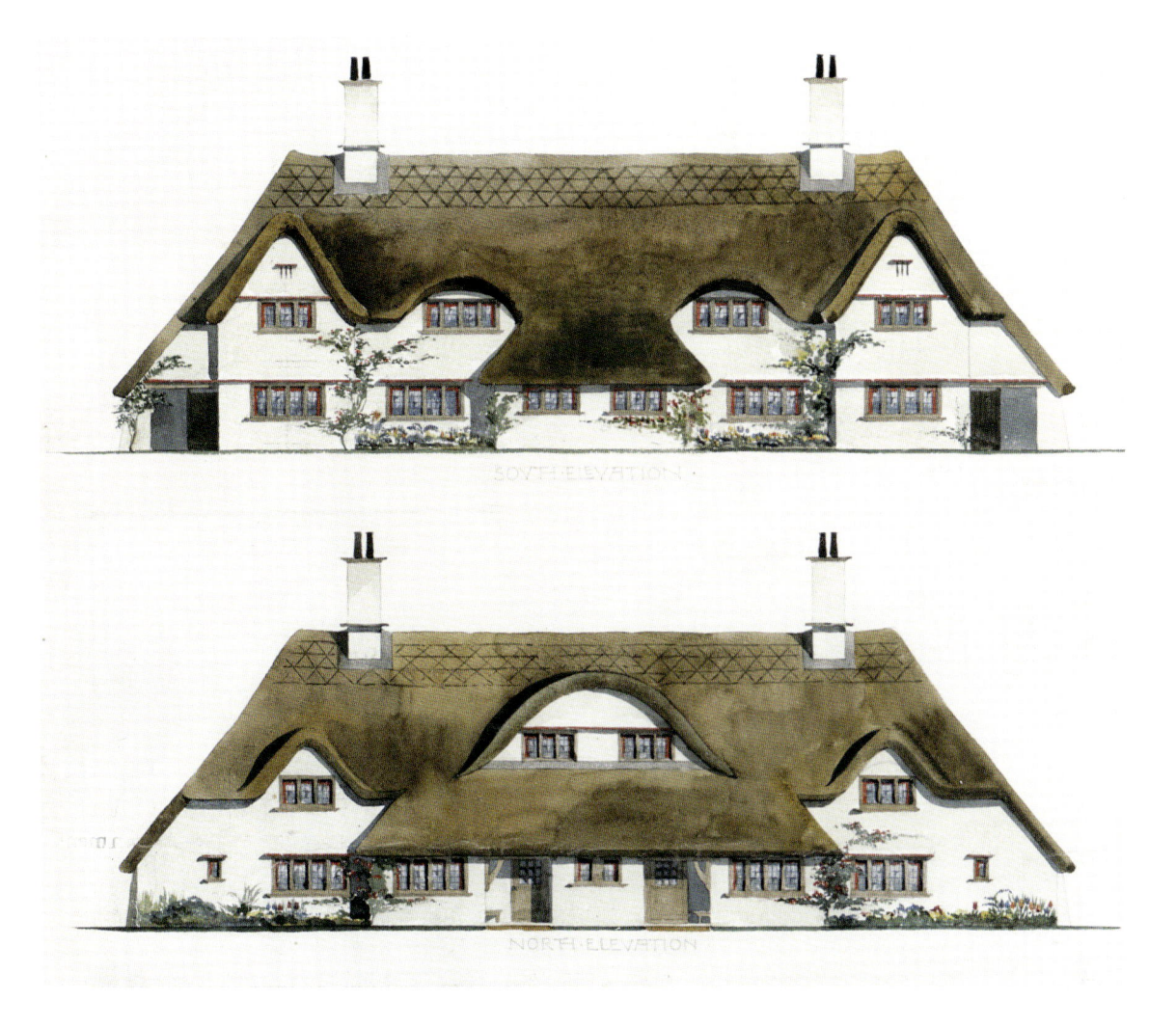

76 A design (unexecuted) for cottages at Madresfield Court, Malvern, Worcestershire, by C.F.A. Voysey (1901), RIBA Collections. Voysey never seemed in much doubt what a cottage should look like. His preference for the type's traditional visuality, so inspiring to the Picturesque's pattern-book architects, could still be seen in designs for estate cottages for A. Heyworth Esq. at Alderley Edge, published in *The Builder*, vol.117, no.3993, 15 August 1919, p.164/VI

most socially open-minded – came from Beresford Pite, Professor at the Royal College of Art and friend of W.R. Lethaby. Pite made, in March 1919,

> a plea that the working classes should, in the design of their homes as in the ornaments of their mantel-pieces, be set free from the authoritative

art of the architect [and be] permitted to exercise and enjoy [their] own characteristic delusions as to ornamentation.[220]

Condescending though this sounds today, Pite at least thought that tenants should be allowed some say in the aesthetics of the cottages they were expected to occupy. Barring occasional comments from Unwin revealing a similar sensitivity to working-class aesthetic preferences, architects of the time demonstrated little interest in the taste of potential cottage occupants.

COTTAGE AESTHETICS IN PARLIAMENT

Christopher Addison's foreword to *The Nation's New Houses*, dated 10 February 1919, sidestepped aesthetics. In March, a deputation from the RIBA – including Hare and Major Harry Barnes MP (*The Architects' Journal* parliamentary correspondent) – went to see the soon-to-become Minister of Health, and reported afterwards:

> he desired to say . . . equal weight must be given to that indescribable element in design, the absence of which in the past had inflicted upon this country the masses of dwellings of . . . supremely dull, dreary and monotonous character.[221]

The opening debate for the 1919 Housing Bill in the House of Commons fell a few days later, on 7 and 8 April 1919. The Health Minister declared that the purpose of his Bill was 'to promote the physical well-being of our people . . . our social stability and industrial content',[222] thus sounding another echo of the Picturesque: Addison as the 'improving landowner', determined to ameliorate by investment the quality of his human stock, whose physical inadequacy (due, at least partly, to abysmal living conditions) had been disappointing government ministers since the South African wars. Wrapping up the second reading of the Bill, Addison's junior minister Major Astor – happy to bandy War Office fitness gradings – left no doubt on this point:

> You have to measure . . . the cost to the community of having thousands of C3 men and women. When we realise what these people have done during the War, in spite of so many of them being C3 . . . we ask: is there any limit to what the people of this country could do if they were an A1 people?[223]

Such instrumental talk of human fitness apparently disturbed no-one. The ensuing debate saw MPs – Sir Martin Conway prominent among them – more eager to address the aesthetics of the people's cottages.

Conway was a remarkable figure. A singularly late-Victorian combination of alpinist and art historian, he was the first occupant (aged 28) of the Roscoe Chair in Art at Liverpool University, by his own account a personal friend of Ruskin,[224] and a devotee of Sidney Addy's 1898 study of autochthonous domestic architecture, *The Evolution of the English House*.[225] He brought that spirit to the subject at hand in April 1919, telling the Commons: 'I do hope that when the country blossoms out with these 500,000 cottages a very serious effort will be made to prevent them being 500,000 eyesores'.[226]

On the first day of the debate, the notorious self-publicist Noel Pemberton Billing MP – whose personal postwar cottage-building plans near his home in Hertford had involved ferro-concrete blocks as a cost-saving measure – had articulated a contrasting anxiety:

> How much money is to be allowed to be spent on making these homes artistic? . . . We cannot afford to spend very much on that aspect today. It is far better to have two sound homes not so artistic, housing two happy families, than to have one artistic home housing one happy family.[227]

There is no definitive evidence that Pemberton Billing's contribution in the House related to the recently launched 'Pemberton Billing System of House Construction' – a licensable set of modular dwelling designs, based on a 30 by 35-foot rectangle, to be built in concrete with the plainest possible elevations. A letter to *The Builder* found 'as many faults as it was possible to produce in the arrangement of the accommodation provided',[228] but anyone determined to become a licensee might have felt compensated by the construction system's readiness to house the innovative Pemberton Billing Single Fire Heating and Cooking system.[229]

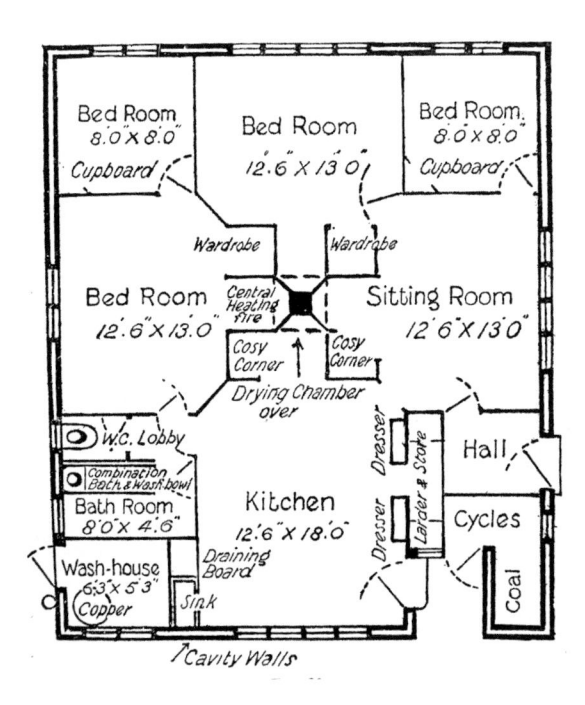

77 Plan of Pemberton Billing's super-austere rectangular dwelling. Two of the bedrooms can only be reached through the sitting room; the fourth (top left) only via the kitchen and another bedroom. Economy clearly prioritised. From Gordon Allen's *The Cheap Cottage & Small House* (London: B.T. Batsford, 1919), fig.88, p.109

In contrast to this possibly self-interested advocate of austerity, Sir Peter Griggs MP hoped for 'pleasant garden suburbs' – revealing himself a friend of the Picturesque;[230] Leslie Scott MP, who would later join the CPRE and campaign to save ancient cottages, wanted to 'save our towns from [the] wicked and hideous monstrosities which disfigure so many of them'.[231] And at much greater length, Sir John Tudor Walters MP spoke of beauty:

> Let us feel that it is a great and worthy task to make England beautiful and attractive and to make the dwellings of the poor things of beauty . . . in building the humble dwellings of the poor we could build a great temple to humanity.[232]

In parallel with the parliamentary discussion, the newspapers displayed a keen interest in the aesthetics of the government's cottage-building plans. On the second day of the housing debate, leader writer 'W.M.', in a *Daily Mirror* editorial, agonised:

> One has a vision of houses everywhere . . . totally unsuited to the character of the county in which ardent philanthropy will have "dumped" them . . . will the official persons warranted to turn out any pattern, to any quantity, at a moment's notice, kindly stay away?[233]

At times, the *Daily Mail* appeared to agree, describing the designs in the LGB *Manual* with a lukewarm 'workmanlike'.[234] The following month, the Prince of Wales would galvanise both newspapers' reservations in a speech at the Royal Academy on 4 May 1919 calling for new dwellings 'not only utilitarian in character but attractive to the eye'.[235] An editorial in *The Daily Telegraph* then picked up the Prince's comments, demanding the awakening of an 'artistic conscience' among 'the bureaucrats of Whitehall' – 'there is a very real danger that the present unexampled opportunity for the provision of beautiful homes for the people may be thrown away'.[236]

More along these lines came from the writer Walter Lionel George,[237] whose novel *Blind Alley* (1919) tackled social changes brought about by war, and who had written an appreciation of the picturesque cottages at Port Sunlight in 1909.[238] In May 1919, he called in *The Daily Mirror* newspaper for a Minister of Fine Arts to 'prevent artistic outrages' and oversee the creation of local authority cottages that would not 'offend our eyes for a century'.[239] Voysey, incidentally, had expressed his distaste for that idea before the war – a 'Minister of Fine Arts . . . set up to impose the Order of the Parthenon'.[240] Over at the *Daily Mail*, the letters desk was inundated: 'Many correspondents are afraid that both the country and the industrial areas may be spoiled by the erection of barrack-like things called homes'.[241]

Emboldened perhaps by the Addison Scheme's Alhambra launch event a few nights earlier, a group of MPs attempted a cottage aesthetics coup at the report stage of Addison's Housing Bill, in the House of Commons on 26 May 1919. Martin Conway told newspapers 'the housing bill threatens to destroy much of the charm and ancient beauty of English towns and villages'.[242] Gillian Darley recounts how Lord Harcourt had been criticised by Uvedale Price in the 1760s for the plainness and ribbon layout of the estate cottages he built at Nuneham Courtenay. The Picturesque movement sought thereafter to instill in landowners a sense of their aesthetic obligation to the landscape,[243] and an echo of this could be heard in Conway's pleadings in 1919. Seconded in the Commons by his Conservative colleague Neville Chamberlain, a veteran of house-planning arguments in Birmingham, Conway tabled an amendment to Clause 1 (Duty of Local Authority to Prepare Housing Schemes) seeking to expand the powers that the Bill gave the government to control the exterior design quality of cottages on local authority estates. The aim of the change, Conway explained, was the promotion and protection of architectural beauty:

> if we could scatter over the country as a result of this housing activity a number of really well-built, well-designed cottages . . . if they were built as 500 years ago they used to be built . . . people seeing what buildings they were, might look back to the persons of today who are busy with these great schemes . . . and regard these houses as . . . a credit to our generation.[244]

MPs speaking for Conway's amendment mostly hunted, shot, and fished in their spare time: Lieutenant-Colonel Sir Archibald Weigall (Conservative and Unionist member for Horncastle, Lincolnshire), Mr Ronald McNeill (Conservative member for Canterbury), and Major George Lane-Fox (Conservative and Unionist member for Barkston Ash, Yorkshire). The Jonathan Swift enthusiast Sir Henry Craik (Conservative MP for the Scottish Universities) made common cause:

> This is going to be a great, epoch-making Bill in regard to the aspect of our country. If it is not

carried out with a due sense of the traditions and the local surroundings of different parts of the country, it will . . . perhaps destroy the whole plan of the country by the erection of some hideous monstrosities.[245]

Countering, the Liberal Health Minister objected:

> It is quite impossible to lay down in a Bill anything that is a matter of taste. . . . in any case where we refuse to approve [a] scheme, we should have to give our reasons for considering that it was injurious to the natural beauties or architectural amenities of the neighbourhood . . . How can you do that? We should have to be setting out a disputation on a work of art. We cannot do that with local authorities.[246]

Conway and Chamberlain's amendment was defeated.

A reverse in the House of Commons did not discourage cottage aesthete Lord Salisbury from attempting a similar amendment in the Lords.[247] Behind the scenes, the SPAB had been in touch with both Conway and Salisbury to lobby for clauses that would protect ancient cottage architecture.[248] But in the upper chamber, the Lord Chancellor pacified Salisbury by praising the Health Ministry's newly appointed architects – 'a number . . . of the greatest eminence' – who could be relied upon to safeguard aesthetic standards.[249] The final form of the Act allowed the government to insist that local authorities employ a RIBA-nominated architect where they believed 'natural amenities' or the 'character of the locality' might be under threat.[250]

FORMAL VERSUS PICTURESQUE IN THE NEWSPAPERS

Parliamentary compromises did not quieten the newspapers. Returning to the subject throughout the first year of the Addison Scheme, *The Daily Mirror* maintained its support for the idea of state-financed dwellings, but worried away at the potential aesthetic consequences. The paper's cartoonist

THE NEW HOUSING SCHEMES: A DANGER.

WHAT LOCAL AUTHORITIES HATE TO SEE

A METAMORPHOSIS DEAR TO THEIR HEARTS

W. K. HASELDEN.

If they are left to the local authorities, experience shows that all thought of beauty will be neglected, and our lovely countryside, with its famous cottages, be turned into a dismal acreage of hideous formal brick.—(By W. K. Haselden.)

78   W.K. Haselden, 'The New Housing Schemes: A Danger', *The Daily Mirror*, 16 June 1919, p.5

One of the great "reconstruction" schemes now being prepared is the building of about a million cottages for returned soldiers. Is it any good hoping that they may be so designed that they do not turn our beautiful countryside into a hideous and monotonous city of bricks and mortar?—(By W. K. Haselden.)

79   W.K. Haselden, 'Will it be like this after the war?', *The Daily Mirror*, 27 August 1918, p.6. A picturesque idyll prior to government intervention in the top frame. Below, a government-mandated formal dystopia. This was the cartoon that partly inspired May Morris to write to the newspaper in June 1919

W.K. Haselden returned to the housing question in June 1919 (fig.78).

His drawing comprised two frames: the first Elysian, with the cottage picturesque ascendant – gables, dormers, prominent chimneystacks, latticed casement windows – labelled 'What Local Authorities Hate To See'. The second frame was dystopian – 'A Metamorphosis Dear To Their Hearts' – in which a uniformed labourer, wearing a curious hat, carried regulation buckets away from the low-pitched roof and square sash windows of a symmetrical modern house. Behind it, a terrace of identical dwellings stretched pitilessly across the horizon.[251] The threat Haselden visualised was twofold: from the local authorities, whose aesthetic preferences many believed the public had 'good reasons not to trust';[252] and from 'hideous formal brick'.

The cartoon was possibly occasioned by another highlight of this well-intentioned English controversy: a letter to The Daily Mirror, published on 14 June 1919, dispatched from that sanctuary of the Arts and Crafts, William Morris's old house on the Thames near Lechlade. From this paragon of traditional domestic architecture, Morris's daughter May – socialist, art-embroiderer, editor of her father's collected works, and member of the governing committee at the SPAB since 1905[253] – wrote her contribution to the cottage aesthetics debate:

Many of us have lived in apprehension since the question of country building was started, knowing how unsympathetically the necessities of housing may be dealt with by local bodies who think that no dwelling for cottage folk can be sanitary or practical unless erected by rule of thumb under their auspices.

Morris's anxiety had been stoked by a previous Haselden cartoon (fig.79) in The Daily Mirror, published in August 1918 – the cartoonist's first visualisation of the government's building plans for 'about a million cottages' representing fears that were widely shared. Morris characterised the dilemma

facing the nation as that between 'the "art" cottage', on the one hand, and 'the . . . "standardised" row of dwellings' on the other. 'Which,' she asked The Daily Mirror's readers, 'shall we choose?'[254]

In letters to The Times, others shared her gloom. RIBA President Hare, on 30 June 1919, warned of the

great danger that one very important consideration may, in the majority of cases, be entirely lost sight of – namely, the necessity for a due regard to the aesthetic and architectural quality of the designs of the houses to be erected.[255]

Hare implied that he already knew what a committee 'of outside experts' – or a putative Minister of Fine Arts – ought to recommend. Being an architect, he had no use for the term 'artistic'; he was ready to use 'picturesque' despite the enthusiasm among establishment architects for formalism: 'No country in the world,' he wrote, 'is so rich as ours in examples of simple and picturesque cottages, establishing a tradition which it is criminal to ignore'.[256] With a Beaux-Arts training and a track record rich in classical-revival libraries and town-halls,[257] Hare was the lynchpin of a RIBA whose panjandra were largely converts to formalism. But in June 1919, he was to be found apparently suggesting the nation's new homes ought to draw on the Picturesque for their aesthetics – the very thing the Tudor Walters Report and LGB Manual had been at pains to discourage.

THE GOVERNMENT RESPONDS TO CRITICISM

Having fought off legislative interventions to make the Health Ministry statutory gatekeeper of council cottage beauty, the government fell silent. But further official reaction to the aesthetics debate can be found. In July 1919, the Ministry of Health launched a fortnightly magazine, Housing, distributing two copies free of charge to every local authority in the country.[258] The first edition included an article titled 'Designs of Cottages', in which Ministry architect S.B. Russell – the man most

80 Plan No. 5, Class B4 (parlour) Urban, LGB *Manual* (1919), The Bodleian Libraries, University of Oxford. Canted bays break the plain rectangular plan. The roof is hipped, and slopes at an angle of just less than 45 degrees – Lutyens's 'ugly angle'

likely to have supervised the *Manual*'s cottages[259] – offered new variations 'on Drawings 1, 2 and 6'.[260] Thus began a process in which *Housing* magazine presented new and adapted designs for Addison Scheme cottages until Sir Alfred Mond shut the publication down in July 1921.

On the same page as Russell's 'Designs of Cottages' was an unsigned article – probably also by Russell[261] – providing further evidence of Ministry thinking about cottage exteriors at this early stage of the housing scheme. 'It is impossible for one person, or collection of persons, to plan a cottage which will disarm all criticism,' the article began. 'The plans in the Manual were offered only as suggestions.' But the anonymous author then reprised the anti-Picturesque refrain of the

81 Cyril Wontner Smith's Second Premium-winning block of two-bedroom (Class C) cottages in the Home Counties Area was one of the designs chosen for the unbuilt London County Council Model Village in Acton. It was dropped due to excessive cost. RIBA Collections

82 W.K. Haselden, 'The Housing Dream and the Reality', *The Daily Mirror*, 27 November 1919, p.5. Whitehall's Addison Scheme was lampooned repeatedly by *The Daily Mirror*. In this case, a picturesque cottage is envisaged as the best-case scenario; low hip-roofed symmetry the probable (and less desirable) outcome

Manual itself, counselling against 'all unnecessary and costly appurtenances, such as outbuildings, outside porches, projecting wings and gables, dormers, broken outlines in roofs, and tall and elaborate chimneystacks'.[262] The article ended by addressing the *Manual*'s 'clamp of bricks' cottage aesthetic: 'The most cutting criticism of the Board's types is that they are boxes with lids. . . . this is not very destructive; at any rate, they are free from architectural pyrotechnics and would make restful habitations'.

But it was a criticism with a pedigree richer than the writer acknowledged. 'Boxes with lids' recalled a dismissive slogan attributed to William Morris.[263] Further, it evoked language that Ruskin had weaponised in his Edinburgh lectures about the dangers of not designing a proper roof for a dwelling – 'making it look like a large packing case with windows in it'.[264]

As local authorities all over the country absorbed the duty to build cottages mandated by the Addison Act, they looked to the government for aesthetic direction. In the first year of the scheme, that guidance came in the potentially contradictory forms of *The Nation's New Houses* and the LGB *Manual*'s type-plans. Nothing about the latter acknowledged the experience of the Ecclesiastical Commissioners in their 1880s redevelopment of slum sites in Walworth and Lambeth, where 'considerable variation' was implemented in dwelling exteriors 'to avoid for the people a monotonous environment which tends so much to stamp out individuality of character'.[265] Neither did the government's *Manual* designs reflect warnings such as Voysey's against 'the mischief of standardizing houses';[266] or from

Baillie Scott, and even from Unwin himself, as to why it might not be ideal to consign the working classes to estates of uniform dwellings, designed with formal purity and economy uppermost in mind – their appearance deliberately at odds with the Picturesque and its traditional domestic inspirations.

One of the National Cottage Competition's winners, back in 1918, had been about as far away in design terms as possible from the LGB *Manual*'s formal aesthetic. In Wontner Smith's Class C cottages (fig.81), steep cross-wing gables dominated each end of the main block, the roof was further complicated by dormers, and the latticed casement windows on the ground-floor even ran to pierced ornamental shutters. Originally selected for the London County Council's model village, the design never made it – along with the rest – beyond the Health Ministry and LCC. The model village was finally cancelled on 24 September 1920.[267] The Local Government Board – soon to become the Ministry of Health – had, however, sent a letter to local authorities across England and Wales in February 1919, putting them on standby to receive a manual of plans 'including premiated designs' from the National Cottage Competition. So, in early 1919 these had not been entirely ruled out.[268]

But would the government recommend cottages of the future – in Adshead's words – or cottages of the past? For all the shapes it had taken, Whitehall's architectural *diktat* was about to be revealed as only one side of the story. Local government, 'the first-line defence thrown up by the community against our common enemies – poverty, sickness, ignorance, isolation',[269] would provide the other.

3

THE COTTAGE DENIED

On the morning of 5 June 1920, a party of 500 delegates to the inaugural meeting of the Inter-Allied Housing and Town Planning Congress made their way to London's Paddington station to catch a special train to Bristol. The Congress had brought together housing experts from 25 allied countries across Europe and the British Empire, all of them bursting to hear news of Britain's radical Addison Scheme. Off the train at Bristol, delegates were met by 'a troop of Boy Scouts and Girl Guides',[1] who whisked them away to the first stop on their itinerary – the new housing estate under construction by Bristol Corporation at Fishponds.

Illustrations published by *The Builder* reveal what was waiting for them (figs 83 and 84). Fishponds was Bristol's first Addison Scheme development. It would remain under construction for ten years, between 1920 and 1930, and by 1939 housed 7,300

83   Addison Scheme cottages under construction at the Fishponds Estate, Bristol, June 1920, *The Builder*, vol.118, no.4036, 11 June 1920, p.694, The Bodleian Libraries, University of Oxford

GROUP OF HOUSES CLASS 'A'
FISHPONDS ESTATE
BRISTOL

1ˢᵗ floor   Gd. floor

84   Block of four Class A cottages on Bristol's Fishponds Estate, the first of their Addison Scheme developments. Note the large cross-wing gables, the porches on the two centre cottages, and the gable ends, *The Builder*, vol.118, no.4036, 11 June 1920, p.694, The Bodleian Libraries, University of Oxford

people.[2] But it was a work in progress that early June day. Three cottage types were going up, under the direction of architects William Watkins and Benjamin Wakefield, both from Bristol and Fellows of the RIBA.[3] Only two dwellings were finished, awaiting occupation by demobbed soldiers' families, but the rest of the new cottages had taken shape sufficiently for the delegates to conclude: 'The elevations, especially of the Class "A" type [were] attractive, and the materials good'.[4]

This chapter sets out to examine how local authorities responded to the government's Addison Scheme requirement for new working-class cottages. Insulated from the cost by Whitehall's agreement to pay for everything beyond the proceeds of a one penny increase in local rates, the councils of England and Wales found themselves in the driving

seat when it came to determining how their new cottages should look. Some held competitions; some hired architects; some gave the task of design to their local surveyors' departments; many proved stubbornly independent when it came to choosing more traditional cottage aesthetics than the government's housing *Manual* had suggested.

As can be seen in *The Builder*'s illustrations, the cottage elevations encountered by Congress delegates in Bristol did not conform to those in the *Manual*. Neither did they comply with its textual recommendations. The Ministry's central guidance in Spring 1919 had boiled down to their Plan No. 7 – an unaugmented rectangle with a low hipped roof.[5] Other Ministry suggestions were enlivened only slightly in plan and perspective by the concession of canted bay windows for the ground storeys at the front. By December 1919, the Ministry had hardened its line even about these: 'Bay windows should only be inserted when they are required to bring the area of a room up to a minimum size'.[6]

In contrast, the cottages going up on Bristol's Fishponds Estate featured large cross-wing gables (in both the semi-detached and block designs); substantial porches, of the sort applauded by Ruskin and Unwin;[7] broken eaves lines and broken plans; and, in the semi-detached cottages, swept catslide roofs at each side that came right down to ceiling level on the ground storey. Aesthetically, these were cottages in the sense that most people at the time would have recognised – their architecture fundamentally picturesque. They were not candidates for the 'boxes with lids' description given to the Health Ministry's 1919 *Manual* plans. Learned visitors, from as far afield as France, Belgium, Poland, Sweden, and Africa, liked what they saw. But picturesque cottages were not the only exhibit on their itinerary. The delegates were rather less impressed by the steel and concrete 'Dorlonco' houses going up on Bristol's Sea Mills estate, a later stop on their tour. There, the visiting experts got their tape measures out and discovered the decorative exterior window shutters on these formal designs were three-quarters of an inch wider than the windows they purported to protect.[8]

In the early months of 1920, the Ministry of Health was under enormous pressure to get things done. They had been given the statutory instrument they needed, in the 1919 Housing Act, to mandate local authority building. The Treasury had agreed to cover the costs of the scheme. And, under pressure from the private sector, they had augmented the primary legislation, via the 'Housing: Additional Powers Act' in December 1919, to introduce a subsidy for private individuals and commercial builders of £130 – £160 per dwelling (later increased by £100) to incentivise them to start building again too.[9]

At the beginning of March 1920, although local authorities had submitted housing schemes for 82,392 dwellings – and the Ministry of Health had approved 75,142 of them – only 511 cottages had actually been built.[10] A Fabian pamphlet described

THE HOUSING PROBLEM.

PEACE. "BUT I THOUGHT I WAS TO HAVE GOT INTO MY TEMPLE LONG AGO." THE OLD ARCHITECT. "EXTREMELY SORRY, MADAM—CONSIDERABLE DIFFICULTIES IN THE BUILDING TRADE. HOPE MY SUCCESSOR HERE WILL HAVE BETTER LUCK."

85   Bernard Partridge, 'The Housing Problem', *Punch*, vol.157, 31 December 1919, p.551, Punch Cartoon Library/TopFoto

progress as 'a staggering disappointment'.[11] With the national shortfall now thought by some to have reached 800,000 dwellings, this was politically problematic for Dr Addison.

New local authority schemes had started to percolate into the public realm, though, allowing *The Builder* to feature a handful that caught its eye. In the 6 February 1920 edition, they published drawings for the first Addison Scheme estates in Royal Leamington Spa. Designed by the Birmingham architects Crouch, Butler & Savage,[12] one of two estates was to be found on the Leicester Street (now Baker Avenue) site of four and three-quarter acres; the other, of 12 acres, at Tachbrook

Road. Both were depicted as garden-suburb islands of *rus in urbe* by the moment's favourite perspectivist Raffles Davison, whose work we have already encountered and who had, in his capacity as associate editor, written advice on architectural drawing for *The Builder* in January 1920.[13]

Like the cottages that were to go up at Fishponds in Bristol later in the year, the Leamington Spa perspectives (fig.86) seemed to ignore the Ministry of Health's 1919 cottage guidance. They too featured large street-facing gables. They had complex roofscapes, prominent chimneystacks, front elevations modulated via a mixture of 'Kenilworth bricks and . . . sandfaced tiles', with white roughcast on the two central gables plus multi-pane casement windows throughout.[14] The cottages at both ends of the estate's entrance blocks were capped with large, asymmetric, street-facing gables, swept so that the roof at one side was brought down in a sort of catslide, in this case over the front door. Even the homes deeper into the estate featured disobedient, decorative street-facing gables.

Further evidence of affection for picturesque cottage architecture amid the first wave of Addison Scheme commissions is easy to find, among rural and urban authorities alike. In the countryside, Wilton Rural District Council in Wiltshire chose the Portman Square architect Norman Evill – who had learned his trade as one of Edwin Lutyens's favourite assistants[15] – to design essentially picturesque cottages in blocks of four and semi-detached pairs. Making use of local stone and including idiomatic but Ministry-discouraged plan breaks (fig.88), they were described as striving 'to keep the local character of the [nearby] villages, with their gables and steep-pitched roofs'.[16]

In urban Folkestone, the Ministry of Health approved a 250-cottage Addison Scheme estate designed by the Borough Engineer and Surveyor A.E. Nichols – utilising concrete bricks and roof tiles fabricated on site with special Vickers machines, to keep costs down.[17] Notwithstanding the innovative choice of materials, and the council's use of their staff surveyor rather than an expensive outside

86   Royal Leamington Spa's first Addison Scheme dwellings, designed for their Leicester Street site by Birmingham architects Crouch, Butler & Savage, *The Builder*, vol.118, no.4018, 6 February 1920, p.162, II and III, The Bodleian Libraries, University of Oxford

87   Close-up of the Royal Leamington Spa Leicester Street Addison Scheme designs. A skilfully handled four-cottage block features key picturesque design elements: the complex eaves line, cross-wing gables and asymmetrical catslide roofs. The Bodleian Libraries, University of Oxford

architect, the aesthetic choices leaned toward the Picturesque once again (fig.89) – dominated by street-facing gables on broken plans with decorative diapering at the apex.

Outside Winchester, the Stanmore Housing Scheme – slow to reach fruition, and not officially opened by the Prince of Wales until November 1923 – exemplified rebellious local authority building at its most picturesque. The architect there, William Curtis Green, had put his love of the ancient English cottage on the record in a Batsford book on the subject in 1908.[18] He ignored the Ministry's 1919 discouragement of gables, prominent chimneystacks, and sweeping roofs (fig.90),[19] to produce one of the most attractive estates in the Addison Scheme – a realisation of the aesthetic generosity with which working-class people might be rehoused, so long as the purse strings were not overly tightened.

Despite the apparent victory of the advocates of formalism in the matter of government aesthetic guidance for Addison Scheme cottages, as expressed in the 1919 housing *Manual*, it was clear that among architects and borough

left

88   Wilton Rural District Council's Addison Scheme cottages, designed by Norman Evill, *The Builder*, vol.118, no.4034, 28 May 1920, p.632, II, The Bodleian Libraries, University of Oxford

below

89   Cottages designed by Borough Surveyor A.E. Nichols for Folkestone Borough Council's first Addison Scheme estate, *The Builder*, vol.118, no.4035, 4 June 1920, p.665, The Bodleian Libraries, University of Oxford

surveyors outside government – and among their local authority patrons – there was no uniform appetite for formality or standardisation in cottage architecture.

The Ministry of Health (MoH) was able to exercise absolute regulatory control over local authority cottage design: formal MoH sign-off for every aspect of a local authority's plans was required (fig.91) to guarantee financial support from central government. But the machinery of regulation – with its 11 District Housing Commissioners, each with teams of architects and administrators[20] – was vulnerable to charges of bureaucratic sclerosis, and the Ministry appears not to have wanted to rely on red tape alone to encourage architects and planners to follow their

104

90   Stuart Crescent on the Stanmore Housing Scheme, Winchester. Cottage design was by William Curtis Green, estate layout by William Dunn, 'Domestic Architecture of Today: The Stanmore Housing Scheme', in *Country Life*, vol.54, no.1400, 3 November 1923, p.627, Future Publishing Ltd

right

91   Official Ministry of Health approval stamp on a London County Council plan for Addison cottages on the Roehampton Estate, South West London, 1 July 1920, London Metropolitan Archives, City of London

guidance. Using *Housing* magazine, their own fortnightly vehicle for injecting reliable thinking into the local authority bloodstream, the Ministry tried exhortatory messages instead. In the 10 November 1919 edition, for example, the writer 'A.E.D.' (probably Ministry of Health staff architect Albert Edward Dixon) ventured:

> If . . . all such features as gables, dormers and even bay windows are left out in some of the types for the sake of economy, it is still possible in, for instance, a Georgian treatment of the elevation, to impart some interest into the design.[21]

In May the following year, an article by 'M.R.' (likely to have been Manning Robertson, appointed as a Temporary Assistant Architect in the LGB's Housing Department in 1919), had more insistent points to make:

> sham half-timber, superabundant gables and bay windows endlessly repeated have been associated with cottage building in the past . . . they are

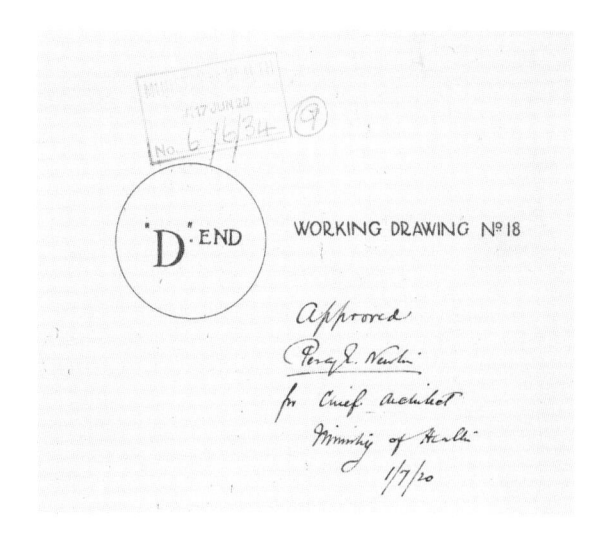

consistent neither with good architecture nor with low prices . . . it can and must be proved that sound and healthy houses are as cheap relatively as the cramped and dark houses of the past.[22]

Robertson's article represents one of the few occasions in *Housing* magazine where government rhetoric about the architectural primacy of simple, unornamented design slipped away, and their underlying concern about economy was exposed. It would have been reasonable for the Ministry to admit that state-funded cottages were going to have to be cheap or they would not get built at all. But such political transparency would have made an uncomfortable bedfellow for the promise of habitations fit for heroes. If the oft-praised heroes turned out to be entitled only to cottages stripped of 'all forms of extravagance',[23] perhaps the sacrifices they and their dead comrades had made would become a locus for resentment and reaction.

The government was not left entirely alone to argue the case for formal aesthetics. In the first weekly edition of *The Builder* of 1920, an anonymous contributor seems to have anticipated local authority enthusiasm for the picturesqueness of 'superabundant gables' and gave vent to a denunciation of garden city cottage design that would not have been out of place in Liverpool University's *Town Planning Review* before the First World War. The writer complained about the way such cottages relied

> for their effect upon a certain character of picturesqueness, which their designers have sought to emulate from medieval examples surviving . . . in the German towns such as Rothenburg, Heidelburg, Hilderheim and Nuremburg.

Focusing specifically on the responsibility of the Picturesque for this unfortunate (and, notably, foreign) state of affairs, the article rejected the Picturesque's tectonic credentials:

> picturesqueness – however great its charm – is most emphatically not an architectural quality,

but something altogether extraneous, having its origin in certain fortuitous circumstances utterly unconnected with the architectural merit of the building.[24]

This critique is familiar for its repudiation of the associationist content of picturesque architecture; and the piece is reminiscent in tone and substance (see Chapter 2) of Geoffrey Scott's *The Architecture of Humanism*. Might it have been written by Scott-disciple and Liverpool alumnus Trystan Edwards, who had criticised picturesque architecture and garden city design in very similar terms in signed pieces for *The Town Planning Review* over the preceding decade? The need for anonymity in this case would be explained by the fact that Edwards had started work the previous year as a Temporary Assistant Architect in Unwin's Housing Department at the Local Government Board.[25]

An Oxford contemporary of Scott, Edwards loved *The Architecture of Humanism*, 'its profound scholarship and elegant prose style'. In December 1914, he had defended the book from a critical review in the *Journal of the RIBA* – Edwards's letter ending with a quotation from Goethe: 'The Classic is health, the Romantic is disease'.[26] That he should have sought to carry on Scott's work would be consistent with his opposition to garden city planning and his theoretical commitment to higher density neo-Georgian terraced housing. But the cottage picturesque, against which Edwards often inveighed, embodied the style of architecture that Scott himself had acknowledged as being where 'modern taste has been concentrated'.[27]

THE HEALTH MINISTRY'S 1920 TYPE-PLANS AND ELEVATIONS

When it came to gables, Trystan Edwards's disciplined vision took a blow, in May 1920, from the arm of central government that had previously seemed most promisingly committed to formalism. The Ministry of Health chose that moment to issue a second manual of designs whose guidance turned away from the formality of its 1919 predecessor. Some slightly more picturesque cottage designs had appeared in the pages of the Ministry's own *Housing* magazine from Autumn 1919 onwards.[28] Swenarton argues that the government's relaxation of its insistence on cottages with low-hipped roofs and pure rectangular plans derived principally from a recognition that tiled roofs – more common in southern England – demanded a steeper pitch due to the roofing material's greater porosity.[29] This in turn called for narrower spans and the historically derived L-shaped plan rather than the 1919 *Manual*'s deeper rectangles – bringing the cross-wing gable back into play.[30] A blanket insistence on slate-only roofs, and the 'box with lid' design they facilitated, might have had cost benefits for the government, but could have slowed building down further because there was a postwar shortage of both slates and the transport needed to move them to non-slate districts.

A determination to accelerate Addison Scheme building can, therefore, fairly be identified as the primary motivation behind the publication of the May 1920 housing *Manual*. Although the Ministry conceded that the designs it contained were 'by no means the last word in cottage planning', it insisted that they were 'the result of working experience in all parts of the country and are so designed as to meet divergent local views and requirements'. They had already 'been adopted by local authorities in various parts of the country [and] a considerable amount of time has been saved'.[31]

The new manual featured 34 designs, 20 of which were unlike anything in the 1919 LGB *Manual* – more picturesque in character, with a typical design repertoire of cross-wing gables, dormer windows, broken plans, and, in many cases, high-pitched roofs enlivened by prominent chimneystacks.[32] Four of the officially sanctioned new designs were obviously neo-Georgian, with sash windows and vestigial doorcases;[33] the other ten came closer to the austere formality of the type-plans presented in the 1919 *Manual* – low hipped roofs, no gables, no dormers, nothing by way of ornamental neo-Georgian detailing. The Ministry's advocacy of

exclusively formalist cottage design had lasted a year at most. But rather than a change in ideology, their new flexibility probably represented resignation. Local authority enthusiasm for more obviously picturesque cottage designs – encountered repeatedly by MoH officials during the approval process – had never been solely a question of access to roofing materials.[34]

Contradictory factors were at work in shaping Addison Scheme cottage aesthetics. Central government, represented by the Ministry of Health, wanted simplicity and the lowest possible cost, within standards set by the Tudor Walters Report. By 1920, thanks to shortages and delay, it also wanted speed. Whitehall's commitment to the formal cottage design adumbrated in the 1919 *Manual* had been lent credibility by the enthusiasm for neo-classicism among an influential section of the architectural profession – practitioners associated with Liverpool University, the RIBA's leadership, the Architectural Association, and *The Architects' Journal* after the turn of the century. In contrast, many of the 1,802 local authorities in England and Wales in 1919–20 seem to have been closer in aesthetic taste to Roger Fry's picturesque-owning neighbours near Guildford (Chapter 2) than they were to Fry himself. Certainly, few local authorities displayed consistent interest in cutting-edge formal architectural fashion, despite often having to deal with pressure from local architectural lobbies. In much of the country, they remained, by contrast, drawn to the acculturated picturesqueness of the cottage examined in Chapter 1. Searching for a middle way, Addison's Ministry found it expedient to bend to councillors' prevailing picturesque enthusiasms – if it meant something actually got built.

THE ADDISON SCHEME IN BIRMINGHAM

The tensions created by the conflict between architectural doctrine and the requirement for speed were evident when it came to Birmingham City Council's first Addison Scheme plans. But in dealing with the 20,000 dwellings Birmingham was estimated to need,[35] the corporation's slowness off the mark also reflected decades of caution in engaging with municipal housing that dated back to their abortive Dalton Street Scheme of 1884.[36]

Prior to the launch of the city's new Housing and Town Planning Committee (H&TPC) in May 1917, a delegation of Birmingham architects led by William Alexander Harvey (of Bournville fame) had attended the old planning committee's regular gathering on 11 May. The architects made suggestions: that the committee should 'exercise a controlling influence over the artistic aspects' of housing, as well as over civic development; and that a competition should be held 'among the Architects of the City' to determine what dwelling types should in future be adopted.[37] The new committee's minutes show resistance to the idea of an architectural competition.[38] Dilatory correspondence with Hayes Fisher's Local Government Board in September 1917 confirmed that housing *would* be a priority after the war, and that the government planned to help with costs – but this only triggered lost weeks of letters about what form such financial support might take.[39]

Finally, in December 1917, Birmingham's planning committee resolved to ask the city council 'to authorise your Committee to purchase . . . any land situate within the City Boundary . . . suitable for Housing Schemes'.[40] And an Advisory Committee got off the ground in April 1918, on which Harvey and two other architects – Joseph Crouch (whose firm's work we have already seen at Leamington Spa) and Herbert Tudor Buckland (one of the designers of the main buildings at St Hugh's College, Oxford) – were invited to join representatives of the Birmingham Building Trades Association and the Birmingham & District House Builders Association.[41] By then, though, the council was being tugged in different directions by both the Local Government Board (Hayes Fisher) and the Ministry of Reconstruction (Addison), neither of which really knew what the other was up to.[42]

Birmingham Corporation's velleity in respect of their housing shortage finally resolved itself at the beginning of 1919 on a tract of seven acres owned by the city at Linden Road and at that time given over to allotments.[43] In January, the planning committee decided the idea of a competition for the site there should be put to one side, and that 16 extant type-plans (for 81 dwellings) drawn up by E.W. Turner's Town Planning Department should be dusted off and sent to the Local Government Board for approval.[44]

On 31 March 1919, a Birmingham delegation consisting of Councillor Siward James (Conservative and Unionist, now chair of the H&TPC), Turner (Town Planning Superintendent), and Mr C. Walker (committee clerk) travelled to Whitehall. They met, as it turned out, no less an authority than Raymond Unwin himself, and were able to discover, face to face, what he thought of their proposals. Unwin was accompanied at this meeting by 'his assistant',[45] the LGB architect Manning Robertson, who would over the coming years use the pages of the government's *Housing* magazine to become one of the more vociferous critics of picturesque cottage architecture.

The main criticism that Unwin made of the Birmingham designs was that some did not have living rooms or principal bedrooms large enough to meet the Local Government Board's new standards. 'Apparently the Board have decided to adopt Tudor Walters' Committee's Report,' remarked the council's minute-taker, suggesting that although the Tudor Walters Report had been published four months previously, no-one had yet told Birmingham it was the new gold standard. Room dimensions out of the way, Unwin's remaining commentary was aimed at discouraging the Birmingham designers' more picturesque leanings.

He began by suggesting that 'some decorative work on one of the gables . . . should be dropped'. Further, he protested that on Plan E the 'angles' were 'expensive'. He proposed that another plan be dropped altogether and replaced by 'something without projecting out-buildings'. Only on Plan H did he soften his formalist stance, suggesting an attic in solution of the space problem (which would surely have led to the normally proscribed dormer windows). Unwin concluded with recommendations concerning the council's approach to the housing scheme more broadly: they should appoint a panel of architects to work, 'in a consulting and advisory capacity', under 'an Architect of experience'.[46]

Birmingham's planners incorporated Unwin's emendations swiftly enough to resubmit the plans and secure government approval by the end of April 1919. The committee then bundled the Linden Road site with three others they had available for 'immediate building' (Belcher's Lane, Cotterill's Lane, and Yardley Road) and recommended to the council that they should be allowed to tender for building work at all four sites as soon as possible 'on the basis of the approved plans of the Linden Road Scheme'.[47]

In July 1919, the H&TPC asked permission from the full council to appoint a temporary Director of Housing – a job that went to Lieutenant-Colonel Frank Cox DSO on a salary of £1,000 per annum. He was immediately given the task of reorganising the council's housing staff.[48] Organisational travails of this kind were a nationwide problem, as Addison acknowledged in a Health Ministry circular to local authorities dated 25 August 1919: 'The Act will make large demands upon councils and their offices, and . . . will place upon its trial the present machinery of Local Government'.[49] In Birmingham, they next found it necessary to replace the Housing and Town Planning Committee with a new Housing and Estates Committee, unifying those responsible for building council estates with those in charge of letting and managing them.[50] This committee met for the first time on Friday 14 November 1919.[51]

Despite a very high estimate, the builder Whitehouse & Sons was given the job at Linden Road, and work there began. But things did not go well. On 19 December 1919, Mr Whitehouse was asked to attend the council's Building and Sites Sub-Committee, where he was told that councillors were 'very disappointed at the slow progress being made'. The contractor blamed the labour difficulties that were general all over the country, 'principally the shortage of bricklayers'.[52] Work had started on only 23 of the 81 dwellings specified, but construction speed did not improve the following year: the Linden Road development stood at 29 commenced and none

completed by 23 February 1920. Across the city, of the 2,927 dwellings approved by the Ministry of Health, only 16 were finished;[53] and by May 1920, the council had run out of patience with Messrs Whitehouse. The company's contract would be terminated after they had completed 41 of the original 81 dwellings commissioned, on the west side of Linden Road. The rest of the building would proceed, with the Ministry of Health's blessing, via Direct Labour.[54]

During his first months, Frank Cox had made good progress with a departmental reorganisation, which – as well as increasing the annual departmental running cost from £10,000 to £15,000 per annum[55] – demoted the council's previous architectural supremo, Town Planning Superintendent E.W. Turner, and allowed Cox to bring in Lieutenant-Colonel Wilfrid Travers as Corporation Architect and Deputy Director of Housing. The department's new creative team then produced its own dwelling designs (the Birmingham builder Charles Haugham later described Travers's cottage plans as 'lovely from the architectural point of view'[56]) and these were submitted to Whitehall for approval. Birmingham's Housing and Estates Committee, meanwhile, welcomed the space on Linden Road, now freed from the lethargic attentions of Messrs Whitehouse, as an opportunity, at last, 'for the erection of a row of houses which will be a credit to the Committee'.[57] Thus a new generation of 'estate owners' kept one eye on posterity.

For all the trouble Birmingham had experienced with the Linden Road site, the place remained particularly rich in meaning. The road runs south from the suburb of Selly Oak out to the village green and polygonal Rest House of Harvey's Cadbury estate at Bournville.[58] To build social housing on Linden Road in 1920 was, therefore, to make an unavoidable statement of some sort about your relationship with the past. And Birmingham Corporation trod carefully with the second phase of building there. From April 1920 onwards, they tried to embrace the future without abandoning their local architectural history.

Ten of the Direct Labour dwellings that Cox's team had agreed upon were to be constructed

92   (above) a panoramic view of the new Birmingham dwellings on Linden Road – an even-handed mix of gabled Picturesque and cut-price neo-classical; (left) detail showing the Birmingham Type Design 1920/10, 'Dorlonco Houses', seen at the centre of the Linden Road panorama, designed by Wilfrid Travers, *The Builder*, vol.119, no.4041, 16 July 1920, p.66(V), The Bodleian Libraries, University of Oxford

using the steel-frame and concrete Dorman Long System[59] – known as the 'Dorlonco' house – a design pioneered during the war in the industrial village of Dormanstown, near Redcar, in north-eastern England. It was approved for Addison Scheme use by the Health Ministry at the end of 1919.[60] The new Corporation Architect, 37-year-old Travers – trained in the offices of Sir Aston Webb,[61] and a collaborator in 1907–8 with Liverpool University's Charles Reilly in his campaign to systematise architectural training[62] – supervised Birmingham's version of the Dorlonco. It was to be built in semi-detached pairs, with a symmetrical formal plan and elevation, a low-pitched roof (gabled not hipped) and squat chimneystacks. Gibbsian quoining on the block corners (fig.92) articulated the houses' low-key neo-classical pretensions.

The other type of dwelling designed for Linden Road would have settled more comfortably into Harvey's Bournville. Credited by *The Builder* to Housing Director Frank Cox, it was to be built using standard brick construction; and in this case, the elevations were more picturesque, echoing Courtney Crickmer's work at Hampstead Garden Suburb.[63]

This more traditional cottage vision employed large street-facing gables, articulating a plan break at the centre of the blocks. Rendered with roughcast, their roofs swept down in catslides to ground-floor ceiling height, sheltering the front doors on either side. There were other plan breaks too, some half-hipped, the overall picture generating a complex (and expensive) roofscape (fig.94). Casement windows added a cottagey finishing touch.

The Health Ministry in London had striven originally to discourage such irregularities: 'slight and unnecessary projections, when treated with gables, are the source of enormous expense, and again are not good architecture because they are the result of straining after effect'.[64] Here again we see Ministry arguments for economy camouflaged

93 Courtenay Crickmer's cottages at the junction of Willifield Way and Temple Fortune Hill, Hampstead Garden Suburb (1909). Inspiration perhaps for Frank Cox's picturesque designs on Linden Road (see fig.94)

94 Birmingham Type Design 1920/24, on the Linden Road development near Bournville, 'Illustrations: Birmingham Housing Scheme', *The Builder*, vol.119, no.4041, 16 July 1920, p.66 (V), The Bodleian Libraries, University of Oxford

by normative assertions about 'good architecture'. But the end-dwellings on some of Linden Road's rebelliously picturesque blocks broke further with Whitehall guidance by featuring mansard roofs and dormer windows.[65] Health Ministry bureaucrats liked dormers no more than they did broken plans: 'Roof cutting is notoriously costly'.[66]

In a historical context, Birmingham Council's Linden Road experiment takes us back to Robert Kerr and Geoffrey Scott's theoretical distinction between the two great architectural types: formal/classical and Picturesque. Building varieties of both as municipal housing in the same road meant councillors left the argument unresolved. Save for the absence of hipped roofs, the concrete Dorlonco houses complied entirely with the 1919 LGB *Manual*'s vision: rectangular in plan, no outshots, no dormer windows, minimal ornamentation. The origin of the design – Chapple calls it Neo-Georgian *maison-type*[67] – lay with the 1917 Dormanstown houses (which had been given canted ground-floor bay windows, and slightly elaborated neo-classical doorcases) designed by the Liverpool-nurtured formalists Adshead, Ramsey, and Abercrombie. By contrast, the new brick-built cottage blocks on Linden Road ignored as many of the Tudor Walters and 1919 *Manual*'s aesthetic recommendations as the Dorlonco houses observed. They could just about be seen as compliant with the more Picturesque-friendly guidance of *Type Plans and Elevations* (1920) – depending on whether you regarded their plan breaks as motivated by aesthetic preference or by material necessity in achieving the Tudor Walters Report's specified square footages.

Birmingham's experience with Addison Scheme building was similar to England's as a whole. Like everywhere else, the city was obliged to seek Health Ministry approval for its design plans because without it they would not be eligible for Treasury subsidy. But they were also under pressure from local architects not to neglect 'artistic aspects' or 'aesthetic considerations'. Cox had ended 1919 by reassuring the Birmingham Architectural Association that he was entirely 'in sympathy with . . . the necessity for variety of design', and that it

would not be his department's policy 'to turn out stock designs'.[68] Linden Road was just one place where these hopes, promises, plans, and arguments were put to the test.

In the end, Birmingham commissioned *some* Dorlonco houses because they were cheap, used modern mass-producible construction techniques, conformed with government aesthetic guidance as set out in the 1919 LGB *Manual*, and played a part in the council's broader experimental approach to Addison Scheme building.[69] They refused to use Dorloncos alone, however, because of their questionable aesthetic impact. Councillors believed that an estate consisting solely of concrete houses like the Dorloncos would be 'detrimental to the amenities of the site'. Here again there are historical echoes – councillors, like rural landowners before them, striving to discharge their picturesque responsibility to the landscape. More hard-headedly, they also minuted: 'variety in building is paramount if the value of the property is to be maintained'.[70]

In Birmingham, therefore, tension between formal and Picturesque in cottage design was not straightforwardly explicable as the state lobbying for the former and the council preferring the latter. Birmingham acknowledged government guidance and sought to follow it, at least up to a point. But having functioned as a cottage landlord since September 1890 – when the council built and let 22 three-bed cottages in Lawrence Street (later Ryder Street)[71] – and being responsible thereafter for setting and collecting cottage rents, they had perhaps a greater cultural insight into the public's aesthetic preferences (or 'amenity', as councillors were wont to call it) than many in Whitehall.

Raymond Unwin at the Ministry of Health surely understood – not least due to his collaboration with Henrietta Barnett at Hampstead – that it was not ideal to offer cottages entirely lacking in 'comeliness' to the public. He certainly shared, at one time, D.H. Lawrence's conviction that 'the human soul needs actual beauty even more than bread'.[72] But his encounter with the Birmingham Council delegation in March 1919 suggests he had, by that stage, become a convert to what was then close to scripturalisation in the formalist credo of the 1919 LGB *Manual*. Addison's Ministry of Health had resolved that it should commission TWR-compliant cottages, but people there knew they had to economise too. Fashionable formalism, shared by an influential architectural *avant garde*, made such economies easier to proselytise. But where did it leave potential tenants?

Writing in the Architectural Association's student magazine *Harlequinade* six years later, the pseudonymous correspondent 'Felix' provided a glimpse of the profession's abiding scepticism about popular taste when he disparaged the public's 'lamentable desire for the "old world" and the picturesque'.[73] Yet the closer that officials involved in delivering the Addison Scheme were situated, professionally, to the 'heroes' their policy was supposed to cater for, the more alert they became to the public's potential lack of enthusiasm for 'boxes with lids'. And that must be, at least in part, the explanation for Birmingham's not wanting to lumber itself with Addison Scheme estates whose aesthetic monotony and lack of variety would make their dwellings difficult to let (and later, perhaps, difficult to sell). In commissioning two contrasting designs for their pioneering Linden Road development, councillors clearly concluded that the way to get dwellings that might 'be a credit to the Committee' was to rely, for at least some of them, on the traditions of the Picturesque.

GABLES, THE PICTURESQUE, AND THE ADDISON SCHEME

Cottages built under the Addison Scheme were approved by the Health Ministry in the comparatively narrow window of 1919 to the first half of 1921. Swenarton estimates that of the 176,000 cottages completed, around 90,000 were built with elevations reflecting the more picturesque aesthetics of the Ministry's 1920 *Type Plans and Elevations*.[74] A ledger inscribed 'Ministerial Types' and kept by Ministry of Health assistant architect Samuel Pointon Taylor[75] records Class B (parlour type) local

authority dwellings approved for construction and contracted across England and Wales between February 1920 and April 1921. The designs listed were Local Government Board or Health Ministry originals. Some were obediently formal – hip-roofed, strictly rectangular in plan – such as the 414 cottages in blocks of four, on Plan No. 119, ordered *inter al.* by Plymouth Urban District Council (fig.95).

Many were more picturesque. The 426 cottages in semi-detached pairs, ordered by Bexley Urban District Council on Plan No. 167 (fig.96), featured cross-wing gables on a double L-shaped plan, with ornamental arrow loops at the gable apex, and catslide roofs sheltering ground-floor porches. Expressed across three bays, each individual dwelling was asymmetrical – a cut-price Kelmscott for the local authority tenant.

Similarly reminiscent of Henry Roberts's muted Picturesque (fig.38) were the blocks of four cottages (fig.97), built as Plan No. 172, ordered by Frimley Urban District Council and West Dean Rural District Council. The block plan was a shallow E-shape, allowing the cottages at each end to project gables towards the street. These were linked by a complex two-level roofline, including a prominent central

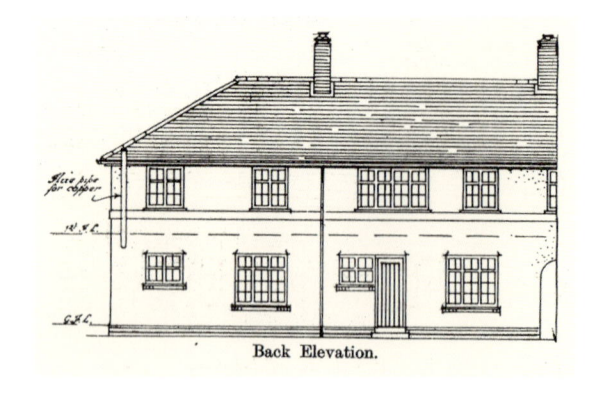

Back Elevation.

95 Addison Scheme block of four Class B cottages, on Health Ministry Plan No. 119. Plans and elevations were pasted into a Ministry of Health ledger by staff assistant architect Samuel Pointon Taylor. Plan No. 119 was commissioned by 15 local authorities between 1920 and 1921. Image from ledger kept by Samuel Pointon Taylor, 1920–21. Image courtesy of Professor Simon Pepper

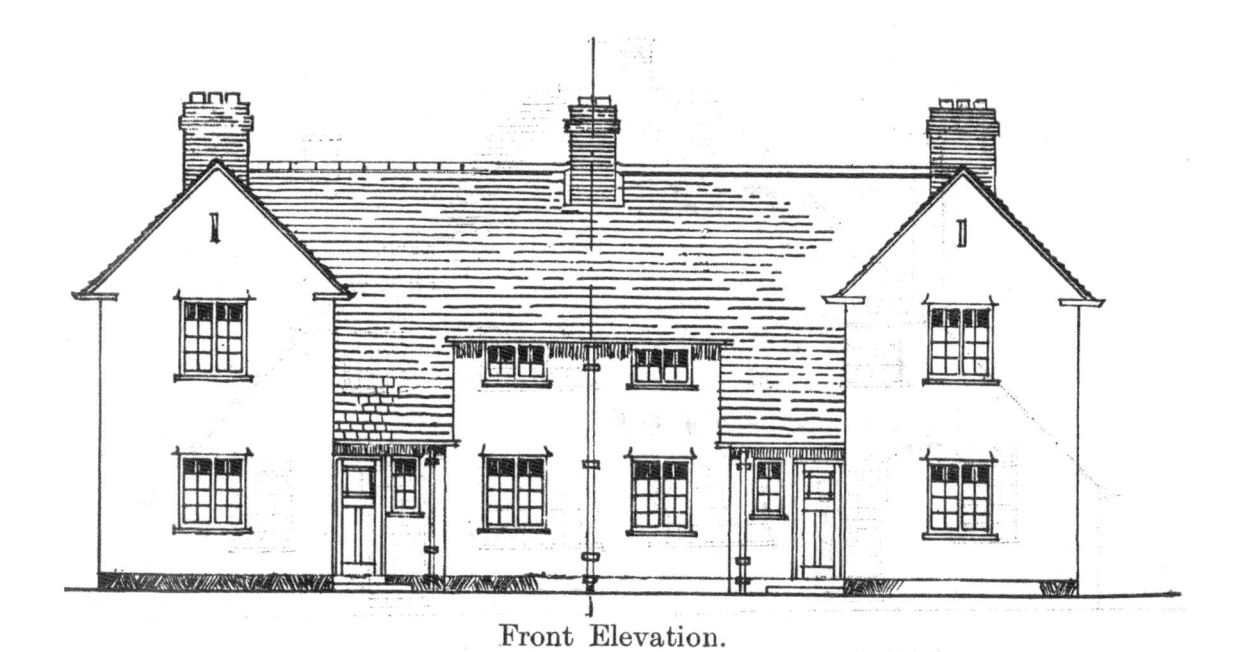

Front Elevation.

96   Addison Scheme semi-detached Class B cottage pair, on Health Ministry Plan No. 167. The design was commissioned by a mixture of nine urban and rural local authorities in 1920–21. Image from ledger kept by Ministry of Health architect Samuel Pointon Taylor, 1920–21. Image courtesy of Professor Simon Pepper

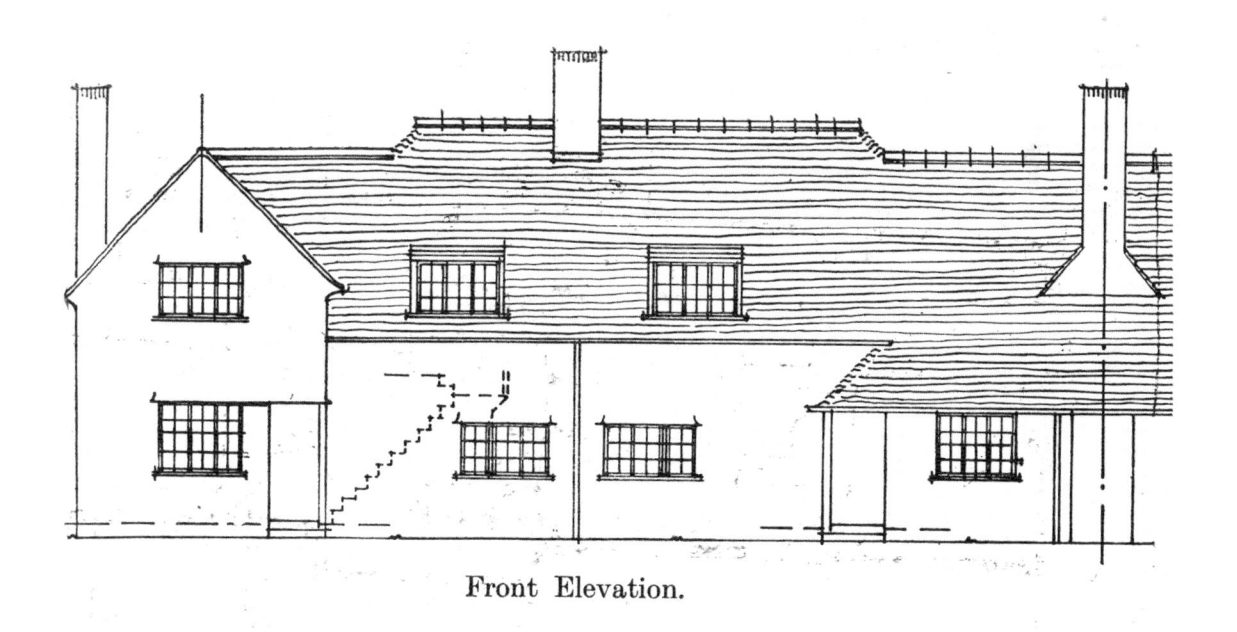

Front Elevation.

97   Addison Scheme block of four Class B cottages, Plan No. 172. This Health Ministry design was commissioned by Frimley Urban District Council and West Dean Rural District Council, but comparatively rarely used. Image courtesy of Professor Simon Pepper

chimney (whose roof-cutting and lead flashing would have been costly) with catslides brought down over the projecting twin porches below it. Ministerially frowned-upon dormer windows lit the stairwells in the centre.[76]

There is some evidence as to how this kind of exterior design was received by tenants. In the early weeks of January 1921, *Housing* magazine reported on Crowmarsh Rural District Council's completion of a small development of Addison Scheme cottages in the Saxon village of Benson in Oxfordshire, on the east bank of the Thames, two miles upstream of Wallingford. The architect was Frederick George Sainsbury, who had won a housing competition for Farnborough in 1914, and later boasted offices in Reading, London, and Copenhagen. At Benson, his five cottage types were 'arranged to group well together, avoiding dull monotony'; and his design for a three-cottage block modelled a 'projecting central porch' – a luxury item saved from scorn in *Housing* because it arose 'from the necessities of the plan and [was] not there merely for external effect'. Unusually, one of the cottages' new tenants was asked for his opinion on the new homes and responded appreciatively: 'Their Elizabethan appearance is a welcome sign of a nation's interest in its countryside'.[77] At this golden moment in the infancy of mass local authority housing, the Picturesque's capacity for association could still work its magic.

THE END OF THE ADDISON SCHEME

Cottages such as these were among the last hurrah of central government-funded interwar Picturesque. Treasury attitudes to the government's housing plans had been sceptical from the outset. To monitor progress, they set up the Goschen Committee on 31 October 1919, which foresaw costs per dwelling rising to £800 or beyond, and heard witnesses 'express doubts as to the possibility of providing so large a number' of dwellings across the period.[78] They were right on both counts. Morgan summarises the challenges faced by the scheme:

Progress in house building was slow . . . local authorities could hardly cope with their massive new responsibilities, and . . . the costs of the Treasury subsidy began to soar, with uncontrolled prices of raw materials leading to apparently open-ended subventions from the state.[79]

The scheme had enemies outside government too. 'We must choose between solvency and downfall, and choose quickly,' trumpeted Lord Rothermere in the *Sunday Pictorial* on 18 April 1920. His aim was to re-energise what had become, since its launch in the summer of 1919, a multifaceted campaign against government 'waste': 'Two more Budgets such as Mr Chamberlain intends to introduce today may mean our extinction as an Empire and a Great Power'. An abridged version of his article was reprinted in the following day's *Daily Mirror* – the Addison Scheme prominent on the charge sheet of extravagances:

it is in the Estimates for the Civil Services and Revenue Departments . . . that the axe should be used remorselessly . . . A new charge in prospect is that of the Government subsidy for making good the loss on uneconomic rents under the new housing scheme, which is said to be likely to amount in the end to £30,000,000 annually.[80]

The campaign had already enlisted the *Daily Mail*, and ran young Esmond Harmsworth (son of Lord Rothermere, nephew of Lord Northcliffe) as a parliamentary candidate pledged to the anti-waste movement (later the Anti-Waste League) in the Isle of Thanet by-election in November 1919.[81] By the end of 1920, localised opposition in the Treasury – fanned by the tireless Harmsworths – had become a fracture in the coalition government between two factions in the Conservative Party: one trying to stay in harness with Lloyd George's Liberals, the other using their own backbenchers' traditional dislike of high taxes and spending as a wedge to break the coalition and promote a pure Conservative government to replace it. Caught between these two was Addison, now facing outright opposition to his housing scheme and its rising costs.[82]

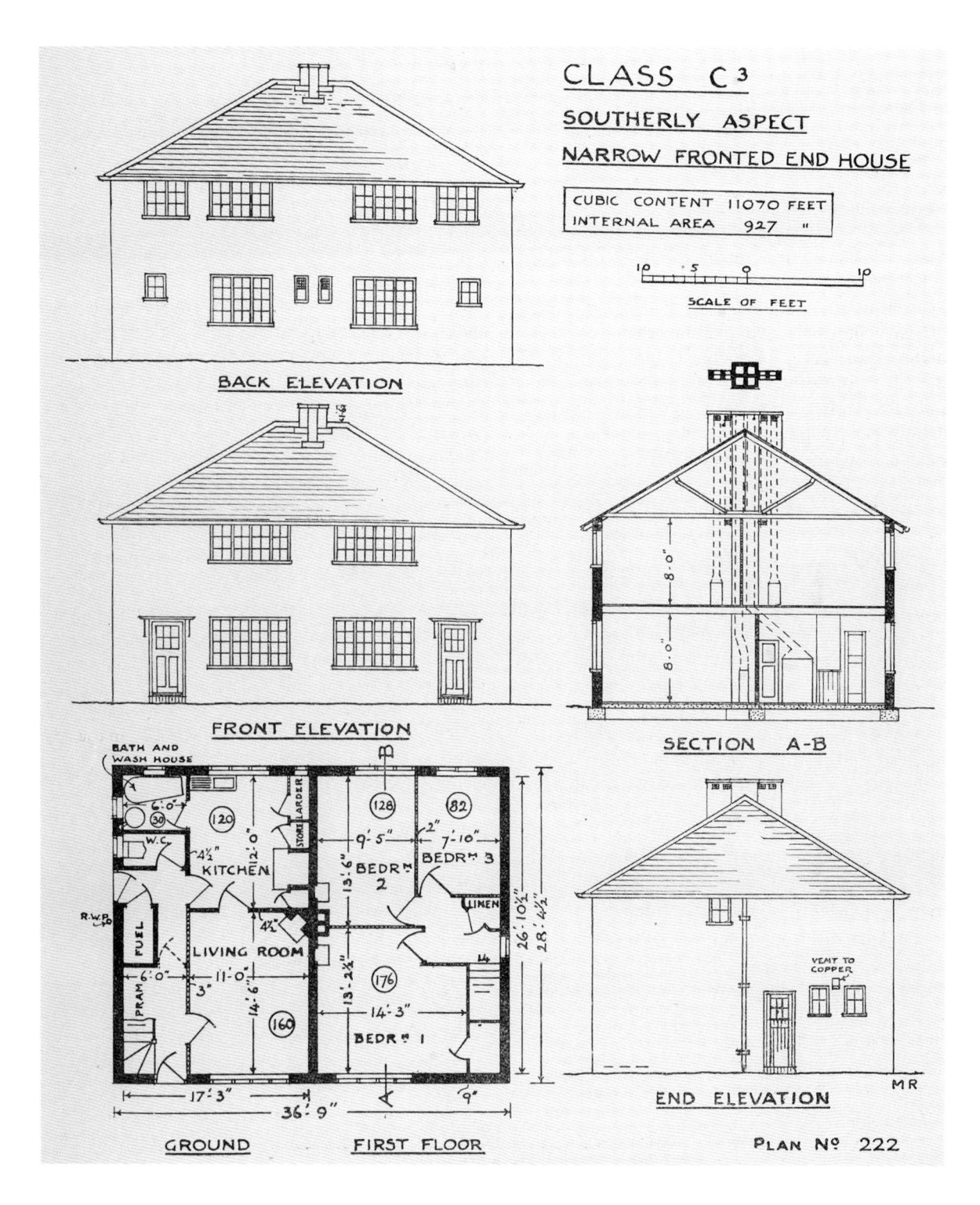

98 Ministry of Health Class C3 semi-detached pair of the new, super-economical 'Kitchen-Scullery' type, Health Ministry Plan No. 222. Designed by 'M.R.' (Manning Robertson?), the living room (at nearly 160ft²) is smaller than the TWR's recommended 180ft² for non-parlour designs; the 'kitchen' larger than recommended for a scullery – 'Class C Houses', in *Housing*, vol.2, no.42, 14 February 1921, p.245, The Bodleian Libraries, University of Oxford

The besieged Health Minister reacted by urging economy on his network of Housing Commissioners. He promoted a new dwelling design early in 1921: Class C3, narrow-fronted, smaller in some key plan dimensions than the Tudor Walters recommendations, and reverting aesthetically to the box-like austerity of the 1919 *Manual*'s type-plans (fig.98).[83] Unwin's former partner Barry Parker added some Class C3s to the Rowntree estate at New Earswick, near York, but thought them 'unusually small and compact'.[84] Such economies were not enough. Correspondence between Addison and the Chancellor of the Exchequer, Austen Chamberlain, reveals the latter's desire to 'wind up' the housing scheme altogether as early as February 1921.[85] With Addison seen by many Conservative coalition members as the '"squander-maniac" *bête noir*',[86] he was forced out of his job as Health Minister in April that year.

Further vigorous cost-cutting was ordered at once in the Health Ministry's housing department, whence a memo was circulated to the Ministry's Housing Commissioners countermanding the local authorities' picturesque penchant for 'unnecessary features such as gables . . . heavy concrete or lead covered wooden hoods to porches . . . unnecessarily tall and over-laboured chimney stacks'.[87] But the die was cast: on 30 June 1921, the Finance Committee of the Cabinet met to finalise 'the suspension of the Government's housing policy'.[88]

Remaining briefly in the Cabinet as Minister without Portfolio, Addison fought to protect his housing initiative. In a memo to the Cabinet on 4 July 1921, he revealed the contending pressures of efficiency, economy, and aesthetic snobbery he had endured while trying to deliver the housing scheme:

> I was being pressed from all quarters to get on faster, although the more drastic the pressure, the more prices went up. When the houses began to appear on all the main roads of the land, then an outcry of the opposite kind arose.[89]

We will return to this 'outcry of the opposite kind', but Addison's appeal made no immediate difference. His successor, Sir Alfred Mond – who had insisted from the outset that he and the Office of Works were better placed to run housing[90] – took the position of Minister of Health and closed the scheme, making, in the words of the *Daily News*, 'a burnt-offering of the housing programme on the altar of economy'.[91] After the Commons passed the Bill suspending his work, Addison resigned from the government on 14 July 1921, with a final plea to the Cabinet: 'I earnestly invite my colleagues to desist from reaching so disastrous a conclusion'.[92]

Mond must have known he was on treacherous ground. In a private memo to the Cabinet in June 1921, he had admitted that his new economy-driven housing policy 'cannot be defended as having any relation to the housing needs of the country'.[93] Alongside Mond's confession, documents in the National Archives reveal the role of senior Treasury civil servant A.W. Hurst in shutting down the scheme.[94] They also provide a glimpse of the way in which aesthetic and typological considerations – the daily bread of architects and architectural journalists at the time – inflected even Treasury attitudes to domestic architecture.

In a memo, hand-written on 8 July 1921 and sent to his colleague R.S. Meiklejohn (Deputy Controller, Supply), copied to the Treasury's Permanent Secretary Sir Warren Fisher, Hurst urged decisive action against the Addison Scheme, opposing 'anything less than a complete stoppage'. He went on to reveal his agitation about the high standard of Addison Scheme building: 'As long as local authorities have a considerable share in it, . . . the standard of materials + design will be kept on an expensive level'. And he followed that with a sentence particularly rich:

> A large proportion of the population lived in "jerry-built" houses before the war + we cannot afford better built houses now, still less the luxury of semi-detached garden-suburb villas.[95]

A prime-ministerial promise of 'habitations fit for the heroes who have won the war' notwithstanding, Hurst's antipathy was to the principle of state/council involvement in the provision of housing.

He favoured revitalising the private sector in the construction of any dwellings required – via subsidy only if absolutely necessary. He was not particularly bothered about the quality of such dwellings.

His assessment as inappropriate of the 'semi-detached garden-suburb villa' exposes both ideological and aesthetic preconceptions – a belief in housing's tendency to express class-structural position and entitlement; a settled view of the role that specific architectural typologies played within that structure; and aesthetic disapproval (common among the Liverpool faction before the war, as discussed in Chapter 2) of the Garden City movement (and, by extension, its predilection for the Picturesque).

Villas were historically understood as a middle-class perquisite. Loudon, in his *Encyclopaedia* (1833), had insisted: 'every man who has been successful in his pursuits and has, by them, obtained pecuniary independence, may possess a villa'.[96] Ruskin characterised the dwellings as gentlemanly territory in 1837.[97] The 1843 *Post Office Directory* recorded a gaggle of 'Esquires' occupying villas on London's Finchley New Road: 'Albert Villa', 'Vernon Villa', 'Cintra Villa', 'Westbourn Villa'.[98] Lord Salisbury, writing about 'Villa Toryism' in 1882, arrogated them as fertile ground for his party's politics.[99] And with the passing of time, the lower-middle classes appropriated the dwelling too: E.M. Forster's 'distressful' Cissie Villa was the work of a speculative builder, and blemished Summer Street in *A Room with a View*.[100] The Bedford Park architect Maurice Adams sneered at the 'ugly boxes called villas used as retreats of retired storekeepers and such like' in his book *Modern Cottage Architecture*.[101]

The Builder would go on to criticise Health Minister Arthur Griffith-Boscawen for his use of the word 'villa' early in 1923: 'associated in England only with bad architecture and pretentious frills'. They called instead for '"middle-class house" . . . an honest name that means what it says'.[102] In *The Road to Wigan Pier*, Orwell saw 'between all the towns of the Midlands . . . a villa civilization indistinguishable from that of the South'.[103] But where Orwell regarded the northward drift of villadom and its upwardly

99 Wates advert for their Contract Department, ready to build 'Anywhere in England', in Wates, Wendover Estate brochure (1930s), Wates Archive. As builders grew larger and widened their sphere of action, housing styles across England were homogenised

mobile occupants as a sign of improving, albeit homogenised, living standards, the Cambridge-educated Hurst (in his 14th year of service at the Treasury) utilised the term 'semi-detached garden-suburb villa' to emphasise the incongruously luxurious standard, in class and material terms, of Addison Scheme dwellings.

Hurst's memorandum shows how fully class and housing types were interwoven in the mind of this key Whitehall policy-maker. Just as *The Builder* had expressed its anxiety about state-aided housing being used to 'invert the order of things' and make the poorest 'the favoured classes' in 1918,[104] Hurst drew on his belief in an underlying class/housing order to make the case against excessive spending on, and excessive expectations among, England's

100 Alfred (A.W.) Hurst, photographed by Walter Stoneman (1941), National Portrait Gallery, London. Hurst was the Treasury's housing specialist in the early 1920s and fought hard to put a stop to the Addison Scheme, which he believed the nation could not afford

working classes in 1921. The Treasury's housing specialist believed that local authorities were not building the kind of dwellings that people might reasonably have expected. Semi-detached villas were a middle-class entitlement.[105] The mandarin's instantiation of the 'garden suburb' tangentially added aesthetics to the critique. He did not make it clear whether the Picturesque that the term tended to connote was objectionable in itself at public expense, or was *de trop* just because it was too expensive to build. Either way, he wanted it stopped. In a nutshell, the working classes had made do with 'jerry-built'[106] dwellings before the war; government need not offer them a higher standard now.

THE WORKING CLASSES

Who did powerbrokers such as Hurst think they were, these people for whom a proverbially poor standard of accommodation was as much as could be expected? Interwar statisticians Carr-Saunders and Caradog Jones set out the difficulties in reaching a classification: 'no measurable characteristic exists which allocates the population into social classes . . . But this does not prove that social classes do not exist'.[107] Others did not share their caution. 'One hears a good deal about the lucky persons who are going to be subsidised as to half their rent,' grumbled the architect and historian of the English Renaissance Alfred Gotch, in January 1919:

> You may abolish slums, but you won't abolish sluts and slatterns so easily. Sluts and slatterns may be expected to carry their natures with them, and in time make their new surroundings somewhat like their old.[108]

Gotch's high octane snobbery was, of course, not reflected in Christopher Addison's drafting for the 1919 Housing Act. The statute simply addressed 'the provision of houses for the working classes',[109] but it was controversial among legislators, and further afield, for those who did not see the post-1918 housing crisis as limited to just one stratum of society.

At the Second Reading of Addison's Housing Bill on 7 April 1919, several MPs raised social class as well as architecture and finance. 'I submit,' said Pemberton Billing,

> that there are classes in this country which today are even in a more precarious and unfortunate position than those who draw a wealthy wage. Those who have been referred to as the "genteel poor" have been the real sufferers during this war. . . . Is it proposed that this housing scheme shall make provision according to social distinction or wage-earning capacity?[110]

Lieutenant-Colonel Sir Assheton Pownall MP (Conservative and Unionist member for Lewisham

East; newly elected in Lloyd George's coupon election of the previous December) suggested that the Bill might be amended

> so that it should apply not only to the working classes but also to what I might call the lower middle, or the middle class, who have been very hard hit by the War, and who are at present no-one's friends.[111]

On the Bill's last day in parliament, Godfrey Locker-Lampson MP (Conservative, Wood Green) pressed Addison on this class point: 'I wish to ask the hon. Gentleman, has he made his mind up as to exactly what he means by working classes?'[112] The Health Minister was characteristically frank in reply:

> I did not find it possible to frame a definition that was good enough . . . the whole scheme is related . . . to the needs of the locality, that is the people who live there, and not people who may want to take a country cottage or anything like that.[113]

As discussed earlier, English society after the First World War generally understood class via a fuzzy triadic model[114] – working, middle, and upper. The fuzziness came from contemporary commentators' readiness, anecdotally, to subdivide each part of the triad, as in Pemberton Billing's 'genteel poor' or Assheton Pownall's 'lower middle class'. Unwin thought he had seen signs, in the trenches, that these strata might, one day, break down. He told the Town Planning Institute on 22 March 1918 that he hoped that the government's new housing scheme could catalyse the change: 'In this great struggle, men of all sorts and conditions had messed and slept and suffered together. Let them do nothing to check this beginning of union'.[115]

In 1919, however, Addison was determined, when it came to deciding who was entitled to the nation's new dwellings, not to discuss precisely what the term 'working classes' meant. On 22 July 1919, in the Conference Room at the Ministry of Health, he met representatives of the Rotary Clubs of Great Britain: 'What is the definition of "a workman", as understood when provision of houses under the Government Scheme is referred to?' asked one. Addison's reply revealed his philosophy:

> I have deliberately and obstinately refrained from giving any definition of 'a workman'. A type of house is sanctioned, and it is left to the local authorities to use their own common sense as to who shall occupy the houses. A workman is a man who works, and it is immaterial to me whether he works as a bank clerk or a navvy.[116]

Addison's Parliamentary Private Secretary, Sir Kingsley Wood MP, had told a meeting in Chatham on 19 June 1919 that 'he did not see why the poorly paid curate or the struggling professional man should not share in the advantages' of the new housing scheme.[117] The Health Minister was determined not to police the borderline between artisan, a word often used to mean the wealthiest tier of the working classes, and 'black-coated' worker or clerk, the poorest tier of the middle classes.[118] One of Addison's senior civil servants at the Ministry of Health, Assistant Secretary E.R. Forber, wrote a letter to a number of rural district councils on 19 August 1919 reinforcing this position: 'It has not been found practical to frame a statutory definition of the term "working classes". That term may be taken generally to include any persons belonging to the classes who work for a living'.[119]

Two signals about what class of tenant would be appropriate for the new dwellings were more freely broadcast. Blackwell Rural District Council in Derbyshire held a meeting in August 1919 where the local Housing Commissioner – Major Douglas Wood, one of Addison's senior staff – was asked: 'Would anyone stand a chance of being accepted as tenant of the houses erected by Local Authorities?' His reply: 'Yes; but preference should be given to returned soldiers'.[120] Big local authorities such as Birmingham followed suit – the city's Housing and Estates Committee proposed: 'preference shall be given to those who have seen service abroad, and to those with the largest families'.[121] The other key filter for Addison Scheme tenants was economic. A member of the West Midlands Housing Commissioner's staff between 1919 and 1921 recounted how rents for the new council dwellings were 'as a rule, much higher than those customarily paid for the best pre-war working-class houses in any district – often twice as high in the towns'.[122] In the first postwar dwellings actually finished in Birmingham, on Cotterill's Lane, four-bedroom rents were set at 17s 6d per week; rent for three-bedroom units at 15s.[123] The brutal economic filter of affordability served to ensure that poorer members of the working classes did not benefit from England's first national council housing initiative.

THE IMPACT OF THE ADDISON SCHEME ON THE MIDDLE CLASSES

Despite Addison's determination not to have his housing scheme become too class-specific an enterprise, the government's stated policy to build cottages for the 'working classes' consolidated housing's place on the list of grievances felt by some among the interwar English middle classes.

Middle-class dislike or fear of those 'beneath' them was not, of course, created by the Addison Scheme. Whereas in 1908 Churchill had seen 'this famous land of ours' as a place where 'there is so little class hatred and jealousy',[124] the writer George Sturt detected significant class tension in his 1912 study of the village where he lived (The Bourne in Surrey): 'Jealousy, suspicion, some fear – the elements of bitter class war in fact – frequently mark the attitudes of middle-class people towards the labouring class'.[125] By 1917, the 'menace of class antagonism' was judged to merit discussion at the top of government, informed by a paper from H.E. Kemp, commissioned and distributed to the cabinet by Philip Kerr, Lloyd George's private secretary:

> Through the distorting lens of "class antagonism", men and women regard any activity on the part of people of another class as a possible attack on one's own position – whether the position be the exalted one of administrators, the hardly-won citadel of the

trade-unionists, the diminishing sphere of the small shop-keepers, or . . . any of the other branches of the "great middle class".[126]

Warwick Deeping's novel *Sorrell and Son* (1925), which would sell no fewer than 34 editions in the interwar period, suggested this antagonism was to become deeply rooted. Sorrell sought to indoctrinate his boy: 'The world has entered on a period of envy and bitterness . . . the social war is going to grow . . . You will be damned by the crowd class – even for having a certain sort of voice and face'.[127]

Kemp had seen class antagonism as a problem not just with the 'crowd class' but across society. *The Builder*, more willing than other architectural periodicals to wade into the grimpen of class relations, worried about the plight of the middle classes:

> We must not forget . . . those who, whilst being comparatively poor so far as money is concerned, are amongst the most intelligent and, let us add, the most law-abiding members of the community . . . What are these people to do for homes? . . . We sometimes wonder how far the thoughts of statesmen carry in the desire to improve the lot of the poor-but-educated and well-balanced folk . . . whose aspirations for wealth lead them no further than the right to live decently without being a burden upon others.[128]

Thus, the Addison Scheme made its own unintended contribution to the exacerbation of class friction in postwar England. The middle classes 'had been comfortable, and now they felt sunk into poverty'.[129] *The Times* reported in March 1919 the foundation of the Middle Class Union – a 'Combination for Self-Defence' – at a crowded meeting in the Cannon Street Hotel in London. Supported by a number of Conservative and Unionist MPs, the new grouping discussed a resolution 'that the existing and intended legislation for housing should be extended to include the requirements of the middle classes'.[130] By November 1919, the new union claimed over 100 branches around the country.[131] McKibbin

Insinuating Stranger. "MAY I PERSUADE YOU TO BECOME A MEMBER OF THE MIDDLE-CLASS UNION?"

Harassed House-Hunter. "DELIGHTED! WHERE IS IT? AND WHEN CAN I MOVE IN?"

101   Cartoon by Lewis Baumer illustrating the connection between middle-class housing difficulties and the formation of the Middle Class Union, *Punch*, vol.157, 3 December 1919, p.465, Punch Cartoon Library/TopFoto

contextualises: 'We tend to overlook just how intense class-consciousness was, especially among the middle class, in the years after the First World War'.[132]

There can be little doubt that some among those middle classes, in 1919–21, harboured resentment about their taxes paying for model cottages that were as good as, or better than, anything they could afford to buy themselves. Key personnel in the Treasury, as we have also seen, clearly believed that bearing down on the cost, quality, and availability of working-class housing was the right course of action from an economic point of view. Its political side-effects might not be unwelcome either.

A contributor with the sobriquet 'Town Clerk', writing in the government's *Housing* magazine in April 1920, identified a political danger of isolating the workers:

> It is not a good thing to have large colonies of these State-Aided houses . . . the tenants might be inclined to form themselves into a class apart from the general community . . . above all, there is the possibility of their exercising a solid and predominant vote in local elections.[133]

Despite the Liverpool contingent's readiness to accept something like this in 1910 – a clearly defined class identity for the occupants of social housing, where new cottages might deliver a 'suppression of the individual taste for the good of the common whole'[134] – Baillie Scott had warned soon after the war against the architecturalisation of social distinction. 'Why should we isolate and segregate our workers like lepers from the community?' he asked. 'In the old village, the squire and parson contrived to exist in close association with their humble neighbours.'[135] This echoed Arthur Wakerley who had told the Leicester Women's Liberal Association in March 1919 that he favoured 'the French system of building large and small houses in juxtaposition as one valuable means of removing class suspicion and prejudice'.[136] By 1930, Henrietta Barnett had come to see segregation of the classes through planning or architecture as one of the great failures of interwar social housing: 'the Government has so arranged that . . . whole areas will be occupied by one class only. What a lost opportunity!'[137]

REFRAMING THE ADDISON SCHEME

Although some at the Treasury in 1921 had seen difficulties in the connection between class entitlement and state expenditure, others did not look far beyond the exchequer's bottom line, believing the main problem with the Addison Scheme was runaway expenditure. One important figure was convinced, however, that aesthetics were a central part of the equation: the new Director-General of Housing at the Ministry of Health, Sir Charles Ruthen. An architect – President of the Society of Architects, no less – he had been a senior inspector for the War Cabinet's Accommodation Committee, where he earned the nickname 'Ruthless Ruthen' for the alacrity with which he commandeered premises that the state required.[138] After the Armistice, he was prominent in discussions of cottage building, advocating, in 1919, economical construction using wooden frames. Then, in July 1921, Sir Alfred Mond appointed him as replacement for Sir James Carmichael in the role of Director-General, Housing.

The following month Ruthen began his duties – for which he drew no salary[139] – with a 'tour of inspection of housing schemes in some of the principal industrial centres'.[140] Birmingham was at the top of his itinerary. He arrived there on 23 August 1921, with his wife and daughter in tow, and was shown around the Direct Labour-built Morris Estate at Washwood Heath by Councillor Siward James, Chairman of the Housing and Estates Committee, and Frank Cox, the city's Housing Director. In a newspaper interview at the end of his visit, the government's new Director-General, Housing pronounced himself 'very pleased' with Birmingham's progress: 'The houses, he said, were of a good type and excellent work had been put into the dwellings'.[141] This

102 Sir Charles T. Ruthen, FRIBA, President of the Society of Architects and Director-General of Housing at the Ministry of Health, 1921–26, photographed by Bassano Ltd (1920), National Portrait Gallery, London

generous response to Addison Scheme building would not last long.

In a controversial address to his own Society of Architects on 12 January 1922, Ruthen unleashed his final version of the project's obituary in altogether less complimentary language:

> Did [the architect] forget his responsibilities to the State . . . his duty to architecture, and allow his pencil to run wild in the dream of the artistic home? . . . The architect must face the prime responsibility for the financial disaster of the great State Housing scheme.[142]

One of Addison's Housing Commissioners, writing anonymously, would describe this apparent

volte-face as 'the private property and invention of Sir Charles Ruthen'.[143] But, ahead of his speech, Ruthen may have caught wind of the first interim report from the Geddes Committee on national expenditure, which excoriated Addison Scheme spending and consolidated the official view of the initiative as a financial catastrophe.[144]

There would remain no political reward in apologising for Addison's work. This left Ruthen free to elaborate a critique that centred on aesthetics. He waxed lyrical on the tectonic features in which he believed architects had indulged, helping drive costs too high; and he situated himself clearly on one side of Kerr's 'great primary division of all architectural art'[145] by singling out, as particularly disastrous, architects' addiction to steep roofs and their recidivist use of gables:

> The architectural profession in its excitement to grasp a great flood of new and unexpected work overreached itself. Set about the designing of ideal homes and ideal lay-outs, the pencil went wild; artistic houses were to be erected at last; steep roof pitches could now be adopted; picturesque gables, and the little artistic features so dear to the heart of the artist, could be incorporated . . .[146]

'Artistic' was often used as a synonym for picturesque, but Ruthen did not hesitate to use the word itself. He boasted that he had seen 'more housing schemes in this country than any living man', and that the best of them 'had not a single gable, or a single projection on the front wall, on the back wall, or the side walls'.[147] Relishing the impact of his own 'hard words', he joined the company of Charles Reilly, Geoffrey Scott, Stanley Adshead, Reginald Blomfield, Trystan Edwards, and Wyndham Lewis in treating 'picturesque' unambiguously as a term of condemnation.

In the discussion that followed his address, society members gave Ruthen the opportunity to moderate his attack. Instead, he renewed his denunciation of qualities intrinsic to the Picturesque: 'It was wrong for the architect to think . . . he should have a bulge here and a break there, and that gables were essential'. He also compounded his accusation that architects should carry the can for the Addison's Scheme's costliness. They were, Ruthen insisted, 'responsible for the high cost of [council cottage] building . . . the architect said: I will get as much architecturally out of this scheme as I can – that was his profiteering effort, and extremely successful it was'.[148]

The speech's impact was profound. Use of the red-rag term 'profiteering' scandalised the architectural profession and brought the story to the attention of *The Times*, the *Daily Mail*, and other national newspapers. One Fellow of the RIBA accused Ruthen of 'bespattering his professional brethren with unprecedented obloquy'.[149] Writing to *The Daily Telegraph*, the Director of the London Master Builders attacked Ruthen's suggestion that the architect's desire to provide dwellings of 'artistic' quality to the working classes should somehow be considered beyond the pale:

> How dare he design houses of an 'artistic' character? The working-class man cannot wish to live in anything better than a benign Ministry of Health will offer him. . . . Why elevate his artistic temperament and give him a 'home fit for a hero'?[150]

With a set of rhetorical questions for Ruthen, *The Architects' Journal* entered the lists to support the profession, so outraged that they reached exclusively for picturesque examples that they might not normally have applauded, all of them antedating the Addison Scheme:

> Does he forget, then, Port Sunlight and the architects that built it? Does he forget what Messrs Cadbury and their architects did at Bournville, or Messrs Rowntree and their architects at York? Has he never heard of Letchworth and Hampstead Garden Suburb and the architects who worked there?[151]

Six days after his address, the Society of Architects called a special meeting of its Council and passed resolutions dissociating itself from Ruthen's views,

registering a loss of confidence in his presidency and suggesting he consider his position.[152] The Society was plunged into confusion – even its annual dinner, long fixed for 22 February 1922, was postponed *sine die*.[153] A week or so after the lecture, Ruthen gave an interview to *The Manchester Guardian* to defend himself: what he had meant to say was that architects had 'tried to obtain artistic effect out of a scheme that would not bear it'.[154] This did not help. The RIBA, which might privately have enjoyed the Society of Architects' discomfiture, attacked Ruthen in his capacity as a government official: 'an undignified departure from the best traditions of the Civil Service . . . an unwarranted attack from an official quarter upon a whole profession'.[155] It was all heading one way. At the Society of Architects' Council meeting on Thursday 26 January 1922, Sir Charles Ruthen tendered his resignation, and it was accepted.[156] But the 'storm went on for weeks and muttered for months'.[157]

Crucially, Ruthen's most powerful ally did not turn on him. Questioned in the Commons, Sir Alfred Mond, Minister of Health, supported his Director-General of Housing. As Mond understood it, Sir Charles had merely rebuked architects for failing to take the opportunities presented by the government's housing scheme. The Health Minister declared himself 'afraid there was ground for thinking this was true of most of the parties concerned'. Mond reinforced this with a personal vote of confidence in Ruthen, declaring his 'services had been of the utmost value to the State'.[158] Thus the government threw its weight behind Sir Charles's anti-Picturesque account of the Addison Scheme's failure – architects, aesthetics, and economics – and helped make it officialdom's final word on the subject. 'Even nineteen years afterwards,' *The Architects' Journal* whispered in 1941, it had 'trepidation in mentioning the *affaire* Ruthen'.[159]

A RECKONING IN BIRMINGHAM

The Addison Scheme ended in tears for Birmingham too. On 5 October 1921, an inquiry led by the

Conservative Alderman Sir David Brooks began its formal investigation into Birmingham's delivery of the scheme, and the 'many charges of waste and extravagance against the Housing and Estates Department of the Birmingham City Council'.[160] In reality, this could be seen as a twin-track political coup – against the liberally minded Housing and Estates Committee, for tribal reasons; but also against its Conservative and Unionist chair, Councillor Siward James, who was a Chamberlain family bannerman and had seconded the resolution that made Neville Chamberlain Lord Mayor of Birmingham in November 1915.[161]

As Ewen Green has recorded, grass-roots opinion within the Conservative Party nationally in 1921–22 was pressing for an end to the coalition with the Liberal Party, whom they blamed for 'squandermaniac' policies like housing. Activists focused much of their dissatisfaction on the then leader of the Conservative Party Austen Chamberlain (Neville's half-brother), who also happened to be Chancellor of the Exchequer in Lloyd George's coalition. The newspapers assailed Austen too. Rothermere's *Daily Mirror* carried a front-page photograph of him, asking: 'When Shall We Again Have a Real Chancellor of the Exchequer?' Inside, an article by Rothermere himself denounced Chamberlain's most recent budget: 'No more disastrous financial blunder is recorded in our political annals'.[162] This was the backdrop to the actions of three Conservative councillors in Birmingham – Messrs Talbot, Teall, and Thornton – who shared their party's discomfort with public spending and were determined to rid their city of the coalition's expensive commitment to municipal housing. They seemed untroubled by the possibility their actions might, in the process, defenestrate the Chamberlain-supporting Chairman of the Housing and Estates Committee, Councillor Siward James.

Talbot, Teall, and Thornton had canvassed the city's builders for months, trawling for criticisms of the council. They were themselves strongly rebuked, before Brooks's inquiry was even convened, in a June 1921 *Birmingham Daily Gazette* editorial that accused

them of 'imperfect evidence or indifference to the public interest'.[163] Undeterred, Alderman Brooks kept this disreputable campaign on the road. Once the inquiry had started, as chairman he showed a tenuous grasp of impartiality – intervening repeatedly after favoured witnesses to say how shocking he found their testimony, and at one point complaining (of his own proceedings) that 'there is too much talking, too much disputing between various witnesses on both sides'.[164] He finally delivered a highly critical report, in February 1922, that concluded 'many of the officials of the Housing Committee are not competent to carry out the duties entrusted to them'.[165]

Brooks's judgement occasioned the final act of this internecine battle, which unfolded at an eight-hour sitting of the full council on 4 April 1922. Siward James defended himself and his committee staff against Brooks's criticisms, but the Conservative majority on the council prevailed in a vote carried by 53 votes to 34. Their successful amendment stripped James's committee of responsibility for building altogether, moving it instead to the Public Works Department. After months in front of a kangaroo inquiry, James could barely contain himself: 'There is no man in the Council more anxious to be relieved of his job than myself'. His deputy on the Housing and Estates Committee, Councillor Tiptaft, provoked laughter by confessing he would positively 'welcome the opportunity to act as critic of the Public Works Department'.[166] Thus the Addison Scheme met its quietus in Birmingham – amid the charges of waste that had fuelled Ruthen's attack in London – helping to forge a future for council housing in England and Wales where an austere formalism (in aesthetics and construction cost) would become the only game in town.

'Steep roof pitches', 'picturesque gables', 'artistic features', 'a bulge here and a break there' . . . Sir Charles Ruthen's charge sheet – colourfully remembered a few years later as including the phrase 'profiteering in gables'[167] – collated many of the key characteristics of the traditional English cottage. Henceforward, for state-funded

103   Kate Greenaway, illustration from *Under the Window: Pictures and Rhymes for Children* (London: Frederick Warne & Co., 1900 [1878]), The Bodleian Libraries, University of Oxford

working-class dwellings across the country, Ruthen had helped define these features as signifiers of architectural extravagance and failure. Over the next two decades, they would be frowned upon for council houses. The people fated to occupy the austere exchequer-subsidised dwellings that predominated hereafter – drawn initially from the artisan tier and then increasingly from overcrowding and slum clearance initiatives – would find themselves demarcated unmistakably in the landscape by the 'boxes with lids' that the state grumpily conceded they *were* allowed to have.

Meanwhile, what of the cottage that Lloyd George had promised to Britain's poorly housed millions in 1918 – by cultural tradition gabled, picturesque;

simultaneously individual *and* universal; beloved of Price, Knight, Ruskin, Wordsworth, Greenaway, Allingham, Octavia Hill; and, once upon a time, even of Raymond Unwin? Ruthen had made it the cottage officially denied.

In class terms, this was a caesura greater than just a new resolution for the visuality of council dwellings. After centuries of ownership, contested though it was, it can also be seen as the latest stage in a process dispossessing the English working classes of the cottage idea. In the next chapter we will see how the middle and upper classes – supported by the shrewd political mythmaking of Stanley Baldwin's government – consolidated their appropriation of the cottage picturesque.

4

THE COTTAGE APPROPRIATED

The demise of the Addison Scheme in July 1921 ended a two-year period during which public discourse had treated the cottage in England as belonging jointly to the working classes and to the architectural profession. The former had been promised 500,000 new cottages; the latter entrusted with their design. The exclusivity of this arrangement was widely recognised and occasionally resented:

> We are filled with envy – we of the Middle Class! We read of a million new houses to be built for the working class with all the nice things we want . . . I am not trying to be funny when I say that every night hundreds of middle-class women cry themselves . . . into a state of despair because they cannot find a home.[1]

There is an academic consensus today that the £190 million cost of Addison's housing subsidy[2] – 'the financial disaster of the great State Housing Scheme'[3] – led to irresistible fiscal, political, and media pressure for the scheme to close. It is less widely recognised that there was also a significant aesthetic dimension to the government's retreat. State-funded housing came close to a dead stop in 1922 – breaking the government's promise to the working classes[4] but leaving cottage architecture's visuality at the heart of the argument. It may not have mattered much to James Bartley, a 33-year-old gas-fitter living with his wife and three children in a single room in Hove, Sussex, who annotated his 1921 Census form: 'Stop talking about your homes for heroes. . . . Start building some houses and let

104   Cottage at Smeeth, near Ashford, Kent. Photograph by W.G. Davie, in Basil Oliver, *The Cottages of England* (London: B.T. Batsford, 1929), plate 73

them at a rent a working man can afford to pay'.[5] But Charles Ruthen, the highest-ranking government architect at the Health Ministry, supported by the Minister in the House of Commons in 1922, could not have been more explicit: state-funded dwellings for the working classes should in future focus on 'healthy and happy existence' rather than architectural 'craft in the artistic or aesthetic sense'.[6]

Impacted by these developments, despite the country's unaddressed working-class housing need, ownership of the cottage idea was about to experience a period of intense contest. The following chapters will examine how it became the subject of interwar appropriations. Evelyn Waugh wrote in 1930: 'the craze for cottages . . . only began as soon as they had ceased to represent a significant part of English life'.[7] But he was only half-right. The Addison Scheme – embodied in the local authorities' appetite for more traditional architecture discussed in Chapter 3 – gave some working-class families a 'cottage', restoring their mythologised domestic birth-right, and making the dwelling, once again, a significant fixture in national life. Thanks not least to Ruthen, the local authority cottage after 1922 was architecturally denatured. It was fixed as something else – the 'box-with-lid' council house – and, thanks to the Treasury, the initiative as a whole was scaled back. This diminution of the working-class stake in new cottage building in the early 1920s left the field clear for middle-class interest groups to compete to redefine the dwelling's identity and associations. For several contending stakeholders, *pace* Evelyn Waugh, the cottage would remain a pillar of English culture.

Private house builders were one clear beneficiary. Ready to start large-scale construction for the domestic market from 1923, they adopted whatever domestic visuality would sell – and that seemed to be houses designed to look like picturesque cottages. Chapter 5 examines this phenomenon in detail. The other key beneficiaries were distinct groups among the English middle and upper classes. This chapter will discuss how one middle-class faction sought picturesque rural cottages as the setting for their weekends in the country – and had the money to buy them. Another subset of the middle and upper classes emerged as committed to cottage conservation, worried that the ancient dwelling had been imperilled by the government's postwar housing legislation and determined to reprioritise the cottage as treasured aesthetic survival in the picturesque landscape for all to enjoy.

In the short-term, other parties retreated from the fray. Scarred by Ruthen's critique, architects found themselves offering services no longer easily afforded by local authorities now required to build dwellings for £300 apiece rather than £800. The other obvious casualty was government. Paralysed by the financial commitments that Addison's policy had entailed for the Treasury, and by the media antagonism they occasioned, Sir Alfred Mond – who had followed Addison as coalition Minister of Health in 1921 – adopted a new housing approach that one contemporary derided as 'the Micawber-Mond *impolicy* of waiting for private enterprise to turn up'.[8] This was part of a wider transformation McKibbin identifies in which British political priority-setting shifted from working- to middle-class interests.[9] The state would not re-enter the cottage conversation, in earnest, until the mid-1920s, ready then to join conservationists in treating the ancient cottage and its associated mythology as a balm with which to soothe a society riven by class conflict. Between them, interwar politics, activism, publishing, and elite and popular culture would shape and reflect the long-term migration of the cottage from working-class essential to middle-class desideratum.

CONSERVATION AND THE COTTAGE PICTURESQUE

Though practically everyone saluted the Addison Scheme's plans to address the country's housing shortage in 1919, one vigilant band – the Society for the Protection of Ancient Buildings (SPAB) – had spotted a problem. The Society's spiritual roots had grown among voluntary preservation organisations founded in the late decades of the nineteenth century: the Commons Preservation Society (1865); SCAPA, the Society for Checking the Abuses of Public Advertising (1893); and the National Trust (1895) among them.[10] SCAPA had placed picturesqueness at the heart of its mission, calling for 'concerted action in defence of the Picturesque and Romantic Elements in our National Life'.[11] The National Trust made early conservationist interventions with traditional architecture, acquiring the Clergy House at Alfriston in 1896, the Joiners' Hall in Salisbury in 1898, and The Old Post Office in Tintagel in 1903.[12] As Melanie Hall suggests, the National Trust's institutional focus was on property that represented traditional forms of community life, rather than individual family dwellings like the cottage.[13] Its burgeoning interest in landscape and the country house left the SPAB – set up by William Morris, the architect Philip Webb, and their friend George Wardle in 1877 – free to dedicate itself to ecclesiastical conservation at first, then to branch out into other traditional architectural forms.

Cottage conservation had roots deep in the Picturesque. In his 1798 *Essay,* Malton had called upon 'gentlemen and persons of cultivated taste . . . to take the Cottage under protection'.[14] A search of the SPAB's cottage preservation archives picks up the story on 17 January 1908, when Thackeray Turner – the 'first really effective Secretary of the SPAB';[15] later its Chairman – wrote to a Dunfermline lawyer to attempt to rescue threatened cottages in the city.[16] He was too late, but he continued to put pen to paper – to *The Times*, in March 1912, to make recommendations on how 'two projecting gables' on a choice 'group of old cottages' on Haslemere High Street might be protected;[17] to *Country Life*, in November 1914, to bring their attention to ancient cottages in Otford, Kent, threatened with demolition;[18] to *The Poole Herald* in October 1917 to warn against the town losing 'such a picturesque and educational building as the old cottage in the High Street'.[19]

Epistolary intervention was sometimes enough. A Turner warning, despatched to *Country Life* in 1912, resulted in a group of sixteenth century cottages on the Guildford to Farnham road being saved from the council's road-widening plans, after 'leading antiquarians and archaeologists . . . penned equally strong letters to the London and local press'.[20] Further activity was piecemeal, reflecting the SPAB's perennial shortage of funds. Soon after the First World War, the Society's leading lights resolved that more concerted protection for ancient cottages was needed.

What they had recognised in Spring 1919 was that dilapidated cottages may have been put at risk by the Addison Housing Act. Designed to pressurise landlords into reconditioning their letting properties, the legislation's Clause 28 gave local authorities the power to insist that properties unfit for human habitation be made fit – at pain of intervention by the authority, which could make any repairs required and then charge the work back to the landlord. The only way out was for owners to register their intention to stop letting an unfit dwelling altogether, at which point the local authority would issue a closing order.[21] For the many landlords without the money to renovate, this was effectively a property death sentence – they could neither let nor repair. SPAB correspondence would become littered with worried references to cottage property under threat of 'closing order'.[22]

Chairman Turner called a Special Committee Meeting at the SPAB in May 1919 to discuss a new strategy to meet this menace. A long-standing committee member, May Morris, sent her apologies from Kelmscott in a state of high alarm – 'I hear that authorities are coming to look at our villages here and I am really miserable with apprehension'.[23] The following month, a letter to *The Times* set out the Society's countermeasures. Alarmed by the Addison Act's apparent binary – new cottages/hygienic; old cottages/insanitary – Turner wrote:

> There are officials in every district whose duty it is to condemn insanitary dwellings. There is no-one in all the land whose duty it is to keep an eye on beautiful old cottages and point out how they may be made fit and right for use . . . There are, indeed, many such cottages that the nation cannot afford to lose.[24]

The SPAB's new policy promised guidance on finding architects to perform surveys and help with co-ordinating visits to groups of threatened cottages. The Society acknowledged that it would not be able to perform these tasks 'without financial assistance from the public interested in the preservation of old cottages'. It declared itself glad, therefore, 'to receive subscriptions to a fund for this express purpose'.[25] Years before the Royal Society of Arts would mobilise Prime Ministers, parliamentarians, and a star novelist to help raise funds for the country's ancient cottages, the SPAB attempted something similar – on a characteristic shoestring.

Donations to the SPAB cottage fund came from over 500 subscribers, including Lady Cynthia Mosley (Sir Oswald's wife), Viscount Astor, the Archbishop of Canterbury, Earl Beauchamp, the Bath Branch of Somerset Architectural Society, and the Honourable Company of Butchers. May Morris promised money. Professor Lethaby pledged and later withdrew;[26] but he did in due course support the campaign in his book *Form in Civilization*: 'To destroy these cottages would be like a preliminary step to asphalting the country all over'.[27]

Lethaby and the rest were participants typical of preservationist cottage activity after the First World War: *bien pensant* members of the middle and upper classes, doing their best to protect the nation's domestic architectural legacy. By portraying the cottage as an emblem of culture, craftsmanship, and history, however – and despite righteous references to making 'insanitary cottages fit for human habitation' – they inadvertently contributed to a softening in the focus on contemporary housing need, privileging instead the cottage's essence as passive object of the picturesque gaze, rendering its appreciation – in Hall's words – 'a genteel leisure pursuit'.[28]

'ONLY TEN MINUTES BY TRAIN FROM TUNBRIDGE WELLS'[29]

Another tribe among the interwar middle and upper classes also committed to genteel cottage gazing did so from a more acquisitive perspective. These were people who wanted to buy and renovate a cottage for weekends in the countryside – members of 'a small class', in the words of Tawney, 'which wears several men's clothes, eats several men's dinners, [and] occupies several families' houses'.[30] Many more who could not afford the extravagance for themselves were fascinated nonetheless, substituting reading and day-dreaming for the activity itself.

The phenomenon antedated the First World War. Tyack finds the novelist Richard Graves complaining about second-home ownership – by 'clerk', 'tradesman', and 'cheesemonger' – as early as 1779.[31] In his 1912 book *Modern Cottage Architecture*,

the Bedford Park and Port Sunlight architect Maurice Adams noted: 'A good many people of late years have purchased old cottages in the country for week-end visits'.[32] The worldwide best-seller of 1916–17, *Mr Britling Sees It Through* by H.G. Wells, introduced us to the 'London journalist' Manning, who 'has a little cottage about a mile over there' and 'comes down for the weekends'.[33] And there was a *Country Life* article during the war on the pleasures of cottage retreat: 'Breakfast with the door opening onto a bright cottage garden. The smell of pinks and roses softly blowing on me as I eat my scrambled egg'. Even the downsides of cottage ownership were first-world: 'The picturesque cottage may be there, but requires a good sum to be spent on it before it is habitable'.[34] When the war ended, cottage escapism was revived – catalysed by a secondary market of book publishers and, in *The Ideal Home*, a newly founded consumer magazine.

Launched in January 1920 (after a pilot edition at the end of the previous year), the new monthly had an editor, Captain G.C. Clarke, who was unequivocal about the class composition of his target audience:

> There is no question of more vital interest than that of housing. The Government and Local Authorities . . . are only dealing with what might be termed "Working or Artisan class houses". The policy of *The Ideal Home* is to cater for the wide circle of the middle class.[35]

The publication's early prospectus – plans and advice for potential home builders from in-house architect Martin Luyken – was subordinated quickly to a photographic and textual celebration of the taste among England's middle and upper classes for acquiring and restoring cottage boltholes in the countryside.

A series of articles by Alan Francis, from April 1920, cast the die that book publishers would subsequently exploit:

> How I made my own little nook in a dilapidated Tudor cottage . . . In our old-fashioned village was found just the right man . . . who knew all about

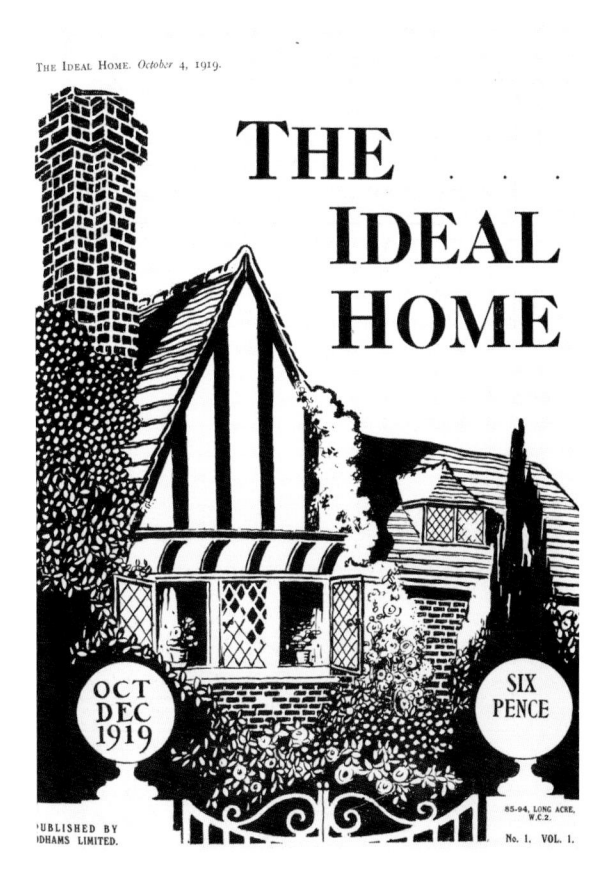

THE IDEAL HOME. *October 4, 1919.*

THE . . .

IDEAL HOME

OCT DEC 1919

SIX PENCE

'UBLISHED BY
IDHAMS LIMITED.

85-94, LONG ACRE,
W.C.2.

No. 1. VOL. 1.

105   Front cover for the pilot edition of *The Ideal Home* magazine, October–December 1919, The Bodleian Libraries, University of Oxford

lattice windows, cleaning old beams, restorations generally . . . I reckoned with hard work and a careful expenditure of a comparatively small amount of money, it would make a capital week-end cottage.[36]

Francis's articles were such a hit that the editor put out a call for more.[37] Classic cottage rescue case-studies included the 'Weekend Cottage of Madame Fifinella', in November 1920. Fifinella was an interwar couturier and court dressmaker, whose cottage was 'local brick-built . . . the eaves . . . hung with weatherboard; the roof . . . of fine Sussex stone slates, well weathered and tinted with patches of vegetable

growth'.[38] In another article, Howard Kemp-Prossor told of his renovation work at an 'ideal cottage with rural surroundings' at Chessington in Surrey. It was 'untouched' – its charm incarnated in 'half-timber and mellow bricks'.[39]

The genre flourished, presenting picturesque cottage rescue, at times, as a kind of middle-class duty. An *Ideal Home* writer, afoot in Sussex in April 1922, lamented 'numbers of charming old cottages all left to the unappreciative labourer because of the northern aspect of the chief rooms'.[40] Guy Church told 'The story of the Transformation of a Seventeenth Century Cottage into a Modern Residence' in January 1923.[41] Cottages crying out for such treatment were advertised in the magazine too: 'For sale with vacant possession . . . This picturesque early 18th Century Cottage . . . capable of conversion . . . within five minutes' walk of Welwyn Garden City Station'.[42] Far from the aestheticism of Geoffrey Scott, picturesqueness was for *The Ideal Home* a cardinal virtue.

Basil Ionides, who would go on to design the interior of the Savoy Theatre in 1929, revealed another rescue project – an 'old-world' cottage under restoration in the hills above Lewes in Sussex. A new gable 'in oak timber framing, filled with plaster' was needed – of course – to create a bedroom over the scullery.[43] The penny would have dropped for even the most inattentive *Ideal Home* reader when a March 1923 article pulled together the threads of the magazine's emergent cottage ideology:

> Many of us build our castles in the air, and how often they simulate the cottage in the country! There seems, somehow, to be a charm which lingers around the very word cottage, a charm which makes a marked appeal to almost all classes.[44]

That this idyll might appeal across the social spectrum is entirely plausible. As a way of life, it was less easily achieved. Cottage rescue implied an amplitude of time and funds. Those with the appetite for the *rus* but without the money might have found a welcome instead in the interwar working-class communities of the Plotlands

106   Mrs Asquith at the window of her converted barn, *The Ideal Home*, vol.2, no.6, December 1920, pp 202–3, The Bodleian Libraries, University of Oxford

– Marlow Bottom, Pett Level, Peacehaven, Canvey Island[45] – fictionalised by Holtby,[46] and studied by Hardy and Ward.[47] The often self-built shanties on these coastal or riverside sites provided cherished rural escape for their tenants but, visually, evoked the sort of scrabbled-together huts erected overnight on the edge of the medieval waste more than they did the kind of cottage *The Ideal Home* chose to celebrate. They were usually makeshift, sometimes converted railway vehicles, and seldom picturesque – notorious rather for 'deform[ing] the choicest spots';[48] a target for caustic preservationist critique from Professor Abercrombie and Clough Williams-Ellis.[49]

Back in the land of moneyed cottage appropriation, one of the first book publishers

to see the writing on the half-timbered wall was Herbert Jenkins Ltd with *The Story of My Ruin* by Marion Cran.[50] She was a gift – a broadcaster for the embryonic British Broadcasting Company, who delivered programmes on 'garden work and flower fun . . . to hundreds of thousands of unseen garden-friends'. She recounted struggles with sullen workmen, and 'a lifetime of waiting', but completed her restoration of a thirteenth-century ruin near Tenterden, in Kent, in a mood of poetic self-realisation:

> The dream is true at last . . . Deeply I have wanted a long, low cottage with a garden – and a hearth where rare bright spirits would meet and be at

home. A place unspotted from the world, won clear by myself, however hardly, from the least brick to the last nail.[51]

Cran's became home rather than a second home after a few years, but she expended few words discussing the consequences for country people of cottage colonisation. People like Cran, Francis, Kemp-Prossor, and Fifinella were 'picturesquely playing at village life', Holdenby had cautioned, 'driving the villager from his home and raising the price of his food'.[52] It was a critique that found its way into fiction in the 1930s, when the Wiltshire farmer-turned-novelist Arthur (A.G.) Street inveighed against the way 'whenever a chance came, the thatched cottages were bought up and renovated to supply this new demand, and their original dwellers were driven into the new slums'.[53] In social-class terms, the process of rural cottage acquisition and improvement was a one-way street. So long as they were sufficiently picturesque, dwellings built for and occupied by agricultural labourers, often for generations, were transacted into the hands of the middle and upper classes.

COTTAGES AND THE LOCAL AUTHORITY AFTER 1922

Middle-class cottage-play was well into its stride during the first few years after the war – a rarely discussed counterpoint to Christopher Addison's coaxing of local authorities into providing tens of thousands of dwellings for people without a single decent place to live.[54] But as conservationists and prospective cottage purchasers toured the countryside in their motorcars, agog with conservationist anxiety or acquisitive rapture, what was happening to social housing?

Aesthetically, the language of weekend cottage ownership – 'half-timber and mellow bricks'; the 'whimsical oak and plaster lines of a little crooked house'[55] – contrasted pointedly with the Health Ministry's injunctions to councils to build unornamented, formal boxes. Notwithstanding the readily attested taste among the middle classes for country cottage aesthetics, the Ministry had never consistently distinguished between urban and rural in its recommended working-class cottage designs

107   Marion Cran's 'ruin' near Tenterden, in Kent, from *The Story of My Ruin* (London: Herbert Jenkins Ltd, 1924), frontispiece, pencil drawing by Eileen Hill, The Bodleian Libraries, University of Oxford

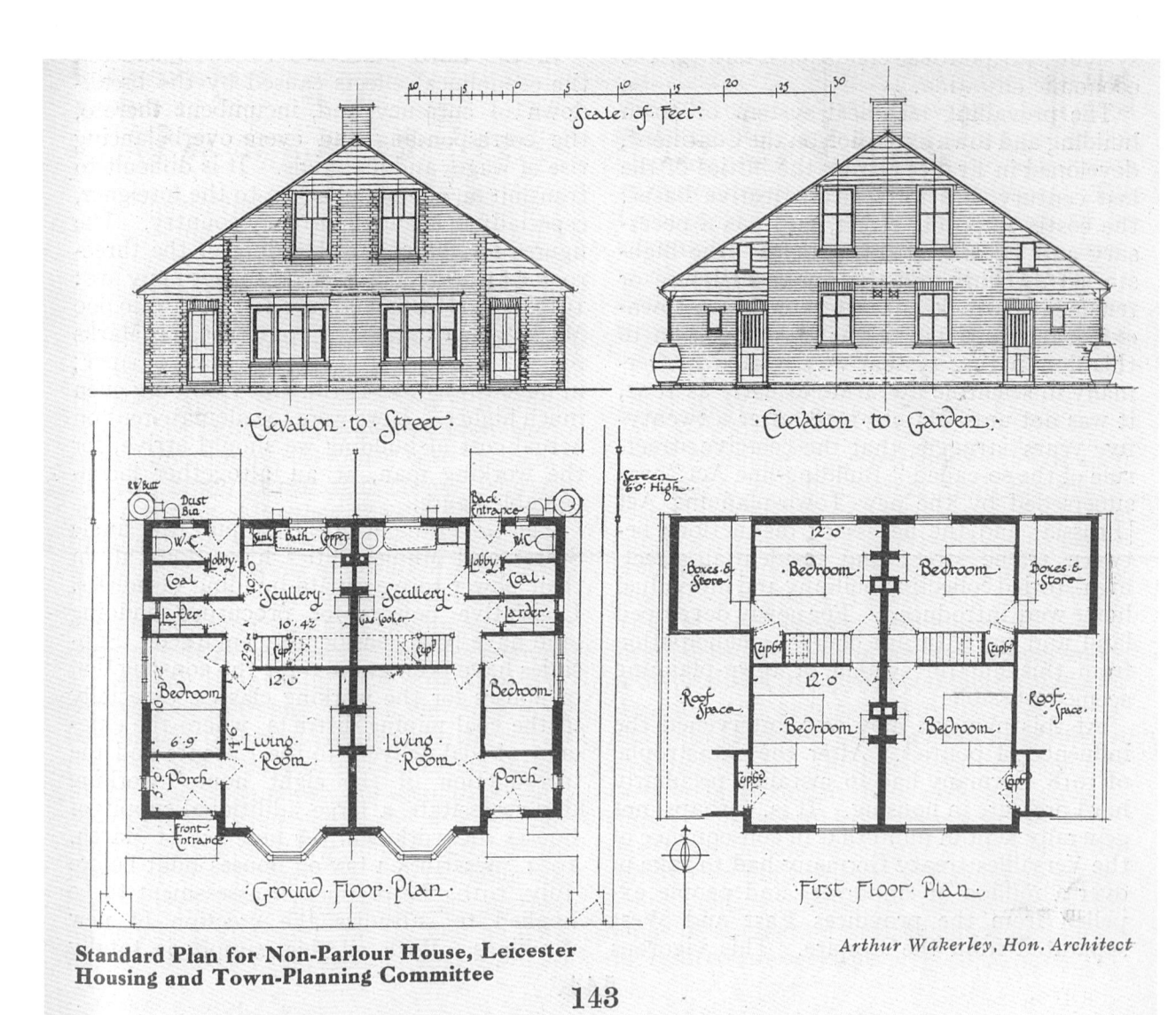

Scale of Feet.

Elevation to Street.

Elevation to Garden.

Ground Floor Plan.

First Floor Plan.

Standard Plan for Non-Parlour House, Leicester Housing and Town-Planning Committee

Arthur Wakerley, Hon. Architect

143

FRONT ELEVATION

left, top

108   A pair of Wakerley's £300 houses (1922), as built, *inter al.*, in Dunster Street, Leicester, in *Garden Cities and Town Planning*, vol.12, no.8, September–October 1922, p.143, Town & Country Planning Association. Posterity has been kinder about them than Wakerley was himself. Grade II-listed, they have a catslide roof, cill- and lintel-bands, and quoining, in dark brick, that together offer more picturesque texturality than perhaps Wakerley feared at the time

bottom

109   Nottingham Corporation design for £300 council houses (Type A36), by T.C. Howitt, ARIBA, in *Garden Cities and Town Planning*, vol.12, no.8, September–October 1922, p.142, Town & Country Planning Association

(see Chapter 2). Many local authorities ignored Whitehall guidance in 1920–21, knowing just as well as Fifinella what a cottage was supposed to look like. They commissioned a majority of more traditional-looking cottages under the state-funded Addison Scheme,[56] and adopted, by and large, garden suburb layouts even for estates close to city centres.

Once the government's subsidy was withdrawn, however, state-funded picturesque cottages with an £800-plus build-price were off the agenda. In Leicester, the chairman of the council's Housing and Town Planning Committee, Arthur Wakerley, told journalists: 'the elevation of the house must be sacrificed if adequate accommodation is to be given at a cost of less than £300'.[57] Previously city mayor,[58] Wakerley had returned to local politics after the war, and, as Leicester's honorary architect in 1922, reluctantly declared that the attempt to build picturesquely had, perforce, to be 'totally abandoned'.[59]

Wakerley's solution for Leicester – a £300 council house, with one of its three bedrooms downstairs (fig.108) – was criticised by *Garden Cities and Town Planning* magazine: 'It is difficult to see how, with this type as a unit, a satisfactory lay-out can be achieved'. Despite acknowledging that Wakerley 'would vastly prefer to build houses of good appearance', they judged his new non-parlour design

to have failed the test. It lacked 'external amenity', they argued. Its aesthetic compromises had been taken too far: 'Whether it is really necessary to "empty out the baby with the bathwater", is open to doubt'.[60]

Another council attracting critical attention for its post-Addison Scheme cottages was Nottingham. In April 1922, the highly regarded city architect T.C. Howitt ARIBA – some of whose Addison Scheme commissions had been notable for their more traditional cottage aesthetics[61] – produced a design (Type A36) for £299[62] whose elevation (fig.109) bespoke an institutional formality reminiscent of Sampson Kempthorne's 1835 workhouses. It was England's first £300 council house, and, in the opinion of *Garden Cities and Town Planning* magazine, 'a reversion to the type . . . that was sadly familiar in every urban area before the war, and from which the framers of the housing policy of 1919 revolted'. The magazine continued: 'If this Nottingham type is Sir Alfred Mond's prize exhibit, we can scarcely be expected to share his pride'.[63]

After the Addison Scheme subsidy was cancelled, the possibility of building municipal working-class dwellings at all was in doubt: only 18 of England and Wales's 1,800 local authorities were able to proceed in 1922 with home building on their own fiscal resources.[64] 'Ideals,' writes Miller, were 'eroded by penny-pinching.'[65] The practical and aesthetic consequences of subsidy loss across the country echoed Nottingham and Leicester's experience. According to *The Builder*, 'sizes of rooms have been whittled down, houses have been more closely packed together, and every amenity has been pared away in a short-sighted scramble for cheapness'.[66] *Garden Cities and Town Planning* ascribed blame *ad hominem*:

Sir Alfred Mond hangs suspended in the political ether . . . emitting all the time a carol of delight at his success in lowering prices. Beneath him, perched conveniently on the withered Homes-for-Heroes tree, Sir Charles Ruthen chants even more blithely than his chief. The burden of their song is that every day, and in every way, houses are getting cheaper.[67]

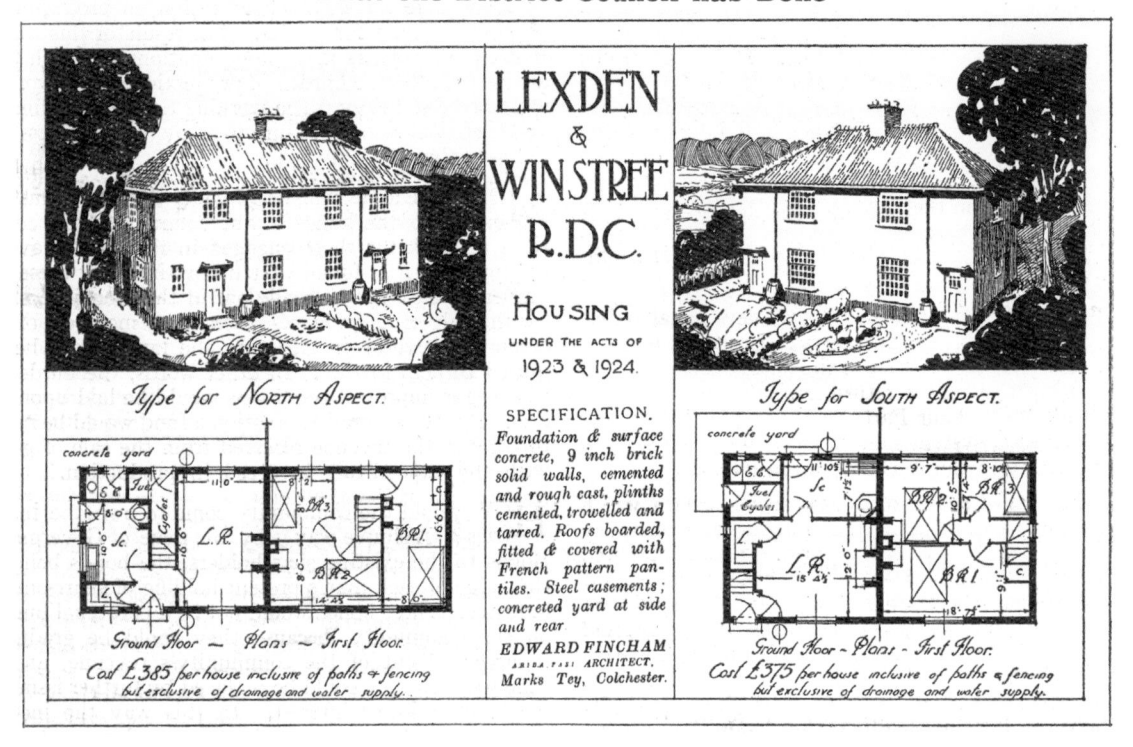

110　New-build council houses from Lexden and Winstree Rural District Council, Essex, *The Land Worker*, vol.6, no.72, May 1925, p.14, Modern Records Centre, University of Warwick

There were architects convinced that the Addison Scheme had delivered aesthetic change for the better in municipal homes. To one, 'the subordination of the picturesque manufactured for theatrical reasons only' was a clear positive.[68] Yet while this may have been true of select Addison developments – like the neat neo-Georgian work that Stanley Adshead oversaw at Moulsecoomb in Brighton[69] – it was not universal. More typical of the way the interwar council house would end up looking were the new 'cottage homes' built by Lexden and Winstree Rural District Council in Essex and featured in the agricultural workers' union magazine *The Land Worker* in May 1925 (fig.110).

Lexden and Winstree was poor – 69,485 acres near Colchester; 19,540 people (146 fewer than in the 1911 Census) – with most of the male workforce employed in agriculture. During 1925, the council's Sanitary Inspector, Mr Hurd, found one family of six people, and another of five, living in single rooms at West Bergholt.[70] To alleviate the problem, the council built 136 cottages under the Addison Act; 30 under the more restrictive conditions of Chamberlain's 1923 Act; and 122 under the 1924 Wheatley Act.[71] Costing around £400 to erect – including site, fencing, and well – letting at 5/6d a week,[72] the later cottages were an undeniable improvement on the district's condemned dwellings. But they were small – no parlour, no bathroom, a living room of around 185ft², three bedrooms. In visual terms, they were the opposite of picturesque. The council's 1923 and 1924 Act designs embodied the aesthetic formality of the Local Government Board's 1919 *Manual* – squat, with low hipped roofs, roughcast over both storeys, front doors articulated by the plainest of doorheads, and otherwise no ornamentation whatever. 'In a stripped-down environment,' writes the sociologist Richard Sennett, 'the more form becomes simple, clear and distinct, the more it defines who belongs there and who doesn't.'[73]

It makes little difference that these were country cottages built by a rural authority. A new, universal, economy type was emerging – the council house – modulated neither by regionality nor distance from the city. Post-Addison Scheme, dwellings like Lexden and Winstree's had been going up in what would become tens of thousands on the LCC's new super-estate at Becontree in north-east London. They were distinctive and easily identified – 'a simplified neo-Georgian style', signifying 'public collectivity'.[74] They did not, in the judgement of the historian John Boughton, amount to 'a pretty estate'.[75]

Councils built houses pretty much like this all over England and Wales before the Second World War, underscoring the difference between private and public sector architectural aesthetics far more than that between town and country. Even with 1924's flexible Wheatley subsidy in place, exchequer support confined local authorities to dwellings smaller than Tudor Walters had recommended, built in the climate of aesthetic repression – without 'craft in the artistic or aesthetic sense'[76] – demanded by the government's housing supremo Sir Charles Ruthen.

PRIVATE ENTERPRISE REVISITS COTTAGE AESTHETICS

It was in contrast with this austere municipal equation that the private buyer and speculative builder's sense of entitlement to cottage-picturesque visuality was consolidated. The opening weeks of 1923 saw the National Federation of House Builders dismiss 1919's Addison Scheme as 'a disastrous . . . experiment in socialism', proposing instead a

111 London County Council houses on the Becontree Estate, Dagenham, 1970, designed by architects under George Topham Forrest. By 1939 it contained 26,000 homes, with a population of 120,000. RIBA Collections

112 The Tibbenham Cottage, photographed at the British Empire Exhibition in July 1925. Two reception rooms, three bedrooms, and a downstairs bathroom at a build cost of £610, in Sir Lawrence Weaver, '"Subsidy" Cottages at Wembley', *Country Life*, vol.58, no.1489, 18 July 1925, p.112, Future Publishing Ltd

cash subsidy that would reanimate the 'infinitely greater agency – private enterprise' in reinvigorating national building.[77] After the collapse of the coalition government, Neville Chamberlain in due course took over as Minister of Health, in March 1923; retained the controversial Sir Charles Ruthen as his unpaid Director-General of Housing; and outlined the country's new housing imperative – getting private builders back on their feet.

This was effected by introducing a Housing Bill, in April 1923, that incorporated a different concept of subsidy, designed to limit exposure for the exchequer. Private sector building was to be supported via the local authorities. The latter would only be entitled to build themselves if they could persuade the Minister that private enterprise was not better placed to do so.[78] Chamberlain's headline subsidy was lower than Addison's,[79] and this had the effect of discouraging construction for rent in favour of construction for

sale. The Health Minister confessed as much to his sister: 'I agree that private enterprise is not now in a position to build houses to let'.[80]

A contemporary described the 1923 Act as 'the charter of private enterprise'.[81] It certainly reflected the broader weakening in 'the centrality of the working class, and its demands, to the popular idea of politics', that McKibbin identifies at the time.[82] Even the ten or so months of minority Labour government under Ramsay MacDonald, from January 1924, did not discourage the builders. Labour's Health Minister John Wheatley passed another Housing Act, in August 1924, that extended the key provisions of Chamberlain's legislation until 1939, introduced a higher subsidy, and greenlit local authorities once again to build the council houses they thought they needed.[83] And while the Conservatives' return to government later that year symbolised for McKibbin 'victory of the middle class over the working class',[84] for Geraint Thomas, in reinstalling Chamberlain at the Ministry of Health, it empowered the politician who 'most embodied the modern working-class Conservatism of the interwar years'.[85] Certainly, the decision not to repeal Wheatley's Housing Act meant a kind of bi-partisan housing policy came into being[86] – and one that seemed productive. By 1925, nearly 200,000 new dwellings had been approved for subsidy by the Health Ministry,[87] two thirds of them private sector built.

In the next chapter, we will see how the inspiration of the cottage picturesque came to define the millions of privately built and purchased houses that abounded across England's suburbs in the 1930s. But it is important to recognise how the Chamberlain and Wheatley subsidies set the ball rolling. Visiting the 'Palace of Housing and Transport' at the 1925 British Empire Exhibition, the former head of postwar land settlement for the Ministry of Agriculture, Sir Lawrence Weaver, found his eye caught by some decidedly picturesque cottage aesthetics. Weaver was interested in the small houses the private sector was developing to qualify for government subsidy. At the show, he noted the 'Tibbenham Cottage' (fig.112), designed by Stanley Hamp, 'which would look normal in any English village . . . the construction [being] genuinely "half-timber"'. Three bedrooms, a tiny parlour, and a downstairs bathroom could be readied for market at a build cost of £610 (or £480 if used on an estate of over 100 dwellings).[88] The Tibbenham's exterior paid an unmistakeable tribute to the kind of aesthetics that wealthy weekenders were finding irresistible, and platoons of anxious conservationists were determined to protect.

COTTAGE RELIGION REACHES THE ROYAL SOCIETY OF ARTS

On 6 May 1926, the loneliness of the SPAB in mounting their cottage conservation vigil was finally relieved. Sir Frank Baines, eminent government architect and Director at the Office of Works, arrived at the Royal Society of Arts (RSA) – on the third day of the General Strike – to give a speech titled 'The Preservation of Ancient Cottages'. He was introduced by Sir Charles Wakefield who set the tone: 'The relentless pressure of present-day conditions would certainly mean the rapid disappearance of many of the picturesque old cottages that at present formed the architectural gems of the country-side'.[89] Sir Frank followed him: 'preservation is called for . . . Our problem to-day is to interest those who are prepared to assist in and devise a scheme which will prevent this waste and destruction in the future'.[90]

Baines has appeared in our story before. Attached from the Office of Works to the Ministry of Munitions, he was responsible, in 1915, for designing the cottage estate for munitions workers, Well Hall, in Eltham, fêted for its picturesqueness.[91] Two years later, he repeated the formula at Roe Green, Kingsbury, for aviation factory personnel. With those feathers in his cap, he was invited in July 1917 to join Raymond Unwin and Sir Aston Webb to help produce the Tudor Walters Report on state-funded cottage building.

Sir Frank's wartime commitment to the cottage picturesque had not dissipated by 1926. Inspired perhaps by Guy Dawber's inaugural address as

incoming President of the RIBA on 2 November 1925 – 'day by day, all over England, old buildings are being pulled down'[92] – Baines's lecture to the RSA was a love-letter to the architectural forms intrinsic to Price, Knight, and Gilpin's late eighteenth-century aesthetic. The speech by the Office of Works supremo luxuriated in cottage visuality: 'swept valleys and stone verges' on roofs in Bradford-on Avon; the 'bay in the gable' on a cottage at Lyddington, Rutland; the 'heavy type of timber frame' and its 'magpie' effect at Eardisley, Herefordshire; 'shaped or crow-stepped' gables in Norfolk; 'tile-hanging' south of Chelmsford; 'diagonal brick-nogging' at Ewhurst, Surrey; and the 'gables or dormers' in the village of Kersey, Suffolk, with their 'coloured, lozenged patterning'.[93] All were presented in celebration of pre-eighteenth century cottage architecture's visuality – the chosen subjects indistinguishable from those that had moved the theorists of the Picturesque over a century before.

Baines's lecture ended with a plea for funds and unity:

> unification of every effort of those who are profoundly concerned with the distinctive possession of this country in its cottage architecture. . . . the Royal Society of Arts has undertaken to initiate and endeavour to organise a movement, directed towards the final preservation of the cottage architecture of this country.[94]

The Builder was impressed, printing an abstract of Baines's talk in June 1926 and expressing the 'genuine hope that something may be done to secure . . . these invaluable possessions, both as a record of old times and for their intrinsic charm'.[95] The speech led directly to the Royal Society of Arts cottage campaign, which would, by enlisting the country's most prominent statesmen, politicise the cottage picturesque – transforming it from neglected rural curiosity into the oriflamme of England's sacred and supposedly contented past. It would officialise, in Urry and Larsen's phrase, the significance of cottages 'as objects upon which the gaze is directed',[96] and cast their preservation as a shared national responsibility. In the process, the idea of the cottage would be subject to the mid-1920s cultural upheaval previously outlined – its class ownership re-contested, and its psychological freehold wrested from its original occupants and taken more firmly into the possession of those for whom it was the perfect symbolic focus for picturesque attention.

Little time elapsed between Baines's speech to the RSA in June 1926 and a commitment of support from the cottage protection frontline at the SPAB. In July, Secretary Albert Powys forwarded a cheque to the RSA for £100 given to its own cottage fund by William Cadbury.[97] The RSA, meanwhile, revealed – even before the formal launch of their project – that there had already been a £250 donation from the Earl of Iveagh, and the promise of money from Sir Alfred Mond. By the end of July 1926, the RSA Fund stood at £1,003 12s, thanks largely to an anonymous donation of £500 from Emslie Horniman (son of the museum's founder).[98] Middle-class cottage activism's enlistment of the genuinely moneyed was gathering momentum.

GOVERNMENT RETURNS TO THE COTTAGE

In the months before Baines's address to the RSA, civil servants in the Ministry of Health had been working on new legislation – the Housing (Rural Workers) Bill, 1926 – that would recuperate government interest in the cottage and move the dwelling from the margins of conservationism into the spotlight of national politics. Baldwin's election address in 1924 had not ignored the housing crisis: 'Next to . . . unemployment, the gravest of our domestic problems still is . . . housing'.[99] But his Health Minister Neville Chamberlain got bogged down in a proposal from the industrialist William Weir to create mass-produced steel homes, which faced opposition from the construction unions.[100] Frustrated in this, and with 'plans on the subject of slum clearances . . . still too vague to form any basis for legislation',[101] Chamberlain turned his attention to the countryside.

Employing a trick he had used before, the Health Minister gave a non-attributable briefing,

on 19 January 1926, to *The Times*'s Alfred Robbins, in which he floated ideas on subsidy for rural cottage reconditioning.[102] Two days later, Robbins wrote them up, making no mention of cottage aesthetics.[103] Then, a letter published in response to the article from one Charles Walston provided the jigsaw's missing piece – 'from the aesthetic point of view . . . help is more urgently required in rural districts'. Without it, 'we should end by losing all our picturesque older villages – one of the most characteristic charms of Old England'.[104] This intervention ensured rural cottage subsidy and its relationship to picturesque cottage aesthetics were effectively launched into the national conversation at the same time.

Mention of the new Housing Bill was agreed for the King's Speech of February 1926,[105] and by the summer, Chamberlain had the wheels of legislative process turning. That a subsidy scheme criticised privately by Health Ministry solicitor M.L. Gwyer in late April 1926 – 'as full of holes as a colander'[106] – was ready for debate in parliament in August is a credit to the Ministry's long-serving housing specialists. The second reading came on 3 August 1926. Introducing the Bill, Chamberlain bruited the official rationale – 'proposals which are designed to try and improve the accommodation for agricultural labourers and for other country workers', offering government financial support for landlords of old cottages, 'to bring them up to modern standards of comfort and sanitation'.[107] At the despatch box, though, the Health Minister expanded on the aesthetic point that Walston had made in his letter to *The Times*:

> Our country villages contain a great deal that is characteristic of Old England in style and material and in the architecture of their cottages. To look at cottages such as you may see in the Cotswold district in Gloucestershire, or in East Kent . . . is a constant pleasure, not only to country dwellers but to town dwellers too, and I must say that it seems to me it would be something like an act of vandalism if we were to destroy these reminders of an older and more picturesque world . . . It is not only an aesthetic question. I cannot help feeling that the

existence of an environment of this kind must do a great deal to preserve what I may call the genius of the place in the minds of the inhabitants.[108]

On one level, here was a Conservative administration seeking to conserve, instrumentalising SPAB philosophy by offering public money to sustain, among other things, the public's right to 'look at cottages'. On another plane – in emphasising the fact that those cottages were, in 'style and material', representative of 'Old England' – the government was attempting something historically more ambitious: co-opting the popular myth of England's rural past to boost the Conservative Party's political appeal across town and country.

The spectator's gaze, associationism, old cottages, Old England – all were present and correct in Chamberlain's speech. Behind them played out, intended or not, one of the deeper original purposes of the Picturesque's late eighteenth-century begetters. As Everett describes it:

> The Picturesque was concerned . . . with the blending together of diversity into harmonious images of connection and mutual dependence. . . . It was a happy characteristic of the picturesque view that it could make all the participants in the landscape more content, the owners of the land as well as the poor.[109]

It was a quintessentially Tory political endeavour. Chamberlain even failed to resist the magic word itself – 'an older and more picturesque world'.[110] Indeed, his allusion to the eighteenth-century poet Alexander Pope – whose phrase 'the genius of the place', in 'Epistle IV, Of the Use of Riches', antedated the theoretical Picturesque – invoked a man who prototyped antipathy to 'the uniformity, narrowness and vanity'[111] of Palladianism, one of the subjects of the Picturesque's original critique: 'Proud to catch cold at a Venetian door; /Conscious they act a true Palladian part, /And if they starve, they starve by rules of art'.[112]

For *The Builder*, government timing was 'opportune' – an editorial in the magazine making the connection between the new Bill and Baines's speech at the RSA a couple of months before.[113] But it is important to recognise that the Conservatives had moved from a coalition commitment in 1918 to build hundreds of thousands of new cottages 'for the heroes who have won the war'[114] – the world's most radical social housing policy – to a pledge of state money for country landlords, aimed in part at preserving the public's right to 'look at' picturesque ancient cottages. The new policy aligned Baldwin's government with the visuality of the ancient cottage – a unifying symbol of national origin and collective moral character.

By the time it was presented in the chamber in August, the Bill went down well both in Whitehall and with Conservative MPs. Chamberlain told his sister Hilda: 'My department is very pleased with the session . . . the Rural Housing Bill has excited something like enthusiasm among the agricultural members'.[115] A contribution in the House from Frank Rye, MP for Loughborough, bore witness:

> We are all very proud of our country. . . . The fact that we have those beautiful cottages in charming surroundings brings a great number of visitors . . . I should hope, if only on this ground, that the Bill will be placed on the Statute Book so that many delightful old cottages, charming to the eye, may be preserved and retained for many years to come.[116]

Rye tabled several amendments at the committee stage, and it was his lobbying that drove Chamberlain to reinforce oratory with an aesthetics clause. The Health Ministry's file-notes show the Minister ready, in November 1926, 'to accept something on the lines of Rye's first amendment'.[117] Protections in the Act ended up afforded to any 'house or building to which any historic, architectural or artistic interest attaches'.[118]

At the second reading, Labour opposition was fierce. What *The Times* described as 'the inexplicable aversion of the Socialists' to the Bill was in fact easily explained.[119] Labour MPs believed that cottage aesthetics and the rural poor were a smokescreen for 'good Tory doctrine' – a plan, sniped Ramsay

113   The Adam Brothers' classical facade at the Royal Society of Arts HQ, 1770s. Institutional classicism sheltered a nest of interwar activists determined to save the cottage picturesque

MacDonald, 'to try to maintain private ownership at the public expense . . . a landlord's measure'.[120] Labour's reaction, Chamberlain thought, 'plainly showed that they were terrified of it'.[121] During the Bill's final reading in December 1926 – reacting to Frank Rye's attempt to fortify the Bill's aesthetic protections – Wilfred Paling, Labour MP for Doncaster, launched an all-out assault that echoed Macaulay's anti-Picturesque arguments with Southey in the 'cottage controversy' of 1829–30:

> Some of these old cottages . . . are only beautiful on the outside. Inside they are equivalent to some of the worst slums in our cities . . . If . . . because of their beauty, these houses had to stop where they are, and

the people had to live in them under conditions of slumdom, I should . . . resist the amendment with all the force of which I am capable.[122]

Chamberlain's Conservative and Unionist colleagues – Archibald Skelton, member for Perth, and the Hon. Charles Rhys (later Eighth Baron Dynevor), MP for Romford – fought back, with helpfully picturesque arguments. Rhys expressed

> the desirability that the countryside should look its best . . . for the sake of the numbers who go out into the country on Saturdays and Sundays and who are a great source of revenue to those who live there.[123]

Skelton dismissed Labour's arguments as fuelled by 'class and party considerations',[124] and the Bill became law in December 1926 – providing a firm footing for Stanley Baldwin at the RSA podium in January 1927 as he fronted the cottage preservation appeal.

The RSA Cottage Fund's organisation had been streamlined during the autumn of 1926 under Secretary G.K. Menzies.[125] A Sub-Committee on the Preservation of Ancient Cottages was formed, and representatives of the SPAB were invited to join to draw up the Cottage Fund's constitution.[126] Whereas the 7 December 1926 launch event for Professor Patrick Abercrombie's landscape-orientated Council for the Preservation of Rural England (CPRE) boasted Health Minister Neville Chamberlain as the star attraction,[127] Menzies at the RSA was able to go one better – telling his colleagues on 21 December that Prime Minister Baldwin would launch the RSA's Cottage Preservation Fund in January 1927.[128]

Williamson contends that 'evocations of the English countryside . . . appeared only rarely in Baldwin's speeches';[129] but one famous address, given at the annual dinner of the Royal Society of St George in May 1924 – 'his definitive statement on national identity'[130] – must have given the RSA confidence that the Prime Minister shared their cause: 'The sounds of England, the tinkle of the hammer on the anvil in the country smithy, the corncrake on a dewy morning . . .'.[131]

Rhetorical gifts were not all that commended Baldwin. The Prime Minister relaxed with the rural writing of Rudyard Kipling (his cousin) and with the novels of the Shropshire writer Mary Webb. He even corresponded with the latter, just before his RSA appearance in January 1927, to thank her for one book in particular – *Precious Bane* – a copy of which he was given by the Deputy Cabinet Secretary, Tom Jones, and had spent the last days of 1926 reading at home. 'I read it at Christmas within sight of the Clee Hills . . . I have not enjoyed a book so much for years.'[132] Prominent in the novel's early nineteenth-century folkloric setting was a thread of cottage nostalgia:

> I never could tell why this cottage drew me . . .
> Three well-whitened steps led up to the door,
> and there was a window of many little panes,
> not bottle-glass . . . there was a second window
> in the living-room that looked over . . . the meadows
> to the mountains.[133]

Another Webb novel – Baldwin's favourite, *The Golden Arrow* [134] – could fairly have been subtitled 'A Tale of Two Cottages':

> John Arden's stone cottage stood in the midst
> of the hill plateau . . . While washing dishes,
> Deborah could see, through the small, age-misted
> pane, counties and blue ranges lying beneath the
> transparent or hazy air.[135]

A penchant for the fiction of 'loam and lovechild'[136] was matched by a biographical quirk that made the Prime Minister an even better collaborator for the RSA's cottage initiative. His mother had family links with William Morris, whose moral example (if not his longing for a socialist utopia) was formative for the Conservative politician. There was a potent nostalgia at the heart of the RSA's cottage campaign that the rhetoric of Morris had prepared Baldwin to exploit. His instinct to treat English pastoral

114 Stanley Baldwin MP, Prime Minister, 1924–29, unknown photographer (1930s), National Portrait Gallery, London. His library boasted the fiction of Mary Webb and his cousin Rudyard Kipling, and even a volume of Raffles Davison's drawings, gifted to the Prime Minister for Christmas in 1927 and signed by Davison himself

as 'symbolic and exemplary'[137] made the initiative an unmissable political opportunity: 'In a world where four-fifths of the population were urban, the principal function of countryside as an icon [was] to represent a timeless England of tradition and stability'.[138]

The occasion to combine upbringing, instinct, and political opportunity came on Wednesday 26 January 1927. Speaking behind the classical entablature of the RSA's West End headquarters in London, Baldwin revealed that architecture was a subject to which he had given at least a little thought:

> It is difficult for us to exaggerate the importance which architecture plays in the national life . . . wherever you go and whatever you do, you are obliged to look at buildings and buildings are obliged to look at you.[139]

The popular view of the Prime Minister – that he was 'always talking about the English countryside'[140] – suggested that he might command the language of cottage conservation like a native. He did not disappoint:

> to those of us who have been brought up in homes amidst some of the most beautiful of the old cottages of England . . . it is difficult to contemplate these survivals without realising that the whole of this architecture is one of the tributaries of the main stream of medieval craftsmanship . . . we want to preserve old cottages . . . We want to bring them back into the main stream of the national life.[141]

The RSA's cottage conference was a grand occasion. According to *The Times,* Baldwin, at the top of the bill, delivered a speech punctuated by laughter and concluding in cheers.[142] There were turns too from the Earl of Crawford and Balcarres (President of the Society of Antiquaries and the brand new CPRE),[143] Sir Alfred Mond (MP for Carmarthen; a year from ennoblement); John Whitley (MP for Halifax; Speaker of the House), and Sir Percy Hurd (Conservative MP for Devizes, and Chairman of the

Association of Rural District Councils). Common to the speakers were two themes: a passion for the aesthetics of picturesque cottages – that outweighed any emphasis on rehousing rural workers – and an undercurrent of distaste towards recent domestic building for the working classes.

Baldwin's comparison of ancient cottages with newer dwellings is difficult not to read, today, as a repudiation that extended to post-First World War council house building. Whereas he saw ancient cottages as having 'an appearance in the country of spontaneous and natural growth', he thought this 'wholly lacking in those abortions of red brick and slate which have arisen with such alacrity since the industrial era began'.[144] Whitley seconded the premier with a rhetorical question about the reputational prospects of contemporary municipal architecture:

> I sometimes think of the year 2027 . . . What will people then be saying of the houses of Dr Addison, of Mr Chamberlain and of Mr Wheatley? I wonder whether they will have in their possession the pride which we have . . . in the older homes of the past.[145]

Mond speculated about whether another 'society' might not soon be needed 'to stop . . . the erection of the most appalling buildings all along our main roads';[146] and Hurd told scare-stories of his home county, Wiltshire, defaced by 'corrugated monstrosities put up in connection with our village cottages'.[147] A group of men at the apex of national politics drew a dividing line between aesthetically acceptable and unacceptable dwellings – between Lord Crawford's 'old world cottages . . . indigenous to the country side'[148] and Baldwin's newer 'abortions of red brick and slate'. It was a foretaste of the class partisanship to come.

The media paid the cottage conference rapt attention. Two mornings' worth of previews had featured in *The Times*, which carried the Prime Minister's entire address the following day. Newspapers from the *Morning Post*, the *Daily Mail*, the *Daily Express* (which parodied Felicia Hemans),[149] and the *Daily Chronicle* in London,

115 'Notice To Quit', *Daily Chronicle*, 28 January 1927, Royal Society of Arts Archive, Cuttings Book 1, PR. EN/100/13/4. The picturesque 'old house' on the hill watches as the formal 'new house' is sent packing by the Royal Society of Arts

to the *Western Morning News*, the *Sheffield Daily Telegraph*, the *Newcastle Journal*, and the *Nottingham Evening Post* gave Baldwin headlines that a modern spin doctor would kill for: 'Mr Baldwin Champions English Countryside';[150] 'Premier Urges Return to Old-Type Houses';[151] 'Vandals of the Countryside – Premier's Onslaught',[152] 'England is slowly awakening'.[153] In *The London Weekly*, Baldwin's 'emerging personality' was heralded as 'constantly revealing him, in the old sense of the term, as an essential Englishman'.[154] Magazines including *The Spectator*, *Country Life*, *Autocar*, *Cycling*, and *Motor World* reported supportively too.[155] Commentary construed Baldwin's priority almost exclusively as aesthetic – rather than as determined to improve standards of rural housing. A cartoon in the *Daily Chronicle* (fig.115) caught the mood of nimbyism *avant la lettre*.

Not everyone fell into line. The Labour MP Ellen Wilkinson – one of only four women in the 1924 parliament – gave a pithy response to the newspapers:

They do not like the modern houses because the modern houses do not look so pretty when their motor cars pass by. They forget that the old English cottages, however pretty they looked from the outside, were dark, insanitary, and inconvenient . . . to talk as though the old English cottage was ideal is just part of the sickly sentimentality that we are getting so accustomed to from Mr Baldwin.[156]

Everything from Baines's RSA speech and the Housing Act of 1926 to Baldwin's address (and others at the conference) at the beginning of 1927 had framed the drive to save picturesque rural cottages as double-barrelled – first, to ensure rural workers had somewhere better to live; and, secondly, to preserve ancient dwellings' aesthetic beauty and architectural value. *The Times* revealed a bigger picture: 'no effort should be spared to keep as large a population as possible contentedly on the soil, and the repair and preservation of old cottages is a means to that end'.[157] Their phraseology reflected briefing material circulating in government at the time – 'to stem the drift from the country to the town'[158] – which highlights today the fundamental picturesqueness of both the policy and the RSA's campaign.

Talk of cottage aesthetics and the satisfaction of the onlooker's gaze was intended literally. But the timing was also crucial. What Mandler calls Baldwin's project to create 'a picture of the English national character' began 'in earnest around the time of the General Strike in 1926'.[159] Here was a Conservative administration using ancient cottage architecture to launch what amounted to a public opinion-forming and legislative initiative – centred on the social and aesthetic merits of the cottage picturesque in a quasi-feudal landscape – just after the nation's cities had contemplated working-class insurrection at the high-water mark of Trades Union influence. In a timely detachment of his party from its aristocratic past, Baldwin must have seen the 1927 RSA initiative as a golden opportunity to play up further 'a gentle, modest, domesticated cottage-loving image that fitted neatly with established trends within the middle class'.[160]

Says Stedman Jones: 'one of the uses of history has always been (in Western society at least) the creation of traditional mythologies attributing a historical sanctity to the present self-images of groups, classes, and societies'.[161] In 1926–27, the historical cottage picturesque was hijacked to serve just such a purpose, propagandising an image of domestic contentedness for the labouring classes in an art-historical landscape that camouflaged – behind the aesthetics of individualism and associative nostalgia – the government's yearning for a calm and obedient populace. With its acculturated mythology, the cottage was the perfect vessel for this socio-political message. But its new role was starkly at odds with the part written for it in 1918–19.

In Lloyd George's original vision, 500,000 new cottages would speak for radical change – each one sheltering a forward-looking working-class family, freed from the burdens of squalor and overcrowding. In Baldwin's 1927 RSA speech, the cottage was ordered back into the rural landscape – once again ancient, once again picturesque, telling

quietly of craftsmanship, tradition, continuity, and social order. Like Eliot's 'significant soil', England's significant cottage – Baldwin seemed to say – was not the one built yesterday by a local authority; it was the cottage of the past.

For those missing newspaper coverage of the Prime Minister's exploits, the RSA printed, in March 1927, 12,000 copies of a pamphlet that reworked the address in the form of a fund-raising letter – 'I now appeal to all those who appreciate the beauty of our old English cottages to contribute'.[162] Baldwin's new text reinforced the now-familiar framing of old/good, new/bad:

> The well-meaning but thoughtless zeal for widening roads has robbed us of many a native homestead, to be replaced by gimcrack bungalows with composition-tiled roofs, or ill-proportioned and bedizened 'villas'.[163]

And although the Prime Minister remembered that poorly housed rural workers were supposed to be a principal beneficiary of the RSA scheme, he gave them just a handful of small print amidst an effusion of touristically inflected picturesque:

> To every motorist, to every cyclist, to every pedestrian who has toured through rural England and whose eye has rested with delight on some lovely old-world cottage, I appeal for a contribution to help this cause.[164]

RSA Secretary Menzies must have been delighted that the most famous of all chroniclers of cottage England's past, the novelist Thomas Hardy, was persuaded to add his voice in the pamphlet to the Prime Minister's:

> I can with pleasure support the appeal of the Royal Society of Arts . . . towards preserving the ancient cottages of England . . . I would . . . urge owners to let as many as are left . . . remain where they are, and to repair them instead of replacing them with bricks, since . . . they have almost always great beauty and charm.[165]

Promoted thus, the Cottage Fund accumulated over £4,607 by the summer of 1927. After a special fund-raising lunch, the Carpenters' Company added £949 14s 6d. More modest sums came from some of the key personalities of interwar cottage debate: £10 10s from Sir Frank Baines; £5 5s from Raymond Unwin; the same from Sir Banister Fletcher; and £2 precisely from W.R. Lethaby. The editorial team at *The Builder* were bowled over by the RSA pamphlet:

> It is possible that there are people . . . inclined to sneer at Mr Baldwin's sentimental appeal to save these cottages . . . there are others who not only think differently but give their time and money freely in their efforts to save us from ourselves. . . . These old cottages are not only beautiful in themselves, they are gems in comparison with our substitutes.[166]

For Baldwin, 1927 would end on a decidedly picturesque note. Among his Christmas presents that year was a book – *Raffles Davison: A Record of his Life and Work from 1870 to 1926*, an eclectic mix of picturesque line drawings ranging from Ightham Mote in Kent to Lakeland cottages – gifted to the Prime Minister with a handwritten dedication by the great perspectivist Davison himself.[167]

THE MINISTRY BACKS COTTAGE CONSERVATION

Geraint Thomas observes of pre-1929 Conservative government: 'Churchill and Chamberlain set the policy, Baldwin set the rhetorical tone'.[168] And although Chamberlain may not have been invited to front the RSA's Cottage Preservation Fund campaign, he wasted no time harnessing the Prime Minister's eloquence to the business of energising local government.

Already in January 1927, a Health Ministry circular to local authorities had told them that it wanted 'the work of reconditioning contemplated by the [1926 Housing] Act . . . to preserve and perpetuate the styles of cottage architecture which have come down to us from former times'.[169] Then, just as the Ministry had in 1919 and 1920, Chamberlain published a Manual that provided detail on the restoration and construction of aesthetically acceptable cottages.

He wrote the foreword himself. Before plotting the course ahead, he conceded: 'especially in rural areas, too little care has been taken to secure that the buildings erected were appropriate in design'.[170] The body of the Manual's copy then quoted Baldwin's RSA appeal, adding the Ministry's voice to the promulgation of picturesque orthodoxy and its antique Tory sentiments concerning the interdependence of populace and landscape:

> The beauty of the English countryside is a heritage which has been handed down from the past. The present generation must recognise a responsibility to pass on this heritage unspoiled for the enjoyment of their successors.[171]

Whose was the government's guiding intelligence here? Probably not Ruthen, who had died in September 1926.[172] Still in the saddle at the Ministry of Health, though, was Raymond Unwin, who had survived the Mond-inspired cull of Housing Department architects in 1921.[173] Compiled with Unwin's participation,[174] the new Manual supplemented the previous year's Housing Act with clear guidance on 'reconditioning old buildings':

> There will be found in all districts choice examples of cottage architecture, sometimes showing elaboration both in design and treatment, which would be very costly if carried out today. The careful preservation of these is of the utmost importance.[175]

More detailed practical advice followed,[176] but the new Manual was determined its readers should understand the Ministry view that not all ancient cottages were distinguished by *decorative* architecture: 'Their pleasing effects depend mainly on their simplicity . . . on the good proportion of the necessary parts'.[177]

This classic of Unwin idiolect evoked Whitehall's Manual from 1919. At the heart of that had been a conspicuous tension: the need to achieve a level of aesthetic acceptability in new municipal cottages while minimising costs. Along with Unwin's conflicted attitude to and understanding of the Picturesque, this tension was still discernible in 1927:

Considerations of cost may exclude the possibility of emulating such charming old buildings as, for example, many of the Cotswold cottages . . . however, it is possible even within the strict limits of economy to avoid the grotesque and unsuitable buildings which so frequently disfigure the English countryside.[178]

Despite abundant talk of picturesqueness and its attractions at the RSA, Health Ministry architectural *diktat* remained hostile. One 1927 Manual paragraph saw 'no virtue in any kind of disorder or irregularity for its own sake'.[179] Surviving from 1919–21, there was an official terror of councils or speculative builders attempting to produce irregularity, that cardinal virtue of the Picturesque. In 1927, the upshot was that those few among the working classes with the prospect of being rehoused by local authorities could still look forward to 'the general uniformity which may be demanded by economy' – an unwitting echo of language used to describe the new workhouses mooted in 1835, which, their advocates had hoped, would model 'the advantages of uniformity'.[180]

The Ministry must have suspected that this did not sound appealing. Mitigation was suggested in the new Manual by a 'carefully placed feature to mark the centre of a group, the termination of a street vista, or the turning of a corner'.[181] But this was planners' talk, not architecture *per se*. Even Abercrombie had come to recognise that the aesthetics of mass housing could not be addressed through grouping alone: 'details of the design, materials and colour of the individual units are as important as their disposition in groups. A single building, if it rises to a grisly eminence of hideousness, can do incalculable harm'.[182] Yet

according to the 1927 Health Ministry Manual, working-class occupants of individual state-subsidised dwellings could not look forward even to 'cheap-looking bays, doorheads, or other features'.

'It is true,' the 1927 Manual conceded,

that there are many beautiful [architectural] relations which are not symmetrical, and consequently good designs for buildings which are not regular. But their virtue arises not from the absence of regularity, but from the presence of definite relations and proportions between the parts, which are frequently much more subtle and difficult to attain than those of regular design.[183]

This was a change from Ministry guidance in 1919, where informality had been deplored in principle.[184] But the new Manual still discouraged picturesque irregularity as too nuanced for mass production, echoing Voysey in June 1912: 'Symmetrical arrangement is more ready to the hand of the unskilled than the harmonious arrangement of differences and unlikeness'.[185] Whitehall agreed. Only those, with 'a clear vision of the more subtle and pleasing relationship and order' they intended to build in place of 'regular order' should be allowed to attempt it.[186] In these instructions, the government was clear that new-build working-class council housing planned for the later 1920s should not really be allowed the aesthetics of the cottage picturesque.

THE ROYAL SOCIETY OF ARTS CAMPAIGN

With the 1927 Manual having made plain to local authorities what was required of them, the RSA's Cottage Fund supporters continued repositioning extant ancient cottages for their new audience. To oversee campaigning efforts, an Advisory Committee had been established, which met for the first time in June 1927 – an agglomeration of influential bodies and individuals including Baines and Unwin from the civil service, Oswald Milne from the RIBA, and representatives of the SPAB, the National Trust, the Town Planning Institute, and others. Through their

116 Ramsay MacDonald, Labour's first Prime Minister, unknown photographer (1937), National Portrait Gallery, London

ministrations, and the more focused attentions of a smaller Executive Committee led by Baines himself (Unwin occasionally chaired the Fund's Executive Committee after Baines fell ill),[187] the Fund would drive considerable cottage rescue activity over the coming years, culminating in its first annual report, presented at the AGM in February 1929, chaired and addressed by the soon-to-be second-time Labour Prime Minister James Ramsay MacDonald.

In 1926, MacDonald had spoken in the Commons in opposition to the government's cottage legislation. But in the rose-tinted spotlight of the RSA three years later, like Baldwin before him, he denounced modern housing efforts – 'So many of our modern dwelling places are absolutely dead from their birth' – and contributed instead one of the cottage picturesque phrasebook's purplest passages:

> perhaps you have been trudging far and fast over delightfully inspiring moorland; . . . as you go down the winding road you are received, as it were, into the arms of a quiet peaceful settlement of thatched cottages. It seems as though somebody had been wandering . . . for generation and generation, and age and age, and had at last found rest in this little nook that had been waiting there for years . . . to receive you as the only pilgrim.[188]

A man who had once mistrusted the Conservative government's instrumentalisation of ancient cottages now found himself 'wandering' sentimentally side by side with Baldwin.

The Society's annual report recorded preservation activity that the Fund had facilitated in its first year or so. At West Tarring, near Worthing, a row of three dwellings known as the Thomas à Becket Cottages – long on the SPAB's watchlist; 'of quite extraordinary beauty and interest'[189] – was bought with the assistance of a £600 loan from the RSA Fund and handed over to the Sussex Archaeological Trust for repair.[190] In 1928, what William Morris believed was 'surely . . . the loveliest village in England'[191] – Bibury

above

117   Arlington Row, Bibury, Gloucestershire, photographed by Sidney Pitcher, FRPS. From Basil Oliver, *The Cottages of England* (London: B.T. Batsford, 1929), plate 29

left

118   The High Street, West Wycombe, Buckinghamshire, from the Royal Society of Arts' pamphlet, *An Appeal to the County of Buckingham* (London: Royal Society of Arts, 1929), p.11, The Bodleian Libraries, University of Oxford

in Gloucestershire (fig.117) – boasted eight fourteenth-century cottages known as Arlington Row whose stone-tiled roofs were in imminent danger of collapse. They were offered to the RSA. Publicity and fund-raising led to a local council decision to buy and help finance the repairs, but the work was not universally applauded. A resident wrote to *The Spectator*: 'It's exactly like the English Village Street in the Ideal Home Exhibition now that the Society of Arts have been busy'.[192] The RSA later transferred the cottages to the care of the Gloucestershire Archaeological Trust, which in turn gave them to the National Trust.[193]

Delighted that the Royal Photographic Society had chosen 'Ancient British Cottages' for their Special Subject Competition in 1928,[194] the RSA Fund's Executive Committee authorised, the following year, their most ambitious project to date – the rescue of an entire village. Sir Lawrence Weaver had pursued this idea for the Society since autumn 1928, though his first bid – Castle Combe in Wiltshire, 'a perfect Tudor village' – saw the owner reject the RSA's overtures.[195] Success came in 1929 at West Wycombe in the Chilterns, home to Sir John Dashwood.

Over 50 cottages, dating from pre-Tudor to Georgian, and a 'lofty column surmounted by a globe at the crossroads [which] informs the traveller that he is thirty miles "from the City" and fifteen "from the University"' were brought to the Society's attention by a letter from Miss Rachael Alexander, who lived down the road at High Wycombe. She called on the RSA to prevent the planned sale (in 60 separate lots) – offering to donate £500 if they could.[196]

Baines had resigned due to ill-health, so Dashwood told the RSA Executive Committee's new chairman Percy Morley Horder – an architect who had designed cottages for Hampstead Garden Suburb[197] – that he was willing to sell freeholds for the entire village at £13,500, a discount of £3,500 on the auctioneer's valuation. An undertaking of this scale demanded referral to the RSA's governing Council, which minuted its approval on 11 March; and, by May 1929, 25 per cent of the agreed price had already been paid to the cash-strapped baronet.

As the total value of the RSA's Cottage Fund stood at only £4,272 by this time, further fund-raising was needed. This called for a specific West Wycombe campaign of such prestige that its expensively printed pamphlet – *An Appeal to the County of Buckingham* – was prefaced by royal endorsement: 'Her Majesty the Queen's interest in the preservation of the beauty of England and its unique traditional building is shown by her acceptance of a copy'.[198] The now-Prime Minister James Ramsay MacDonald again put his shoulder to the wheel: 'to the vast majority of town dwellers for whom the development of modern transport has brought [the country's] remote recesses within reach, it is of vital importance that its beauties should be preserved'.[199]

Almost completely absent by this stage was any talk of rehousing labourers. The government's 1926 Housing Act would result in the reconditioning of only 11,513 cottages by 1936.[200] The agenda for the nation's conservation-minded politicians, and many of its middle and upper classes more widely, had become, in Her Majesty's words, 'preservation of the beauty of England'.[201] And for that, the ancient cottage was essential. From the American Ambassador Charles Dawes, a message to similar effect was featured; as was a list of supporters whose social class was unambiguous: Viscount Astor, the Bishop of Buckingham, and no fewer than four Rothschilds.[202]

In their quest to raise an additional £20,000, the RSA announced it had called 'a halt here to hot red bricks and restless forms' – and that 'no worthier place could be found to restore and preserve as a village of still living beauty'.[203] Three years of preservation work later, having renovated West Wycombe's cottages, shops, inns, and furniture manufactories, the Society handed yet another of its bright beginnings to the National Trust, distinctly harrowed by how difficult the project had turned out to be.[204]

THE COTTAGE DOMESDAY BOOK

The final key RSA initiative in 1929 was to commission a cottage conservation book that would spur 'further propaganda work with regard to . . . the preservation of our ancient cottages'.[205] The writer chosen was one of the Cottage Fund's longest-standing Executive Committee members, the architect Basil Oliver – a committee member at the SPAB and at the Art Workers' Guild, and a teacher on the staff of the LCC's Central School of Arts and Crafts.[206] Lined up to publish was the country-loving B.T. Batsford, where they had been producing cottage literature – such as Guy Dawber's *Old Cottages and Farm-houses in Kent* (1900) and C.R. Ashbee's *A Book of Cottages and Little Houses* (1906) – for decades. Oliver's new study, *The Cottages of England* (1929), his first book for Batsford since 1912,[207] leant on the technical insight of the Hallamshire Group architectural historian Charles Innocent.[208] Stanley Baldwin's address at the RSA's cottage campaign launch in 1927 was reworked to provide a foreword.

For all the lip-service originally paid by the government and by the RSA Cottage Fund to the importance of rural cottages' continuing role in agricultural housing, Oliver predicated a cottage's inclusion in his survey – its suitability for protection – on the grounds of picturesqueness. He conceded that there were other considerations:

> Mr G.K. Chesterton . . . once reminded us that "rose-covered cottages should not colour our conception too much. The roses are all outside such places; the thorns are within" . . . but this aspect of the matter is a subject in itself and cannot be more than hinted at in these pages.[209]

The project was précised, therefore, in Oliver's own words, as 'admiring the external picturesqueness of old cottages'.[210] Despite making no explicit reference to Price and Knight's Picturesque, or Hussey's 1927 book, Oliver connoted traditional fourteenth- to seventeenth-century architecture with picturesqueness of effect – articulated in terms the hierarchs of the Picturesque would surely have embraced.

Oliver's work was reviewed enthusiastically in *The Architects' Journal*: 'The *Cottages of England* is an excellent book, and one that fills a gap, as

the whole field has never before been surveyed'.[211] But this latter claim is debatable. Oliver's was only the latest addition to a shelf of cottage literature replenished by writers who rarely let a year pass without adding to the catalogue. Brace summarises B.T. Batsford's contribution to the broader tide: 'a remarkably coherent, conservative, backward-looking and nostalgic vision of England'.[212] Matless examines landscape literature's share of the vision – from Batsford and others.[213] But behind the texts usually discussed is a sizeable subset of cottage literature. In books from Billing & Sons, Jonathan Cape Ltd, Chapman & Hall, Cobden-Sanderson, Collins, Herbert Jenkins Ltd, and Methuen & Co., as well as Batsford, it is possible to trace, from 1889 at the latest, the key strains of a cottage discourse that helped consolidate the rural labourer's

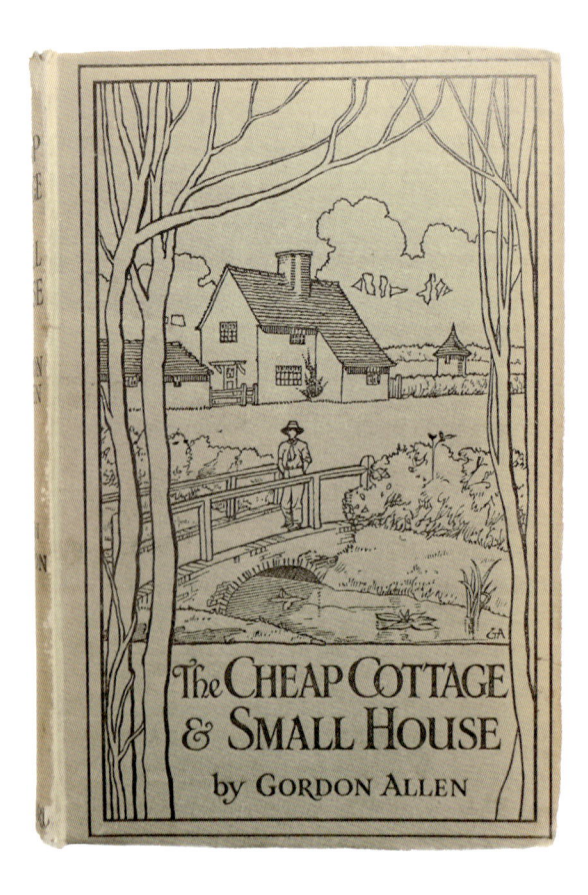

119 Gordon Allen's book was first published by the Letchworth Press in 1912, sold well, and was enlarged and revised for the B.T. Batsford Ltd sixth edition in 1919

picturesque ancient dwelling as a phenomenon of compelling interest to the interwar middle classes.

Many of the key books have been cited in previous chapters. Helen Allingham's *Happy England* (1903) and *The Cottage Homes of England* (1909) celebrated the cottage artistic. Others – Maurice Adams's *Modern Cottage Architecture* (1904), and *The 'Country Life' Book of Cottages* (1913) by Lawrence Weaver – tackled new cottage building and how to do it sensitively. There were pleadings for conservation of the threatened dwelling – Ralph Nevill, *Old Cottage and Domestic Architecture, South West Surrey* (1889) and Albert Powys's *An Old Cottage Saved* (1921) – plus advocacy of modernisation so that a new class of owner could appreciate and enjoy the cottage's charms. Captain P.A. Barron insisted in one such – *The House Desirable* (1929) – that his title referred mostly to the cottage: 'Her charming home [the wealthy woman of today] will describe, very modestly, as her "cottage", for there is something lovable about that term'.[214] The architect Gordon Allen, in *The Cheap Cottage & Small House* (1912), was an early convert to the 'benefits of week-ending',[215] among which he celebrated the urbanite's 'great social use' in 'carrying mental activity into what often are uncivilised districts'.[216]

The list does not include Batsford's topographical 'Face of Britain' series, which encompassed rural architecture; or H.V. Morton's best-selling travelogues from Methuen, which featured numerous passages of cottage nostalgia.[217] Some of the fiction already examined – from Gissing, Webb, Sherriff, et al.; and the autobiographical *Lark Rise to Candleford* by Flora Thompson – also paid homage to the talismanic rural dwelling.

Nearly all of it nostalgic, interwar cottage literature can be seen as meeting demand from the two strains of middle-class cottage enthusiasm set out at the beginning of this chapter – conservationist and acquisitive – and a more general nostalgia. Among the acquisitive, *The Story of My Ruin*'s publishers Herbert Jenkins Ltd had not secured all the early-mover advantage they might have deserved. Major commercial reward

120   Beverley Nichols, author of *Down the Garden Path* (1932), and *A Thatched Roof* (1933), photographed by Bassano Ltd (1937), National Portrait Gallery, London

came to Marion Cran's 1930s' successors: the 'neo-decadent'[218] Beverley Nichols's twin memoirs, in 1932 and 1933, about acquiring and restoring his weekend cottage in Glatton, near Peterborough – *Down the Garden Path* and *A Thatched Roof*; Cecil Roberts's novel *Pilgrim Cottage*, published in 1933, with its seventh reprint in September 1935; and the equally successful sequel, 1934's *The Guests Arrive*, which was given six reprints.

Nichols was 'the epitome of the jazz-age playboy' and moved among celebrities – Cole Porter, Noel Coward, Dame Nellie Melba, and cottage playwright Somerset Maugham.[219] The newly purchased Glatton dated back to 1520, and Nichols's writing about it began magnificently: 'I bought my cottage by sending a wireless to Timbuctoo from the

Mauretania at midnight, with a fierce storm lashing the decks'.[220] Once on dry land, everything became more predictable. His home was, of course, 'an exquisite, thatched cottage . . . with beams that have been twisted by Time into lovely shapes'; the view from the bend in the road was of 'white walls, sturdily timbered'.[221] W.S. Percy called Nichols's Glatton 'the best-known cottage in England today'.[222]

In Cecil Roberts's *Pilgrim Cottage*, the American Mrs Cressington acquires an ancient dwelling near Henley-on-Thames: 'The cottage was shut off by a circular hedge, only the quaint twisted roof, the dormer windows and chimney pots visible'.[223] Mrs C cannot contain herself: 'This cottage must be Elizabethan – you can't find oak like that anywhere else. . . . this is the real thing!'[224] It was certainly close enough to inspire the purchasers of multiple editions. But who were these readers making literary excursions to *Pilgrim Cottage* or to Glatton? Possession of the idea of the cottage was in transition – the traditional shelter of labouring families in the past was slipping further away to find new signification as rural refuge or picturesque weekend space for the middle classes of the future.

The other great discourse of interwar cottage writing was preservationist. Nevill's pioneering *Old Cottage and Domestic Architecture* came in 1889.[225] Then, from 1900 to 1908, Dawber, Ould, Adams, Ashbee, and Curtis Green represented an early Batsford cottage push.[226] More prolific still among the pioneers was the Reverend Peter Hampson Ditchfield, whose first cottage opus – *Picturesque English Cottages and their Doorway Gardens* – arrived in 1905. Ditchfield's prose, inspired by Malton, presaged much that was to come: 'How different are the old cottages of England! . . . of odd, irregular form, with various harmonious colourings, the effects of weather, time and accident'.[227]

Across at least eight further books about English cottages and villages, this emerged as Ditchfield's catechism. In *The Charm of the English Village*, for Batsford, he added a little chauvinism to the mix.[228] *Vanishing England*, published by Methuen, made clear his devotion to Ruskin, but otherwise self-plagiarised. Ditchfield also showed himself

incapable of appreciating the cottage picturesque without disparaging the aesthetics of more recent working-class housing – in the same way that Baldwin and his peers would at the RSA in 1927.[229] The essence of *Vanishing England* was romantic conservation. Ditchfield regretted, as would many after him, 'the bellow of the motor car which like a hideous monster rushes through the old-world villages, startling and killing old, slow-footed rustics'.[230] His aim was 'to check vandalism, to stay the hand of the iconoclast, to prevent the invasion and conquest of the beauties bequeathed to us by our forefathers'.[231]

Another apostle of Basil Oliver's 1929 endeavours had been a collaborator on Ditchfield's *The Charm of the English Village* – Sydney Jones, who provided the book's illustrations. In 1912, Jones was thought worthy of a book all his own: *The Village Homes of England*, in this case published by The Studio. It sustained the Ditchfield credo of cottage adoration: 'old cottages, as we see them . . . fulfil many conditions that make for good architecture, ever present there is a feeling for harmony'.[232]

Ditchfield and Jones were pioneers of the preservationist turn in interwar cottage publishing. Ditchfield became Grand Chaplain of the English Freemasons during the war,[233] but returned pluckily to the cottage conservation front for *The Builder* in 1919, appalled perhaps by the Addison Scheme promise of 500,000 *new* cottages:

> Already many a lovely dell and rustic paradise are disfigured by monotonous rows of hideous cottages, familiar to the denizens of overgrown towns where workmen congregate . . . contrast this with the charming old English thatched and weather-beaten dwellings which visitors to our shores admire so greatly.[234]

A reissue of Gordon Allen's *The Cheap Cottage & Small House* (1919) punctuated a wartime lull in Batsford's new cottage output that came after Oliver's *Old Houses and Village Buildings in East Anglia* (1912) and Ernest Pulbrook's *The English Countryside* (1914). In 1926, Allen's *The Smaller*

House of Today came out. The combination of the government's legislation that year and the RSA's cottage campaign – 'the Government and Royal Society of Arts . . . march together', reported *The Builder* hopefully[235] – seemed to invigorate cottage preservationists. Writing in *The Architectural Review*, John Briarfield saluted the RSA and re-sounded the trumpets: 'public opinion must be roused . . . The cottages of England must be preserved'.[236] Then came Oliver's 1929 book – an adrenaline shot to cottage preservation everywhere.

In the next ten years, Batsford published at least 21 landscape, countryside, or rural architecture titles, encompassing the 'British Heritage' and 'Face of Britain' series – the latter boasting Massingham's *English Downland* (1936) where, even when the cottage was no longer centre stage, it played a supporting role.[237] Sydney Jones's *English Village Homes* (1936) was another of the new Batsford wave – a reworking of his 1912 book – gazetting key cottage survivals, like Oliver; deploying quotation from Mary Webb's *The Golden Arrow*;[238] and distinguishing between 'Picturesque' and 'Solid Georgian' as productively as ever Robert Kerr had done.[239]

Such was the publishers' estimate of public appetite for cottage literature around this time, that they settled for authors who did not always bring the authority of Massingham, Jones, or Oliver. *Strolling through Cottage England*, by W.S. Percy (1936) – one of several *Strolling* titles – came from Collins and is notable less for its scholarship than for the recycling of interwar cottage cliché. 'Evolved from the single great wooden dwelling of the chief of the Saxon invaders,' the English cottage was for Percy – inevitably – 'a part of the soil', 'the most picturesque', 'the work of unknown generations of English workmen', and 'a reflection of the people'. It 'owed its attractiveness to the old porch . . . covered with climbing roses or honeysuckle', and was – when 'time and weather have mellowed and moulded [it] into beauty' – a dwelling of 'indescribable charm'.[240]

In 1938, having sold around 300,000 countryside books in the 'British Heritage' series alone, as Batsford's proprietor, Harry Batsford ventured *The English Cottage* – his fourth collaboration with long-standing friend and company editor Charles Fry[241] – his first to address the sacred dwelling directly. Their preface laid out campaigning ambitions:

> to stimulate the public to a more united effort to defend the rather precarious existence of these little buildings which, often beautiful in themselves, are nearly always a vital ingredient in the beauty of their patch of landscape.[242]

Today, the book is invaluable as a compendium of interwar cottage non-fiction's key themes. It was deeply nostalgic, of course. In 'recalling a time when the English house was almost literally hewed out of the English forest', it had a penchant for mythology. It employed a subtle political mode too: 'the old cottages stand as emblems of that sense of "rugged individualism" which had its roots in the village'. And there were less generous passages too: 'The Rothschild estates, with their fretted bargeboards, bogus timbering, and lurid brick.' Batsford and Fry could never quite resist a snipe – 'old cottages, now falling into disuse and dilapidation . . . an almost endless theme for the musings of the poetaster and the facile brush of the maiden lady'.[243] Most striking today, though, is the book's class-consciousness. Sillars (2022) sees the preservationists' world as 'under threat from excursionists, and in this a class-consciousness is implicit'.[244] But the enemy for Batsford and Fry was not just excursionists. The authors aped Baldwin's habit of celebrating the past by repudiating the present – openly scorning those who lived in recently created working- and lower-middle-class housing.

They began by chastising England's 'vast lethargic public' for stimulating builder and craftsman to produce substandard goods. 'Gullible droves of tourists' were then ticked off for falling for the 'Christmas calendar prettiness' of places like Old Warden in Bedfordshire, and Ickwell, its neighbour. In the countryside, 'the box-like growth of featureless brick cottages . . . like a red and yellow fungus' was mournfully noted.[245] A crescendo of displeasure mounted:

From here it is but a step to the mean little "council houses" which seem nowadays to perch with such malevolent intention to spoil the patch of country in which they stand, the gabled "villas" of the village fringes, and those later "bungalows" whose flushed asbestos roofs lend such disharmony to the rustic half-tones.[246]

The authors concluded:

How one longs nowadays, when moving about the country, to sweep away the litter of the last hundred years or so, the "council houses", the "villas" and the "bungalows" . . . and restore to the solid nuclei of our villages something of that time-honoured seemliness in colour, texture and design achieved by many centuries of quiet usage and destroyed by the incontinence of one.[247]

No fate was specified for the occupants of dwellings that Batsford and Fry wanted swept away. But the authors' fulminations must be considered alongside those of others at the time. W.B. Yeats had given the genre early endorsement in his 1919 edition of *The Wild Swans at Coole*. Enraptured by his newly acquired tower-house, Thoor Ballylee in Galway, the poet cursed any 'limb of the devil' who might 'destroy' his view 'by . . . setting up a cottage/ Planned in a government office'.[248] Without the excuse of poetic licence, Clough Williams-Ellis (1928) would widen the critique to 'mean and perky little houses that surely none but mean and perky little souls should inhabit with satisfaction'.[249] Barron (1929) deplored 'new houses that can only be described as hideous';[250] D.H. Lawrence, the same year, 'a mean and petty scrabble of paltry dwellings called "homes"'.[251] Street (1932) denounced 'Hideous rows of glaring slums';[252] Massingham (1934) regretted dwellings 'built by the County Council . . . diabolically inspired by a cult of ugliness';[253] and even Orwell (1939) bemoaned 'houses, houses, little red cubes of houses all alike'.[254]

It is hard to avoid the suspicion that the besetting sin of the home-loving interwar public, in the minds of the Batsford commentariat and

beyond, was to have dared become visible at all. 'The more we spread out,' wailed *The Builder*, 'the bigger is the blot on the landscape.'[255] Although there was a consensus that the cottage picturesque should be preserved under the control of those who understood 'time-honoured seemliness', new homes for the displaced seemed fated to be held in contempt – demanding, in an Orwellian phrase from *The Times*, 'critical control for the suppression of outrage'.[256]

The two main tendencies of middle-class interwar cottage appropriation, profitably reflected and exploited by England's publishers, began their journeys separately. Their distinct purposes – for one, that the cottage's purchase and renovation should create a picturesque leisure asset to help moneyed weekenders decompress from the tensions of the *urbs*; for the other, that the ancient rural cottage should be preserved to prolong its picturesque architectural value, sustain its contribution to the landscape, and, if possible, rehouse agricultural labourers – started out in contradiction. By the end of the 1930s, they had begun to coalesce. At the RIBA in March 1937, Patrick Abercrombie, founder of the CPRE, was ready to champion the second home, even when it meant rural families moving out: 'I maintain that it is quite possible to put a house which is not suitable to be reconditioned for a working-class family to . . . the use of that much less difficult person to cater for, the weekender'.[257]

Country Life magazine insisted that anyone would see 'in picturesque cottages the most desirable objects in the countryside' and concurred with Abercrombie: 'There can be no doubt that it is better for the rural population to be housed in more up-to-date quarters'. But,

besides their aesthetic value, old cottages play an increasingly important part in modern life by affording an escape . . . to the far more numerous and equally deserving urban workers. By all means, let the new cottages be built; but let the old ones . . . be preserved and made available for holiday purposes.[258]

Let 'new cottages be built' indeed – cottages Abercrombie regarded as 'too often . . . by no means so good as they ought to be'[259] – be built and then disparaged by a multitude from Harry Batsford's address book. With Abercrombie and *Country Life* together in the weekender's corner, middle-class annexation of the rural labourer's traditional cottage was nearly complete.

A 1944 report for the government's Central Housing Advisory Committee would declare: 'we do not think that this taking over of old cottages by the better-to-do is necessarily a bad thing'. It went on to recommend a division of the spoils implicitly on class lines (with my annotations): 'an adequate supply of new cottages [for the working classes] is of course especially necessary wherever this diversion [to the middle classes] of older cottages is taking place'.[260] Lexden and Winstree Rural District Council was just one local authority that had already demonstrated what those 'new cottages' might look like. In other words, here was Whitehall at it again – effectively suggesting that the Picturesque was best saved for the 'better-to-do'.

Unless there was an alternative: a way for 'ordinary' people to recover their (possibly imaginary) lost Elysium; new-build speculative homes with picturesque aesthetics that were beyond the controlling writ of the Ministry of Health. Could such things satisfy a nation's atavistic yearning? The 1930s would answer yes – if you could afford a mortgage. And the next chapter will give an account of this, the cottage picturesque's last and perhaps most consequential phase of interwar significance – manifesting itself to the mass market as the predominant aesthetic in suburban spec-building; available to the middle classes, of course, but, in making itself affordable enough for some among the working classes too, facilitating a kind of social class re-ordering based on domestic aesthetics rather than just employment or income.

5

THE COTTAGE COMMERCIALISED

When it comes to identifying the aesthetic origins of the interwar period's explosion in speculative house building, Christopher Hussey's 1927 insight is invaluable – 'the modern speculating builder's six-roomed house'[1] was indeed essentially picturesque. This chapter discusses how the highly successful interwar construction company Wates Limited – who worked in an architectural style typical of most spec-builders – catered effectively for public taste when they produced homes prefigured by the late eighteenth/early nineteenth-century aesthetics of the cottage picturesque. We will also see how architecture's professional leadership, in refusing to reconcile themselves to such houses, remained defiantly out of sympathy with public preferences.

In Wates's houses, the cottage aesthetics that had been effectively forbidden to the working classes

in social housing found an enduring incarnation. Whereas the weekend boltholes and conservation cases discussed in Chapter 4 both symbolised middle-class appropriation of the cottage idea, the suburban house – inspired by the cottage picturesque – made real bricks and timber available to the millions who could not afford restoration projects as costly as Marion Cran's cottage in Kent. 'Raised close to a spiritual intensity by traditions of literature and painting',[2] the interwar English homemaker's *penchant* for the quasi-mythical dwelling of their ancestors would bring success and standing to Wates's founders.

This emphasis on the Picturesque is not where analysis of interwar speculative building has clustered. Stamp, Scott, Barrett and Phillips, Ballantyne and Law in *Tudoresque*, and Sugg Ryan in *Ideal Homes*, all prefer Tudorism as the key to understanding interwar speculative house aesthetics.[3] Goodhart-Rendel, however, agrees with Hussey: 'In the twenty years between the two last wars . . . whatever the little houses that lined our new roads may not have been, they were undeniably picturesque in intention'.[4]

This was an interpretation shared by numerous commentators at the time. 'We have only to turn,' wrote Percy, 'to the thousands of new suburbs . . . to find that the builders are adopting much of the picturesqueness of the old cottage'.[5] The private-sector style that architect, Unwin-*protégé*, and past-President of the National Housing and Town Planning Council T. Alwyn Lloyd saw around him, he described as:

121   Card No. 11, 'Kingsland, Herefordshire', Player's Cigarettes, *Picturesque Cottages* (1929)

symbolical of some incurable sentimentality of which the Englishman is so often accused . . . he wants his new suburban home to have something about it that he associates with his idea of the country cottage.[6]

Randal Phillips, editor of *Homes and Gardens*, recognised the same *leit-motif*: 'the traditional manner of the English country cottage'.[7] Outsiders saw it too. Harvard philosopher George Santayana believed that England's architecture became more 'English in growing picturesque'.[8] The Danish architect and town planner Steen Eiler Rasmussen concluded in 1937 that the English 'do not want to live in street houses any longer . . . they want a cottage . . . with old oak beams looking as if it had been inherited from the great-grandparents'.[9] A recognition of the ubiquitous visual appeal of cottage picturesque abounded even in contemporary fiction – from Aldous Huxley in 1921 to George Orwell in 1939. Huxley's character Scogan pontificates in *Crome Yellow*:

> civilized and sophisticated men have solemnly played at being peasants. Hence quaintness, arts and crafts, cottage architecture and all the rest of it. . . . reduplicated in endless rows, studiedly quaint imitations and adaptations of the village hovel.[10]

Eighteen years later, Orwell made his hard-to-like George Bowling grumble about the same thing: 'As for the picturesqueness, the sham countrified stuff . . . it merely gives me the sick. Whatever we were in the old days, we weren't picturesque'.[11] Towards the end of the Second World War, John Gloag, stalwart of the interwar design commentariat, consolidated these impressions of the twentieth-century English suburb: a 'form of romantic architecture . . . satisfying the householder's desire for picturesque and cosy surroundings. Suburban villas . . . like enlarged cottages'.[12]

Shaw, Voysey, Baillie Scott – proponents of nineteenth-century Old English (a term employed by the Picturesque's theorists in the 1820s[13]) – had all built in the picturesque tradition without

necessarily acknowledging it. Brittain-Catlin records Philip Webb's embarrassment about the 'affected picturesqueness' of his own work at Morris's Red House in Bexleyheath.[14] On the eve of the First World War, it was the cottage that Geoffrey Scott singled out as problematic: 'While the Georgian taste sought to impart to the cottage the seemly distinction of the manor, the modern preference is to make the manor share in the Romantic charm of the cottage'.[15]

Today, utilising this nexus of cottage visuality and the Picturesque as a heuristic for the aesthetics of interwar private-enterprise homes usefully helps interrogate the Tudor consensus while revealing the links between speculative building, arguments about council cottage aesthetics in 1918–22, and the multiplex appropriation of the cottage picturesque by the middle classes in the 1920s.

ARCHITECTS AND THE COTTAGE

At the turn of the 1920s and 1930s, domestic aesthetics for the masses were not securely under the direction of English architecture's ruling cabal at the RIBA. Architects had gone from congratulating themselves on seizing control of the popular cottage's future in 1918[16] to a bitter divorce from those golden prospects at the instigation of the government's Director-General of Housing, Sir Charles Ruthen, in January 1922.[17] The years afterwards were a time for wound-licking – during which the 'New Old-World House'[18] sprang up around almost every town in the country.

RIBA-approved professionals carried on designing higher-end bespoke homes, and coffee-table books celebrated their achievement – from the Architectural Press, edited by Frederick Chatterton in 1926; and from *Country Life*'s publishers, edited by Randal Phillips (as Hon. ARIBA, a tribune of the architectural profession) from 1923 to 1936.[19]

In the 1924 Phillips collection *Small Family Houses*, the architect-survivors of Addison Scheme cottage building were to be found re-fighting old battles between formal and Picturesque. Of the 35 designs featured, ranging in build-cost from £1,000 to £3,000, 15 were neo-Georgian – and a third of those were drawn up by old friends Adshead and Ramsey or by Samuel Bridgman Russell. The anti-picturesque fervour of the latter, no longer on the staff at the Health Ministry, was undimmed. What is almost certainly his commentary, accompanying his design for a neo-Georgian six-bedder, disparaged 'houses tricked out with little bay windows and leaded oriels, and well barge-boarded in keeping with a hazy notion of "old-worldness"'.[20] The book's introduction, written by Phillips, seemed inadvertently to confirm that English architects continued to listen to the public with a tin ear: 'striving after effect is always a bad thing to do in building a house, as we may see in many an effort which is aggressively Olde Englishe'.[21]

In the 1927 round-up – *The Modern English House* – anti-picturesque rhetoric was given another outing: 'Worst of all is that modern method of building . . . which consists of nailing strips of wood to a brick fabric and putting a lick of plaster between'.[22] And there was no let-up the following year. *The 1,000 Pound House* in 1928 offered an £1,100, three-bedroom design by Longden & Venables, garlanded for its freedom 'from the false trappings that disfigure so many of the small houses now being erected all over the country – chiefly the work of builders who have no sense of architectural values'.[23]

Possibly because of this endless criticism, by 1934 RIBA architects were winning, according to the Institute's journal, as little as 5 per cent of house design work in England and Wales.[24] Between the Armistice and 31 March 1934, 2.33 million new dwellings had gone up.[25] If the RIBA's 5 per cent figure was right, much of that building did not generate an architect's fee.

Awareness among RIBA's leadership that the profession might benefit from connecting better with the public on a range of topics had led to the foundation of the Institute's Public Relations Committee in May 1933.[26] One of its principal concerns from the outset was what members saw as the poor standard of speculative house building. In February 1934, a RIBA Journal editorial commented:

> it is generally agreed that the design of the majority of the small houses built in speculative schemes is deplorably low . . . Every house built by the speculative builder according to the popular notions – half-timber and all that – is another brick on the awful monument of bad precedent.[27]

RIBA's Public Relations Committee formed a Sub-Committee to undertake research into the phenomenon – No. 3, on House Design – which was charged with trying to understand how such horrors could possibly appeal to the house-buying public.[28] Was it all, Trystan Edwards wondered later, just 'some big, blind delusion'?[29] The RIBA's implied hypothesis was Marxian. A false consciousness had taken root in people's minds: 'The builder does it because the public likes it; the public is persuaded to like it because it is all he is given; the builder does it again because the public seemed to like it the first time, and so on'.[30]

The Sub-Committee appointed as convener the formalist Stanley Ramsey, who we first encountered working with Adshead on the Duchy of Cornwall's cottages in Kennington around 1911. Ramsey had featured in Randal Phillips's 1927 book, working again with Adshead, to offer a plain neo-Georgian house with 'an outer skin of metal sheathing, encased in cement plaster and an inner skin of breeze concrete slabs', plus a roof 'also of concrete and steel overlaid with tiles'.[31] Fellow members of the Sub-Committee included other RIBA insiders – *inter al.*, T. Alwyn Lloyd and Arthur Kenyon (both implicated in the disappointing sales at Laing's Sunnyfields Estate at Mill Hill, north London, from 1935)[32] and Charles Holloway James.[33] Lloyd, it must be said, did not begin the RIBA inquiry in 1934 with a completely open mind. He thought speculative builders' houses

> devoid of taste or suitability to modern requirements. They are either vulgarly ostentatious, with a riot of ill-proportioned gables and windows, or merely dull replicas of the pre-war suburban street. . . . it is almost impossible to find a gable that is without its restless barge boards or mock

122 An example of non-approved house building from the RIBA's House Design Sub-Committee investigations in April 1934, 'The Architect and Housing by the Speculative Builder', *Journal of the Royal Institute of British Architects*, vol.41, no.12, 28 April 1934, p.650, The Bodleian Libraries, University of Oxford

half-timber. Why is it that house purchasers, even those of some education and discrimination in other matters, have a liking for such "features" as these?[34]

Rhetoric like this had grown more common through the 1920s. The Irish essayist Robert Wilson Lynd, a columnist at the *New Statesman*, mused in 1926: 'It is a strange thing that . . . no-one has ever thought of making building a crime'.[35] Clough Williams-Ellis – architect and CPRE activist – published the highly regarded *England and the Octopus* in 1928, in which he insisted that it was 'the English people [who] need mass psycho-analysis . . . False values and insensitiveness – particularly to beauty – these are probably at the root of the problem'.[36] The honorary legal counsel at the CPRE, Sir Leslie Scott (a Conservative MP until 1929), agreed: 'the meaningless ornamentation of post-war villadom . . . demonstrate[s] in so many of the general public an almost complete absence of taste'.[37] And in the early 1930s, design reformer John Gloag let rip with a now famous outburst: 'Why are you, or perhaps your neighbours, living in an imitation Tudor house, with

stained wooden slats shoved onto the front of it to make it look like . . . a half-timbered house?'[38]

Was this anything more than snobbery? The social-climbing novelist Evelyn Waugh had taken against 'Elizabethan' architecture as early as 1925, 'owing to the vulgarities of Stratford-upon-Avon'.[39] He lent his prejudices to the fictional Margot Beste-Chetwynde, who could not 'think of anything more bourgeois and awful than timbered Tudor architecture'.[40] In 1950, Lutyens's daughter Ursula, Lady Ridley – sufficiently above the salt even for Waugh – went so far as to welcome the demolition of her father's Papillon Hall, near Market Harborough, on the grounds of its 'Kingston By Pass manner in roughcast, which is always ugly, and a lot of half-timber bogosity'.[41] Sacheverell Sitwell protested by adopting the term 'magpie', so completely did he believe that the suburbs had debased black and white half-timber.[42] Enthusiasm for such things among the masses seems to have created what Macarthur calls 'objects of phobic disgust'[43] – architectural targets for an intelligentsia ('a very ugly word for a

123 An example of approved house architecture that the public would not buy – from the RIBA's House Design Sub-Committee investigations, April 1934, 'The Architect and Housing by the Speculative Builder', *Journal of the Royal Institute of British Architects*, vol.41, no.12, 28 April 1934, p.652, The Bodleian Libraries, University of Oxford

very ugly thing', quipped Baldwin[44]) repelled by the tastes of the less expensively educated.

When the RIBA's House Design Sub-Committee lodged its first report in April 1934, snobbery and speculation were forced to defer to research. Committee members had 'inspected a number of recent speculative estates [covering] all sizes and prices of house and all kinds of development from the semi-rural to the urban'.[45] They particularly 'endeavoured to appreciate the point of view of the builders and their public', reported RIBA's Journal, 'and as a result have come to some interesting conclusions'.[46]

The first was that the builder 'prefers to build what he knows he can sell' – a lesson surely worth assimilating. The Sub-Committee also found there was little jerry-building going on: 'A large class of speculative builder builds very soundly, if simply, and provides good value' – another canard laid to rest.[47] Then the report worked through a series of photographs. The terraced houses shown in their Figure 5 (fig.122), sold 'readily' at about £550, and

'belong . . . to a very popular type'. Their dwarf cross-wing gables, token timbering, gabled porches, and two-storey bow windows all paid asymmetric tribute to the cottage picturesque, but they were busy enough to antagonise RIBA purists. 'The elevations may not appeal to an architect, who may want to clean up or remove the "features". None the less, they represent good value to the lower-paid clerk.'[48]

It got worse. Not only did the 'lower-paid clerk' like the *wrong* thing, but they had complex 'psychological' reasons for disliking the right thing. Of the RIBA's Figure 10 (fig.123), Ramsey's sub-committee said: 'these houses are the kind of thing which the speculative builder finds hard to sell'. Further:

> They are, in fact, too like the municipal housing scheme to live in, which implies that one belongs to a lower social class. Many speculative builders have in the past employed architects only to find . . . that the latter's production will not sell because it resembles a "council" house.[49]

A difficult finding, it was one the Sub-Committee reported twice. The 'fussy, "feature"-bespattered elevation'[50] – which the building societies were happy to fund, builders happy to build, and the public seemed happy to buy – kept on selling because, among other things, it did not 'look like municipal housing – a psychological point which it is fatal for the speculative builder to overlook'.[51] The report's author knew that they were delivering an uncomfortable message. Their attempt to ensure it was heard is worth quoting at length:

> It is easy to raise hands in pious horror, to jeer at bad taste or stigmatise apparently unworthy social ideas. It is much more difficult to understand causes and to find cures for poor design . . . Looking at some of these illustrations, readers may be inclined to exclaim "What awful houses to find in the pages of the RIBA Journal!" It is much worse that they are to be found all over England. To examine the causes of, and to find cures for, this state of affairs is one of the difficult tasks before the RIBA Public Relations Committee.[52]

This is an admission of sorts that the leaders of the architectural profession had become estranged from the public. Rapidly absorbing the RIBA report, the house builders' trade journal *The National Builder* responded in June 1934: 'It is the fashion in certain quarters to condemn this gigantic effort to provide better homes for our fellow citizens'. The RIBA's finding about the subjective unattractiveness of many council houses was endorsed – 'the English public is by nature conservative and snobbish' – and a bullish conclusion reached: 'it is useless to lecture the builder . . . the first task of architects is to convince [him] that they have something . . . valuable to contribute to his enterprise'.[53]

The RIBA was left squarely to confront the fact that the public did not seem to share its leadership's taste for stripped-back formality in small-house aesthetics. Academic researchers Whitehand and Carr suggest RIBA's figure of 5 per cent involvement for architects in speculative house-building (re-estimated in 1938 by Stanley Ramsey at 20 per cent)[54] was also wrong. Study of planning applications for the interwar period in Birmingham shows – even with the definition of architect narrowed to RIBA membership – that more like 35 per cent of spec-housing schemes had architect involvement.[55] In the mid-1930s, this was a state of affairs either not known to the RIBA or too unpleasant to acknowledge. The conclusion that significant numbers of RIBA architects were engaged in designing for spec-builders allows us to infer that part of the profession had a perfectly serviceable understanding of what builders wanted. For the 1934 RIBA research to come as a surprise to the organisation's upper echelons suggests a profession split between an ideologically purist leadership and a rank-and-file readier to turn their hand to whatever picturesqueness the builder believed was needed.

There are echoes here of where we began – with the RIBA-belittled architect entrants to the government's 1918 cottage design competition, who had produced predominantly picturesque designs; 'the cottage of the past', in Adshead's cursory dismissal.[56] Thanks to the House Design Sub-Committee, it was now clear that those competitors were not wrong about public aesthetic enthusiasms. Perhaps their efforts had deserved a more considered response than Health Ministry pabulum in 1919 and 1920 about the 'simple lines and good proportion'[57] of the formal architecture that government and the profession's leadership favoured.

RIBA's research suggests the Local Government Board/Tudor Walters aesthetic formula had been a municipal-housing recipe for class alienation. Mass construction of state-funded council dwellings for the working classes was an undertaking radical enough in 1919 without an insistence on designing the new cottages to look decidedly different from the culturally established English home. The importance of government architect Manning Robertson's *ukase*, in 1920, against cottages with 'sham half-timber, superabundant gables and bay windows endlessly repeated'[58] can be seen more clearly in this light. Public architectural

124   Peter Behrens's revolutionary house 'New Ways' (1926) in the Northampton suburbs contrasted starkly with its picturesque neighbours (just as Roger Fry's formalist 'Durbins' had in Guildford). Some among RIBA's leadership hoped modernism would prove more appealing to the house-buying masses than stripped down neo-Georgian formalism had done, *The Architectural Review*, vol.60, no.360, November 1926, p.177

preferences, revealed by operation of the market after 1923, *were* understood by the Health Ministry's architects immediately after the war. RIBA's research exposes architecture's leadership as more interested in its own preferences – in 1934 as in 1918 – than it was in the aesthetic leanings of the home-making classes.

Rather than force the profession to reflect on all this, the Sub-Committee offered the RIBA a way out. Alwyn Lloyd had previewed it in his February 1934 article: 'some argue that modernism . . . is the right solution'. He was worried though that 'Flat roofs, glass fronts and the other motifs associated with it are too big a departure from . . . tradition and practice'.[59] Two months later, the House Design Sub-Committee rediscovered Alwyn Lloyd's

lifeboat and clambered aboard. It was, they said, 'in the growing demand for "modern" houses [the architect] can do most'. They had 'no doubt that . . . the "modern house" is just what [the owner] wants', so long as it was not too 'arty' and did not border on the 'bizarre'.[60] This was the RIBA, in a kind of slow motion, threatening to compound one mistake about public taste with its next.

Why were the profession's leaders so convinced that suburban Picturesque was beyond the pale? Was it because its informality and lack of hard-learned rules devalued their professional training and expertise? Beresford Pite had foreseen the difficulty in 1919. Writing in *The Architects' Journal*, he had called on architects back then for 'the surrender of the exterior' – continuing: 'even the ambitions and painful ornaments beloved of the cheap house builder will in due course pass from the ridiculous to the sublime'.[61] After the Second World War, the architectural journalist J.M. Richards captured the empowered mood of a Labour-electing *demos* by daring to ask whether anything blameworthy had actually occurred. Of the vilified, interwar, spec-built suburban house, he observed:

> Most significant . . . is the universality of its appeal . . . If democracy means anything, it means deciding – for a change – to pay some attention to the expressed preference of the majority, to what people themselves want, not what we think they ought to want.[62]

People had, by and large, liked this kind of house well enough to buy it. At a RIBA gathering in 1938, the architect Ingham Ashworth, later professor of architectural design at the University of Sydney, admitted as much: 'I have come to the conclusion . . . that the public are getting what they really want'.[63] Was the fact that RIBA architects had not been very much involved – or worse still, that they had been involved and the Institute's leaders did not want to know – really a problem for anyone but the RIBA? A contemporary verse from the novelist (and Kensington vicar) George Birmingham encapsulates the debate:

> *Ah! Me! With wider vision*
> *Perhaps I should forgive*
> *The horrid little houses*
> *Where happy people live!*[64]

'WATES-BUILT IS WELL-BUILT'

In 1935 came George V's rapturously welcomed Silver Jubilee. Wates Limited – a family building company in the London suburb of Norbury, by this time probably the second largest house builder in the country[65] – decided to mark the occasion. Celebrating a perhaps less-familiar interval, the company produced a photographic capriccio, '34 Years of Quality Building', for inclusion in its estate sales brochures (fig.125). It depicted just the kind of houses – 'where happy people live' – that Wates had been building since 1901.[66]

The image was a montage of the irregular suburban Picturesque that had triggered Hussey's epiphany in 1927. Gables abounded, as did roughcast, and bay windows (canted, rectangular, and bow), most of them tile-hung. There were catslide roofs, pent-roofed porches, prominent chimneystacks, jettied first storeys, casement windows, round windows, dormer windows – even gablets. Across the 34 years, Sitwell's abhorred suburban black and white timbering was conspicuous too – on a cross-wing gable or a swept-roof porch; sometimes ornamenting much of a first storey. The whole image makes unignorable the aesthetic legacy of the Picturesque. This was mass-produced scenographic or facadist architecture that the Arts and Crafts – with its emphasis on craft skills, local traditions, authentic materials, and practitioner fulfilment – simply does not elucidate.

Wates's visual *précis* of their architectural history also displayed the key aesthetic tropes in popular, owner-occupier home building that the government's Director-General of Housing, Sir Charles Ruthen, had effectively ruled out for council tenants in 1922. It was a visual tribute to – or parody of, depending on your perspective – the appearance of the ancient cottage architecture that the government and the Royal Society of Arts had spent 1926 onwards trying to protect.

A decade earlier, in *The Architectural Review*, W.G. Newton summarised popular taste in domestic architecture as 'natural man's home picture':

> The house he pictures as the background of his life must be pretty . . . He likes plenty of sugar in his tea and in his house as well. So, we will have a base course or plinth of bright red bricks, pebble-dashed walls above, and a hint of half-timber in the jaunty small gable . . . a front door with a round-glazed opening, for variety and to get away from straight lines as much as possible; for straight lines are ugly.[67]

34 YEARS OF QUALIT

1901

1908

1925

1926

1928

1929

1932

1934

BUILDING

1916

1927

1930

1935

125 Wates photographic capriccio showing houses from estates built between 1901 and 1935, Wates Archive, Box WA19, Item 452

Newton's view was a snobbish but largely accurate description of spec-builder output. Horsey corroborates it in his work later, outlining the dominant private-sector domestic exterior – in the trade language of the time, the 'so-called spec style'. It was a visuality whose origins could be traced jointly, says Horsey, to 'the Queen Anne style of Shaw and Godwin' and to 'a primitive vernacular, in the work, notably, of Voysey and Baillie Scott'.[68] Hussey, though, had ventured a more totalising interpretation in 1927, rooted in a more choate English domestic architectural tradition: 'Blenheim is picturesque,' he had written; 'so is the modern speculating builder's six-roomed house, with its sham half-timbering, unbalanced fenestration, bay window, and terra-cotta dragon on the gable'.[69] Hussey encapsulates the Wates aesthetic in its entirety, invoking also the designs of Picturesque movement cottage architects such as James Malton and Thomas Frederick Hunt.

It is worth remembering how Malton's 1798 *Essay on British Cottage Architecture* had described the ideal cottage:

> of odd, irregular form, with various, harmonious colouring, the effect of weather, time and accident . . . A porch at entrance; irregular breaks in the direction of the walls; one part higher than another; various roofing of different materials, thatch particularly, boldly projecting; fronts partly built of . . . brick, partly weatherboarded and partly brick-noggin dashed; casement window lights . . .[70]

Minus the thatch, Malton could have been describing a 1936 Wates semi in Beulah Hill. Ballantyne and Law describe Malton's book as 'most significant for the developing sense of the Tudoresque',[71] but Malton had little use for the word 'Tudor' – he cited Price and Knight, and referred repeatedly to the Picturesque. That his version of cottage ideality prefigured Wates Limited's successful commercial architecture by over 120 years is very much the point.

126 The most active family members in the early days of Wates. Clockwise from top left: Edward, Arthur, Ronald Wallace and Norman Edward. Photographs from Wates's Briardene Estate brochure (1936), Wates Archive, Box WA19, Item 452

A FAMILY BUSINESS

Tradition dated Wates's first house building experiment to a 'modest commencement' in 1901[72] – the work of company founder Edward Wates (1873–1944), third born in a family of 11 children. A resourceful Streatham salesman who specialised in furnishing and removals, he was joined in 1904 by his brother Arthur (1880–1956) to establish the partnership Messrs E. & A. Wates,[73] which opened

127   Wates's third Head Office, at 1258–1260 London Road, Norbury, London SW16, by Fry, Drew & Partners; architectural formality for their institutional HQ from providers, almost exclusively, of the domestic Picturesque. Wates's Olympia brochure (1938), Museum of Domestic Design and Architecture, Middlesex University

128   From Wates's Olympia brochure (1938), p.39, Museum of Domestic Design and Architecture, Middlesex University

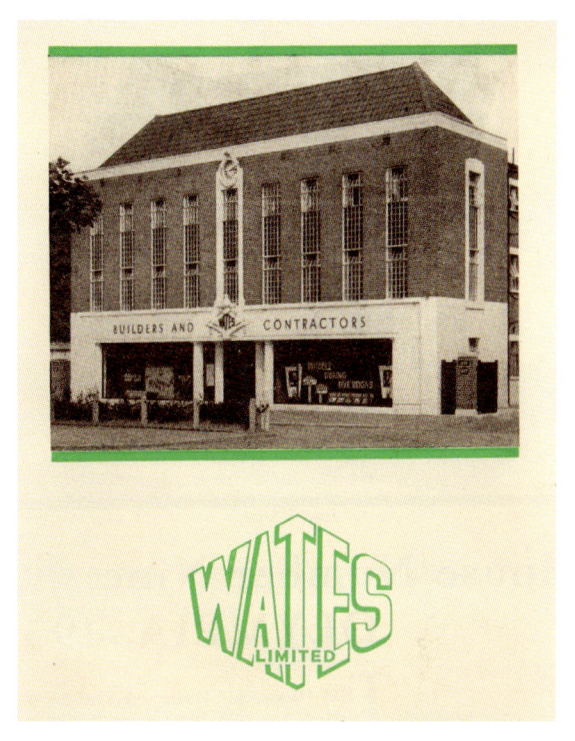

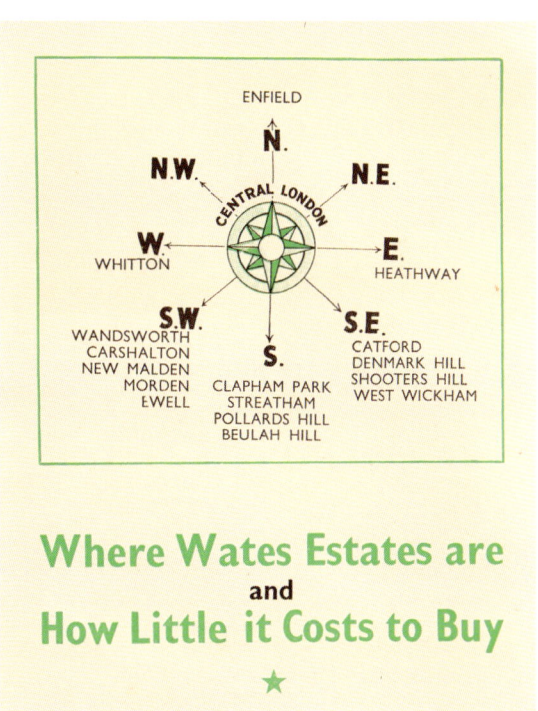

a furniture shop on Mitcham Lane in 1905. In 1909, they were joined by a third brother, William (1883–1924), and house construction became their principal concern.[74]

The Wates brothers, and in due course Edward's sons Norman Edward (1905–69) and Ronald Wallace (1907–86), turned out to have a considerable gift for the trade. By the late 1930s, they were directors of a major building company. They had a handsome, architecturally formal head office in the London suburb of Norbury, designed by Fry, Drew & Partners (fig.127); and a reorganisation between 1934 and 1935[75] that had given the firm separate departments for legal affairs, surveying, architecture, road-making, sewerage, procurement, and accounts.[76] It was this organisational structure that they credited with enabling construction on a score or more housing estates simultaneously. The company newsletter for 19 November 1938 boasted '26 estates engaged in normal building activities, giving employment to thousands of men in seven different counties (Kent, Surrey, Middlesex, Essex, London, Warwickshire and Oxfordshire)'.[77]

Every new Wates estate was set up as a distinct organisational entity, its material requirements – the 4,824,000 bricks, 1,211,500 roof tiles, 838,000 feet of roof battens, and over 50 miles of mouldings required, for example, by the Wilverley Park Estate, in New Malden, Surrey, under construction 1934–35[78] – serviced by the company's specialist teams. At the same time as the reorganisation, the company launched a staff

WATES HOUSE NEWS

No 1.   JUNE 1935   PRICELESS.

Building for the Future

THE FIRST ISSUE OF A
JOURNAL PRODUCED BY
AND IN THE INTERESTS
OF THE STAFF OF THE
HOUSE OF WATES

magazine, *Wates House News*, first published in June 1935 and edited by staffer Charles Mitchell, who would go on to become the company's General Manager.[79] Intended to promote communication across the silos of a complex business, the magazine was baptised with a message from Norman Edward, one of the second-generation directors: 'Good luck to Wates House News! . . . there is a real need for a journal which will help to knit us together'.[80]

Also contributing to that first edition was the man behind the external aesthetics of Wates homes in the 1930s, the company's Chief Architect Kenneth William Bland. Before joining Wates in 1933 as a 24-year-old, Bland served his articles (1925–28) with the Camberley architect and watercolourist Briant Poulter, and attended lectures at the London County Council School of Building (1925–29) and the Royal Academy Schools (1929–34).[81] In common with many more established architects, he considered 'current public taste in Architecture decidedly capable of improvement'.[82] But more of his thinking was to be found in the article that he wrote for the launch edition of *Wates House News*. Headlined 'We can still learn from the Past', it revealed his primary aesthetic inspiration as the ancient English cottage:

131   'Collingwood' at Bagshot Heath in Surrey. More Picturesque from Kenneth Bland's mentor Briant Poulter, in *The Studio Yearbook of Decorative Art* (1911), p.65, The Bodleian Libraries, University of Oxford

overleaf, pp 174–5

132   House at Streatham for Messrs Wates Ltd, designed by Kenneth W. Bland (1937). The influence of his tutor Briant Poulter is apparent in key picturesque features: asymmetric swept gable over porch, prominent chimneystacks, tile-hanging, canted two-storey bay, and leaded casements, RIBA Archive RAN 54/F/1

> This being Jubilee year . . . it is particularly suitable that some reference should be made in these pages to the oldest and strongest of our traditions . . . Nothing illustrates the English character so clearly as our wealth

HOUSE AT STREATHAM FOR MESSR.

ATES LTD.

GROUND FLOOR

FIRST FLOOR

KENNETH W. BLAND
ARCHITECT. 1937

133 Wates's competitor New Ideal Homesteads Ltd's brochure displays off-the-peg picturesque in their 'A' and 'LC' type interwar houses. Museum of Domestic Design and Architecture, Middlesex University

of cottages built by the forefathers of the present day man-in-the-street . . . Our cottage building tradition has remained practically unchanged from earliest times . . . old buildings always look just right.[83]

We see Bland positioning Wates's houses here as part of an aesthetic tradition established by the Picturesque's revival and commoditisation of the medieval English cottage at the beginning of the nineteenth century. A Wates house's external visuality was in no sense an innovation. Neither was it a reaction to the Health Ministry's council house designs of 1919 (though its aesthetic differences from such designs were crucial). Rather, it represented a proud and self-conscious continuity in the essential visuality of the English cottage home – as analysed by the theorists of the Picturesque; as propagated by the writers of early nineteenth-century cottage pattern books; as sustained by Shaw, Devey, Voysey, and Baillie Scott; and as debated to and fro by critics and enthusiasts ever since the turn of the nineteenth and twentieth centuries.

Proud of Wates's commitment to fundamentals – 'sound, straightforward building, without unnecessary frills' – Bland would show in his designs of the late 1930s (fig.132) an attachment to the Picturesque, as practised by his mentor Briant Poulter across Kent and Surrey (figs 130 and 131), that left little doubt as to where his heart lay.

WATES'S BRIARDENE ESTATE

Spring 1935 came amid the most vigorous phase of England's interwar private-sector building boom. Well over 50 per cent of new-builds went up in the six years between 1933 and 1938,[84] and one of the Wates estates joining the stampede was Briardene in 'lovely' Carshalton, among London's southern suburbs.[85] In 1936, R.C. Sherriff – author of the anti-war play *Journey's End* – wrote a novel, *Greengates*, in which his characters Mr and Mrs Baldwin (the name no coincidence, surely) leave their mid-Victorian terrace in the metropolis for a new suburban house. Sherriff caught the mood of the moment:

> Estates jostled with each other and pushed their attractions eagerly . . . The Meadow Hall Estate was exquisitely situated in a centuries old garden; the Pitberry Hill Estate offered a glorious view over three of nature's most favoured counties; the Chawley Down Estate invited one to enjoy a breeze that blew one's cares away.[86]

Just as in *Greengates*, potential purchasers needing a lift to see a Wates show house were invited to make use of the company's luxury car service (fig.134). And the dwellings they would have been shown on arrival at Briardene were more affordable than the £1,250 the fictional Mr Baldwin was ready to spend.[87]

134 The Wates Car Service offered potential purchasers a lift to see the show houses, Briardene Estate brochure, Wates Archive, Box WA19, Item 452

Built in short terraces of four or six, they were marketed as 'Type B' for the 'centre house', and 'Type A' for the end-of-terrace – 'virtually semi-detached'. Type As sold at £570 freehold or £420 for a 99-year lease.[88] Wates called them 'To-day's greatest value in modern building achievement'. Both had three bedrooms and two reception rooms, but the accommodation was cramped. The Type A's 'Drawing Room' at 119ft^2, and its 'Best Bedroom' at 114.5ft^2, were both smaller than the Tudor Walters

Report's cottage recommendations.[89] Furthermore, the affordable selling price meant there was little spare money for the external frills or ostentatious features that Kenneth Bland professed to find objectionable in competitors' work.[90]

The basic architectural vocabulary was, nonetheless, asymmetric cottage picturesque. Externally, Type A end-houses on Briardene (fig.135) were distinguished by large tile-hung cross-wing gables, decorative arrow-loops at the apex, jettied out over the ground storey on Voysey-esque brackets.[91] Type B houses, in the centre of the blocks, were similarly eclectic, rendered in white-painted roughcast throughout, with two-storey canted bay windows. Round-arched front-door apertures articulated by facing brick surrounds completed the stylistic *pot-pourri*. The windows were casements – 'wood . . . of approved type' at the front; 'Crittall Guaranteed Metal Framed Windows' at the back.[92] *In toto*, Briardene's architecture most recalls the cottages designed by Pearson and Sutcliffe at Brentham Garden Suburb in Ealing – the same concoction of gables, canted bays, tile-hanging, render, and red facing bricks[93] – a 'healthy and picturesque environment', in the 1912 words of the Ealing suburb's promoters.[94]

Wates, like the builders RIBA had interviewed in Spring 1934, believed house appearance mattered to potential buyers. Their 1930s' brochures extolled the exterior visuality of their homes: 'the greatest possible thought and care have been devoted to both the external appearance and the internal planning'.[95]

135 Wates's Type A and B houses – Briardene Estate brochure, March 1935, Wates Archive, Box WA19, Item 452

Type As at Briardene were blessed with 'a wide, sweeping gable, giving the front elevation a most attractive and imposing appearance'. The tile-hanging provided 'a pleasing variation to the adjoining houses' – granting the customer with deeper pockets than his Type B neighbour a little more picturesque for his money.[96] Type Bs were saved from betraying their economical origins altogether by that Ruskinian essential, 'wide bays extending up to the eaves – presenting delightful elevations'.[97] Echoing the way that house aesthetics at Briardene were mediated using the language of the Picturesque, so too was their location in the suburbs:

> with its quaint setting of old-world houses, the visitor to Carshalton would find it hard to realise that this delightful spot is less than 30 minutes from the City . . . to-day it successfully blends the charm of the past with the demands of the future. The Town Centre is probably unique in its picturesque beauty.[98]

RUNNING THE COMPANY

Aesthetics were a matter for the company architect and the marketing department – not, it appears, the day-to-day concern of Wates's directors. In this, the company was not unique. Interviewed for *The National Builder* in 1933, Harold Neal, of the smaller London building firm Messrs Harry Neal Ltd, was asked about his houses' exterior style, and had only a little to say: 'We find that a good bay is still appreciated'.[99] At Wates, the directors' Day Book, covering the years 1932–38, records senior management's quotidian preoccupations. Meetings were usually attended by Edward, his brother Arthur, and Edward's sons Norman Edward and Ronald Wallace. Occasionally, Edward's third son, Allan Charles – who joined the company in 1930 and took control of the contracting business in 1935 – turned up too.

Early in the 1930s, the assembled directors debated the houses themselves and their pricing – a possible new small type for the Rosedene Estate in Croydon, which would sell for £495 freehold (cheaper even than Briardene's Type Bs);[100] and a more expensive three-bed house, possibly for the Newstead Estate near West Wickham, which they discussed selling leasehold at £1,095 (on a build cost of £625; a handsome profit).[101] The main recurring theme, though, was land. In August 1932, Ronald Wallace was deputed to offer £12 10s per square foot for ground the directors fancied at Beckenham; Norman Edward was tasked with offering Merton College, Oxford, up to £500 per acre for 20 acres of land at New Malden.[102] They needed it – plans for 1934 envisaged erecting 2,252 houses.[103]

Wellings describes the company as 'brilliantly led in the interwar period'.[104] Second-generation director Norman Edward was renowned among Wates's staff for his dynamism, his 'electric air'.[105] This was evident in Wates's in-house magazine from 1935. The company's founder directors Edward and Albert were salesmen, pioneering an early form of direct marketing by door-to-door distribution of illustrated postcards (fig.136) for their pre-1914 houses. *Wates House News* in September 1935 showed the company's commercial philosophy had not grown flabby with age: 'Wates build houses in order to sell them . . . before deciding on a piece of land we have to make sure the market's there and build the right type of house to attract the buyer'.[106]

'It's Action That Counts,' roared a correspondent in the same edition: 'You salesmen – when next you meet a prospective purchaser, don't wait for him to buy a house – walk right up to him and sell him one.'[107]

Wates prized its sales force. Incentivisation of salesmen appeared on the agenda for directors;

136   Postcard used for door-to-door marketing by E. & A. Wates for their pre-1914 estate development around Croydon, in Nick Barratt, *Wates: A Family Business* (London: Profile Editions, 2022), p.28, Wates Archive

THE KING OF SALESMEN

Ever Felt Like This ?

His recipe:
Six wives in
one life.

Our recipe:
Six sales in
one day.

137   Motivational cartoon in the Tudor style, aimed at the sales team, *Wates House News*, No. 2, September 1935, Wates Archive, Box WA67, Item 46 (PD/WN/6)

motivational cartoons featured in the company magazine; and the expense of joining the Ideal Home Exhibition's model village was regarded as a sage investment in new sales leads: 'thousands of happy seekers of homes and free samples . . . pouring through the turnstiles and . . . through our own noble edifice'.[108] The company's Sales Manager in the mid-1930s, A.W. Madger, told the in-house magazine: 'I really do not know of more pleasant products to sell than Wates-built houses'.[109] But he knew he had to keep his sales force hungry too. At the 'Quotabusters' Dinner' in December 1937, target-beating colleagues were treated to supper at the Florence Restaurant in London's Rupert Street, W1. 'To say everybody enjoyed themselves would be putting it mildly,' reported *Wates House News*: 'Mr Wildsmith excelled himself at the piano and with a story concerning an elephant'; 'Mr Madger's contribution received a roar of applause'; and 'Frank (de-la-Zouche) Ashby' provided what the magazine called 'special music . . . rendered on his piano-accordion'.[110]

WATES'S WILVERLEY PARK ESTATE, 1935

Representatives of this vaudevillian sales team had been hard at work marketing another new Wates estate back in 1935 – Wilverley Park in Malden – further west in London's southern suburbs than Briardene and more upmarket. 'Houses of to-day in the Tranquillity of Yesterday,' promised the brochure; 'at Wilverley Park the air blows fresh and clean from the sunny south.'[111]

Briardene's mini terraces were not the staple here. Top of the billing instead was 'that misshapen key to the English suburb – the semi-detached house'.[112] And retail prices for the range of dwellings available – from the three-bed, two-reception Tudor Major (TMP) semi at £649, and Tudor DeLuxe (TDL) semi at £680; to the semi-detached, three-bed, two-reception Chalet-type SC3 at £819; or the fully detached, four-bed, two-reception Chalet-type C4 at £920 (all freehold prices) – allowed Wates's architect Kenneth Bland free rein with his predilection for cottage picturesque.

House Number Nine
OLYMPIA, 1938

THIS 'Wakefield' House, exhibited by Wates Ltd. at the 1938 Ideal Home Exhibition, is designed in a restrained architectural style which reflects the substantial principles of construction on which it is based. There is an unobtrusively classical suggestion in the pillared porch, the gable is well balanced, and ample windows promise good light and comfort within. The Hall, where first impressions count for so much, is of good size, which is emphasized by a wide staircase finished on a modern note with a graceful metal handrail.

The two Reception Rooms are of generous dimensions—most welcome for entertaining—and are

138   Wates Ltd's 'Wakefield' design, featured in their brochure for the 1938 Ideal Home Exhibition, p.2, Museum of Domestic Design and Architecture, Middlesex University. A case-study in the stylistic heterogeneity of spec-builder housing. Picturesque in asymmetric plan and fenestration, steep gables, canted bay, and prominent chimneystacks, the design adds a pedimented classical doorcase to signify elevated social-class ambitions

Wilverley Park's showstopper was the Wates Chalet. It made its debut in 1934 and was presented by the company at the 1935 *Daily Mail* Ideal Home Exhibition. The dwelling was considerably more spacious than the houses on Briardene – its drawing room (at 185.25ft^2 in both semi- and detached versions) over half as large again as that in

above

(left) 139 and (right) 140   Wates's detached Chalet-type C4 offered on the Wendover Estate, New Malden (1936), Wates Archive

right

141   As the 1930s wore on, Wates gave names to their house designs. The Briardene Estate's Types A and B were renamed 'Avondale' and 'Beverley', granting the 'buyer of moderate means' a little more cachet, Wates's Olympia brochure (1938), Museum of Domestic Design and Architecture, Middlesex University

from
17'9
Weekly
Including
ALL RATES
Repayments
Insurance
EVERYTHING

•

Available at :—
CATFORD
HEATHWAY
CARSHALTON
MORDEN
WHITTON
SHOOTER'S HILL
ENFIELD
*for prices
see end of Book*

Avondale and Beverley Houses

Sensibly planned for maximum comfort, with the finish, fittings and equipment of much more expensive houses, these splendid types were designed to enable the buyer of moderate means to possess a home of individuality and character at prices hitherto considered impossible.

The Avondale Type, being end houses, are virtually semi-detached and have wide, sweeping gables, giving an imposing front elevation. Beverley are the centre houses of groups of four or six houses, and have wide bays extending right up to the eaves.

Each house has a separate porch opening into a fine entrance hall with an easy-going stairway. There is a comfortable Drawing Room, a Dining Room over sixteen feet in length, and full Kitchenette equipment. The three Bedrooms are spacious, airy and comfortable, and the Bathroom is fully tiled.

Briardene's Type A. Wilverley Park's 'Tudor'-styled houses were only a little smaller than the Chalets, the DeLuxe having a drawing room 171.5ft^2 in floor area.[113]

While offering a variation on cottage aesthetics in almost every house design, Wates's marketing literature did not use the word 'cottage' itself. There seems to have been a view in the sector that the word retained some of its less fortunate connotations. A cosy-sounding alternative – like *chalet*, a French, German, or Swiss synonym (from the land of the architecture that had entranced Octavia Hill) – squared the circle;[114] though conservationists sometimes used *chalet* to specify disapproved-of, gimcrack plotland dwellings. By the late 1930s, Wates would solve the problem altogether by giving names to their houses (as did other builders), such as the upmarket 'Wakefield', Wates's star at Olympia in 1938; the 'Windsor', available in the London

142 Wates Chalet-type SC3 semi-detached, today – Hollington Crescent, Old Malden, Kingston

143   'Labourer's Cottage', plate 2, W.F. Pocock, *Architectural Designs for Rustic Cottages* (London: J. Taylor, 1807), The Bodleian Libraries, University of Oxford. The design's asymmetry and catslide recall Wates's Chalet. See fig.142

suburb of Wandsworth (quite an outlay at £1,395 freehold); the 'Westcombe', the 'Warwick', and the 'Jerningham'. Briardene Estate's rather prosaic sounding As and Bs were renamed 'Avondale' and 'Beverley'.[115] Harold Neal told *The National Builder* that his company gave estate nomenclature careful consideration,[116] but the Wates Archive holds no clues as to how names were chosen. On the eve of the Second World War, Pevensey, Quentin, Welbeck, and Verwood joined Wates Limited's 1939 *Book of*

Plans[117] – a selection whose guiding principle is not easy to discern.

The C4 Detached Chalet and SC3 Semi-detached version (figs 140 and 142) at Wilverley Park and on other estates were similar in appearance, both assertively asymmetrical, with a catslide roof plunging down from the main hipped slope (with gablet) to ground storey ceiling height on one side – 'the sweeping roof lines which are so charming a feature'.[118] Other picturesque staples included the fenestration: a tile-hung dormer window over the main entrance to one side (on the SC3), a ground-floor oriel on the front elevation of both, a small porthole window above, and casements throughout, with leaded panes to the front.

The two-storey canted bay was tile-hung on the first floor, and in exposed brick at ground floor level. Voysey-esque white roughcast covered nearly all the houses' other external wall surfaces, but this sometimes varied within estates or from one estate to another. The Brockley Estate Chalets used more facing brick and little roughcast.[119] The mixture of materials amounted to a variety of picturesque surface modulations that Malton himself would have celebrated. Even devotees of the Arts and Crafts might have applauded, so long as they had not learned of Norman Wates's appetite for airfreighting in consignments of 'Flemish Wirecuts' – good-value Belgian bricks. Wates did not build in the tradition of local materials or regional grammar;[120] they wanted houses to look good so they would sell fast. The Picturesque's unashamed emphasis on visual effect is quite the best way to understand their aesthetics.

A 1938 company brochure included an encomium for the Chalet's exterior styling: 'beautifully proportioned bays, perfect harmony of tiling and rendered walls softened by sweeping roof lines, proclaiming a masterpiece in design'.[121] On the cover of Wates's *Wilverley Park Estate* brochure (fig.144), the Chalet was deliberately sequestered from its real-life surroundings – indulging the gaze of the owner with eyes only for their own property; 'the importance of the individual house *within* the pair'[122] – rendering it the perfect evocation of Ruskin's dream cottage: 'looking out of the woody dingle with its eye-like window . . . sending up the motion of azure smoke between the silver trunks of aged trees'.[123]

While the Chalets certainly were picturesque, they did not obviously lend themselves to being marketed as Tudor; and Wates had spotted 'Houses designed in the Tudor period style are proving more and more popular every day'.[124] For customers with that yearning – 'all the beauty of old-world

144 Cover illustration, Wates's Olympia Brochure (1938), Museum of Domestic Design and Architecture, Middlesex University. The Wates Chalet is presented as Ruskin's perfect cottage: 'looking out of the woody dingle with its eye-like window . . . sending up the motion of azure smoke between the silver trunks of aged trees'

145 The Tudor Major, cheaper of the two designs that Wates marketed specifically as 'Tudor' around 1935, Wates, Wilverley Park Estate brochure, Wates Archive

quaintness . . . that mellow appearance that only Tudor style can give'[125] – the company offered two designs, available across their estates in the mid-1930s including at Wilverley Park.

The exteriors of the two houses are tricky to differentiate, but the Tudor DeLuxe three-bed, two reception semi was about 20 per cent more spacious across its principal rooms than the Tudor Major.[126] And because the DeLuxe was larger on plan – resulting in a wider semi-detached pair – half-timbering was used to cover the first storey wall-space between the two houses, whereas it was not in the smaller Tudor Major (fig.145). Incidentally, whether either of Wates's 'Tudor' designs can accurately or usefully be described as Tudor raises a bigger question, to which we will come.

WATES'S COMPETITORS

Aesthetically, there was little to choose between Wates's version of suburban cottage picturesque and the domestic visuality offered by their rivals. Among the volume interwar speculative builders, only Laing – who produced half as many houses as Wates during much of the 1930s[127] – shied consistently away from the Picturesque. Proprietor John Laing said in 1933: 'the public . . . desire simplicity of design and warmth of colour. They dislike meaningless ornamentation'.[128] These convictions were not shared by Laing's competitors. An experiment by Laing (1933–35) at the Sunnyfields Estate, Mill Hill, north London, might have given even them pause for thought. In a bid for professional approval, the company offered an estate to the Architectural Association (AA) for a 'Competition for the Design of Small Villa Property'.[129] The adjudicating architects, Arthur Kenyon and Thomas Alwyn Lloyd (who, as we have seen, served on the RIBA's House Design Sub-Committee in 1934), designed most of the houses, but left space for three successful newcomers. Laing's anti-picturesque tradition set the tone: no roughcast, half-timbering, or elaborate chimneystacks. The resulting architecture was formal in the cheaper dwellings, with marked steps

taken towards Modern movement fenestration throughout, but with suburban staples like the tile-hung canted bay retained in places. The AA approved – its journal talking of 'restraint, dignity and charm' – the public less so. When Sunnyfields house-types were introduced on other Laing estates, 75 per cent of the time traditional alternatives were chosen.[130] Sunnyfields turned out to be the slowest selling estate in Laing's history.[131]

'Competitors there are,' wrote C.G. Allsopp in *Wates House News*, 'and although the best standard of many of them is below our worst, there is no guarantee they will stay there.'[132] New Ideal Homesteads – later known as Ideal Homes – was Wates's volume rival. In 1935, they sold 5,500 houses compared with Wates's 1930s' peak average, in second place, of 2,000 a year.[133]

Ideal was run by former Erith Urban District Council surveyor Leo Meyer, and built their houses on similar aesthetic lines to Wates – conforming to Gibberd's summary with their cottage-style asymmetries, bay windows, swept roofs, roughcast, tile-hanging, and half-timbered gables.[134] They dubbed themselves 'Britain's best and biggest builders' and offered '50 types of home' on 20 estates.[135] In the mid-1930s, their 'LB' type (fig.146) could be bought freehold for £425 – undercutting Wates's economy offers – from Sidcup in Kent to Edmonton and Ponders End in the northern suburbs of London. Accommodation was tight: the buyer would have to make do without a parlour, and with a 13 ft by 15 ft 5 in living room instead, plus kitchen/diner downstairs, and two bedrooms on the first floor (or three if you could afford to upgrade to the 'LC' type, at £465 freehold).

Visually, the houses are familiar – and doubtless could be squeezed into the broad category 'Tudor' by virtue of their massive, half-timbered cross-wing gables, shared between two dwellings at the opposite ends of a six-house terrace. But, as with the Wates Tudor Major and Tudor DeLuxe, Ideal's were not Tudor designs in any scholarly sense. They were a picturesque hotchpotch, achieving their effect through structural outline and the vaguest of historical evocations. The combination of

"LB" TYPE

from

10/5

WEEKLY

£425

FREEHOLD

146   'LB' type row house, New Ideal Homesteads brochure,
Museum of Domestic Design and Architecture, Middlesex University

"K" TYPE

from

14/4

WEEKLY

£575

FREEHOLD

"Q" TYPE

from

15/-

WEEKLY

£595

FREEHOLD

147 'K' type house and 'Q' type semi, New Ideal Homesteads brochure,
Museum of Domestic Design and Architecture, Middlesex University

"DBI" Bungalow

from

18/9

WEEKLY

£750

FREEHOLD

"MW" Bungalow

from

13/11

WEEKLY

£550

FREEHOLD

148   'DBI' and 'MW' type bungalows, New Ideal Homesteads brochure,
Museum of Domestic Design and Architecture, Middlesex University

roughcast, timbered gables, two-storey rectangular bays, porthole windows to light the hall, pent-roofed porches, and casement windows recalled the aesthetic eclecticism of Malton's and Robinson's picturesque designs.

If New Ideal Homesteads had an aesthetic signature, it was one that further challenges the usefulness of classifying interwar houses as Tudor. Instead of a rectangular or canted bay, New Ideal Homesteads often used what they called a 'circular bay',[136] more precisely a two-storey bow window. This featured on their types 'A', 'K', and 'Q', two- or three-bed semi-detached and terraced houses, ranging in price from £575 to £725 freehold (fig.147) and available on pretty much all New Ideal Homesteads estates. Ideal also used it in a single-storey version on their two- or three-bed bungalow types 'MW' and 'DBI' (fig.148) – priced freehold at £550 and £750 – again widely available across the company's estate portfolio. The trademark casemented bow almost invariably sat beneath a large timbered gable, but New Ideal Homesteads' combination of the bow window with the rest of the ragbag of stylistic elements that they favoured demands to be viewed with picturesque eyes.

Indeed, very few spec-builders' houses were intended as exercises in stylistic authenticity. 'We are nearly always selling just . . . the idea that this will be the prospect's future home',[137] said A.W. Madger from Wates. Like Wates houses, New Ideal Homesteads' were oneiric. Their visuality – its 'many historical architectures . . . a complex additive aesthetic'[138] – was meant to give buyers a sense of homely, cottage belonging and nostalgic historical connection, not to satisfy the codifications of house-bibbing scholars in the decades to come.

TUDOR OR NOT?

It is wrong to ignore the way 'Tudoresque', 'Neo-Tudor', 'sham-Tudor', 'Mock Tudor', 'Tudorbethan', and 'Tudoristic' abound in today's discussions of interwar architecture. None of them intrinsically problematic, they are descriptions that only become

so if treated as a totalising explanation of spec-housing's aesthetics between 1919 and 1939.

In 1981, publication of pioneering texts from Arthur Edwards (*The Design of Suburbia*), and Oliver, Davis and Bentley (*Dunroamin*) saw relatively nuanced discussion predominate as to how far the Tudor idea could be taken. For Edwards, Tudor was important, but only one of four styles to be found in the interwar suburb: 'the Tudor, the mièvre, the neo-Georgian and the debilitated Queen Anne'.[139] For *Dunroamin*'s authors, Tudor inflections in suburban architecture were qualified: 'hints only, connotative of uncertain echoes of the Tudor style rather than direct imitations'.[140] More recently, broader descriptions have proliferated. Barrett and Phillips discuss 'the style chosen by the builders . . . mock Tudor or "Jacobethan"'.[141] Ballantyne and Law call 'Tudoresque' the 'default choice of architectural style' for new speculative houses post-1918.[142] Gavin Stamp goes furthest: 'it is safe to say, almost all of these houses built by speculative builders conformed to models which can be described as being in the Tudor style'.[143]

The argument is not a modern one. In 1929, in the mind of Captain P.A. Barron, co-editor of *Automobiles of the World* in 1921 and one-time motoring correspondent for *The Ideal Home* magazine, houses like those from Wates and Ideal did not deserve the description 'Tudor':

> We have today many designers of half-timbered houses which are usually described as Tudor, though I could not say why they should be so named, as half-timbering was not peculiar to the Tudor period, nor was it universal in that era.[144]

Barron's 1929 scepticism is valuable today. The claim about the interwar speculative suburb from Stamp – 'almost all of these houses . . . can be described as being in the Tudor style' – is surely too strong.

Clearly he was not referring to the small number of modernist or moderne spec-houses built in the late 1920s and 1930s. New Ideal Homesteads flirted briefly with the style but without commercial success.[145] Wates tried it too – at Barnfield, New

Malden – building modernist homes designed by R.A. Duncan, a RIBA committee member, and the architect behind the 'House of the Future' at the 1928 Ideal Home Exhibition.[146] The style enjoyed another flurry of success at the same exhibition in 1931, in the form of 'The House that Jack Built'.[147] Smaller builders, such as Howard Houses in Molesey, south-west of London, marketed modernist houses using the 'Sun-Trap' tag. Even in the later stages of Hampstead Garden Suburb, enclaves of moderne houses designed by the likes of G.C. Winbourne appeared.[148] But, in mass-market terms, 'the Modern Movement style was little favoured in Britain' for anything other than elite commissions.[149]

Yet most more-traditionally designed interwar houses should not really be swept up in a Tudor drag-net either. The *sine qua non* of picturesque suburban architecture was the two-storey canted bay, an early Perpendicular model for which can be found on Grevel's House, in Chipping Campden, thought to date from around 1400.[150] There is a three-storey version on the George Hotel (Pilgrims Inn) in Glastonbury, tentatively dated at around 1470. As for bow windows, although Ideal's two-storey version almost invariably appeared under a large, half-timbered cross-wing gable, the bow itself was not a Tudor form either, becoming common in English domestic architecture around the mid-eighteenth century.[151] Timbering also antedated the Tudors in historical dwellings – Lower Brockhampton in Herefordshire (*c.*1400) and Ockwells Manor in Berkshire (*c.*1440s–60s), for example – being widespread from the fourteenth century.[152] Albert Powys, Secretary of the SPAB, mentioned in 1929 'evidence that the custom of darkening the oak work in half-timber houses did not begin before the seventeenth century'.[153] All these are architectural features, either pre-1485 or post-1603, perhaps too readily generalised as Tudor in the interwar context.

Wates's Chalets on Wilverley Park, and their Type As and Bs on Briardene, were not conspicuously Tudor in style. But the company chose to market two houses from their mid-1930s range specifically as Tudor – deliberately differentiating them from their other designs. And even these were architecturally

right

149   Exterior of Cerne Abbey Guest House, Cerne Abbas, Dorset, probably built under Abbot John Vanne (1458–70) before the first Tudor monarch, Henry VII, came to the throne. The north elevation oriel is canted – an architectural technique much beloved of interwar domestic builders for their ubiquitous bay windows

debatable. The front-door porch apertures on the Tudors Major and DeLuxe would surely have been given a four-centred treatment or a Tudor Arch[154] by any designer determined to live up to his sales department's brochures. 'Most suburban Tudorists,' says Pinney, 'had to be content with "Tudorbethan" details stuck onto ordinary semi-detached houses.'[155]

The unifying thread in interwar spec-built architecture is, I contend, less the Tudors than the continuity of medieval English architecture more broadly. The poet John Drinkwater, writing towards the end of the First World War, seemed to understand: 'I see the little cottages that keep /Their beauty still where since Plantagenet /Have come the shepherds happily to sleep'.[156] The aesthetics of most interwar domestic architecture are better understood not as scrupulously historical but as impressionistic, associative, decorative. Frederick Gibberd's 1938 history of English architecture suggested:

> Most of the houses built by private enterprise are decorated rather than designed – that is, proportion and suitability to purpose are secondary to the trimmings, such as imitation half-timbering, tiles hung on bay windows, and panels of coloured cement.[157]

There was another interwar trend in home-building that also suggests we should be careful about lavishing the description Tudor on *all* 1920s and 1930s suburbia: namely, the interwar builders who promised to build genuinely accurate revival Tudor homes – smaller, niche companies, charging higher prices. In March 1923, at the *Daily Mail* Ideal Home Exhibition, the star exhibit was from John I. Williams & Sons of Oxted in Surrey, branded the 'Tudor Cottage':

PERSPECTIVE ELEVATION

150   John I. Williams & Sons' 'Tudor Cottage' took pride of place at the *Daily Mail* Ideal Home Exhibition in March 1923, from J.I. Williams's booklet, *In Tudor Times*, Museum of Domestic Design and Architecture, Middlesex University

ELEVATION MAIN ENTᴿᴱᴱ.

Tudor Cottage
at the
Ideal Home Exhibition
OLYMPIA
1923
By
John I. Williams
& Sons
OXTED
SURREY

151   Main entrance elevation of J.I. Williams's Tudor Cottage. From *In Tudor Times*, p.2, Museum of Domestic Design and Architecture, Middlesex University

partly half-timbered with oak, partly weather-tiled with old tiles; base of old stone and brick; roofed with old roofing tiles; leaded lights in diamond and oblong panes; small gabled porch with a low arched entrance [and] a small room above with a quaint oriel window.[158]

This was an upmarket proposition, priced at £1,750 (before panelling, at £100 per room, and the cost of the land to build on). But J.I. Williams & Sons were well regarded in the high-end restoration world, having worked on the thirteenth-century Chirk Castle in the Welsh Marches and on Compton Wynyates in Warwickshire.[159] At Olympia, they were proposing to build, from scratch, a 'faithful reproduction on traditional lines' of a Tudor cottage.[160]

Builders for the middle and upper-middle classes of expensive neo-Tudor like this – Blunden Shadbolt,[161] and Edgar Ranger with his 'high quality archaisms' in the Thanet area of Kent, were two more[162] – did not attract scorn from the commentariat in the same way that their mass-market peers tended to. Even Randal Phillips was prepared to countenance expensive Tudor Revival under certain strict conditions. It could 'only be successful if it is done in a thorough-going way, with no make-believe about it, and, above all, with some appreciation of the craft-spirit which permeated the times from which its inspiration is derived'[163] – which can be translated as 'do not attempt this on the cheap'. Phillips echoed the government's 1927 housing *Manual* in suggesting that traditional architectural styles were not for those with limited resources.

Interwar domestic elevations in England did, of course, evoke the preceding century's historical enthusiasms. What Peter Mandler calls 'the Olden Time' – and, later, 'Tudorism' – he identifies starting as early as the 1820s, a phenomenon arising towards the end of the Picturesque's architectural theorisation. We saw in Chapter 1 how the picturesque architect T.F. Hunt helped visualise the cottage picturesque in his 1825 book *Half a Dozen Hints on Picturesque Domestic Architecture*. His later work, *Exemplars of Tudor Architecture Adapted to Modern Habitations* (1830), made explicit and appreciative reference to the theories of Price and Knight, positioning Tudor aesthetics as the means to achieving a picturesque end.[164] In part because 'elite culture's longstanding disregard of national history in favour of classicism . . . gave the past an intrinsically democratic appearance',[165] the Olden Time remained salient in English popular culture for most of the nineteenth century. Its aesthetics were prominent, reports Jonathan Woodham, in British contributions to international design exhibitions in France and the USA in the 1860s and 1870s,[166] and were re-energised at the beginning of the twentieth century in the 1910 Ideal Home Exhibition's 'Tudor Village', and at Mrs George Cornwallis-West's blockbuster show *Shakespeare's England* in 1912.[167] Tudorism undoubtedly exercised a powerful fascination during the interwar period, but in domestic architecture it makes sense to see it as one among several continuities rather than as the definitive signifier for spec-building in the 1920s and 1930s.

CLASS AND THE PICTURESQUE

This book's first chapter explored how the interwar English had been subject to over a century of picturesque domestic-architectural acculturation – 'The viewer, subconsciously trained in an appreciation of picturesque landscapes through the observation of thousands upon thousands of images'.[168] Advertising for the Metropolitan Railway Company during the 1920s and 1930s worked to similar effect. Its role in the development of suburban estates near new stations around London went hand-in-hand with an overpowering preference for cottage picturesque – as John Betjeman remembered in a television commentary of the 1970s: 'Child of the First War, forgotten by the Second, we called you Metro-land. We laid our schemes, lured by the lush brochure – down byways beckoned, to build at last the cottage of our dreams'.[169]

In class terms, though, who exactly did the brochure beckon to buy their 'cottage' in this

METRO-LAND

PRICE TWO-PENCE

left

152 *Metro-land* guidebook cover (1921), illustration
by C.A. Wilkinson for the Metropolitan Railway,
London Transport Museum

right

153 One of the kinds of family that Wates tried to
persuade to buy their houses. This image was used
across Wates estate brochures in the 1930s. Does it
represent how the buyers saw themselves at the moment
of purchase or who they might become after purchase?
Wates brochures (various), *c.*1935, Wates Archive

interwar vision of the suburban landscape?
Scholarship has seen a shift in the answer to this
question. Earlier work, by Swenarton and Taylor,
concluded: 'The boom in owner-occupation in this
period was overwhemingly a middle-class process'.[170]
Subsequent research by O'Carroll in Edinburgh, and
Byrne on Tyneside,[171] suggests lower prices outside
London made new houses accessible to more
working-class buyers. Speight, more recently, agrees:
'more working-class households became owner
occupiers . . . than Swenarton and Taylor allow . . .
[buying] many of the new houses built during the
1930s'.[172]

People between the wars addressed this question
too. In 1939, the sociologically inclined Stanley
Ramsey wrote: 'It is very difficult to draw a hard-
and-fast line between the houses for the working
classes and those of the . . . middle classes, but if
we fix the figure at £400, this gives an approximate
indication'.[173] A writer in *The Economist* claimed in 1936
that purchasers of new houses in the interwar period
emerged 'from the lower middle class, the clerk and
artisan class, numerically very much smaller than
the unskilled labouring class'.[174] The RIBA 1934 report
on spec-built houses had, of course, recognised 'the
lower paid clerk' as a significant presence in the
market.[175] But work done by the Ministry of Health
under Sir Hilton Young in 1933 showed that 38 per
cent of new private-enterprise houses built across
England and Wales in the preceding 12 months were
at the affordable end of the market, with rateable

values below £13 (or £20 in the Metropolitan Police
Area of London). Such dwellings, Young said, 'are . . .
of the type usually occupied by manual workers'. He
also revealed that 19 of that 38 per cent had, in 1933,
been sold rather than let.[176]

That the housing market was suddenly open to
this influx of new buyers was a function, first, of a
fall in construction costs that began in the mid-
1920s, reflecting lower labour and commodity prices;
and, second, of the 'Pool' system – a revolution in
home-purchase financing. The Pool was a trade
arrangement that required builders to lodge money
of their own with building societies to indemnify
them against any losses they might incur on
defaulting loans above the 75 to 80 per cent Loan-to-
Value ratio that the societies normally lent at. This
meant borrowers could make a purchase with much
less than the 20 to 25 per cent deposit they would
normally have needed (sometimes paying as little as
£25 on a £500 house, rather than £100 or £125).[177] In
class terms, this inevitably opened house purchase
to people not previously able to afford it – the 'black-
coated class', identified in Graves and Hodge's
contemporary history of the interwar years as the
least well-off among the middle classes; and the

Their happiness can be yours ..

154 Close-up from a National Building Society advert, *c*.1935, Museum of Domestic Design and Architecture, Middlesex University. The image makes no bones about the aspirational qualities of home ownership – a sun-dappled vision of perfect family life is only a mortgage away

'artisans', traditionally seen as the most prosperous among the working classes.[178] In 1934, the builder John Laing said that he believed the Pool system had increased the quantum of potential buyers threefold.[179]

In meeting the demand for housing, local authorities, building societies, and speculative builders comprehensively remade England's domestic architectural landscape during the interwar years, changing the country's socio-spatial complexion in the process. It is important to consider what the nation's class system looked like *after* this great domestic resettlement. For this, a relatively recent strain of sociology is invaluable: 'whereas occupation used to define social class, now it is residential location that increasingly does so . . . we are thus witnessing nothing less than the *spatialization of class'.*[180] Mike Savage and his team from Manchester University write:

> One's residence is a crucial, possibly the crucial identifier of who you are . . . Rather than seeing wider social identities as arising out of the field of employment it would be more promising to examine their relationship to residential location.[181]

Thus the four million new homes of the interwar years can be seen as both cause *and* location of a significant upheaval in class terms.[182] New tiers among the middle classes had emerged during the Edwardian period, Forster's Leonard Bast one of their earliest literary incarnations. They needed somewhere to live. The window of home affordability that opened in the 1920s allowed people on the cusp of the middle and working classes – and many from deeper working-class backgrounds – to relocate themselves simultaneously in spatial and in class terms. New lifestyles – ranging from the responsibilities of the mortgage-payer, recently resident on a spec-built estate with its cottage-picturesque styling, to those of the council rent payer, in one house among a more formally styled multitude at Becontree, Speke, or Wythenshawe – bespoke distinct class identities. Both contexts made class visible in a new way.

155   Wates Tudor-Major semi on Wilverley Park Estate today: Chilmark Gardens, Old Malden, Kingston

A black-coated worker or artisan who had gone out on a limb to service a mortgage consolidated a step firmly into the middle class. Peter Scott explores this: 'Owner-occupation . . . promoted the

156   An interwar council estate in F. Gibberd and F.R.S. Yorke, *The Modern Flat* (London: The Architectural Press, 1937), p.15

No. 6. CLASS B—URBAN—SOUTHERLY ASPECT.

157 LGB *Manual*, Plan No. 6 (Class B parlour cottages), modelled for the 'Model Homes Exhibition', May 1919, Museum of Domestic Design and Architecture, Middlesex University

adoption of longer-term planning horizons and strategies . . . act[ing] as a catalyst for one of the most fundamental breaks [with] the "traditional" working-class household'.[183] The picturesque aesthetics of the newly acquired house asserted this new status to the outside world. Subtle external differences from the dwellings next door or across the road – 'largely cosmetic variations in design'[184] – articulated the desire for distinction and autonomy.

For the arrival on one of England's growing council estates – experiencing perhaps the dislocation inherent in the loss of social networks from the place they used to live,[185] and subject to a clear aesthetic declaration from the council that, in terms of 'plainer houses in near-identical rows',[186] everybody around them was more or less the same – the opposite was true. Whatever nuances may have informed their previous social standing, as council tenants they became fixed – in the opinion not least of the RIBA House Design Sub-Committee, and those in the building trade that they had interviewed – as from 'a lower social class'. The aesthetics of individual council houses served to declare this identity to the world outside, effacing individuality in just the way that Reilly, Adshead, et al. had theorised it should. As the anthropologist James Duncan remarks: 'often the landscape a group inhabits is one of the few things that other social worlds know about that group'.[187]

Critically, the withholding of the Picturesque in council dwellings denied tenants the aesthetics of the English cottage that over a century of acculturation had conditioned so many people to value – that, as council tenants could see, millions on spec-built estates continued to choose. Thus were council-house tenants segregated – not just by estate location or paucity of communal facilities, but by aesthetics; by the fact that, from the end of the Addison Scheme, an easily legible visuality differentiated their homes. In Lynsey Hanley's words: 'You could no longer look at a council house without knowing it was one'.[188]

This was recognised as early as the 1930s. The chairman of the Abbey Road Building Society, Sir Harold Bellman, confessed in 1938: 'as one drives round the countryside one need not have any . . . professional qualifications to be able to discern "the council house"'.[189] Others were less coy. Captain Barron, the motoring correspondent, saw council houses as among the 'most hideous of all buildings erected within the memory of man'.[190] Sacheverell Sitwell, in 1945, seemed to extend his disdain to their inhabitants: 'Is ours to be a world only of dog-races and the cup final? When we consider the spiritual values in our council houses, should we not envy the Papuan and the black fellow of the Torres Straits?'[191]

The interwar story of the cottage picturesque came to an end in this world of haves and have-nots. For those who could afford a mortgage, Wates, New Ideal Homesteads, and the legion other speculative builders delivered millions of suburban dwellings whose aesthetics offered purchasers a widely valued, deeply acculturated vision of home. Those unable to buy were rarely allowed this modern version of the Picturesque. A still-vital eighteenth-century aesthetic – largely responsible for carrying domestic architectural visuality from medieval England into the radio age – was built selectively into the landscape, sorting private-sector owner-occupiers from local authority estate tenants in an unambiguously divisive aesthetic display.

CONCLUSION

It was shrewd electoral politics for the British government to promise a new cottage home to the nation's ill-housed working classes in 1918. A war-weary people longed for Samuel Rogers's 'dear abode of peace and privacy',[1] whose aesthetics – in Beresford Pite's 1919 description, 'a poetic illusion evolved in not less than a century and a half'[2] – most had been acculturated to understand as picturesque. But although Lloyd George had inaugurated a truly radical social housing policy, government use of the term 'cottage' invoked architectural continuity. Centuries old, the picturesque cottage aesthetics that many architects and local authorities originally believed suitable for the government's scheme would prove expensive to build and amount ultimately to a greater fiscal commitment than politicians were prepared to honour. The evolution of interwar housing began thus with a marriage of new policy and an old idea – the cottage picturesque, a concept whose visuality and potent reification of home are invaluable in attempting to understand the morphology of domestic architecture in the period 1919 to 1939.

As I argue in Chapter 1, these two ideas – cottage and Picturesque – belong together. 1918's National Cottage Competition revealed the cottage picturesque as the dwelling many English (and Welsh) architects believed should be built for the country's working classes after the First World War. It was the dwelling argued against for that role by the government, and deprecated by the coterie of influential architects whose thinking we have examined between 1910 and 1919. It was the dwelling

158   Cottage at Hopton Castle, south-west Shropshire, photograph by B.C. Clayton, in Basil Oliver, *Cottages of England* (London: B.T. Batsford, 1929), plate 44, The Bodleian Libraries, University of Oxford

that many local authorities were determined to build anyway under the Addison Scheme between 1919 and 1921. And it was the dwelling whose aesthetics – 'steep roof pitches . . . picturesque gables . . . artistic features . . . a bulge here and a break there'[3] – the government's Director-General of Housing Sir Charles Ruthen publicly anathematised, in 1922, as responsible for the scheme's collapse.

Officially disapprobated as the model for working-class social housing aesthetics, the cottage picturesque became subject to middle-class and political-class appropriation – inspiring what Evelyn Waugh called 'the craze for cottages'.[4] Sought after by the moneyed as rural weekend retreat;

159 Brochure from north London builder A.W. Curton (1939), Museum of Domestic Design and Architecture, Middlesex University

subject to sedulous campaigning as conservation imperative by the great and good at the Society for the Protection of Ancient Buildings and the Royal Society of Arts, the cottage picturesque was further seized upon in 1926–27 by Stanley Baldwin's government as a talisman for the spirit of shared origin, peace, and unity that the Tories feared had been lost to the collectivism of the General Strike. Around the same time, the Picturesque – as Christopher Hussey discerned it – reasserted itself as the fundamental aesthetic inspiration for interwar, mass-market speculative house builders. The outskirts of every conurbation in the country, from 1923 to 1939, were decorated with the textures, asymmetries, and associations of this still-potent eighteenth-century aesthetic.

Conceptually, the cottage picturesque illuminates the interconnectedness of these interwar developments. Adopting it as an heuristic for the period also allows us to see patterns emerging that would extend beyond the Second World War. When the group of architects who had campaigned against picturesque cottages after 1910 was joined in the 1920s by a cabal of design critics (the likes of Gloag, Bertram, and Boumphrey), a new assault began on

the aesthetics of interwar spec-built houses that was essentially an attack on the same old target – the deeply acculturated visuality of the traditional cottage. Critics resented being able neither to purge its aesthetics from contemporary house building nor 'improve' them. And it led to a frustration that set epistocratic architects at odds with the market's consensual aesthetic in a way that would be repeated after the Second World War. When he was criticised for what the *avant garde* saw as his too-traditional social housing at Harlow New Town in the 1950s, Frederick Gibberd denounced modernist architects' determination to '[give] people what you think they ought to want'.[5] Ortolano discusses similar forces at work in Milton Keynes in the 1970s.[6]

Opposition to cottage-picturesque visuality in social housing after 1922 collaterally weakened the ancient relationship between the cottage and England's labouring classes – a dispossession with implications for the future. The 'affaire Ruthen' of 1922 (as *The Architects' Journal* later called it[7]) placed the term 'cottage' under a high degree of lexical strain. How could the same small word go on denoting simultaneously the cut-price, formal rectangle of Ruthen's preference – without 'craft in the artistic or aesthetic sense'[8] – *and* the asymmetric cynosure of the picturesque imagination treasured by weekend cottagers, the Society for the Protection of Ancient Buildings, and the Royal Society of Arts?

A resolution with long-term consequences emerged between the wars in the form of a new label for local authority-built working-class dwellings. Prior to 1920, the expression 'Council House' referred exclusively to a council headquarters building and meeting place – notable examples going up in Coventry in 1920, and in Nottingham in 1929.[9] In 1920, however, *The Times* newspaper used the expression 'council houses', with its modern meaning, for the first time (as far as I can ascertain).[10] In the period 1920–23, the newspaper then used 'council house(s)' with the same new meaning on 12 occasions, followed by a further 47 uses in the years 1924–28. Searches of the *Daily Mail* online archive show modern usage of 'council house' four times between 1920 and 1923, growing to 41 for the period 1924–28. As a regional comparison, the *Nottingham Evening Post* did not employ the expression with its modern meaning at all in 1920 but used it an average of 32 times a year between 1930 and 1939, peaking with 52 in 1932.[11]

Google NGram analysis of their digitised database of British books shows use intensity of 'council house(s)' at 847 per cent higher as an average for the 1930s than it was in 1921. The expression 'cottage estate' persisted; and modernist ideologues returned to the word 'cottage' in the 1930s for dismissive rhetorical purposes.[12] But it is striking that local authority single-family homes started to be called 'council houses' – a designation that would become the standard term of reference after the Second World War – at around the same time in the early 1920s that the government made clear its determination that council dwellings should not be permitted the aesthetics of the cottage picturesque. The new language persists to this day. Jack Young's 2022 survey of local authority domestic architecture is titled simply *The Council House*.

After 1939, the Picturesque – unpopular for so long among architectural *cognoscenti* – shrugged off the disapproval of Geoffrey Scott and his followers and found new favour with one particular group of modernists. Already quoted, Ivor de Wolfe's letter to Christopher Hussey in 1950 illuminates what has become a well-studied episode in the Picturesque's later career – what its progenitors called 'a programme for the renewal of architecture and town-planning under the title "Townscape: A Plea for an English Visual Philosophy founded on the true rock of Sir Uvedale Price"'.[13] After 1944, a campaign was organised at *The Architectural Review* – led by de Hastings, Pevsner, Cullen, and Nairn – to use the Picturesque to give their fundamentally modernist vision of architecture's future an incontestably English pedigree; in Pevsner's formulation, 'an account of how this theory and this tradition influenced the nineteenth century in England and might influence the twentieth'.[14] Macarthur examines what Townscape's advocates believed the Picturesque could do for them – mitigating modernism's 'unpopularity' and the 'divergence of taste between the public and the [architectural] profession'.[15]

But as Aitchison, another student of the episode, makes clear, Pevsner built his theoretical approach on a misconception. He was convinced that the Picturesque was a landscape theory; that its founding fathers had written little about architecture;[16] and that new thinking focused on land- and streetscape could therefore be used freely to reconcile modernist architecture with public preferences in traditional street layout for postwar town planning. Townscape began life as a determination to legitimise – as Whyte has noted – a modernist architectural future recognised as controversial to the public in terms of a sentimentally appealing past that they were believed to find congenial.[17] But it did little to address directly how people expected their homes to look.

In addition to helping us acknowledge the vitality, post-First World War, of the late eighteenth-century's key aesthetic theory, see more clearly how the evolution of interwar domestic architecture was sequenced, and understand the early dynamics of relationships between architects, social housing, and the public, the cottage picturesque also emerges

160 'The Bride's Home', from Morrell Builders Ltd, *c*.1933, Museum of Domestic Design and Architecture, Middlesex University

as useful in the task of classifying the aesthetics of interwar spec-build houses today.

The consensus traditionally resorts for this to one variety or another of 'Tudor'. But, as Chapter 5 argues, this has limitations. Few interwar suburban houses were built in a conscientiously Tudor style.

161 Card No. 14, 'Pembridge Herefordshire', Players Cigarettes, *Picturesque Cottages* (1929)

Apart from on spec-build estates with some more formal architecture (such as Laing's poorly selling Sunnyfields Estate at Mill Hill, London, from 1933) – and the few, also rather less successful, modernist developments – interwar spec-builders 'designed' for the most part by choosing from a menu of traditional exterior ingredients, blending, as budgets allowed, cross-wing gables, gablets, timbering, roughcast, casement windows, variegated bricks, pentice roofs, dormers, catslides, oriels, two-storey canted bays, bow windows, circular windows, tile-hanging, and arched doorways. The pick-and-mix aggregation of these elements makes no real sense viewed through the lens of the 'styles'. By contrast, Malton's cottage picturesque – with its essential asymmetry, variety, and particolouration – accounts convincingly for their aesthetics. Hussey recognised this in 1927. Few apart from Richards and Goodhart-Rendel tracked the Picturesque's enduring influence thereafter.

Identifying cottage picturesque as the visuality fought over between builders and the RIBA between the wars also helps us understand how crucial domestic-architectural aesthetics were to the interwar period's spatialisation of class – the unintended consequence of England's interwar dwelling settlement. Picturesque architecture was overwhelmingly valorised in the purchase, between 1923 and 1939, of millions of suburban houses by the private buyer. But it remained effectively denied to the majority of council tenants. The resulting polarity requires a new iteration of the concept of 'housing classes' posited in the 1960s' work of Rex and Moore.

Theirs is 'a hierarchy of values concerning housing in Britain, ranging from debt-free home-ownership, through mortgaged ownership, and the various forms of renting, to lodging in rooms'.[18] For those seeking to understand the class dimensions of interwar England's emergent domestic-architectural landscape, this class-inflected hierarchy of tenure should be supplemented by an hierarchy of aesthetics. Whereas the picturesque middle-class rural bolthole, and the *homage* to the cottage picturesque put up by the suburban spec-builder, were available to the homebuyer, they shared the kind of appearance deliberately made off-limits to those renting the majority of council houses built after 1922. Cottage picturesque and its derivatives came thus to function as a new class marker.

There are some broad brushstrokes here, of course. Not all interwar spec-building was picturesque – though experiments in modernism did not tend to prosper commercially.[19] Some among the middle classes moved to council estates in 1920–21 (at the LCC's Roehampton Estate they were gradually encouraged to leave) but when they stayed they tended to be among the least contented.[20] Only 14 per cent of people in England and Wales lived in council property by 1939; and, as Clapson reminds us, most lived happy and 'decent' lives, too often subject to the 'condescension of posterity'.[21] Class within private and municipal estates should never be regarded as homogeneous

– hierarchies have always prospered intra- as well as inter-class.[22]

Yet prior to 1919, Unwin and Barnett had shared a progressive vision for social-housing where, as Unwin put it, the architecture might have 'such a standard of amenity that the smallest types of houses would afford no justification, by their lack of comeliness, for the well-to-do to live out of sight of them'.[23] Addison Scheme cottage building in 1919–21 had the potential to deliver such a moment – on a national scale. The best of its architecture did not lack comeliness; the need for housing at the time crossed class boundaries; and the notion of a government-subsidised, council-owned dwelling was sufficiently novel not to bring established class semiotics automatically into play. Yet government determination from 1921 onwards to minimise spending on social housing squandered this opportunity. Civil servant Alfred Hurst sounded the eternal Treasury tocsin in 1921: 'a large proportion of the population lived in "jerry-built" houses before the war + we cannot afford better built houses now'.[24] Mond and Ruthen reacted by economising thereafter, countenancing only an ultra-plain, visually unambiguous version of the council house.

'Like a child's drawing . . . crude in shape . . . no distinguishing features,' was Margaret Forster's description of the two-bed 1931 specimen where she was born and grew up on the Raffles council estate in Carlisle.[25] So legible was their aesthetic disparity from England's nineteenth-century home-building tradition, as theorised and perpetuated by the Picturesque, that these plain new dwellings imposed upon their inhabitants a manifestation of social apartness that Forster experienced and resented in Carlisle,[26] and that Barnett believed she had witnessed at Becontree – '90,000 people of the same class . . . "housed" in what must be annoying monotony'.[27] Between the wars, a new, constructionally objectified social class was created – council house tenant[28] – visually overdetermined by the cut-price formality of the domestic architectural exteriors that government was prepared to finance, and by the time-honoured aesthetics of cottage picturesque that were wittingly denied them.

NOTES

INTRODUCTION

1 Card No.19, 'Amberley, Sussex', Player's Cigarettes, *Picturesque Cottages*, 1929. Text quotes Thomas Moore's poem 'Ballad Stanzas' – *The Lady's Weekly Miscellany*, vol.14, no.4, 16 November 1811 (New York). The poem was originally about a Canadian cottage.

2 Evelyn Waugh, *Labels* (London, 1985 [1930]), p.46.

3 Osbert Lancaster, *Homes Sweet Homes* (London, 1939), p.68.

4 Professor A.E. Richardson, in 'Vote of Thanks and Discussion', *Journal of the Royal Institute of British Architects*, vol.45, no.11, 11 April 1938, p.538.

5 *Twentieth Annual Report of the Ministry of Health 1938–39*, Cmd. 6089 (London, 1939), pp 86–7.

6 Henry Hare, 'Good Building', *The Times*, 1 July 1919, p.8.

7 Karl Silex, *John Bull at Home* (London, 1931), p.39.

8 Adrian Tinniswood, *Life in the English Country Cottage* (London, 1997), p.10.

9 *OED* analysis uses Google Books Ngram data (version 2) from several million books published between 1500 and 2010; and online news sources for more recent data. Use frequency of the word 'cottage': 14.5 instances per million (1920–30); 5.9 instances per million (2017–23); https://www.oed.com/dictionary/cottage_n?tab=frequency/8035931.

10 'Manifesto of Mr Lloyd George and Mr Bonar Law', in F.W.S. Craig, ed., *British General Election Manifestos* (London, 1975), pp 28–9.

11 John Burnett, *A Social History of Housing, 1815–1985* (London, 1986), pp 267–8.

12 'The £300 House', *Garden Cities and Town Planning*, vol.12, no.8, September–October 1922, p.143.

13 Rosemary Hill, *God's Architect: Pugin and the Building of Romantic Britain* (London, 2007), p.16.

14 Uvedale Price, *An Essay on the Picturesque* (London, 1796), p.175.

15 John Macarthur, *The Picturesque: Architecture, Disgust and Other Irregularities* (Abingdon, 2007), p.131. Lars Spuybroek, *The Sympathy of Things: Ruskin and the Ecology of Design* (London, 2016), pp 167–8.

16 Christopher Hussey, *The Picturesque: Studies in a Point of View* (London, 1927), p.186.

17 Terence Conran, ed., *The House Book* (London, 1982 [1974]), p.25.

18 *Homes and Gardens*, vol.5, no.7, December 1923, p.xxxiii.

19 Maurice Adams, 'Appreciation of the Picturesque', *The British Architect*, March 1918, p.26.

20 Lynsey Hanley, *Estates: An Intimate History* (London, 2012), p.ix.

21 Raymond Unwin, 'Town Planning Institute', *The Builder*, vol.114, no.3922, 5 April 1918, p.209.

22 Charles Reilly, 'The Immediate Future in England', in *The Transactions of the Royal Institute of British Architects Town Planning Conference, London, 10–15 October 1910* (Abingdon, 2011), p.342.

23 Reginald Blomfield, *The Touchstone of Architecture* (Oxford, 1925), p.127.

24 Wyndham Lewis, *The Caliph's Design* (Santa Barbara, 1986 [1919]), p.23.

25 W.R. Lethaby, *Architecture: An Introduction to the History and Theory of the Art of Building* (London, 1911), p.251.

26 Stanley Baldwin, 'The Torch I Would Hand On', in *The Service of Our Lives* (London, 1938), p.163.

27 Alison Light, *Forever England: Femininity, Literature and Conservatism between the Wars* (London, 1991), p.19.

28 Stuart Sillars, *Picturing England Between the Wars: Word and Image 1918–1940* (Oxford, 2022), pp ix and 3.

29 D.H. Lawrence, 'Nottingham and the Mining Countryside' (1930), in James T. Boulton, ed., *Late Essays and Articles*, Cambridge Edition of the Works of D.H. Lawrence (Cambridge, 2014), p.293.

30 Ross McKibbin, 'Reviews: "The People: The Rise and Fall of the Working Class 1910–2010"', *Twentieth Century British History*, vol.25, no.4, 2014, p.651.

31 Captain G.C. Clarke, 'Foreword', *The Ideal Home*, vol.1, no.1, January 1920, p.1.

32 Laurence Gomme, *Housing of the Working Classes, 1889–1912* (London, 1913), pp 7–10.

33 Ministry of Reconstruction, Housing (Financial Assistance) Committee, *Interim Report on Public Utility Societies*, Cd. 9223 (London, 1918), p.12.

34 L.T. Hobhouse, *The Elements of Social Justice* (London, 1922), p.163; L.T. Hobhouse, *Social Development: Its Nature and Conditions* (Oxford, 2010 [1924]), p.365.

35 A.M. Carr-Saunders and D. Caradog Jones, *A Survey of the Social Structure of England and Wales* (Oxford, 1937 [1927]), p.67.

36 Morris Ginsberg, *Sociology* (London, 1934), pp 166–70.

37 David Cannadine, *The Rise and Fall of Class in Britain* (New York, 1999), p.110.

38 R.H. Tawney, *Equality* (London, 1983 [1931]), p.71.

39 Allen Hutt, *The Condition of the Working Class in Britain* (London, 1933), p.226.

40 Howel Evans, 'Where are we to find Good Houses?', *The Daily Mirror*, 15 January 1919, p.7.

41 Ross McKibbin, *The Ideologies of Class: Social Relations in Britain, 1880–1950* (Oxford, 1991), p.284.

42 John Pretyman Newman MP, Letter to the Editor: 'The Middle Classes', *The Times*, 14 November 1919, p.8.

43 John Rex and Robert Moore, *Race, Community and Conflict* (London, 1967), pp 273–4. Robert Moore, 'Forty-Four Years of Debate: The Impact of Race, Community and Conflict', *Sociological Research Online*, vol.16, no.3, August 2011, pp 194–201.

44 M. Savage, G. Bagnall and B. Longhurst, in Rowland Atkinson, 'Padding the Bunker: Strategies of Middle-class Disaffiliation and Colonisation in the City', *Urban Studies*, vol.43, no.4, April 2006, p.822.

45 C.F.A. Voysey, 'The Artisan's Cottage', *The Builder*, vol.116, no.3976, 18 April 1919, p.379.

46 P.A. Barron, *The House Desirable* (London, 1929), p.2.

47 Winifred Holtby, *South Riding* (London, 1936), p.15.

48 Raymond Williams, *Keywords: A Vocabulary of Culture and Society* (London, 1988), p.15.

49 Karen Sayer, *Country Cottages: A Cultural History* (Manchester, 2000).

50 Peter Burke, 'Review of "The History of Political and Social Concepts: A Critical Introduction" by Melvin Richter (New York, 1995)', *History of European Ideas*, vol.23, no.1, 1997, p.56. Reinhart Koselleck, in *The Meaning of Historical Terms and Concepts: New Studies of Begriffsgeschichte*, German Historical Institute Occasional Paper, 15th edition (Washington, DC, 1996), pp 61 and 67.

1 THE COTTAGE PICTURESQUE

1 Keith Tribe, 'Intellectual History as Begriffsgeschichte', in Richard Whatmore and Brian Young, eds, *A Companion to Intellectual History* (Chichester, 2016), p.61.

2 *First Report of Her Majesty's Commissioners for Enquiring into the Housing of the Working Classes*, C. 4402 (London, 1885), p.4.

3 Editorial – 'Housing without Hands', *The Times*, 31 March 1919, p.13.

4 Herbert Samuel MP, *Hansard*, 20 March 1914, c. 2455.

5 Birmingham Corporation Medical Officer of Health, 'Memo A', Meeting 28 June 1918, *Minutes of the Housing and Town Planning Committee*, Birmingham City Council, pp 295–6; BCC1/BL/1/1/2.

6 'Chronicle', *Journal of the Royal Institute of British Architects*, vol.22, no.12, 24 April 1915, p.308.

7 G.N. Barnes MP, *Commission of Enquiry into Industrial Unrest: Summary of the Reports of the Commission* (London, 1917), p.6.

8 Ministry of Reconstruction, *Housing in England & Wales: Memorandum by the Advisory Housing Panel on the Emergency Problem*, Cd. 9087 (London, October 1917), p.1.

9 Mervyn Miller, *Raymond Unwin: Garden Cities and Town Planning* (Leicester, 1992), p.162.

10 *Journal of the Royal Institute of British Architects*, vol.22, no.5, 9 January 1915, p.118.

11 Ministry of Reconstruction, *Housing in England & Wales*, pp 3–4.

12 Ministry of Reconstruction, Housing (Financial Assistance) Committee, *Interim Report on Public Utility Societies*, Cd. 9223 (London, 1918), p.4.

13 Kenneth O. Morgan, 'Addison, Christopher, First Viscount Addison (1869–1951)', *Oxford Dictionary of National Biography* (Oxford, 2011).

14 Letter from D. Lloyd George, Prime Minister, to All Government Departments, in Christopher Addison, *Four and a Half Years*, Vol. II (London, 1934), p.423.

15 Christopher Addison, 'Wednesday September 12, 1917', *Four and a Half Years*, p.428.

16 'Answers to the Questions Submitted by Dr Addison to the Housing Panel', August 1917, p.1; The National Archives, RECO 1/467.

17 'Answers to the Questions', p.1.

18 Henry Roberts, *The Dwellings of the Labouring Classes: Their Arrangement and Construction* (London, 1850), p.20.

19 Sheila Marriner, 'Sir Alfred Mond's Octopus: A Nationalised House-Building Business', *Business History*, vol.21, no.1, January 1979, pp 23–44 (p.41, n.26).

20 Christopher Turnor, Board of Agriculture Smallholdings Report, Cd. 6708 (London, 1913), pp 36–8.

21 Sir John Tudor Walters MP, Tudor Walters Report, Cd. 9191 (London, 1918), p.25.

22 Local Government Board, *Manual on the Preparation of State-Aided Housing Schemes* (London, 1919), pp 8 and 29.

23 Ebenezer Howard, Letter to the Editor: 'Garden Cities and Suburbs', *The Times*, 26 March 1919, p.7.

24 Manning Robertson, 'Architectural Education', *Housing*, vol.1, no.23, 24 May 1920, p.311.

25 Sydney R. Jones, *The Village Homes of England* (London, 1912), p.3.

26 M.H. Baillie Scott in 'Life and Labour – Cheap Cottages', *Daily News*, 17 August 1905, p.5.

27 J.M. Richards, *The Castles on the Ground* (London, 1946), p.23. Rosalind Blakesley, *The Arts and Crafts Movement* (London, 2009), p.131.

28 Karen Sayer, *Country Cottages: A Cultural History* (Manchester, 2000), p.209.

29 Nathaniel Kent, *Hints to Gentlemen of Landed Property*, 1st edn (London, 1775), p.232.

30 Roberts, *Dwellings of the Labouring Classes*, pp 4 and 21.

31 para. 15, *Labourers' Cottages Improvement Act, 1861*, 27 June 1861, p.4.

32 The Earl of Shaftesbury, 11 March 1884, para. 19, 'Minutes of Evidence and Appendix as to England and Wales', in *Royal Commission on the Housing of the Working Classes* (London, 1885), p.2.

33 Raymond Unwin, *Cottage Plans and Common Sense*, Fabian Tract 109 (London, 1902), pp 11–13.

34 Raymond Unwin, 'Cottage Building in Garden City', *The Garden City*, vol.1, no.5, June 1906, pp 108–9.

35 Turnor, Board of Agriculture Report, pp 683–99.

36 Ministry of Reconstruction, *Housing in England & Wales*, p.5.

37 'Manifesto of Mr Lloyd George and Mr Bonar Law', in F.W.S. Craig, ed., *British General Election Manifestos* (London, 1975), pp 28–9.

38 James Malton, *An Essay on British Cottage Architecture* (London, 1798), p.4.

39 Samuel Johnson, *A Dictionary of the English Language* (London, 1755), p.505.

40 James A.H. Murray, *A New English Dictionary on Historical Principles*, Vol. II, Part VII (Oxford, 1893), p.1042.

41 Murray, 'Prefatory Note', in *New English Dictionary*, Vol. II, Part VII, p.v.

42 Paul Readman, *Storied Ground: Landscape and the Shaping of English National Identity* (Cambridge, 2018), pp 10–14.

43 James Stevens Curl, *Victorian Architecture* (Newton Abbott, 1990), p.20.

44 Arthur Bryant, *English Saga 1840–1940* (London, 1940), p.45.

45 Sir Leslie Stephen, *Hours in a Library*, Vol. III (London, 1991 [1892]), p.165.

46 H.V. Morton, *In Search of England* (London, 1935), p.viii. C.R. Perry, 'In Search of H.V. Morton', *Twentieth Century British History*, vol.10, no.4, 1999, p.433, n.3.

47 Stanley Baldwin, 'The Beauty of England: A Treasure in Our Keeping', in *The Torch I Would Hand to You* (London, 1937 [1928]), pp 95–6.

48 Richard Griffiths, *Fellow Travellers of the Right: British Enthusiasts for Nazi Germany, 1933–39* (London, 1980), pp 317–19. G.C. Webber, *The Ideology of the British Right, 1918–1939* (London, 1986), pp 57–9. Patrick Wright, *The Village that Died for England: The Strange Story of Tyneham* (London, 1995), pp 170–75.

49 Alun Howkins in Simon Miller, 'Urban Dreams and Rural Reality: Land and Landscape in English Culture, 1920–45', *Rural History*, vol.6, no.1, 1995, p.90.

50 Bryant, *English Saga*, p.42.

51 Urania Cottage, the 'Home for Homeless Women', was set up by Dickens and Burdett-Coutts in Shepherd's Bush. They called it a cottage, despite its being a small Regency house, to typologise its ambitions for domesticity and moral reform – Jenny Hartley, 'Undertexts and Intertexts: The Women of Urania Cottage, Secrets and *Little Dorrit*', *Critical Survey*, vol.17, no.2, Dickens and Sex, 2005, pp 63–76.

52 Peter Higginbotham, 'Cottage Homes', *The Workhouse: The Story of an Institution*; https://www.workhouses.org.uk/cottagehomes/.

53 Thomas Sharp, *Town and Countryside* (Oxford, 1932), p.7.

54 Henry Lord Brougham, *Historical Sketches of Statesmen*, Vol. 1 (London and Glasgow, 1858), p.42.

55 Benjamin Disraeli (1848), in William Monypenny and George Buckle, *The Life of Benjamin Disraeli*, Vol. II (London, 1929), p.709.

56 'Manifesto of Mr Lloyd George and Mr Bonar Law', in F.W.S. Craig, ed., *British General Election Manifestos* (London, 1975), pp 28–9.

57 Thomas Macaulay, 'Horatius', *Lays of Ancient Rome* (New York, 1871), p.50. Mrs Cecil Frances Alexander, 'All Things Bright and Beautiful', *Hymns for Little Children* (London, 1849).

58 Charles Innocent, *The Development of English Building Construction* (Donhead St Mary, 1999 [1916]), pp 5 and 11.

59 Colin Ward, *Cotters and Squatters: Housing's Hidden History* (Nottingham, 2005), pp 5–13, 41–3.

60 J.L. Hammond and Barbara Hammond, *The Village Labourer* (London, 1978 [1911]), p.5. G.E. Mingay, *Parliamentary Enclosure in England: An Introduction to its Causes, Incidence and Impact, 1750–1850* (London, 1997), p.13. Danae Tankard, 'The Regulation of Cottage-Building in Seventeenth-Century Sussex', *The Agricultural History Review*, vol.59, no.1, 2011, p.30.

61 William Gilpin, *Remarks on Forest Scenery*, Vol. II (London, 1791), p.39.

62 Tankard, 'Regulation of Cottage-Building', pp 19–20.

63 George Ewart Evans, *Ask the Fellows Who Cut the Hay* (London, 2018 [1956]), pp 251–3. Flora Thompson, *Lark Rise to Candleford* (Harmondsworth, 1982 [1939]), p.18. Ward, *Cotters and Squatters*, pp 63–70.

64 John Woodforde, *The Truth about Cottages* (London, 1969), pp 11–12.

65 Clauses I–III, 'An Act against the Erecting and Maintaining of Cottages' (31 Eliz. c7, 1589) in *The Statutes at Large from the First Year of the Reign of King Edward the Fourth to the End of the Reign of Queen Elizabeth* (London, 1963), p.664.

66 Keith Wrightson, *English Society 1580–1680* (London, 1988), p.166. Tankard, 'Regulation of Cottage-Building', p.19.

67 Steve Hindle, *On The Parish? The Micro-Politics of Poor Relief in Rural England* (Oxford, 2004), p.304.

68 Oliver Goldsmith, 'The Deserted Village' (1769) in E.T. Stevens, ed., *Annotated Poems of English Authors* (London, 1876).

69 John Clare, 'The Fallen Elm', *John Clare*, ed. Paul Farley (London, 2011), p.42.

70 Gilpin, *Remarks on Forest Scenery*, p.46.

71 E.P. Thompson, *The Making of the English Working Class* (Harmondsworth, 1982), p.243.

72 Benjamin Disraeli, *Sybil* (Oxford, 2020 [1845]), p.50.

73 H.J. Massingham, 'Our Inheritance from the Past', in Clough Williams-Ellis, ed., *Britain and the Beast* (London, 1937), pp 9–10.

74 Revd George Crabbe, *The Village: A Poem* (London, 1783).

75 John Barrell, *The Spirit of Despotism: Invasions of Privacy in the 1790s* (Oxford, 2006), pp 220–25.

76 Simon Bainbridge, *British Poetry and the Revolutionary and Napoleonic Wars: Visions of Conflict* (Oxford, 2003), pp 40–41.

77 William Cobbett, *Cobbett's Cottage-Economy* (London, 1822), p.3. Alice Chandler, *A Dream of Order: The Medieval Ideal in Nineteenth-Century English Literature* (London, 1971), pp 61 and 77.

78 Patrick Joyce, *Visions of the People: Industrial England and the Question of Class, 1848–1914* (Cambridge, 1991), pp 32–3.

79 Matthew Roberts, 'Richard Oastler, Toryism, Radicalism and the Limitations of Party, 1807–1846', *Parliamentary History*, vol.37, no.2, 2018, pp 250–73.

80 W.G. Hoskins, *The Making of the English Landscape* (Harmondsworth, 1985), p.155.

81 'The Cottage Problem', *The Spectator*, vol.83, no.3723, 4 November 1899, p.652.

82 Christopher Hussey, *The Life of Sir Edwin Lutyens* (London, 1950), p.187.

83 Edward Hubbard and Michael Shippobottom, *A Guide to Port Sunlight Village* (Liverpool, 2009), p.4.

84 Nicholas Taylor, *The Village in the City: Towards a New Society* (London, 1973), p.66.

85 'Democratic Control of Society', *The Times*, 3 January 1918, p.3.

86 Special Correspondent, 'The Election: Labour at Deptford', *The Times*, 12 December 1918, p.9.

87 G.R. Searle, 'Billing, Noel Pemberton', *Oxford Dictionary of National Biography* (Oxford, 2015).

88 'MP's Housing Scheme', *The Times*, 8 January 1919, p.3.

89 Lord Conway, *Episodes in a Varied Life* (London, 1932), pp 38–9.

90 Martin Conway MP, *Hansard*, 8 April 1919, p.1916.

91 Major Astor MP, *Hansard*, 8 April 1919, p.1947.

92 Jill Allibone, *George Devey: Architect 1820–1886* (Cambridge, 1991), pp 46–7.

93 'No Gossip for Cottagers', *Daily Mail*, 29 August 1919, p.4.

94 'The Duke of Bedford and Lord Northcliffe and their Cottages', *The Spectator*, vol.123, no.4766, 1 November 1919, p.12.

95 Roberts, *Dwellings of the Labouring Classes*, pp 19–20.

96 Alison Ravetz, *Council Housing and Culture: The History of a Social Experiment* (London, 2001), p.5.

97 John Ruskin, 'Lecture I, Architecture', *Lectures on Architecture and Painting*, Library Edition, *The Works of John Ruskin*, Vol. XII, ed. E.T. Cook and A. Wedderburn (London, 1903–9), p.33.

98 Virgil, 'Eclogue I', in Raymond Williams, *The Country and the City* (London, 1985 [1973]), p.16. Daniel Maudlin, *The Idea of the Cottage in English Architecture, 1760–1860* (Abingdon, 2015), pp 17–21.

99 Freya Gowrley, *Domestic Space in Britain, 1750–1840: Materiality, Sociability and Emotion* (London, 2022), p.1.

100 Edith Hall and Henry Stead, *A People's History of Classics: Class and Greco-Roman Antiquity in Britain and Ireland 1689–1939* (London, 2020), pp 533 and 24–33.

101 Maudlin, *The Idea of the Cottage*, pp 22–3.

102 John Milton, 'L'Allegro', *The English Poems of John Milton* (London, 1958 [1631/2]), p.22.

103 Sarah Lloyd, 'Cottage Conversations: Poverty and Manly Independence in Eighteenth-Century England', *Past & Present*, vol.184, 2004, p.70.

104 Samuel Ireland, *Picturesque Views on the Upper or Warwickshire Avon* (London, 1795), p.225.

105 Andrew Sanders, *In the Olden Time: Victorians and the British Past* (London, 2013), pp 60–62. Andrea Zemgulys, 'Henry James in a Victorian Crowd: "The Birthplace" in Context', *The Henry James Review*, vol.29, 2008, pp 245–56.

106 Katherine West Scheil, 'Anne Hathaway's Cottage: Myth, Tourism and Diplomacy', in Clara Calvo and Coppélia Kahn, eds, *Celebrating Shakespeare: Commemoration and Cultural Memory* (Cambridge, 2015), p.330.

107 Samuel Taylor Coleridge, 'Fears in Solitude', in Herbert Read, ed., *The English Vision – An Anthology* (London, 1933 [1798]), p.150.

108 Sidney K. Robinson, *Inquiry into the Picturesque* (Chicago, 1991), pp 67–8.

109 William Wordsworth, 'The Excursion: Book First, The Wanderer', *Complete Poetical Works* (Oxford, 1936 [1814]), p.602.

110 George Ford, 'Felicitous Space: The Cottage Controversy', in U.C. Knoepflmacher and G.B. Tennyson, eds, *Nature and the Victorian Imagination* (Berkeley, 1977), p.32.

111 Robert Southey, 'Colloquies on the Progress or Prospects of Society' (1829), in Thomas Macaulay, *Critical and Historical Essays Contributed to the Edinburgh Review* (London: Longman, Green and Roberts, 1830).

112 Samuel Rogers, *The Pleasures of Memory* (London, 1806 [1792]), pp 21 and 173–4.

113 Gary Kelly, 'Introduction', *Felicia Hemans, Selected Poems, Prose, and Letters* (Peterborough, Ontario, 2002), p.15.

114 Felicia Hemans, 'The Homes of England', *The Poetical Works of Felicia Hemans* (London, 1873), p.284.

115 Sir Walter Scott, Introduction, Canto IV, 'Marmion', *The Poetical Works of Sir Walter Scott* (Edinburgh, 1848), p.106.

116 Peter Mandler, *The Fall and Rise of the Stately Home* (London, 1997), pp 22–8.

117 'On the Choice of a Labouring Man's Dwelling', *The Penny Magazine*, vol.1, no.2, 7 April 1832, pp 15–16.

118 Charles Dickens, *Oliver Twist* (London, 2004 [1837]), p.269.

119 Charles Dickens, *Little Dorrit* (London, 2003 [1857]), p.600.

120 Charley Dickens, 'Anne Hathaway's Cottage', *All the Year Round*, vol.7, no.174, 30 April 1892, p.418.

121 George Eliot, *Middlemarch* (London, 1998 [1872]), p.31. Heather Miner, 'Reforming Spaces: The Architectural Imaginary of "Middlemarch"', *Victorian Review*, vol.38, no.1, 2012, pp 193–209.

122 Thomas Hardy, *Under the Greenwood Tree* (London, 1927 [1872]), pp 14, 120–21. Thomas Hardy, *Tess of the D'Urbervilles* (1891), in Sydney R. Jones, *English Village Homes* (London, 1936), p.5. Alexander M. Ross, *The Imprint of the Picturesque on Nineteenth-Century British Fiction* (Waterloo, Ontario, 1986).

123 'Notes – Mr Thomas Hardy, Hon. Fellow RIBA', *The Builder*, vol.118, no.4036, 11 June 1920, p.680.

124 Jonathan Rose, *The Intellectual Life of the British Working Classes* (London, 2002), pp 116–45, 162, 373–4.

125 William Whitley, *Thomas Gainsborough* (London, 1915), pp 40–41.

126 Barrell, *Spirit of Despotism*, pp 213–14, 225. Ann Bermingham, ed., 'Introduction: Gainsborough's Cottage Door', *Sensation & Sensibility: Viewing Gainsborough's 'Cottage Door'* (London, 2005), pp 1–4.

127 Susan Sloman, '"Innocence and Health": Nursing Women in Gainsborough's Cottage-door paintings', in Bermingham, ed., *Sensation & Sensibility*, p.37.

128 Elizabeth Helsinger, *Rural Scenes and National Representation: Britain, 1815–1850* (Princeton, NJ, 1996), pp 58–64.

129 Frances Spalding, *The Real and the Romantic: English Art Between Two World Wars* (London, 2022), p.264.

130 John Dixon Hunt, 'The Cult of the Cottage', in *The Lake District: A Sort of National Property* (London, 1986), p.78.

131 Tom Taylor, *Birket Foster's Pictures of English Landscape* (London, 1863), p.40. David Watkin, *The English Vision: The Picturesque in Architecture, Landscape and Garden Design* (London, 1982), p.147.

132 M.H. Spielmann and G.S. Layard, *Kate Greenaway* (London, 1905), p.2.

133 John Ruskin, Letter to Kate Greenaway, 15 January 1880, in Spielmann and Layard, *Kate Greenaway*, p.83.

134 Kate Greenaway, Letter to John Ruskin, 30 November 1886, in *Kate Greenaway*, pp 160–61.

135 Helen Allingham, in *Kate Greenaway*, p.173.

136 A Practising Architect, 'Modern English Architecture', *The Builder*, no.124, no.4172, 19 January 1923, p.114.

137 George Gissing, *The Private Papers of Henry Ryecroft* (London, 1903), p.84.

138 Ruskin, 'Lecture IV – Fairy Land: Mrs Allingham and Kate Greenaway', in *The Art of England*, Library Edition, *The Works of John Ruskin*, Vol. XXXIII, ed. E.T. Cook and A. Wedderburn (London, 1903–9), pp 327–49.

139 Jennifer Schacker, 'Unruly Tales: Ideology, Anxiety, and the Regulation of Genre', *The Journal of American Folklore*, vol.120, no.478, 2007, pp 381–400.

140 'Country Cottages: The Lost Art of Building', *The Times*, 28 November 1917, p.9.

141 Stewart Dick and Helen Allingham, *The Cottage Homes of England* (London, 1909), p.8.

142 Anne Helmreich, 'The Marketing of Helen Allingham: The English Cottage and National Identity', in Steven Adams and Anna Greutzner Robins, eds, *Gendering Landscape Art* (Manchester, 2000), p.57.

143 'Minutes of Evidence and Appendix as to England and Wales', Vol. II, *Royal Commission on the Housing of the Working Classes* (London, 1885), p.162. See also, Lord William Compton, para. 726, p.38.

144 C.F.G. Masterman, *The Condition of England* (London, 1960 [1909]), p.89.

145 John Boughton, 'Municipal Housing in Liverpool before 1914: The "First Council Houses in Europe"', *Municipal Dreams*; https://municipaldreams.wordpress.com/2013/10/08/liverpool-first-council-houses-in-europe/.

146 Laura Wright, *Sunnyside: A Sociolinguistic History of British Place Names* (Oxford, 2020), p.57.

147 Kenneth Grahame, *The Wind in the Willows* (London, 2012 [1908]), p.107.

148 Christopher Holdenby, *Folk of the Furrow* (London, 1913), pp 49–50.

149 'The Stoics of Mayfair' by V.L.C. Booth, *Punch*, vol.133, no.3490, 30 October 1907, p.319.

150 C.F.A. Voysey, 'London Street Architecture and its Possibilities', *The Architectural Association Journal*, vol.20, no.215, January 1905, p.2.

151 Roger White, *Cottages Ornés: The Charms of the Simple Life* (London, 2017), pp 6–8.

152 W.G. Horseman, 'Cottages', *Journal of the Royal Institute of British Architects*, vol.21, no.6, 31 January 1914, p.197.

153 Lawrence Weaver, 'Preface', *The 'Country Life' Book of Cottages* (London, 1913).

154 Gordon Allen, *The Cheap Cottage & Small House* (Letchworth, 1912), pp 6–8.

155 Hussey, *Life of Sir Edwin Lutyens*, p.78.

156 Rebecca Tropp, 'The Interior Topography of the Picturesque', *Architectural History*, vol.66, 2023, p.156.

157 John Macarthur, *The Picturesque: Architecture, Disgust and Other Irregularities* (Abingdon, 2007), p.131. Lars Spuybroek, *The Sympathy of Things: Ruskin and the Ecology of Design* (London, 2016), pp 167–8.

158 Wilfrid Travers, *Architectural Education* (London, 1908), pp 8–9.

159 Robert Kerr, *The Gentleman's House, or How to Plan English Residences from the Parsonage to the Palace* (Cambridge, 2012 [1864]), p.360.

160 Stanley Adshead, 'Romford Garden Suburb, Gidea Park', *Town Planning Review*, vol.2, no.2, July 1911, pp 125–6.

161 Henry-Russell Hitchcock compares Price and Knight's writings 'more than favourably with those of contemporary French architect-academicians such as A.C. Quatremère de Quincy (1755–1849)', *Early Victorian Architecture in Britain* (London, 1954), p.24.

162 Andrew Ballantyne and Andrew Law, *Tudoresque* (London, 2011), p.12.

163 *OED* analysis reports the use frequency of 'Tudoresque' at a very low average 0.0027 instances per million published words between 1920 and 1940. 'Tudoresque, adj.', *Oxford English Dictionary*, Oxford University Press, September 2023; see https://www.oed.com/dictionary/tudoresque_adj?tab=frequency.

164 Ivor de Wolfe, Letter to Christopher Hussey, 12 October 1950; National Trust, Scotney Castle Archive, File 2/2/6/8 (Box 3/4).

165 Mathew Aitchison and John Macarthur, 'Pevsner's Townscape', in Aitchison, ed., *Visual Planning and the Picturesque* (Los Angeles, 2010), p.24.

166 Nikolaus Pevsner, in Aitchison, ed., *Visual Planning and the Picturesque* (Los Angeles, 2010), p.145.

167 Sigrid de Jong, *Rediscovering Architecture: Paestum in Eighteenth-Century Architectural Experience and Theory* (London, 2014), p.74.

168 Reyner Banham, *Theory and Design in the First Machine Age* (London, 1988 [1960]), pp 32–3.

169 J. Mordaunt Crook, *The Dilemma of Style: Architectural Ideas from the Picturesque to the Post-Modern* (London, 1987), pp 41–6.

170 Rosemary Hill, *God's Architect: Pugin and the Building of Romantic Britain* (London, 2007), p.116.

171 Andrew Saint, *Richard Norman Shaw* (London, 2010), pp 86–9. Hussey, *Life of Sir Edwin Lutyens*, p.78.

172 Christopher Hussey, *The Picturesque: Studies in a Point of View* (London, 1927), pp 7–12.

173 Hussey, *The Picturesque*, p.186.

174 Hussey, *The Picturesque*, p.217.

175 Banham, *Theory and Design*, p.21.

176 Joshua Reynolds, 'Discourse Thirteen', in *Discourses on Art* (London, 1969 [1786]), p.212.

177 William Gilpin, *Observations on the River Wye* (London, 1782). Kim Ian Michasiw, 'Nine Revisionist Theses on the Picturesque', *Representations*, no.38, Spring 1992, pp 81–2.

178 Uvedale Price, *An Essay on the Picturesque* (London, 1796), pp 49–67. Richard Payne Knight, *An Analytical Inquiry into the Principles of Taste*, 1st edn (London, 1805), pp 164–218.

179 Humphry Repton, 'The Cottage', in *The Red Book of Blaise Castle* (Bristol, 1795–96), Bristol City Council Fine Art Collection, Mb2400.

180 Nikolaus Pevsner, *Studies in Art, Architecture and Design, Volume I: From Mannerism to Romanticism* (London, 1968), pp 79–82. Andrew Ballantyne, *Architecture, Landscape and Liberty: Richard Payne Knight and the Picturesque* (Cambridge, 1997), p.208.

181 Daniel Elsea, ed., *Pragmatics of the Picturesque: Strategies for the Contemporary City* (London, 2021).

182 de Jong, *Rediscovering Architecture*, p.74.

183 T.F. Hunt, *Half a Dozen Hints on Picturesque Domestic Architecture* (London, 1841 [1825]), p.i. A reaction, perhaps, to Gilpin's interest in further ruining ruins – Hussey, *The Picturesque*, p.195.

184 Price, *An Essay*, p.61.

185 Stephen Daniels and Charles Watkins, 'Picturesque Landscaping and Estate Management: Uvedale Price and Nathaniel Kent at Foxley', in Stephen Copley and Peter Garside, eds, *The Politics of the Picturesque* (Cambridge, 1994), p.19.

186 Michasiw, 'Nine Revisionist Theses', pp 84, 89 and 99 (n.50).

187 J.T. Smith, *Remarks on Rural Scenery* (London, 1797), pp 5 and 12.

188 Francis Stevens, *Views of Cottages and Farm-Houses in England and Wales* (London, 1815).

189 Gilpin, *Remarks on Forest Scenery*, Vol. I (London, 1791), 216.

190 Price, *An Essay*, p.175.

191 Richard Payne Knight, *The Landscape: A Didactic Poem* (London, 1794), p.36.

192 Repton, 'The Cottage'. Nigel Temple, *John Nash and the Village Picturesque* (Gloucester, 1979), pp 50–51.

193 P.F. Robinson, *Rural Architecture, or A Series of Designs for Ornamental Cottages* (London, 1823), p.201.

194 Ann Bermingham, *Landscape and Ideology: The English Rustic Tradition 1740–1860* (Berkeley, 1986); Nigel Everett, *The Tory View of Landscape* (New Haven and London, 1994); Macarthur, *The Picturesque*; Spuybroek, *The Sympathy of Things*.

195 Humphry Repton, 'A Letter to Uvedale Price, Esq', in *A Letter to H. Repton, Esq* (London, 1798), p.10.

196 Michasiw, 'Nine Revisionist Theses', pp 86 and 94. Robinson, *Inquiry*, p.120.

197 Copley and Garside, 'Introduction', in *Politics of the Picturesque*, p.6.

198 Robinson, *Inquiry*, p.126.

199 Spuybroek, *The Sympathy of Things*, p.169.

200 Hitchcock, *Early Victorian Architecture*, pp 24–8. Macarthur, *The Picturesque*, p.131.

201 John Macarthur, 'The Picturesque: Architecture and Urbanism', in Elsea, ed., *Pragmatics of the Picturesque* (London, 2021), p.17.

202 Malton, *An Essay*, p.1.

203 Malton, *An Essay*, p.5.

204 Hunt, *Half a Dozen Hints*, p.ii.

205 George Gilbert Scott, *Remarks on Secular & Domestic Architecture* (London, 1857), p.4.

206 Kenneth Clarke, *The Gothic Revival* (London, 1928), p.206.

207 J. Mordaunt Crook, 'John Nash and the Genesis of Regent's Park', in Geoffrey Tyack, ed., *John Nash: Architect of the Picturesque* (Swindon, 2013), pp 81 and 91.

208 Nigel Temple, 'In Search of the Cottage Picturesque', *The Georgian Group Report and Journal*, 1988, p.74.

209 White, *Cottages Ornés*, pp 178–82.

210 Kent, *Hints to Gentlemen of Landed Property*. J. Wood, *A Series of Plans for Cottages or Habitations of the Labourer* (London, 1806 [1781]). Daniel Maudlin, 'Habitations of the Labourer: Improvement, Reform and the Neoclassical Cottage in Eighteenth-Century Britain', *The Journal of Design History*, vol.23, no.1, 2010, p.8.

211 Roberts, *Dwellings of the Labouring Classes*, p.vii.

212 Gilbert Laing Meason, *On the Landscape Architecture of the Great Painters of Italy* (London, 1828), pp 65–6.

213 Eric Mercer, *English Vernacular Houses: A Study of Traditional Farmhouses and Cottages* (London, 1975), p.75.

214 Hunt, *Half a Dozen Hints*, p.i.

215 'The Picturesque was a long time dying', in Adrian Tinniswood, *Life in the English Country Cottage* (London, 1997), p.195.

216 H.S. Goodhart-Rendel, *English Architecture since the Regency: An Interpretation* (London, 1953), p.227.

217 William Wordsworth, 'Tintern Abbey', *Complete Poetical Works* (Oxford, 1936), p.164.

218 Ruskin, 'Poetry of Architecture', Library Edition, *The Works of John Ruskin*, Vol. I, ed. E.T. Cook and A. Wedderburn (London, 1903–9), pp 11–12.

219 Ruskin, 'Lecture I, Architecture', in *Lectures on Architecture and Painting*, Library Edition, *The Works of John Ruskin*, Vol. XII, ed. E.T. Cook and A. Wedderburn (London, 1903–9), pp 32–3.

220 Ruskin, para. 205, 'The Eagle's Nest', in *Ten Lectures on the Relation of Natural Science to Art*, Library Edition, *The Works of John Ruskin*, Vol. XXII, ed. E.T. Cook and A. Wedderburn (London, 1903–9), p.263.

221 Ruskin, para. 11, 'Lamp of Memory', in *Seven Lamps*, Library Edition, *The Works of John Ruskin*, Vol. VIII, ed. E.T. Cook and A. Wedderburn (London, 1903–9), p.235.

222 Hussey, *Life of Sir Edwin Lutyens*, p.78.

223 Ruskin, para. 24, 'The Lamp of Power', in *Seven Lamps*, Library Edition, *The Works of John Ruskin*, Vol. VIII, ed. E.T. Cook and A. Wedderburn (London, 1903–9), p.136. Blomfield particularly disapproved of this passage – *The Mistress Art* (London, 1908), p.92.

224 Spuybroek, *The Sympathy of Things*, p.189.

225 Ruskin, 'Lecture I, Architecture'; Ruskin, para. 11, 'Lamp of Memory', pp 34 and 33.

226 Ruskin, 'Lamp of Memory', p.36.

227 Nicholas Taylor, *Village in the City*, p.7.

228 Ruskin, 'Lamp of Memory', p.43.

229 Ruskin, 'Lamp of Memory', pp 49 and 50.

230 Hussey, *The Picturesque*, pp 193–4. Chris Brooks, *The Gothic Revival* (London, 1999), p.93. Olive Cook, *The English House through Seven Centuries* (Harmondsworth, 1984 [1968]), p.280.

231 J. Mordaunt Crook, *William Burges and the High Victorian Dream* (London, 2013), p.90.

232 A.W.N. Pugin, *The True Principles of Pointed or Christian Architecture* (London, 1841), pp 1–2.

233 Elizabeth Helsinger, *Ruskin and the Art of the Beholder* (Cambridge, MA, 1982), pp 83–4.

234 Hill, *God's Architect*, p.425.

235 Ruskin, in Maudlin, *Idea of the Cottage in English Architecture*, p.128.

236 Ruskin, para. 7, 'The Lamp of Sacrifice', in *Seven Lamps*, Library Edition, *The Works of John Ruskin*, Vol. VIII, ed. E.T. Cook and A. Wedderburn (London, 1903–9), p.39.

237 Saint, *Richard Norman Shaw*, p.75.

238 Meason, *On the Landscape Architecture*, p.65.

239 Allibone, *George Devey*, pp 23 and 28–33.

240 Mark Girouard, *The Victorian Country House* (London, 1990), p.312.

241 Saint, *Richard Norman Shaw*, p.43.

242 J. Mordaunt Crook, 'The Pre-Victorian Architect: Professionalism & Patronage', *Architectural History*, vol.12, 1969, p.62.

243 Girouard, *Victorian Country House*, p.312.

244 George Santayana, *Soliloquies in England* (New York, 1923), p.74.

245 P.F. Robinson, 'Design XX', in *Rural Architecture*, p.245.

246 Allibone, *George Devey*, p.56.

247 Spuybroek, *The Sympathy of Things*, p.168.

248 'The Inspirations of Our Fathers', *The Builder*, vol.115, no.3950, 18 October 1918, p.237.

249 John Betjeman, in Edward Mirzoeff, *Metro-Land with John Betjeman* (BBC, 1973). Film, Voysey from 36mins 20secs; Shaw from 22mins 56secs.

250 Kate Greenaway, Letter to Mrs Severn, in M.H. Spielmann and G.S. Layard, *Kate Greenaway* (London, 1905), p.143.

251 Philip Webb in Mark Girouard, *Sweetness and Light: The Queen Anne Movement, 1860–1900* (Oxford, 1977), p.120.

252 Mordaunt Crook, *William Burges*, p.102.

253 Not Joseph Gandy's – *Designs for Cottages, Cottage Farms, and other Rural Buildings* (London, 1805). His were a mixture of neo-classical and picturesque Italianate.

254 Richard Norman Shaw, 'Preface', *Architectural Sketches from the Continent* (London, 1858). Saint, *Richard Norman Shaw*, pp 9–10.

255 Girouard, *Victorian Country House*, p.312.

256 Saint, *Richard Norman Shaw*, pp 75 and 321.

257 Geoffrey Scott, *The Architecture of Humanism* (London, 1961 [1914]), p.90.

258 Charles Whibley, 'Ruskin Reversed', *Daily Mail*, 8 February 1919, p.4.

2   THE COTTAGE CONTESTED

1 Beresford Pite, 'Architects and the Architecture of Cottages', *The Architectural Review*, vol.49, no.1262, 12 March 1919, p.149.

2 Julienne Hanson, *Decoding Homes and Houses* (Cambridge, 1998), p.307.

3 Pite, 'Architecture of Cottages', p.149.

4 Henry Hare, 'Good Building', *The Times*, 1 July 1919, p.8.

5 Guy Dawber, *Old Cottages and Farmhouses in Kent and Sussex* (London, 1900), p.28.

6 William Whyte, 'Memorialists', *Oxford Dictionary of National Biography* (Oxford, 2007).

7 Robert Kerr, *The Gentleman's House, or How to Plan English Residences from the Parsonage to the Palace . . .* (Cambridge, 2012 [1864]), p.360.

8 Patrick Zamarian, *The Architectural Association in the Postwar Years* (London, 2020), p.14; Alan Powers, *Modern: The Modern Movement in Britain* (London, 2005), p.13.

9 'Working Class Housing Schemes and Architects', *Journal of the Royal Institute of British Architects*, vol.24, August 1917, p.244.

10 'National Housing and National Life', *Journal of the Royal Institute of British Architects*, vol.25, June 1918, p.170.

11 'Answers to the Questions Submitted by Dr Addison to the Housing Panel', August 1917, p.2; The National Archives, RECO 1/467.

12 'Answers to the Questions', p.1.

13 'National Housing and National Life', p.170.

14 'National Cottage Competition: South Wales Area', *The Builder*, vol.114, no.3916, 22 February 1918, p.123.

15 'Presidential Address of Henry T. Hare to the RIBA, November 1918', *The Builder*, vol.115, no.3953, 8 November 1918, p.296.

16 Mark Swenarton, *Homes Fit for Heroes: The Politics and Architecture of Early State Housing in Britain* (London, 1981), p.90. Mervyn Miller, *Raymond Unwin: Garden Cities and Town Planning* (Leicester, 1992), p.166.

17 'Cottage Competitions', *Journal of the Royal Institute of British Architects*, vol.25, November 1917, p.11; *The Town Planning Review*, vol.8, no.1, April 1919, p.57.

18 'National Cottage Competition: South Wales Area', p.123.

19 Local Government Board/The Royal Institute of British Architects, 'Housing of the Working Classes in England and Wales – Cottage Competitions', 1917; Local Government Board/The Royal Institute of British Architects, 'Supplementary Particulars in Response to Questions by Competitors', 1918 – The National Archives, RECO 1/634.

20 Local Government Board/The Royal Institute of British Architects, 'Supplementary Particulars', 1918.

21 'Cottage Competitions', 1917; The National Archives, RECO 1/634.

22 'A Stand against Standardisation', *The Builder,* vol.114, no.3909, 4 January 1918, p.2.

23 'National Cottage Competition: South Wales Area', p.123.

24 'The National Housing Competition', *Journal of the Royal Institute of British Architects*, vol.25, June 1918, p.178.

25 Sidney F. Harris, Letters – 'Architects and Reconstruction', *The Architects' Journal*, vol.93, no.2410, 3 April 1941, p.225. 'National Cottage Competition', *The Builder,* vol.114, no.3917, 1 March 1918, p.137. 'National Cottage Competition: South Wales Area', p.123.

26 Bank of England Inflation Calculator.

27 Royal Institute of British Architects, *Cottage Designs Awarded Premiums in the Competitions Conducted by the Royal Institute of British Architects with the Concurrence of the Local Government Board* (London, 1918), p.11.

28 Stanley Adshead, Letters – 'Architects and Reconstruction', *The Architects' Journal*, vol.93, no.2410, 3 April 1941, p.224.

29 Gavin Stamp, *The Great Perspectivists* (London, 1982), pp 17, 19–20.

30 RIBA, *Cottage Designs Awarded Premiums*, p.12.

31 Nigel Temple, 'In Search of the Cottage Picturesque', *The Georgian Group Report and Journal* (1988), p.74.

32 'Country Cottages: The Lost Art of Building', *The Times*, 28 November 1917, p.9.

33 Charles Reilly, *Representative British Architects of the Present Day* (London, 1931), p.22.

34 Stanley Adshead, in 'National Housing and National Life', *Journal of the Royal Institute of British Architects*, vol.25, June 1918, p.170.

35 'Notes – The RIBA Housing Competition', *The Builder*, vol.114, no.3922, 5 April 1918, p.208.

36 'Cox, Alfred', *Who's Who in Architecture 1923*, ed. Frederick Chatterton (London, 1924), p.64.

37 'Notes – The RIBA Housing Competition', p.208.

38 Alexander Harvey, *The Model Village and its Cottages: Bournville* (London, 1906), p.5. See also, 'The Model Village and its Cottages, Bournville', *The Architectural Association Journal*, vol.21, no.229, March 1906, p.69.

39 Adam Voelcker, 'The Close, Llanfairfechan', 2009; https://coflein.gov.uk/en/site/409754/. Julian Holder, *Arts and Crafts Architecture: Beauty's Awakening* (Ramsbury, 2021), p.162.

40 'North, Herbert Luck', *Who's Who in Architecture 1926* (London, 1927), p.220.

41 Harold Hughes and Herbert L. North, *The Old Cottages of Snowdonia* (Bangor, 1908), p.54.

42 Hughes and North, *Old Cottages*, p.59.

43 Katie Carmichael, 'Civic and Civilian Architecture', in Wayne Cocroft and Paul Stamper, eds, *Legacies of the First World War* (Swindon, 2018), p.152.

44 'A Government Housing Scheme', *The Builder*, vol.114, no.3909, 4 January 1918, p.7.

45 John Ruskin, para. 12, 'Lamp of Memory', *The Seven Lamps of Architecture*, Library Edition, *The Works of John Ruskin*, Vol. VIII, ed. E.T. Cook and A. Wedderburn (London, 1903–9), p.237.

46 Uvedale Price, *Dialogue* (1801), in Christopher Hussey, *The Picturesque: Studies in a Point of View* (London, 1927), p.73.

47 'National Housing and National Life', p.170.

48 'LGB Cottage Competition', *The Builder*, vol.114, no.3925, 26 April 1918, p.252.

49 'National Cottage Competition: South Wales Area', p.123.

50 'National Cottage Competition: Manchester, Liverpool and North Wales', *The Builder*, vol.114, no.3916, 22 February 1918, p.124.

51 'The Housing Competition at the RIBA', *The Builder*, vol.114, no.3922, 5 April 1918, p.207.

52 'Housing Competition at the RIBA', p.207.

53 RIBA, *Cottage Designs Awarded Premiums*, pp 12–13.

54 H.S. Goodhart-Rendel, 'Planning the Five-Roomed Cottage', *The Architects' and Builders' Journal*, vol.49, no.1260, 26 February 1919, p.114.

55 William Whyte, 'Introduction', in *The Transactions of the Royal Institute of British Architects Town Planning Conference, London, 10–15 October 1910* (Abingdon, 2011), p.1.

56 John Burns MP, 'Welcome', in *Transactions*, p.66.

57 Charles Reilly, 'The Immediate Future in England', in *Transactions*, p.341.

58 Reilly, *Representative British Architects*, pp 57–8, 61 and 67.

59 Reilly, 'The Immediate Future in England', p.342.

60 John Ruskin, 'Lecture I, Architecture', in *Lectures on Architecture and Painting*, Library Edition, *The Works of John Ruskin*, Vol. XII, ed. E.T. Cook and A. Wedderburn (London, 1903–9), p.46.

61 Wilfrid Travers, *Architectural Education* (London, 1908), p.67.

62 Reginald Blomfield, *The Mistress Art* (London, 1908), p.92.

63 Trystan Edwards, *Good and Bad Manners in Architecture* (London, 1924), p.117.

64 Octavia Hill, 'Cottage Property in London', *Fortnightly Review*, vol.6, no.36, November 1866, p.862. 'Octavia Hill', *The Spectator*, 24 August 1912, p.7.

65 Octavia Hill, 'Letter, 1879', in Robert Whelan and Anne Hoole Anderson, eds, *Octavia Hill's Letters to Fellow Workers, 1872–1911* (London, 2005), p.121.

66 Gillian Darley, 'Octavia Hill: Lessons in Campaigning', in Elizabeth Baigent and Ben Cowell, eds, *'Nobler Imaginings and Mightier Struggles': Octavia Hill, Social Activism and the Remaking of British Society* (London, 2016), p.37.

67 Octavia Hill, 'Letter, 1886', in Whelan and Hoole Anderson, *Letters to Fellow Workers*, pp 201–2.

68 Bridget Cherry, 'Introduction', in *The Buildings of England: London 2: South* (London, 1990), p.76.

69 William Whyte, '"Beauty Is for All": Art in the Life and Work of Octavia Hill', in Baigent and Cowell, *'Nobler Imaginings and Mightier Struggles'*, p.61.

70 Gillian Darley, *Octavia Hill: A Life* (London, 1990), p.212.

71 David Watkin, *The English Vision: The Picturesque in Architecture, Landscape & Garden Design* (London, 1982), p.195.

72 Octavia Hill, 'Letter, 1905', *Letters to Fellow Workers*, pp 546–7.

73 Peter Richmond, 'The Call to Order: Neo-Georgian and the Liverpool School of Architecture', in Julian Holder and Elizabeth McKellar, eds, *Neo-Georgian Architecture 1880–1970: A Reappraisal* (Swindon, 2016), p.29. Charles Reilly, *Scaffolding in the Sky* (London, 1938), pp 91 and 113.

74 Stanley Adshead, 'Romford Garden Suburb, Gidea Park: Cottage Exhibition and Town Plan', *The Town Planning Review*, vol.2, no.2, July 1911, pp 125–6.

75 Timothy Brittain-Catlin, *The Edwardians and their Houses* (London, 2020), p.113.

76 Patrick Abercrombie, 'The Square House', *The Town Planning Review*, vol.4, no.1, April 1913, pp 35–6.

77 Trystan Edwards, 'A Criticism of the Garden City Movement', *The Town Planning Review*, vol.4, no.2, July 1913, pp 152–3.

78 Reilly, *Representative British Architects*, pp 57–8, 61 and 67. The book made numerous critical references to the Picturesque.

79 'Appreciation of the Picturesque', *The British Architect*, vol.87, no.3, March 1918, p.26.

80 Reginald Blomfield, in Louise Campbell, 'A Call to Order: The Rome Prize and Early Twentieth-Century British Architecture', *Architectural History*, vol.32, 1989, p.133.

81 Reginald Blomfield, 'Address to Students', *Journal of the Royal Institute of British Architects*, vol.21, no.7, 14 February 1914, p.210.

82 Reyner Banham, *Theory and Design in the First Machine Age* (London, 1988 [1960]), p.48.

83 Geoffrey Scott, *The Architecture of Humanism* (London, 1961 [1914]), pp 91–2.

84 C.F.A. Voysey quoted Ruskin: 'Good taste is a moral quality' – *Individuality* (London, 1915), p.22.

85 Scott, *Architecture of Humanism*, p.133.

86 Scott, *Architecture of Humanism*, pp 134–9.

87 Robert Macleod, *Style and Society: Architectural Ideology in Britain 1835–1914* (London, 1971), p.130.

88 'The Architecture of Humanism', *The Architectural Review*, vol.36, September 1914, p.65.

89 Kenneth Clarke, 'Letter to Michael Sadleir', in *The Gothic Revival* (London, 1964 [1928]), p.xiv.

90 Reginald Blomfield, *Modernismus* (London, 1934), pp 16–32.

91 Louise Campbell, *Studio Lives* (London, 2019), pp 58–9.

92 Scott, *Architecture of Humanism*, pp 66, 208 and 91.

93 Scott, *Architecture of Humanism*, pp 91 and 69.

94 Adshead thought it 'was originated by Mr Norman Shaw' – 'Romford Garden Suburb, Gidea Park: Cottage Exhibition and Town Plan', p.125.

95 Reilly, *Scaffolding in the Sky*, p.126.

96 Cherry, 'Introduction', pp 76–7.

97 John Ruskin, *Poetry of Architecture,* Library Edition, *The Works of John Ruskin*, Vol. I, ed. E.T. Cook and A. Wedderburn (London, 1903–9), p.11.

98 Stanley Adshead, 'The Standard Cottage', *The Town Planning Review*, vol.6, no.4, 1 April 1916, p.249.

99 Reilly, *Scaffolding in the Sky*, pp 40–42.

100 Peter Mandler, *The Fall and Rise of the Stately Home* (London, 1997), p.278.

101 'The Liverpool School of Architecture', *Who's Who in Architecture 1914*, ed. Frederick Chatterton (London, 1915), p.260.

102 Charles Reilly, 'Letter to Wilfrid Travers', in Travers, *Architectural Education*, p.37.

103 Reilly, 'The Immediate Future in England', in *Transactions*, pp 342, 341 and 344.

104 Neal Shasore, "A Stammering Bundle of Welsh Idealism": Arthur Trystan Edwards and Principles of Civic Design in Interwar Britain', *Architectural History*, vol.63, 2018, pp 177–9.

105 Roger Scruton, 'David Watkin and the Classical Idea', in Frank Salmon, ed., *The Persistence of the Classical: Essays on Architecture Presented to David Watkin* (London, 2008), p.65.

106 D.H. Lawrence, 'Nottingham and the Mining Countryside' (1930), in James T. Boulton, ed., *Late Essays and Articles* (Cambridge, 2014), pp 292–3. Alan Powers, 'Edwardian Architectural Education: A Study of Three Schools', *Architectural Association Files*, vol.5, 1984, p.50.

107 Adshead, 'The Standard Cottage', p.244.

108 Swenarton, *Homes Fit for Heroes*, pp 63–4.

109 Reilly, *Representative British Architects*, p.61.

110 E.M. Forster, *Howard's End* (Harmondsworth, 1961 [1910]), p.111.

111 John Carey, *The Intellectuals and the Masses: Pride and Prejudice among the Literary Intelligentsia, 1880–1939* (London, 1992), pp 24–5.

112 Edwards, *Good and Bad Manners*, pp 28–31 and 38.

113 Stanley Adshead, *Town Planning and Town Development* (London, 1923), pp 9–10.

114 Roger Fry, *Letters of Roger Fry*, ed. Denys Sutton (London, 1972), pp 31 and 329. Campbell, *Studio Lives*, pp 59–60.

115 Roger Fry, 'A Possible Domestic Architecture', in *Vision & Design* (Harmondsworth, 1937 [*Vogue*, 1918]), pp 222–3.

116 Nikolaus Pevsner, Ian Nairn and Bridget Cherry, *Surrey*, The Buildings of England (London, 2002 [1962]), pp 288–9.

117 Fry, 'A Possible Domestic Architecture', p.224.

118 J. Mordaunt Crook, *The Dilemma of Style: Architectural Ideas from the Picturesque to the Post-Modern* (London, 1987), p.74.

119 Edith Hall and Henry Stead, *A People's History of Classics: Class and Greco-Roman Antiquity in Britain and Ireland 1689-1939* (London, 2020), pp 126–7.

120 C.R. Ashbee, *Where the Great City Stands* (London, 1917), pp 26–8.

121 Ashbee, *Where the Great City Stands*, p.28.

122 W.R. Lethaby, 'Observations and Suggestions: The Essence of the Renaissance', *The Builder*, vol.118, no.4005, 7 November 1919, p.463.

123 Kathryn Morrison, *The Workhouse: A Study of Poor-Law Buildings in England* (Swindon, 1999), pp 46 and 53. Allan Brodie, Jane Croom and James Davies, *English Prisons: An Architectural History* (Swindon, 2002), pp 37–41, 40, 46, 271, n.38.

124 Nina Harkrader, 'Building for the Poor and the Pauper: Architecture, Morality and Medical Models in Victorian London, 1850–1900', p.10 (PhD thesis; ProQuest Dissertations Publishing).

125 W.G. Newton, 'Bases of Criticism: V – Natural Taste', *The Architectural Review*, vol.56, no.332, July 1924, p.1.

126 M.H. Baillie Scott, 'The Charm of Natural Planning', *The Architectural Review*, vol.46, August 1919, p.43.

127 Lynsey Hanley, *Estates: An Intimate History* (London, 2012), p.ix.

128 Henrietta Barnett, *Matters that Matter* (London, 1930), pp 106–10.

129 Raymond Unwin, 'Town Planning at Hampstead', *Garden Cities and Town Planning*, vol.1, no.1, January 1911, p.7.

130 Swenarton, *Homes Fit for Heroes*, pp 92–111. Miller, *Raymond Unwin*, pp 164–70.

131 Sir John Tudor Walters MP, *Hansard*, 8 December 1919, h. 1037.

132 Octavia Hill, para. 9019, 9 May 1884, 'Minutes of Evidence', *Royal Commission on the Housing of the Working Classes*, Vol. II (London, 1885), p.300.

133 Maud Bell, *Report of Meeting Held by Miss Maud Bell at Plaistow* and *Report of Meeting Held by Miss Maud Bell at Camberwell*; The National Archives, RECO 1/631 (Pt. 1), IV, WH38. Mrs Sanderson Furniss, *Report of Enquiry Conducted by the Women in the Labour Party (The Women's Labour League)*; The National Archives, RECO 1/631 (Pt. 1), IV, WH71, p.6.

134 para. 85, Tudor Walters Report, Cd.9191 (London, 1918), p.25.

135 Christopher Turnor, Board of Agriculture Smallholdings Report [Board of Agriculture Report], Cd. 6708 (London, 1913), pp 36–8.

136 Winifred Holtby, *South Riding* (London, 1936), p.15.

137 Pamela Gerrish Nunn, 'The Cottage Paradise', *Victorian Review*, vol.36, no.1, 2010, pp 190–92.

138 Nicholas Taylor, *The Village in the City: Towards a New Society* (London, 1973), p.24.

139 Tudor Walters Report, pp 19 and 37.

140 para. 147, Tudor Walters Report, p.36.

141 'Charivaria', *Punch*, vol.157, 16 July 1919, p.61.

142 'Search for Houses', *The Times*, 3 January 1919, p.3.

143 'Demobilised Unable to Find Homes', *The Daily Mirror*, 22 February 1919, p.13.

144 'Coalition to Continue', *The Times*, 13 November 1918, p.9.

145 '£100,000,000 Housing Plan', *The Daily Mirror*, 4 January 1919, p.4.

146 'Village of Model Houses', *Daily Mail*, 10 January 1919, p.6.

147 Henry Hare, 'The Cottage Competition', *The Builder*, vol.115, no.3953, 8 November 1918, p.296.

148 'Notes – The LGB and Housing', *The Builder*, vol.116, no.3963, 17 January 1919, p.64.

149 'General News – Model Cottages for the LGB', *The Builder*, vol.116, no.3966, 7 February 1919, p.126.

150 'Report of the RIBA Council for the Official Year 1918–19', *The Builder*, vol.116, no.3979, 9 May 1919, pp 456–7.

151 'Advert – The Nation's New Houses', *Sheffield Independent*, 7 April 1919, p.8.

152 'Reviews – More about Houses', *The Common Cause*, 25 July 1919, p.195.

153 'The Whirligig: Comments on Men and Matters', *The Illustrated Leicester Chronicle*, 12 April 1919, p.4. Advertisement (*The Nation's New Houses*) – *Sheffield Independent*, 19 April 1919, p.9; *Nottingham Journal & Express*, 23 April 1919, p.3; *Birmingham Daily Gazette*, 1 May 1919, p.7 (The British Newspaper Archive).

154 Christopher Addison, 'Foreword', in Raymond Unwin, ed., *The Nation's New Houses* (London, 1919), p.1.

155 Unwin, *Nation's New Houses*, p.3.

156 Unwin, *Nation's New Houses*, pp 4–6.

157 Jan Ward, *Raffles and Rupert Davison* (Caterham, 2016), pp 10 and 22.

158 T. Raffles Davison and William Axon, *Rambling Sketches* (London, 1883), pp 57 and 159.

159 G.A.T. Middleton, *The Principles of Architectural Perspective* (London, 1907), p.1.

160 Charles Reilly, in Powers, 'Edwardian Architectural Education', p.55.

161 Stamp, *The Great Perspectivists*, p.11.

162 Aston Webb, 'Foreword', in Maurice Webb and Herbert Wigglesworth, eds, *Raffles Davison: A Record of his Life and Work from 1870 to 1926* (London, 1927), p.xiii.

163 Reginald Blomfield, 'Introduction', in Webb and Wigglesworth, *Raffles Davison*, p.xiv.

164 Stamp, *The Great Perspectivists*, p.17.

165 Hussey, *The Picturesque*, p.207.

166 Ann Bermingham, ed., 'Introduction: Gainsborough's Cottage Door', *Sensation and Sensibility: Viewing Gainsborough's 'Cottage Door'* (London, 2005), pp xiii–xviii.

167 'Houses on the Film', *Westminster Gazette*, 21 May 1919, p.6.

168 'Garden Cities Film', *The Daily Telegraph*, 23 May 1919, p.6.

169 'The Alhambra Meeting', *Garden Cities and Town Planning*, vol.9, no.6, June 1919, p.120.

170 Local Government Board, *Manual on the Preparation of State-Aided Housing Schemes* (London, 1919), p.8.

171 Local Government Board, *Manual*, p.8.

172 Local Government Board, *Manual*, pp 8–9.

173 Raymond Unwin, 'Cottage Building in Garden City', *The Garden City*, vol.1, no.5, June 1906, pp 108–9.

174 Turnor, Board of Agriculture Report, p.6 [566], p.123 [683].

175 Miller, *Raymond Unwin*, p.166.

176 *The Daily Express & Sunday Express 'Model Homes Exhibition' Official Catalogue* (London, 1919), p.5; Museum of Domestic Design and Architecture, Middlesex University, BADDA 1132.

177 Raymond Unwin, 'Cottage Plans and Common Sense', Fabian Tract 109 (London, 1902), p.12.

178 Roger White, *Cottages Ornés: The Charms of the Simple Life* (London, 2017), p.44.

179 Uvedale Price, *An Essay on the Picturesque* (London, 1796), p.216.

180 'Ubique', 'Government Housing Manuals', *Country Life*, vol.45, no.1171, 14 June 1919, p.734.

181 'Ubique', p.734.

182 'The New Homes', *Daily Mail*, 14 April 1919, p.5.

183 'The LGB Manual', *The Builder*, vol.116, no.3976, 18 April 1919, p.369.

184 'On Cottage Design', *The British Architect*, vol.86, no.9, September 1917, p.101.

185 Ralph Nevill, *Old Cottage and Domestic Architecture: South West Surrey* (Guildford, 1889), p.30. Dawber, *Old Cottages and Farmhouses in Kent and Sussex*, pp 19 and 21. William Curtis Green, *Old Cottages & Farmhouses in Surrey* (London, 1908), p.22.

186 Raymond Unwin, 'Housing: The Architect's Contribution', *The Architects' and Builders' Journal*, vol.49, no.1252, 1 January 1919, p.10.

187 Timothy Mowl, *Stylistic Cold Wars: Betjeman versus Pevsner* (London, 2000), p.17.

188 'Memorandum to Housing Commissioners, No. 7' (Local Government Board, 16 April 1919), p.1; The National Archives, HLG 31/1. 'Notes – Housing Appointments', *The Builder*, vol.116, no.3973, 28 March 1919, p.293.

189 John Burnett, *A Social History of Housing 1815–1985* (London, 1986 [1978]), p.228.

190 'Russell, Samuel Bridgman', *Dictionary of Scottish Architects 1660–1980* (2016); http://scottisharchitects.org.uk/architect_full.php?id=100338.

191 Macleod, *Style and Society*, pp 88–97.

192 Geoffrey Tyack, 'Ruskin and the English House', in Rebecca Daniels and Geoff Brandwood, eds, *Ruskin and Architecture* (Reading, 2003), p.114.

193 Unwin, 'Cottage Plans and Common Sense', p.15.

194 Raymond Unwin, 'The Art of Designing Small Houses and Cottages', Lecture VIII, in *The Art of Building a Home* (London, 1901), p.128.

195 Unwin, 'Housing: The Architect's Contribution', pp 49–64.

196 Unwin, 'The Art of Designing Small Houses and Cottages', pp 109–10.

197 Raymond Unwin, 'Town Planning Institute', *The Builder*, vol.114, no.3922, 5 April 1918, p.209.

198 Mrs Alwyn Lloyd, *Women's Housing Sub-Committee, Investigation IV, Gretna Green and East Riggs, Dumfries*; The National Archives, RECO 1/631, IV, WH70, p.2.

199 'Gidea Park House Competition', *The British Architect*, vol.76, no.19, 17 November 1911, p.345. Brittain-Catlin, *Edwardians and their Houses*, pp 110–18.

200 Michael Stratton and Barrie Trinder, *Twentieth Century Industrial Archaeology* (Abingdon, 2013), p.99.

201 Sir Robert Lorimer, 'Country Homes: Gretna – The Home of an Industrial Army', *Country Life*, vol.44, no.1128, 17 August 1918, pp 137–8. Miller, *Raymond Unwin*, pp 158–9.

202 Walter Creese, *The Legacy of Raymond Unwin* (Cambridge, MA, 1967), p.18.

203 Raymond Unwin, 'Co-operation in Building (Lecture VII)', *The Art of Building a Home* (London, 1901), p.92.

204 Unwin, 'Co-operation in Building (Lecture VII)', p.94.

205 Frank Jackson, *Raymond Unwin: Architect, Planner and Visionary* (London, 1985), pp 90–94. Raymond Unwin, *Town Planning in Practice* (London, 1909), p.ix.

206 para. 56, Tudor Walters Report, p.12.

207 'Report on the Proceedings of the RIBA', *The Builder*, vol.116, no.3964, 24 January 1919, p.87.

208 Alfred Tennyson, 'Aylmer's Field', in *Enoch Arden &c.* (Boston, 1865), p.69.

209 'Report on the Proceedings of the RIBA', p.87.

210 'Ubique', 'Government Housing Manuals', p.734.

211 Editorial, 'Mr Arnold Bennett's Housing Suggestions', *The Architects' and Builders' Journal*, vol.49, no.1260, 26 February 1919, p.112.

212 Goodhart-Rendel, 'Planning the Five-Roomed Cottage', p.114.

213 Arthur Stratton, 'Plea for a Classic Tradition', *The Architects' Journal*, vol.49, no.1261, 5 March 1919, p.128.

214 Hermann Muthesius, *Das Englische Haus* (New York, 1987 [1904]), p.42.

215 Julian Holder, *Arts and Crafts Architecture: 'Beauty's Awakening'* (Ramsbury, 2021), p.105.

216 C.F.A. Voysey, 'Patriotism in Architecture', *The Architectural Association Journal*, vol.28, no.304, June 1912, p.25. C.F.A. Voysey, 'On Town Planning', *The Architectural Review*, vol.46, July 1919, p.26.

217 Voysey, 'On Town Planning', p.26.

218 'Artistic Houses', *The Times*, 4 April 1919, p.19.

219 'Professor Adshead on Cottage Building', *The Architectural Review*, vol.46, October 1919, p.91.

220 Pite, 'Architecture of Cottages', p.150. Brian Hanson, 'Pite, Arthur Beresford', *Oxford Dictionary of National Biography* (Oxford, 2007).

221 Major Harry Barnes MP, 'Architects and Housing Schemes: RIBA Deputation to Dr. Addison', *The Architects' Journal*, vol.49, no.1264, 26 March 1919, p.193.

222 Christopher Addison MP, 'Housing and Town Planning Etc Bill, 1919, Second Reading', *Hansard*, 7 April 1919, c. 1713.

223 Major Waldorf Astor MP, *Hansard*, 8 April 1919, c. 1955–1956.

224 Lord Conway, *Episodes in a Varied Life* (London, 1932), pp 83, 115–17.

225 Sir Martin Conway, 'The Oldest Type of English Cottage', *Country Life*, vol.36, no.913, 4 July 1914, pp 8–10.

226 Sir Martin Conway MP, *Hansard,* 8 April 1919, c. 1916.

227 Noel Pemberton Billing MP, *Hansard,* 7 April 1919, c. 1784.

228 S.E. Tomkins, Letter, 'Plans of a "Model" House', *The Builder*, vol.116, no.3966, 7 February 1919, p.127.

229 *The Daily Express & Sunday Express 'Model Homes Exhibition' Official Catalogue* (London, 1919), pp 41–2; Museum of Domestic Design and Architecture, Middlesex University, BADDA 1132.

230 Sir Peter Griggs MP, *Hansard*, 7 April 1919, c. 1794.

231 Leslie Scott MP, *Hansard*, 7 April 1919, c. 1820.

232 Sir John Tudor Walters MP, *Hansard*, 8 April 1919, c. 1907.

233 W.M., 'Beautiful Houses?', *The Daily Mirror*, 8 April 1919, p.5.

234 'The New Homes', *Daily Mail*, 14 April 1919, p.5.

235 'Prince on Pretty Homes', *Daily Mail*, 5 May 1919, p.8.

236 'Editorial', *The Daily Telegraph*, 5 May 1919, p.10.

237 'George, Walter Lionel', *Who Was Who* (Oxford, 2019).

238 W.L. George, *Labour and Housing at Port Sunlight* (London, 1909), p.69.

239 W.L. George, 'Beauty in House Building', *The Daily Mirror*, 14 May 1919, p.7.

240 C.F.A. Voysey, 'Patriotism in Architecture', p.21.

241 W.B.T., 'Architects' Prize-Winning Designs', *Daily Mail*, 15 May 1919, p.10.

242 Our London Correspondent, 'To Save the Picturesque', *Sheffield Daily Telegraph*, 23 May 1919, p.4.

243 Gillian Darley, *Villages of Vision* (London, 1978), pp 28 and 15–24.

244 Sir Martin Conway MP, 'Housing Bill 1919, Report Stage', in *Hansard*, 26 May 1919, c. 884.

245 Sir Henry Craik MP, *Hansard*, 26 May 1919, c. 889–890.

246 Christopher Addison MP, *Hansard*, 26 May 1919, cc. 885–886.

247 The Marquess of Salisbury, 'Housing Bill 1919, House of Lords Committee Stage', *Hansard*, 8 July 1919, c. 289.

248 A.R. Powys and Sir Martin Conway MP, Letters, Powys (Secretary, Society for the Protection of Ancient Buildings) to Lord Salisbury; Conway to Powys, 4–8 July 1919; The Society for the Protection of Ancient Buildings Archive, Folder: Cottages II – 1919.

249 Lord Birkenhead, *Hansard*, 8 July 1919, c. 293.

250 Clause 1 (3), *Housing, Town Planning, &c. Act, 1919 Chapter 35*, p.2.

251 W.K. Haselden, 'The New Housing Schemes: A Danger', *The Daily Mirror*, 16 June 1919, p.5.

252 'Editorial', *The Daily Telegraph*, 5 May 1919, p.10.

253 The Society for the Protection of Ancient Buildings, *Twenty-Eighth Annual Report, May 1905* (London, 1905), p.3; Society for the Protection of Ancient Buildings Archive.

254 May Morris, 'Fight for the Beauty of England!', *The Daily Mirror*, 14 June 1919, p.5.

255 Hare, 'Good Building', p.8.

256 Hare, 'Good Building', p.8.

257 Geoffrey Tyack, *The Making of Our Urban Landscape* (Oxford, 2022), p.228.

258 Christopher Addison, 'Housing and Peace', *Housing*, vol.1, no.1, 19 July 1919, p.1. Minutes, 8 August 1919, 'Housing Publication', in *City of Nottingham Housing Committee Minute Book No. 7*, p.395; Nottinghamshire Archives, CA/CM/49/7.

259 Burnett, *Social History of Housing*, p.227.

260 S.B. Russell, 'Designs of Cottages', *Housing*, vol.1, no.1, 19 July 1919, p.6.

261 'Some Notes on the House Plans in the Ministry of Health's Manual', *Housing*, vol.1, no.1, 19 July 1919, p.6. 'Designs of Cottages', on the same page, was credited 'SBR'. In 1924, after he left the Ministry, Russell contributed designs to a book edited by *Homes and Gardens* editor Randal Phillips. In the commentary (again unsigned), familiar phrases appeared: 'One sometimes hears a house contemptuously referred to as "a box with a lid". This criticism usually comes from those . . . who think that the really "pretty" house is the sort which the speculative builder has inflicted on a helpless suburbia' – Phillips, *Small Family Houses* (London, 1924), pp 55–6.

262 'Some Notes', *Housing*, vol.1, no.1, 19 July 1919, p.6.

263 Sir Robert Lorimer credited 'brick box with the slate lid' to Morris – Lorimer, 'Country Homes', p.137.

264 Ruskin, 'Lecture I, Architecture', p.33.

265 'The Ecclesiastical Commissioners' Housing of the Working Classes' (1906), Appendix 3, in Whelan and Hoole Anderson, *Letters to Fellow Workers*, p.749.

266 Voysey, 'On Town Planning', p.25.

267 'Minutes, 6 October 1920', in *London County Council, Minutes of Proceedings of the Housing Committee, January 1920 to December 1920* (London, 1921); London Metropolitan Archives, LCC/MIN/07277, p.552.

268 H.C. Monro, Secretary Local Government Board, 'Circular on Housing', *The Architects' and Builders' Journal*, vol.49, no.1258, 12 February 1919, p.95.

269 Holtby, *South Riding*, pp v–vi.

3 THE COTTAGE DENIED

1 'Bristol Housing Scheme', *The Builder*, vol.118, no.4036, 11 June 1920, p.694.

2 Rosamond Jevons and John Madge, *Housing Estates: A Study of Bristol Corporation Policy and Practice between the Wars* (Bristol, 1946), p.17.

3 Ministry of Health, 'Supplement', *Housing*, vol.1, no.23, 24 May 1920.

4 'Bristol Housing Scheme', p.694.

5 Local Government Board, *Manual* (London, 1919).

6 Ministry of Housing, 'Notes on House Plans', *Housing*, vol.1, no.11, 8 December 1919, p.145.

7 John Ruskin, 'Lecture I, Architecture', *Lectures on Architecture and Painting*, Library Edition, *The Works of John Ruskin*, Vol. XII, ed. E.T. Cook and A. Wedderburn (London, 1903–9), p.49. Raymond Unwin, 'Housing: The Architect's Contribution', *The Architects' and Builders' Journal*, vol.49, no.1252, 1 January 1919, p.10.

8 'Bristol Housing Scheme', p.694.

9 'Timber Frame Houses', *The Builder*, vol.117, no.4000, 3 October 1919, p.339.

10 'Housing and Town Planning Notes: Weekly Housing Return', *The Builder*, vol.118, no.4025, 26 March 1920, p.369.

11 C.M. Lloyd, *Housing*, Fabian Tract 193, May 1920 (London, 1920), p.6.

12 Julian Holder, *Arts and Crafts Architecture: 'Beauty's Awakening'* (Ramsbury, 2021), p.135.

13 Raffles Davison, 'Some Thoughts on Drawing', *The Builder*, vol.118, no.4013, 2 January 1920, p.21.

14 'Illustrations: Leamington Housing Scheme', *The Builder*, vol.118, no.4018, 6 February 1920, p.162.

15 Christopher Hussey, *The Life of Sir Edwin Lutyens* (London, 1950), p.161.

16 'Illustrations: Cottages, Wilton Housing Scheme', *The Builder*, vol.118, no.4034, 28 May 1920, p.632.

17 'Folkestone Housing Scheme', *The Builder*, vol.118, no.4035, 4 June 1920, p.664.

18 William Curtis Green, *Old Cottages & Farmhouses in Surrey* (London, 1908).

19 Randal Phillips, 'Domestic Architecture of Today: The Stanmore Housing Scheme', *Country Life*, vol.54, no.1400, 3 November 1923, p.627.

20 Local Government Board, *Manual*, p.52.

21 'A.E.D.', 'Architectural Character', *Housing*, vol.1, no.9, 10 November 1919, p.122.

22 'M.R.' (Manning Robertson?), 'Hints on Cottage Design', *Housing*, vol.1, no.23, 24 May 1920, p.305.

23 'M.R.', 'Hints on Cottage Design', p.305.

24 'A Plea for Street Architecture', *The Builder*, vol.118, no.4013, 2 January 1920, p.13.

25 *Forty-Eighth Annual Report of the Local Government Board, 1918–19*, Cmd. 413, p.150.

26 Trystan Edwards, 'Correspondence: The Architecture of Humanism', *Journal of the Royal Institute of British Architects*, vol.22, no.5, December 1914, p.68.

27 Geoffrey Scott, *The Architecture of Humanism: A Study in the History of Taste* (London, 1961 [1914]), pp 91–2.

28 Henry W. Allardyce, 'Suggestion for Parlour Type Cottages, No. 92' (dated August 1919), *Housing*, vol.1, no.5, 13 September 1919, p.83. Also, 'C.H.B.', 'Drawing No. 97', *Housing*, vol.1, no.8, 25 October 1919, p.107.

29 Mark Swenarton, *Homes Fit for Heroes: The Politics and Architecture of Early State Housing in Britain* (London, 1981), pp 148–51.

30 'R.T.', 'Building in Tile Districts', *Housing*, vol.1, no.23, 24 May 1920, p.303.

31 Ministry of Health, *Type Plans and Elevations of Houses Designed by the Ministry of Health in Connection with State-Aided Housing Schemes* (London, 1920), A2.

32 'Plates 2–4, 13 and 13A – Plan Nos. 135, 137, 168 and 170', in Ministry of Health, *Type Plans and Elevations*.

33 'Plates 19–20 – Plan Nos. 159 and 175', in Ministry of Health, *Type Plans and Elevations*.

34 Swenarton, *Homes Fit for Heroes*, p.146.

35 Minute 24547, Meeting 7 October 1919, *City of Birmingham, Proceedings of the Council, 9th November 1918 to 21st October 1919* (Birmingham, 1919), p.633.

36 E.V. Hiley, 'The Housing Work of the Council', p.17, in Minute 1, Meeting 30 July 1913, *Minutes of the Housing Inquiry Committee*, pp 1–2, Birmingham City Council, BCC1/BR/1/1/1.

37 Minute 850, Meeting 11 May 1917, *Minutes of the Town Planning Committee*, pp 161–2; BCC1/BL/1/1/2.

38 Minute 879, Meeting 1 June 1917, *Minutes of the Housing and Town Planning Committee*, pp 180–81; BCC1/BL/1/1/2.

39 Minutes 920–930, Meetings 4 September 1917 and 2 October 1917, *Minutes of the Housing and Town Planning Committee*, pp 200–208; BCC1/BL/1/1/2.

40 Minute 983, Meeting 14 December 1917, *Minutes of the Housing and Town Planning Committee*, p.240; BCC1/BL/1/1/2.

41 Minute 1076, Meeting 26 April 1918, *Minutes of the Housing and Town Planning Committee*, p.285; BCC1/BL/1/1/2.

42 Meeting 28 June 1918, *Minutes of the Housing and Town Planning Committee*, pp 295–7; BCC1/BL/1/1/2.

43 'Bournville Allotments Wanted for Housing', *Birmingham Daily Gazette*, 23 July 1919, p.3.

44 Minute 1276A, Meeting 17 January 1919, *Minutes of the Housing and Town Planning Committee*, p.88; BCC1/BL/1/1/3.

45 Minute 1353, Meeting 14 April 1919, *Minutes of the Housing and Town Planning Committee*, p.144; BCC1/BL/1/1/3.

46 Minute 1353, Meeting 14 April 1919, *Minutes of the Housing and Town Planning Committee*, p.144; BCC1/BL/1/1/3.

47 Minute 1378, Meeting 25 April 1919, *Minutes of the Housing and Town Planning Committee*, p.171; BCC1/BL/1/1/3.

48 Minute 24687, Meeting 2 December 1919, *City of Birmingham, Proceedings of the Council, 10th November 1919 to 20th October 1920* (Birmingham, 1920), p.63.

49 Minute 24547, Meeting 7 October 1919, *City of Birmingham, Proceedings of the Council, 9th November 1918 to 21st October 1919*, p.633.

50 Minute 24560, Meeting 21 October 1919, *City of Birmingham, Proceedings of the Council, 9th November 1918 to 21st October 1919*, pp 675–7.

51 Minute 1600, Meeting 14 November 1919, *Minutes of the Housing and Estates Committee*, p.17; BCC1/AM/1/1/25.

52 Minute 644, Meeting 19 December 1919, *Minutes of the Building and Sites Sub-Committee* (of the Housing and Estates Committee), p.36; BCC1/AM/10/1/2.

53 Minute 24816, Meeting 2 March 1920, *City of Birmingham, Proceedings of the Council, 10th November 1919 to 20th October 1920*, p.271.

54 Minute 25009, Meeting 9 June 1920, *City of Birmingham, Proceedings of the Council, 10th November 1919 to 20th October 1920*, pp 545–6.

55 Minute 24718, Meeting 6 January 1920, *City of Birmingham, Proceedings of the Council, 10th November 1919 to 20th October 1920*, p.97.

56 'City Housing "Farce"', *Birmingham Daily Gazette*, 23 November 1921, p.3.

57 Meeting 20 April 1920, *Minutes of the Housing and Estates Committee*, p.19; BCC1/AM/1/1/26.

58 Mervyn Miller, *English Garden Cities* (Swindon, 2010), pp 10–11.

59 Birmingham Type 1920/10 'Dorlonco Houses' in 'Illustrations: Birmingham Housing Scheme', *The Builder*, vol.119, no.4041, 16 July 1920, p.66 (V).

60 'Dorman Long & Co's Steel-Frame System of House Construction', *Housing*, vol.1, no.12, 22 December 1919, p.165. Cheryl Buckley, 'Modernity, Tradition and the Design of the "Industrial Village" of Dormanstown 1917–1923', *The Journal of Design History*, vol.23, no.1, 2010, pp 28–31.

61 'Travers, Wilfrid, OBE, FRIBA', *Who's Who in Architecture 1923*, ed. Frederick Chatterton (London, 1924), p.251.

62 Wilfrid Travers, *Architectural Education* (London, 1908), pp vii & 37.

63 Miller, *English Garden Cities*, p.52.

64 'M.R.', 'Hints on Cottage Design', p.305.

65 Birmingham Type Design 1920/24, in 'Illustrations: Birmingham Housing Scheme', p.66 (V).

66 'R.T.', 'Building in Tile Districts', p.303.

67 Nick Chapple, 'C.H. James: Neo-Georgian – from the Small House to the Town Hall', in Julian Holder and Elizabeth McKellar, eds, *Neo-Georgian Architecture 1880–1970: A Reappraisal* (Swindon, 2016), p.96.

68 Minute 1754, Meeting 23 December 1919, *Minutes of the Housing and Estates Committee*, p.140; BCC1/AM/1/1/25.

69 'Architects' Ban', *Birmingham Daily Gazette*, 19 February 1919, p.5.

70 Meeting 20 April 1920, *Minutes of the Housing and Estates Committee*, pp 19–20; BCC1/AM/1/1/26.

71 E.V. Hiley (Town Clerk), 'The Housing Work of the Council', in Minute 1, Meeting 30 July 1913, *Minutes of the Housing Inquiry Committee*, pp 17–18; BCC1/BR/1/1/1.

72 D.H. Lawrence, 'Nottingham and the Mining Countryside' (1930), in James T. Boulton, ed., *Late Essays and Articles* (Cambridge, 2014), p.292.

73 'Felix' (F.B.R. Browne), 'After-Dinner Architecture or What the Student Sees', *Harlequinade* (Architectural Association student magazine), Two/Six, July 1924, p.11.

74 Swenarton, *Homes Fit for Heroes*, p.148.

75 The ledger was kindly lent to the author by Professor Simon Pepper of Liverpool University. Samuel Pointon Taylor is listed in *Who's Who in Architecture 1914*, ed. Frederick Chatterton (London, 1915), p.219.

76 Samuel Pointon Taylor, *Ministerial Types*, Ministry of Health Addison Scheme ledger (London, 1920–21).

77 'Housing at Benson', *Housing*, vol.2, no.39, 3 January 1921, pp 198–9.

78 'Interim Report of the Treasury Committee on Housing Finance', 27 November 1919, p.3, The National Archives, CAB 24/94/27.

79 Kenneth Morgan, 'Addison, Christopher, First Viscount Addison (1869–1951)', *Oxford Dictionary of National Biography* (Oxford, 2011).

80 Lord Rothermere, 'Solvency or Downfall? – The Choice', *The Daily Mirror*, 19 April 1920, p.7. 'The First List of "Waste" MPs', *The Daily Mirror*, 3 December 1920, p.2.

81 '"Stop Waste" Fight in Thanet Election', *The Daily Mirror*, 21 October 1919, p.3.

82 E.H.H. Green, *Ideologies of Conservatism: Conservative Political Ideas in the Twentieth Century* (Oxford, 2008), pp 122–5.

83 'Class C Houses', *Housing*, vol.2, no.42, 14 February 1921, p.229.

84 'The Joseph Rowntree Village Trust, Earswick', *Housing*, vol.2, no.43, March 1921, p.248.

85 Christopher Addison MP, Letter to the Rt Hon Austen Chamberlain MP, Chancellor of the Exchequer, 22 February 1921; The National Archives, HLG68/29.

86 Green, *Ideologies of Conservatism*, p.125.

87 Ministry of Health, 'Memorandum to Housing Commissioners, No. 136', 25 June 1921, p.4; The National Archives, HLG 31/1.

88 Christopher Addison, 'Cabinet Memorandum: Housing Policy' (CP3108), 4 July 1921, p.1; The National Archives, T161/132.

89 Addison, 'Cabinet Memorandum', p.2.

90 Sir Alfred Mond MP, 'Housing of the Working Classes – Memorandum from the First Commissioner of Works to the War Cabinet', 23 December 1918, p.1; The National Archives, CAB 24/72/53 (GT-6552). 'Architects and State Housing', The Times, 12 February 1919, p.8.

91 'The Housing Fiasco', Daily News, 15 July 1921, p.1.

92 Addison, 'Cabinet Memorandum', p.4.

93 Sir Alfred Mond MP, 'Reduction of Public Expenditure – Memorandum by the Minister of Health – Secret (CP 3067)', 22 June 1921, p.5; The National Archives, T161/132.

94 'Hurst, Sir Alfred', Who Was Who (Oxford, 2020).

95 A.W. Hurst (HM Treasury), Memorandum to R.S. Meiklejohn (Deputy Controller, Supply, HM Treasury), cc. Sir Warren Fisher (Permanent Secretary, HM Treasury), 8 July 1921; The National Archives, T161/132.

96 J.C. Loudon, An Encyclopaedia of Cottage, Farm and Villa Architecture (London, 1834), p.763.

97 John Ruskin, 'Poetry of Architecture', Library Edition, The Works of John Ruskin, Vol. I, ed. E.T. Cook and A. Wedderburn (London, 1903–9), p.74.

98 Laura Wright, Sunnyside: A Sociolinguistic History of British Place Names (Oxford, 2020), p.48.

99 Lewis Baston, 'Rising Damp in the Suburbs. Or "Whatever Happened to the Villa Tory?"', The Political Quarterly, vol.90, no.1, January – March 2019, p.65. Osbert Lancaster, With an Eye to the Future (London, 1967), pp 133–5.

100 E.M. Forster, A Room with a View (Harmondsworth, 1983 [1908]), pp 120–21 and 135.

101 Maurice Adams, Modern Cottage Architecture (London, 1912), pp 14–15.

102 'Notes – The Villa', The Builder, vol.124, no.4177, 23 February 1923, p.306.

103 George Orwell, The Road to Wigan Pier (Harmondsworth, 1975 [1937]), p.94.

104 'The Housing Competition at the RIBA', The Builder, vol.114, no.3922, 5 April 1918, p.207.

105 After the Second World War, Nye Bevan agreed that managers in the newly privatised coal industry deserved the distinction of 'villa-style' houses – Selina Todd, The People: The Rise and Fall of the Working Class, 1910–2010 (London, 2014), pp 168–9.

106 W.A. Forsyth, 'The Conversion of the Jerry Builder', The Architectural Association Journal, vol.21, no.228, February 1906, p.39.

107 A.M. Carr-Saunders and D. Caradog Jones, A Survey of the Social Structure of England and Wales (Oxford, 1937), p.67.

108 J. Alfred Gotch, 'Common-Sense Housing Schemes', The Architects' and Builders' Journal, vol.49, no.1256, 29 January 1919, p.57.

109 Housing, Town Planning, &c., Act, 1919 (London, 1919), Clause 1 (1).

110 Noel Pemberton Billing MP, Hansard, 7 April 1919, c. 1782.

111 Sir Assheton Pownall MP, Hansard, 7 April 1919, c. 1796.

112 Godfrey Locker-Lampson MP, Hansard, 27 May 1919, cc. 1174.

113 Christopher Addison MP, Hansard, 27 May 1919, cc. 1181.

114 David Cannadine, 'Beyond Class? Social Structures and Social Perceptions in Modern England', British Academy's Raleigh Lecture on History, (London, 1998), pp 95–118. George Orwell, The Lion and the Unicorn (Harmondsworth, 1982 [1941]), pp 55–70.

115 'Town Planning Institute', The Builder, vol.114, no.3922, 5 April 1918, p.209.

116 'Rotary Clubs of Great Britain', Housing, vol.1, no.2, 2 August 1919, pp 22–3.

117 'The Working Classes', The Times, 20 June 1919, p.10.

118 R. Graves and A. Hodge, The Long Weekend: A Social History of Great Britain, 1918–39 (London, 1991 [1940]), pp 64–6.

119 E.R. Forber, 'Points Raised by Rural District Councils', Housing, vol.1, no.4, 30 August 1919, p.60.

120 'Questions at Meetings', Housing, vol.1, no.4, 30 August 1919, p.52.

121 'Report of the Housing and Estates Committee . . . 2 December 1919', p.7; Birmingham City Council, BCC/1/AM/1/1/25.

122 A. Sayle, The Houses of the Workers (London, 1924), p.163.

123 Minute 1703, Meeting 9 December 1919, Minutes of the Housing and Estates Committee, p.98; BCC1/AM/1/1/25.

124 Winston S. Churchill MP, 'Unemployment – Speech at Dundee, 10 October 1908', in Liberalism and the Social Problem (London, 1909), p.198.

125 George Bourne [Sturt], Change in the Village (London, 1955 [1912]), pp 107–8.

126 H.E. Kemp, 'Class Antagonism: A Study in Temper', 1917; Churchill Archive, CHAR 15/106, Image 112.

127 Warwick Deeping, Sorrell and Son (London, 1964 [1925]), pp 161–2.

128 'Notes – The Middle Classes', The Builder, vol.118, no.4014, 9 January 1920, pp 50–51.

129 Samuel Hynes, A War Imagined: The First World War and English Culture (London, 1990), p.359.

130 'Middle Class Union Formed', The Times, 7 March 1919, p.7.

131 John Pretyman Newman MP, Letter to the Editor: 'The Middle Classes', The Times, 14 November 1919, p.8.

132 Ross McKibbin, Classes and Cultures: England 1918–1951 (Oxford, 2000), pp 528–9.

133 'A Town Clerk' in 'Notes on Housing', *Housing*, vol.1, no.20, 12 April 1920, p.270.

134 Charles Reilly, 'The City of the Future: The Immediate Future in England', *The Town Planning Review*, vol.1, no.3, October 1910, p.197.

135 M.H. Baillie Scott, 'The Charm of Natural Planning', *The Architectural Review*, vol.46, no.273, August 1919, p.43.

136 'The Housing Question', *Leicester Daily Post*, 7 March 1919, p.2.

137 Henrietta Barnett, *Matters that Matter* (London, 1930), p.106.

138 'Housing Chief of Britain – Death of Sir Charles Ruthen', *The Western Mail*, 20 September 1926, p.8.

139 *Third Annual Report of the Ministry of Health, 1921–1922*, Cmd. 1713 (London, 1922), p.46.

140 'City's First Thousand', *Birmingham Daily Gazette*, 24 August 1921, p.3.

141 'City's First Thousand', p.3.

142 Sir Charles T. Ruthen, 'The Architect and the State', *Journal of the Society of Architects*, vol.15, no.4, February 1922, pp 87–8. 'Architects and Housing Costs', *The Times,* 28 January 1922, p.5.

143 A Former Housing Commissioner, *The Housing Question* (London, 1922), p.53.

144 The first of three interim Geddes Committee reports (Cmd. 1581) had been in circulation since 14 December 1921 – Geoff Burrows and Phillip Cobbin, 'Controlling Government Expenditure by External Review: The 1921–22 "Geddes Axe"', *Accounting History*, vol.14, no.3, 2009, pp 205–10.

145 Robert Kerr, *The Gentleman's House, or How to Plan English Residences from the Parsonage to the Palace* [. . .] (Cambridge, 2012 [1864]), p.360.

146 Ruthen, 'The Architect and the State', p.88.

147 Ruthen, 'The Architect and the State', p.92.

148 Ruthen, 'The Architect and the State', pp 92–3.

149 Major Harry Barnes MP, Letter to the Editor: 'Sir C. Ruthen and Architects', *The Daily Telegraph*, 23 January 1922, p.6.

150 Ernest J. Brown, Letter to the Editor: 'Profiteering Architects', *The Daily Telegraph*, 14 January 1922, p.7.

151 'Sir Charles Ruthen and the Profession', *The Architects' Journal*, vol.55, no.1412, 25 January 1922, p.155.

152 18 January 1922. 'The Architect and the State', *Journal of the Society of Architects*, vol.15, no.4, February 1922, p.94.

153 'Annual Dinner Postponed', *Journal of the Society of Architects*, vol.15, no.4, February 1922, p.113.

154 'Sir Charles Ruthen and the Architects', *The Manchester Guardian*, 21 January 1922, p.9.

155 'Sir Charles Ruthen and National Housing', *Journal of the Royal Institute of British Architects*, vol.29, no.6, 28 January 1922, p.188.

156 'Sir Charles Ruthen', *Daily Mail*, 27 January 1922, p.7. 'Resignation of the President', *Journal of the Society of Architects*, vol.15, no.4, February 1922, p.94.

157 'Small Houses and Architects: 1', *The Architects' Journal*, vol.93, no.2412, 17 April 1941, p.253.

158 'The Architect and the State', *Journal of the Society of Architects*, vol.15, no.5, March 1922, p.138.

159 'Small Houses and Architects: 1', p.253.

160 'City Housing Inquiry', *Birmingham Daily Gazette*, 22 November 1921, p.3.

161 'Son of a Famous Father', *Birmingham Daily Gazette*, 10 November 1915, p.1.

162 Green, *Ideologies of Conservatism*, pp 114–31. 'Has the Day of Reckoning Come?', *The Daily Mirror*, 9 December 1920, pp 1 and 9.

163 'The Wrong Spirit', *Birmingham Daily Gazette*, 8 June 1921, p.4.

164 'Housing in the City', *Birmingham Daily Gazette*, 17 November 1921, p.2.

165 'End of Birmingham Housing Committee', *Birmingham Daily Gazette*, 5 April 1922, p.5.

166 'End of Birmingham Housing Committee', p.5.

167 Edwin Gunn, 'The Speculative Architect', *The Architects' Journal*, vol.77, 5 April 1933, p.462.

4   THE COTTAGE APPROPRIATED

1 Howel Evans, 'Where are we to find Good Houses?', *The Daily Mirror*, 15 January 1919, p.7.

2 *Third Annual Report of the Ministry of Health, 1921–1922*, Cmd. 1713 (London, 1922), p.42.

3 Charles Ruthen, 'The Architect and the State', *Journal of the Society of Architects*, vol.15, no.4, February 1922, p.87.

4 Sir Alfred Mond MP, 'Reduction of Public Expenditure – Memorandum by the Minister of Health – Secret (CP 3067)', 22 June 1921, p.5; The National Archives, T161/132.

5 Sanchia Berg, '"Can You Help Us?" – 100-Year-Old Census Secrets Unearthed', *BBC News Online*, 6 January 2022; https://www.bbc.co.uk/news/uk-59879470.

6 Ruthen, 'The Architect and the State', p.86.

7 Evelyn Waugh, *Labels* (London, 1985 [1930]), p.46.

8 'A Conspectus of Housing Policies', *Garden Cities and Town Planning*, vol.12, no.10, December 1922, p.182.

9 Ross McKibbin, *Parties and People: England 1914–1951* (Oxford, 2010), pp 36–64.

10 David Matless, *Landscape and Englishness* (London, 1998), p.25.

11 Patrick Abercrombie, *The Preservation of Rural England* (Liverpool, 1926), p.43.

12 Melanie Hall, 'Affirming Community Life: Preservation, National Identity and the State, 1900', in Chris Miele, ed., *From William Morris: Building Conservation and the Arts and Crafts Cult of Authenticity 1877–1939* (London, 2005), pp 139–43.

13 Hall, 'Affirming Community Life', pp 136 and 141.

14 James Malton, *An Essay on British Cottage Architecture* (London, 1798), p.11.

15 Jenny West, 'Appendix II, The Society for the Protection of Ancient Buildings Committee Members', in Miele, *From William Morris*, p.331.

16 Thackeray Turner, Letter to Dr Ross, Carnegie Dunfermline Trustees, 17 January 1908; Society for the Protection of Ancient Buildings Archive, Folder: Cottages I, 1915–23.

17 Thackeray Turner, Letter to the Editor: 'Old Houses in Haslemere', *The Times*, 19 March 1912, p.11.

18 Thackeray Turner, Letter to the Editor: 'Threatened Kentish Cottages', *Country Life*, 7 November 1914; Society for the Protection of Ancient Buildings Archive, Folder: Cottages I, 1915–23.

19 Chairman, Society for the Protection of Ancient Buildings, Letter to the Editor, *The Poole Herald*, 6 October 1917; Society for the Protection of Ancient Buildings Archive, Folder: Cottages I, 1915–23.

20 Letter to the Editor: 'Guildford's Old-World Cottages Saved', *Country Life*, vol.32, no.815, 17 August 1912, p.242.

21 Clause 28 (1–3), *Housing, Town Planning, &c., Act, 1919*.

22 H. Bell, Letter to A.R. Powys (Secretary, Society for the Protection of Ancient Buildings), 8 February 1923. Assistant Clerk, Sevenoaks Council, Letter to A.R. Powys (Secretary, Society for the Protection of Ancient Buildings), 28 July 1923 – both Society for the Protection of Ancient Buildings Archive, Folder: Cottages I, 1915–23.

23 May Morris, Letter to A.R. Powys (Secretary, Society for the Protection of Ancient Buildings), 21 May 1919, p.1; Society for the Protection of Ancient Buildings Archive, Folder: Cottages II, 1919.

24 Thackeray Turner, Letter to the Editor: 'Old English Cottages', *The Times*, 9 June 1919, p.6.

25 Turner, 'Old English Cottages', p.6.

26 'Cottage Fund Members', pp 1–22; Society for the Protection of Ancient Buildings Archive, Folder: Cottage Fund Members.

27 W.R. Lethaby, *Form in Civilization: Collected Papers on Art & Labour* (London, 1922), p.41.

28 Hall, 'Affirming Community Life', p.146.

29 Alan Francis, 'New Lamps for Old', *The Ideal Home*, vol.1, no.4, April 1920, p.136.

30 R.H. Tawney, *The Acquisitive Society* (London, 1923), p.41.

31 Geoffrey Tyack, *The Making of Our Urban Landscape* (Oxford, 2022), p.243.

32 Maurice Adams, *Modern Cottage Architecture* (London, 1912), p.34. Anthony King, *The Bungalow: The Production of a Global Culture* (London, 1984), p.120.

33 H.G. Wells, *Mr Britling Sees It Through* (London, 1916), p.73.

34 'K', 'A Cottage and Its Economies', *Country Life*, vol.38, no.972, 21 August 1915, pp 253–4.

35 Captain G.C. Clarke, 'Foreword', *The Ideal Home*, vol.1, no.1, January 1920, p.1.

36 Francis, 'New Lamps for Old', pp 135–7.

37 The Editor, 'Ancient and Modern', *The Ideal Home*, vol.2, no.4, October 1920, p.132.

38 The Editor, 'Somewhere in Sussex – The Week-End Cottage of Madame Fifinella', *The Ideal Home*, vol.2, no.5, November 1920, pp 172–4.

39 H. Kemp-Prossor, 'An Old-Time Cottage', *The Ideal Home*, vol.3, no.5, May 1921, pp 169–72.

40 Basil Ionides, 'Creating a Southern Aspect', *The Ideal Home*, vol.5, no.4, April 1922, p.189.

41 Guy Church, 'Comfort, Taste and Beauty', *The Ideal Home*, vol.7, no.1, January 1923, pp 4–6.

42 Advertisement, *The Ideal Home*, vol.7, no.4, April 1923, p.259.

43 Ionides, 'Creating a Southern Aspect', pp 189–90.

44 Lulie James, 'Cottage Simplicity', *The Ideal Home*, vol.7, no.3, March 1923, p.220.

45 Colin Ward, *Cotters and Squatters: Housing's Hidden History* (Nottingham, 2005), p.156.

46 Winifred Holtby, *South Riding* (London, 1936).

47 Dennis Hardy and Colin Ward, *Arcadia for All* (Nottingham, 2004).

48 Patrick Abercrombie, 'The Preservation of Rural England', *The Town Planning Review*, vol.12, no.1, May 1926, p.23.

49 Clough Williams-Ellis, *England and the Octopus* (London, 1996 [1928]), pp 140–42.

50 Marion Cran, *The Story of My Ruin* (London, 1924).

51 Cran, *Story of My Ruin*, pp 230–31, 57 and 305.

52 Christopher Holdenby, *Folk of the Furrow* (London, 1913), p.60.

53 A.G. Street, *Strawberry Roan* (London, 1932), p.310.

54 Deborah Sugg Ryan does address it – see *Ideal Homes: Uncovering the History and Design of the Interwar House* (Manchester, 2020), pp 68–9.

55 Cran, *Story of My Ruin*, p.11.

56 Mark Swenarton, *Homes Fit for Heroes: The Politics and Architecture of Early State Housing in Britain* (London, 1981), p.148.

57 'The £300 House', *Garden Cities and Town Planning*, vol.12, no.8, September–October 1922, p.143.

58 'Municipal Elections', *Leicester Daily Post*, 13 October 1919, p.2. 'Here and There – Mr Arthur Wakerley', *Leicester Daily Post*, 27 October 1919, p.3.

59 'The £300 House', p.143.

60 'The £300 House', p.143.

61 Chris Matthews, *Homes and Places: A History of Nottingham's Council Houses* (Nottingham, 2015), pp 28–30. T. Cecil Howitt, *Nottingham Housing Schemes 1919–1928* (Nottingham, 1929), pp 54–7.

62 Howitt, *Nottingham Housing Schemes*, p.22.

63 'Editorial Comments', *Garden Cities and Town Planning*, vol.12, no.7, July–August 1922, p.105. Also, A. Sayle, *The Houses of the Workers* (London, 1924), p.17.

64 'Editorial Comments', *Garden Cities and Town Planning*, vol.13, no.2, February 1923, pp 19–20.

65 Mervyn Miller, *Raymond Unwin: Garden Cities and Town Planning* (Leicester, 1992), p.180.

66 'Notes – The New Minister of Health', *The Builder*, vol.124, no.4180, 16 March 1923, p.430.

67 'Editorial Comments', *Garden Cities and Town Planning*, vol.12, no.8, September–October 1922, pp 133–4.

68 A Practising Architect, 'Modern English Architecture', *The Builder*, vol.124, no.4172, 19 January 1923, p.114.

69 Ben Jones, *The Working Class in Mid-Twentieth-Century England: Community, Identity and Social Memory* (Manchester, 2012), p.83.

70 Lexden and Winstree Rural District Council, *Annual Report – Medical Officer of Health* (Colchester, 1925), pp 4–5 and 21; Wellcome Collection.

71 Lexden and Winstree Rural District Council, *Annual Report*, p.20.

72 Emily Digby, 'A Cottage Home for Every Family', *The Land Worker*, vol.6, no.72, May 1925, pp 14–15; Warwick University Modern Records Centre.

73 Richard Sennett, *Building and Dwelling: Ethics for the City* (London, 2019), p.129.

74 Sugg Ryan, *Ideal Homes*, p.60.

75 John Boughton, *Municipal Dreams: The Rise and Fall of Council Housing* (London, 2018), p.36.

76 Ruthen, 'The Architect and the State', p.86.

77 Norman McKellen, 'The National Housing Policy', *The Builder*, vol.124, no.4170, 5 January 1923, p.44.

78 Robert Self, *Neville Chamberlain: A Biography* (Aldershot, 2006), p.91.

79 Neville Chamberlain MP, *Housing, &c (No. 2) Bill,* 1923, 13 GEO. 5, p.2

80 Neville Chamberlain, Letter to Hilda, 18 May 1924, in Robert Self, ed., *The Neville Chamberlain Diary Letters,* Vol. 2 (Aldershot, 2000), p.223. Robert Self, 'Introduction: Neville Chamberlain, 1921–1927', in *Chamberlain Diary Letters,* Vol. 2, p.10.

81 Lt. Col. F.E. Fremantle, *The Housing of the Nation* (London, 1927), p.44.

82 McKibbin, *Parties and People*, pp 36–7.

83 *Sixth Annual Report of the Ministry of Health, 1924–1925*, Cmd. 2450 (London, 1925), p.48.

84 McKibbin, *Parties and People*, p.64.

85 Geraint Thomas, *Popular Conservatism and the Culture of National Government in Inter-War Britain* (Cambridge, 2020), p.42.

86 Charles Loch Mowat, *Britain between the Wars 1918–1940* (Boston, 1971), p.206. Thomas, *Popular Conservatism*, p.40.

87 Keith Feiling, *The Life of Neville Chamberlain* (London, 1946), p.103.

88 Sir Lawrence Weaver, '"Subsidy" Cottages at Wembley', *Country Life*, vol.58, no.1489, 18 July 1925, p.112.

89 Sir Charles Wakefield, 'Introduction', in Sir Frank Baines, 'The Preservation of Ancient Cottages', *Journal of the Royal Society of Arts*, vol.74, no.3838, 11 June 1926, p.706.

90 Baines, 'The Preservation of Ancient Cottages', pp 711–12.

91 S.L.G. Beaufoy, 'Well Hall Estate, Eltham', *The Town Planning Review*, vol.21, no.3, October 1950, p.264.

92 Guy Dawber, 'The Inaugural Address, Ninety-Second Session 1925–26', *Journal of the Royal Institute of British Architects*, vol.33, no.1, 7 November 1925, p.5.

93 Baines, 'The Preservation of Ancient Cottages', pp 715–21.

94 Baines, 'The Preservation of Ancient Cottages', p.725.

95 'Notes – Preservation of Old Cottages', *The Builder*, vol.130, no.4348, 4 June 1926, p.900.

96 John Urry and Jonas Larsen, *The Tourist Gaze 3.0* (London, 2011), p.120.

97 G.K. Menzies (Secretary, Royal Society of Arts), Letter to A.R. Powys, 10 July 1926; Society for the Protection of Ancient Buildings Archive, Folder: Cottages V – RSA Appeal.

98 G.K. Menzies, 'Preservation of Ancient Cottages – List of Donations', 1926; Society for the Protection of Ancient Buildings Archive, Folder: Cottages V – RSA Appeal.

99 Stanley Baldwin, *The 1924 Conservative Party General Election Manifesto*; http://www.conservativemanifesto. com/1924/1924-conservative-manifesto.shtml.

100 'The Steel House', *Country Life*, vol.57, no.1461, 3 January 1925, pp 8–10.

101 M.L. Gwyer, Ministry of Health Solicitor's Department, Letter to W. Graham-Harrison, Office of the Parliamentary Counsel, 28 April 1926; The National Archives, HLG 29/149.

102 Neville Chamberlain, 'Secret Diary 1922–1926', 22 January 1926; Birmingham University, Cadbury Research Library, NC 2/21.

103 Our Parliamentary Correspondent, 'Housing . . . Help for Rural Owners', *The Times*, 21 January 1926, p.14.

104 Charles Walston, Letter to the Editor: 'Rural Housing', *The Times*, 22 January 1926, p.8.

105 Maurice Hankey, 'The King's Speech' (CP9 (26)), 2 February 1926, p.2; The National Archives, CAB 24-178-9.

106 M.L. Gwyer, Ministry of Health Solicitor, Letter to W. Graham-Harrison, Office of the Parliamentary Counsel; The National Archives, HLG 29/149.

107 Neville Chamberlain MP, 'Second Reading, Housing (Rural Workers) Bill, 1926', *Hansard*, 3 August 1926, c. 2839–2842.

108 Chamberlain, *Hansard*, 3 August 1926, c. 2841.

109 Nigel Everett, *The Tory View of Landscape* (London, 1994), pp 104–5.

110 Chamberlain, *Hansard*, 3 August 1926, c. 2841.

111 Everett, *Tory View of Landscape*, p.104.

112 Alexander Pope, 'Epistle IV, Of the Use of Riches. To Richard Boyle, Earl of Burlington', in *Four Ethic Epistles* (Glasgow, 1731), p.55.

113 'Rural Housing and Folk Architecture', *The Builder*, vol.131, no.4357, 6 August 1926, p.195.

114 'Coalition to Continue', *The Times*, 13 November 1918, p.9.

115 Neville Chamberlain, Letter to Hilda, 10 August 1926; Birmingham University, Cadbury Research Library, NC 18/1/539.

116 Frank Rye MP, *Hansard*, 3 August 1926, c. 2891.

117 E.R. Forber, Letter to W. Graham-Harrison, Office of the Parliamentary Counsel, 10 November 1926; The National Archives, HLG 29/149.

118 Clause 2. (3), *Housing (Rural Workers) Act, 1926* [16 and 17 GEO. 5 CH 56], p.3.

119 'Small Holdings Bill in the Lords', *The Times*, 7 December 1926, p.16.

120 Ramsay MacDonald MP, *Hansard*, 3 August 1926, c. 2901–2903.

121 Chamberlain, Letter to Hilda, 10 August 1926.

122 Wilfred Paling MP, 'Third Reading, Housing (Rural Workers) Bill, 1926', *Hansard*, 6 December 1926, c. 1744.

123 Charles Rhys, MP, *Hansard*, 6 December 1926, c. 1745.

124 Archibald Skelton MP, *Hansard*, 6 December 1926, c. 1745.

125 'Menzies, George Kenneth', *Who Was Who* (Oxford, 2021).

126 G.K. Menzies, Letter to The Society for the Protection of Ancient Buildings, 22 October 1926; Society for the Society for the Protection of Ancient Buildings Archive, Folder: Cottages V – RSA Appeal.

127 Patrick Abercrombie, Letter to the Editor: 'Rural England', *The Times*, 6 December 1926, p.15.

128 G.K. Menzies, Letter to A.R. Powys (Secretary, Society for the Protection of Ancient Buildings), 21 December 1926; Society for the Protection of Ancient Buildings Archive, Folder: Cottages V – RSA Appeal.

129 Philip Williamson, *Stanley Baldwin* (Cambridge, 1999), p.243.

130 Simon Miller, 'Urban Dreams and Rural Reality: Land and Landscape in English Culture, 1920–45', *Rural History*, vol.6, no.1, 1995, p.89.

131 Stanley Baldwin, *On England and Other Addresses* (London, 1927), pp 6–7.

132 Stanley Baldwin, Letter to Mary Webb, 14 January 1927, in Mary Webb, *Armour Wherein He Trusted* (London, 1929), pp 9–11. Stuart Sillars, *Picturing England Between the Wars: Word and Image 1918–1940* (Oxford, 2022), p.172. Claud Cockburn, *Bestseller* (Harmondsworth, 1975), p.186.

133 Mary Webb, *Precious Bane* (London, 1978 [1924]), p.73.

134 Williamson, *Stanley Baldwin*, p.244, n.3.

135 Mary Webb, *The Golden Arrow* (London, 1916), p.1.

136 Simon White and Owen Davies, 'Tradition and Rural Modernity in Mary Webb's Shropshire: *Precious Bane* in Context', *The Space Between*, vol.15, no.1, 2019, p.10.

137 Williamson, *Stanley Baldwin*, p.246.

138 Miller, 'Urban Dreams and Rural Reality', p.94.

139 Stanley Baldwin, 'Conference on the Preservation of Ancient Cottages', in *Journal of the Royal Society of Arts*, vol.75, no.3873, 11 February 1927, p.305.

140 Clough Williams-Ellis, *Architect Errant* (Portmeirion, 1991 [1971]), p.181.

141 Baldwin, 'Conference on the Preservation of Ancient Cottages', pp 305–6.

142 'Ancient English Cottages', *The Times*, 27 January 1927, p.7. 'The Preservation of Ancient Cottages', *The Wiltshire Times*, 29 January 1927; Society for the Protection of Ancient Buildings Archive, Folder: Cottages V – RSA Appeal.

143 'Notes – The Preservation of Rural England', *The Builder*, vol.131, no.4375, 10 December 1926, p.934.

144 Baldwin, 'Conference on the Preservation of Ancient Cottages', p.305.

145 John Whitley MP, 'Conference on the Preservation of Ancient Cottages', *Journal of the Royal Society of Arts*, vol.75, no.3873, 11 February 1927, p.309.

146 Sir Alfred Mond MP, 'Conference on the Preservation of Ancient Cottages', *Journal of the Royal Society of Arts*, vol.75, no.3873, 11 February 1927, p.312.

147 Sir Percy Hurd MP, 'Conference on the Preservation of Ancient Cottages', *Journal of the Royal Society of Arts*, vol.75, no.3873, 11 February 1927, p.314.

148 Earl of Crawford & Balcarres, 'Conference on the Preservation of Ancient Cottages', *Journal of the Royal Society of Arts*, vol.75, no.3873, 11 February 1927, p.308.

149 'By The Way', *Daily Express*, 28 January 1927, p.8.

150 'Mr Baldwin Champions English Countryside', *Morning Post*, 28 January 1927, p.7.

151 'Beautiful Homes – Premier Urges Return to Old-Type Houses', *Sheffield Daily Telegraph*, 27 January 1927, p.5.

152 'Vandals of the Countryside', *Daily Mail*, 27 January 1927, p.7.

153 'Rural Cottages', *Western Morning News*, 27 January 1927, p.6.

154 *The London Weekly*, 5 February 1927, p.173; Royal Society of Arts Archive, Cuttings Book 1, PR.EN/100/13/4.

155 Royal Society of Arts Archive, Cuttings Book, p.1.

156 'Ancient Cottage Architecture', *The Manchester Guardian*, 28 January 1927, p.5; Royal Society of Arts Archive, Cuttings Book 1, PR.EN/100/13/4.

157 'Old Cottages', *The Times*, 25 January 1927, p.15.

158 Ministry of Health, Housing (Rural Workers) Bill – Second Reading Brief, 3 August 1926, p.1; The National Archives, HLG 29/149.

159 Peter Mandler, *The English National Character: The History of an Idea from Edmund Burke to Tony Blair* (London, 2006), p.150.

160 Peter Mandler, *The Fall and Rise of the Stately Home* (London, 1997), p.241.

161 Gareth Stedman Jones, in Edith Hall and Henry Stead, *A People's History of Classics: Class and Greco-Roman Antiquity in Britain and Ireland 1689–1939* (London, 2020), p.8.

162 Stanley Baldwin, *The Preservation of Ancient Cottages* (London, 1927), p.5; Society for the Protection of Ancient Buildings Archive, Folder: Cottages V – RSA Appeal.

163 Baldwin, *Preservation of Ancient Cottages*, p.9.

164 Baldwin, *Preservation of Ancient Cottages*, p.12.

165 Thomas Hardy, 'Note by Thomas Hardy, OM', in *The Preservation of Ancient Cottages* (London, 1927), pp 13 and 16.

166 'The Preservation of Ancient Cottages', *The Builder*, vol.132, no.4391, 1 April 1927, p.511.

167 The book, with dedication, is in the author's possession, acquired from a dealer who confirmed the provenance as Baldwin's family.

168 Thomas, *Popular Conservatism*, p.44.

169 Ministry of Health, *Circular on the Housing (Rural Workers) Act, 1926* (London, 1927), p.8; The National Archives, AO 30/45.

170 Neville Chamberlain, 'Foreword', in *Housing Manual on the Design, Construction and Repair of Dwellings* (1927 Manual), (London, 1927), p.ii.

171 para. 2, 1927 Manual, p.2.

172 'Housing Chief of Britain – Death of Sir Charles Ruthen', *The Western Mail*, 20 September 1926, p.8. 'Absent Grand Jurors', *Nottingham Evening Post*, 23 September 1926, p.1.

173 Swenarton, *Homes Fit for Heroes*, p.141.

174 Miller, *Raymond Unwin*, p.182.

175 para. 14, 1927 Manual, p.4.

176 paras 17–21, 1927 Manual, pp 4–5.

177 para. 15, 1927 Manual, p.4.

178 para. 3, 1927 Manual, p.2.

179 para. 12, 1927 Manual, p.4.

180 W.O. Hammond, *An Address to the Churchwardens, Guardians, Overseers of the Poor and Rate Payers of the Wingham Division of Saint Augustine* (Canterbury, 1835), p.10.

181 para. 13, 1927 Manual, p.4.

182 Abercrombie, 'The Preservation of Rural England', p.24.

183 para. 12, 1927 Manual, p.4.

184 'M.R.', 'Hints on Cottage Design', *Housing*, vol.1, no.23, 24 May 1920, p.305.

185 C.F.A. Voysey, 'Patriotism in Architecture', *The Architectural Association Journal*, vol.28, no.304, June 1912, p.25.

186 para. 12, 1927 Manual, p.4.

187 Royal Society of Arts, Preservation of Ancient Cottages – Executive Committee Meeting, 19 April 1928, *Minutes of Committees – Cottages 1928–31*, p.1.

188 Ramsay MacDonald, 'Fund for the Preservation of Ancient Cottages', *Journal of the Royal Society of Arts*, vol.77, no.3982, 15 March 1929, p.451.

189 'Fund for the Preservation of Ancient Cottages – First Annual Report', *Journal of the Royal Society of Arts*, vol.77, no.3982, 15 March 1929, p.463.

190 'The Preservation of Ancient Cottages', *The Architectural Association Journal*, vol.69, no.1786, 10 April 1929, p.572.

191 William Morris, in 'Arlington Row, Bibury', *The Architectural Review*, vol.63, no.377, 1 April 1928, p.lxxxviii.

192 M. Washbourn, 'Points from Letters: "The Most Beautiful Village in England"', *The Spectator*, vol.143, no.5291, 23 November 1929, p.771.

193 'Fund for the Preservation of Ancient Cottages – First Annual Report', pp 464–5.

194 Minute, Royal Society of Arts, Preservation of Ancient Cottages – Executive Committee Meeting, 19 April 1928, *Minutes of Committees – Cottages 1928–31*, pp 2–3.

195 Minute, Royal Society of Arts, Preservation of Ancient Cottages – Executive Committee Meeting, 25 October 1928, *Minutes of Committees – Cottages 1928–31*, p.13.

196 Minute, Royal Society of Arts, Preservation of Ancient Cottages – Executive Committee Meeting, 13 February 1929, *Minutes of Committees – Cottages 1928–31*, p.22.

197 Raymond Unwin and M.H. Baillie Scott, *Town Planning and Modern Architecture at Hampstead Garden Suburb* (London, 1909), p.34.

198 Royal Society of Arts, *An Appeal to the County of Buckingham* (London, 1929), p.3.

199 Royal Society of Arts, *An Appeal*, p.3.

200 'Re-conditioning of Cottages', *Journal of the Royal Institute of British Architects*, vol.44, no.4, 19 December 1936, p.185.

201 'Preface', Royal Society of Arts, *An Appeal*, p.3.

202 Royal Society of Arts, *An Appeal*, pp 2 and 4–5.

203 Royal Society of Arts, *An Appeal*, p.12.

204 Minutes, Royal Society of Arts, Preservation of Ancient Cottages – Executive Committee Meeting, 3 September

1930, *Minutes of Committees – Cottages 1928–31*, pp 67–73.

205 'Publication of a Book on Cottages', in 'Fund for the Preservation of Ancient Cottages – First Annual Report', p.469.

206 'Oliver FRIBA, Basil', *Who's Who in Architecture 1926*, ed. Frederick Chatterton (London, 1927), pp 222–3.

207 Basil Oliver, *Old Houses and Village Buildings in East Anglia, Norfolk, Suffolk and Essex* (London, 1912).

208 Elizabeth McKellar, 'All Roof, No Wall', *Architectural History*, vol.62, 2019, pp 238–9.

209 Basil Oliver, *The Cottages of England* (London, 1929), p.2.

210 Oliver, *Cottages of England*, p.2.

211 Grahame B. Tubbs, 'Some Books of the Year', *The Architects' Journal*, vol.71, no.1825, 8 January 1930, p.105.

212 Catherine Brace, 'Publishing and Publishers: Towards a Historical Geography of Countryside Writing, *c.*1930–1950', *Arena*, vol.33, no.3, 2001, p.293.

213 Matless, *Landscape and Englishness*, pp 47–67.

214 P.A. Barron, *The House Desirable* (London, 1929), p.2.

215 Gordon Allen, *The Cheap Cottage & Small House* (Letchworth, 1912), pp 8–9.

216 Allen, *The Cheap Cottage & Small House*, 6th edn (London, 1919), p.8.

217 H.V. Morton, *In Search of England* (London, 1935 [1927]), pp 77–82.

218 Samuel Hynes, *A War Imagined: The First World War and English Culture* (London, 1990), p.390.

219 Brian Connon, 'Foreword', in Beverley Nichols, *Down the Garden Path* (Portland, 2005 [1932]), pp vii–viii.

220 Nichols, *Down the Garden Path*, p.15.

221 Nichols, *Down the Garden Path*, pp 16–20 and 23.

222 W.S. Percy, *Strolling through Cottage England* (London, 1936), p.88.

223 Cecil Roberts, *Pilgrim Cottage* (New York, 1933), p.16.

224 Roberts, *Pilgrim Cottage*, pp 17–18.

225 Ralph Nevill, *Old Cottage and Domestic Architecture – South West Surrey* (Guildford, 1889).

226 Guy Dawber, *Old Cottages and Farmhouses in Kent and Sussex* (London, 1900). E.A. Ould, *Old Cottages, Farmhouses . . . in Shropshire, Herefordshire, and Cheshire* (London, 1904). Maurice Adams, *Modern Cottage Architecture* (London, 1904). C.R. Ashbee, *A Book of Cottages and Little Houses* (London, 1906). W. Curtis Green, *Old Cottages & Farm-Houses in Surrey* (London, 1908).

227 Peter Hampson Ditchfield, *Picturesque English Cottages and their Doorway Gardens* (Philadelphia, 1905), p.15.

228 P.H. Ditchfield, *The Charm of the English Village* (London, 1908), p.1.

229 Ditchfield, *Vanishing England* (London, 1910), pp 69–70.

230 Ditchfield, *Vanishing England*, p.2.

231 Ditchfield, *Vanishing England*, p.398.

232 Sydney Jones, *The Village Homes of England* (London, 1912), p.3.

233 'Ditchfield, Rev. Peter Hampson', *Who Was Who* (London, 2007).

234 P.H. Ditchfield, 'The Destruction of Country Cottages', *The Builder*, vol.117, no.3997, 12 September 1919, p.267.

235 'Rural Housing and Folk Architecture', *The Builder*, vol.131, no.4357, 6 August 1926, p.195.

236 John Briarfield, 'Cottage Groups', *The Architectural Review*, vol.62, no.372, 1 November 1927, p.167.

237 H.J. Massingham, *English Downland* (London, 1936), p.110.

238 Sydney Jones, *English Village Homes* (London, 1936), p.33.

239 Jones, *English Village Homes*, figs 69 and 70, pp 66–7. Robert Kerr, *The Gentleman's House, or How to Plan English Residences from the Parsonage to the Palace* (Cambridge, 2012 [1864]), p.360.

240 Percy, *Strolling*, pp 14, 31, 40, 46, 66, 98.

241 Brace, 'Publishing and Publishers', p.293.

242 Harry Batsford and Charles Fry, *The English Cottage* (London, 1944 [1938]), p.v.

243 Batsford and Fry, *The English Cottage*, pp 1, 7, 108, 105.

244 Sillars, *Picturing England Between the Wars*, p.20.

245 Batsford and Fry, *The English Cottage*, pp 1, 107–8 and 109.

246 Batsford and Fry, *The English Cottage*, p.109.

247 Batsford and Fry, *The English Cottage*, p.110.

248 W.B. Yeats, 'A Prayer On Going Into My House', in Alain Le Garsmeur and Bernard McCabe, *Images of Ireland* (London, 1991), p.90.

249 Clough Williams-Ellis, *England and the Octopus* (London, 1996 [1928]), p.15.

250 Barron, *The House Desirable*, pp 2–3.

251 D.H. Lawrence, 'Nottingham and the Mining Countryside' (1930), in James T. Boulton, ed., *Late Essays and Articles* (Cambridge, 2014), p.293.

252 Street, *Strawberry Roan*, p.309.

253 H.J. Massingham, *Country* (London, 1934), p.129.

254 George Orwell, *Coming Up for Air* (Harmondsworth, 1975 [1939]), p.198.

255 'Ugliness', *The Builder*, vol.131, no.4372, 19 November 1926, p.809.

256 'Rural England', *The Times*, 7 December 1927, p.11.

257 Patrick Abercrombie, in G.H. Jack, 'The Working of the Advisory Panels System' – Vote of Thanks and Discussion, *Journal of the Royal Institute of British Architects*, vol.44, no.10, 20 March 1937, p.494.

258 'Cottages' Charter', *Country Life*, vol.81, no.2102, 1 May 1937, p.474.

259 Abercrombie, in Jack, 'The Working of the Advisory Panels System', p.494.

260 *Rural Housing,* Third Report of the Rural Housing Sub-Committee of the Central Housing Advisory Committee (London, 1944), paras 154 and 156; The National Archives, AO 30/45.

5 THE COTTAGE COMMERCIALISED

1 Christopher Hussey, *The Picturesque: Studies in a Point of View* (London, 1927), p.186.

2 Stuart Sillars, *Picturing England Between the Wars: Word and Image 1918–1940* (Oxford, 2021), p.13.

3 Gavin Stamp, 'Neo-Tudor and Its Enemies', *Architectural History,* vol.49, 2006, pp 1–33. Peter Scott, *The Making of the Modern British Home: The Suburban Semi and Family Life between the Wars* (Oxford, 2013), p.5. Helena Barrett and John Phillips, *Suburban Style: The British Home 1840–1960* (London, 1988), pp 15 and 128. Andrew Ballantyne and Andrew Law, *Tudoresque* (London, 2011). Deborah Sugg Ryan, *Ideal Homes: Uncovering the History and Design of the Interwar House* (Manchester, 2020), pp 191–7.

4 H.S. Goodhart-Rendel, *English Architecture since the Regency: An Interpretation* (London, 1953), p.228.

5 W.S. Percy, *Strolling Through Cottage England* (London, 1936), p.30.

6 T. Alwyn Lloyd, 'The Architect and Housing by the Speculative Builder', *Journal of the Royal Institute of British Architects,* vol.41, no.8, 24 February 1934, p.387.

7 Randal Phillips, *Houses for Moderate Means* (London, 1936), p.5.

8 George Santayana, *Soliloquies in England* (New York, 1923 [1922]), pp 79–80.

9 Steen Eiler Rasmussen, *London: The Unique City* (London, 1937), p.304.

10 Aldous Huxley, *Crome Yellow* (London, 1989 [1921]), p.54.

11 George Orwell, *Coming Up for Air* (Harmondsworth, 1975 [1939]), pp 209 and 176.

12 John Gloag, *The Englishman's Castle* (London, 1944), p.156.

13 T.F. Hunt, *Half a Dozen Hints on Picturesque Domestic Architecture* (London, 1841 [1825]), p.i. Gilbert Meason, *On the Landscape Architecture of the Great Painters of Italy* (London, 1828), p.65.

14 Timothy Brittain-Catlin, 'Britain and Ireland, 1830–1914', in Murray Fraser, ed., *Sir Banister Fletcher's Global History of Architecture 21st Edition* (London, 2020), p.629.

15 Geoffrey Scott, *The Architecture of Humanism: A Study in the History of Taste* (London 1961 [1914]), p.90.

16 'National Housing and National Life', *Journal of the Royal Institute of British Architects,* vol.25, June 1918, p.170.

17 'Sir Charles Ruthen and National Housing', *Journal of the Royal Institute of British Architects,* vol.29, no.6, 28 January 1922, p.188.

18 The Architectural Editor, 'A New Old-World House', *The Ideal Home,* vol.10, no.5, November 1924, p.352.

19 *Houses, Cottages and Bungalows,* ed. Frederick Chatterton (London, 1926). Randal Phillips, *The House You Want* (London, 1923); *Small Family Houses* (London, 1924); *The Modern English House* (London, 1927); *The 1000 Pound House* (London, 1928); *Houses for Moderate Means* (London, 1936).

20 Phillips, *Small Family Houses,* pp 55–6.

21 Phillips, *Small Family Houses,* p.9.

22 Phillips, *The Modern English House,* p.x.

23 Phillips, *The 1000 Pound House,* pp 23–5.

24 'Journal', *Journal of the Royal Institute of British Architects,* vol.41, no.8, 24 February 1934, p.383.

25 Ministry of Health, *Fifteenth Annual Report, 1933–1934,* Cmd. 4664 (London, 1934), p.153.

26 Neal Shasore, *Designs on Democracy: Architecture and the Public in Interwar London* (Oxford, 2022), p.118.

27 'Journal', *Journal of the Royal Institute of British Architects,* vol.41, no.8, 24 February 1934, p.383–4.

28 'Journal', *Journal of the Royal Institute of British Architects,* vol.41, no.12, 28 April 1934, p.603.

29 Trystan Edwards, 'Journal', *Journal of the Royal Institute of British Architects,* vol.44, no.1, 7 November 1936, p.3.

30 'Journal', *Journal of the Royal Institute of British Architects,* vol.41, no.8, 24 February 1934, p.384.

31 Phillips, *The Modern English House,* p.151.

32 Miles Horsey, 'London Speculative Housing of the 1930s: Official Control and Popular Taste', *The London Journal,* vol.11, no.2, 1985, p.157.

33 'Report of the Public Relations Committee', *Journal of the Royal Institute of British Architects,* vol.41, no.12, 28 April 1934, p.633.

34 Alwyn Lloyd, 'The Architect and Housing by the Speculative Builder', p.387.

35 Robert Lynd, 'The Empty House', in *The Little Angel* (London, 1926), p.21.

36 Clough Williams-Ellis, *England and the Octopus* (London, 1996 [1928]), p.22.

37 Sir Leslie Scott, 'Preservation of the Countryside', in Ernest Betham, ed., *House Building, 1934–36* (London, 1934), p.32.

38 John Gloag, *Design in Modern Life* (London, 1946 [1934]), p.19.

39 Jane Mulvagh, *Madresfield* (London, 2009), pp 52–3. 'Friday 11th September 1925', in *The Diaries of Evelyn Waugh* (Harmondsworth, 1984), p.220.

40 Evelyn Waugh, *Decline and Fall* (London, 2001 [1928]), p.109.

41 Gavin Stamp, *Edwin Lutyens Country Houses* (London, 2001), p.127.

42 Sacheverell Sitwell, *British Architects and Craftsmen* (London, 1945), pp 14–15.

43 John Macarthur, *The Picturesque: Architecture, Disgust and Other Irregularities* (Abingdon, 2007), p.115.

44 Stanley Baldwin, 'Education and National Life', in *Our Inheritance* (London, 1928), p.124.

45 RIBA (House Design Sub-Committee), 'The Architect and Housing by the Speculative Builder', *Journal of the Royal Institute of British Architects*, vol.41, no.12, 28 April 1934, p.649.

46 'Journal', *Journal of the Royal Institute of British Architects*, vol.41, no.12, 28 April 1934, p.604.

47 RIBA, 'The Architect and Housing by the Speculative Builder', pp 650–51.

48 RIBA, 'The Architect and Housing', p.651.

49 RIBA, 'The Architect and Housing', p.652.

50 RIBA, 'The Architect and Housing', p.652.

51 RIBA, 'The Architect and Housing', p.651.

52 RIBA, 'The Architect and Housing', p.653.

53 B.S. Townroe, 'A Tribute to House Builders', *The National Builder*, vol.13, no.11, June 1934, p.387.

54 Stanley Ramsey, 'Speculative House Building', *Journal of the Royal Institute of British Architects*, vol.45, no.11, 11 April 1938, p.534.

55 J.W.R. Whitehand and Christine Carr, 'The Creators of England's Interwar Suburbs', *Urban History*, vol.28, no.2, August 2001, p.228.

56 'National Housing and National Life', p.170.

57 Local Government Board, *Manual* (London, 1919), p.8.

58 'M.R.', 'Hints on Cottage Design', *Housing*, vol.1, no.23, 24 May 1920, p.305.

59 Alwyn Lloyd, 'The Architect and Housing by the Speculative Builder', p.389.

60 RIBA, 'The Architect and Housing', pp 652–3.

61 Beresford Pite, 'Architects and the Architecture of Cottages', *The Architects' Journal*, vol.49, no.1262, 12 March 1919, pp 149–50.

62 J.M. Richards, *The Castles on the Ground* (London, 1946), p.15.

63 Ingham Ashworth, in 'Vote of Thanks and Discussion', *Journal of the Royal Institute of British Architects*, vol.45, no.11, 11 April 1938, p.537.

64 Sydney Jones, *English Village Homes* (London, 1936), p.9. R.J. Moore-Colyer, 'From Great Wen to Toad Hall', *Rural History*, vol.10, no.1, 1999, p.116.

65 Fred Wellings, *Dictionary of British Housebuilders* (Beckenham, 2006), p.153.

66 Wates Limited, *34 Years of Quality Building*, 1935; Wates Archive, Box WA19, Item 452.

67 W.G. Newton, 'Bases of Criticism: V – Natural Taste', *The Architectural Review*, vol.56, no.332, July 1924, p.1.

68 Horsey, 'London Speculative Housing of the 1930s', p.156.

69 Hussey, *The Picturesque*, p.186.

70 James Malton, *An Essay on British Cottage Architecture* (London, 1798), p.5.

71 Ballantyne and Law, *Tudoresque*, p.48.

72 Wates, *Briardene Estate* brochure (London, 1935); Wates Archive, Box WA19, Item 452.

73 'Partnership Deed, Messrs E. & A. Wates, Furnishing Department', 10 October 1906, 1; Wates Archive, Box WA82, Item 1563.

74 'Partnership Deed, Messrs E. & A. Wates, Building Department', 13 December 1909, 1; Wates Archive, Box WA82, Item 1564.

75 'Editorial', *Wates House News*, No. 2, September 1935, p.1; Wates Archive, Box WA67, Item 46 (PD/WN/6).

76 Wates, *Wilverley Park Estate* brochure (London, 1935); Wates Archive.

77 'Ramifications', *Wates News Sheet*, 19 November 1938, p.1; Wates Archive, Box WA67, Item 440 (PD/WN/7).

78 'These Figures Will Surprise You', *Wates House News*, No. 1, June 1935, p.6; Wates Archive, Box WA67, Item 46 (PD/WN/6).

79 Nick Barratt, *Wates: A Family Business* (London, 2022), p.56; Wates Archive.

80 Norman Wates, 'A Personal Message', *Wates House News*, No. 1, June 1935, p.1; Wates Archive, Box WA67, Item 46 (PD/WN/6).

81 RIBA Nomination Papers (Associate), 19 June 1945.

82 'Potted Personalities No. 9', *Wates News Sheet*, No. 20, 3 September 1938, p.2; Wates Archive, Box WA67, Item 440 (PD/WN/7).

83 K.W. Bland, 'We Can Still Learn from the Past', *Wates House News*, No. 1, June 1935, p.3; Wates Archive, Box WA67, Item 46 (PD/WN/6).

84 George Speight, 'Who Bought the Inter-War Semi? The Socio-Economic Characteristics of New-House Buyers in the 1930s', in *University of Oxford Discussion Papers in Economic and Social History*, vol.38, 2000, p.4.

85 Wates, *Briardene Estate* brochure.

86 R.C. Sherriff, *Greengates* (London, 2015 [1936]), pp 131–2.

87 Sherriff, *Greengates*, pp 162 and 174.

88 Wates, *Briardene Estate* brochure.

89 Wates, *Briardene Estate* brochure. Tudor Walters Report (London, 1918), p.29.

90 Bland, 'We Can Still Learn from the Past', p.4.

91 Stuart Durant, *C.F.A. Voysey* (London, 1992), pp 85, 88–9, 92–3.

92 Wates, *Briardene Estate* brochure.

93 Brentham Society, 'Brentham Garden Suburb Virtual Tour'; http://www.brentham.org.uk/tour/html/virtual_tour.html.

94 *The Pioneer Co-Partnership Suburb* (London, 1990 [1912]), p.12.

95 Wates, *Station Estate* brochure (London, 1935); Wates Archive, Box WA19, Item 452.

96 Wates, *Briardene Estate* brochure.

97 Wates, *Briardene Estate* brochure. John Ruskin, 'Lecture I, Architecture', *Lectures on Architecture and Painting*, Library Edition, *The Works of John Ruskin*, Vol. XII, ed. E.T. Cook and A. Wedderburn (London, 1903–9), p.50.

98 Wates, *Briardene Estate* brochure.

99 'Houses for Sale – Messrs Harry Neal Ltd', *The National Builder*, vol.13, no.5, December 1933, p.164.

100 Messrs Wates, '5th August 1932', *Directors' Day Book*, p.3; Wates Archive, Box WA82, Item 565.

101 Messrs Wates, '29th June 1934', *Directors' Day Book*, p.72.

102 Messrs Wates, '8th August 1932' and '15th August 1932', *Directors' Day Book*, pp 5–10.

103 Messrs Wates, '8th December 1933', *Directors' Day Book*, p.70.

104 Wellings, *Dictionary of British Housebuilders*, p.286.

105 Barratt, *Wates: A Family Business*, p.52.

106 'It was a Nice House but the Builder Couldn't Sell It!', *Wates House News*, No. 2, September 1935, p.18; Wates Archive, Box WA67, Item 46 (PD/WN/6).

107 L. Smith, 'It's Action That Counts', *Wates House News*, No. 2, September 1935, p.2; Wates Archive, Box WA67, Item 46 (PD/WN/6).

108 L. Smith, 'The Lighter Side of Olympia', *Wates House News*, No. 1, June 1935, p.10; Wates Archive, Box WA67, Item 46 (PD/WN/6).

109 A.W. Madger, 'Selling Houses Is Pleasant', *Wates House News*, No. 1, June 1935, p.8; Wates Archive, Box WA67, Item 46 (PD/WN/6).

110 'The Quotabusters' Dinner', *Wates House News*, No. 4, December 1937, p.32; Wates Archive, Box WA67, Item 46 (PD/WN/6).

111 Wates, *Wilverley Park Estate* brochure.

112 Andrew Saint, 'The Quality of the London Suburb', in Julian Honer, ed., *London Suburbs* (London, 1999), p.15.

113 Wates, *Wilverley Park Estate* brochure.

114 Elizabeth McKellar, 'All Roof, No Wall', *Architectural History*, vol.62, 2019, p.237. 'The little white cottage among the apple-trees – the chalet, as Madame Münster always called it' – Henry James, *The Europeans* (Oxford, 1996 [1878]), p.45.

115 Wates house-type brochure (London, 1938); Museum of Domestic Design and Architecture Archive, Middlesex University Archive, BADDA 4619.

116 'Houses for Sale – Messrs Harry Neal Ltd', p.164.

117 Barratt, *Wates: A Family Business*, pp 48–9.

118 Wates, *Wilverley Park Estate* brochure.

119 Wates, *Wilverley Park Estate* brochure.

120 Barratt, *Wates: A Family Business*, p.44.

121 Wates house-type brochure (London, 1938), p.16.

122 Paul Oliver, Ian Davis and Ian Bentley, *Dunroamin: The Suburban Semi and its Enemies* (London, 1981), p.117.

123 John Ruskin, 'Poetry of Architecture', Library Edition, *The Works of John Ruskin*, Vol. I, ed. E.T. Cook and A. Wedderburn (London, 1903–9), pp 11–12.

124 Wates, *Wilverley Park Estate* brochure.

125 Wates, *Station Estate* brochure.

126 Tudor Major floorspace was about 578ft^2 across the bedrooms and reception rooms, versus 699ft^2 in the Tudor DeLuxe – Wates, *Wilverley Park Estate* brochure.

127 Wellings, *Dictionary of British Housebuilders*, pp 165 and 287.

128 'Houses for Sale – Interview with Mr J. Laing', *The National Builder*, vol.13, no.3, October 1933, p.84.

129 Simon Pepper, 'John Laing's Sunnyfields Estate', in Boris Ford, ed., *Early 20th Century Britain*, Vol. 8 (Cambridge, 1992), p.300.

130 Pepper, 'John Laing's Sunnyfields Estate', pp 303–5.

131 Horsey, 'London Speculative Housing of the 1930s', p.157.

132 C.G. Allsopp, 'The Builders of Homes', *Wates House News*, No. 1, June 1935, 14; Wates Archive, Box WA67, Item 46 (PD/WN/6).

133 Wellings ranks interwar output in the 1930s: New Ideal Homesteads peaking at an average 6000 houses a year; Wates at 2000; Henry Boot at 2000; Taylor Woodrow at 1500; Davis Estates at 1200; Wimpey at 1200; Laing at 1000 – 'The Rise of the National Housebuilder', unpublished PhD (University of Liverpool, 2005), p.46; British Library EThOS, ID: 416083.

134 Frederick Gibberd, *The Architecture of England* (London, 1945 [1938]), p.42.

135 New Ideal Homesteads, *Homebuilders*; Museum of Domestic Design and Architecture, Middlesex University Archive, BADDA 460.

136 New Ideal Homesteads, *Homebuilders*.

137 Madger, 'Selling Houses Is Pleasant', pp 8–9.

138 Ian Bentley gives a perfect definition of the Picturesque here without using the word; see Oliver, Davis and Bentley, *Dunroamin*, p.66.

139 Arthur Edwards, *The Design of Suburbia: A Critical Study in Environmental History* (London, 1981), p.128.

140 Oliver, Davis and Bentley, *Dunroamin*, p.162.

141 Barrett and Phillips, *Suburban Style*, p.15.

142 Ballantyne and Law, *Tudoresque*, p.116.

143 Stamp, 'Neo-Tudor and Its Enemies', p.19.

144 P.A. Barron, *The House Desirable* (London, 1929), pp 102–3.

145 Horsey, 'London Speculative Housing of the 1930s', p.158.

146 Sugg Ryan, *Ideal Homes*, p.213.

147 Tim Benton, *The Modernist Home* (London, 2006), pp 14–15.

148 Mervyn Miller, *English Garden Cities* (Swindon, 2010), pp 54–6.

149 Greg Stevenson, *The 1930s Home* (Princes Risborough, 2000), p.14. Barrett and Phillips, *Suburban Style*, p.133.

150 Olive Cook, *The English House through Seven Centuries* (Harmondsworth, 1984), pp 51–2.

151 Charles O'Brien, *Houses* (London, 2016), p.130.

152 O'Brien, *Houses*, pp 25 (fig.14), 28 (fig.17). Harold Priestley, *The English Home* (London, 1971), pp 58–79.

153 A.R. Powys, *Repair of Ancient Buildings* (London, 1929), p.68.

154 O'Brien, *Houses*, p.36.

155 Mark Pinney, 'Architecture', in *Little Palaces: House and Home in the Inter-War Suburbs* (Barnet, 2003), p.24.

156 John Drinkwater, 'The Midlands', in *Tides* (London, 1918), p.32.

157 Gibberd, *The Architecture of England*, p.42.

158 'Tudor Cottage', in *1923 Ideal Home Exhibition Catalogue* (London, 1923), p.149; V&A Collections, Archive of Art and Design, GB73 AAD/1990/9/5.

159 Barron, *The House Desirable*, p.104.

160 John I. Williams & Sons, *In Tudor Times* (Oxted, 1923), Museum of Domestic Design and Architecture, Middlesex University Archive, BADDA 117.

161 Barron, *The House Desirable*, pp 168–80.

162 Timothy Brittain-Catlin, 'Picturesque, Modern, Tudor-Style: Edgar Ranger in Thanet', in *Houses: Regional Practice and Local Character* (London, 2015), p.38.

163 Randal Phillips, *Small Family Houses* (London, 1924), p.9.

164 Hunt, *Half a Dozen Hints*, pp 27 and 68–9.

165 Peter Mandler, *The Fall and Rise of the Stately Home* (London, 1997), pp 28–9.

166 Jonathan Woodham, 'Twentieth-Century Tudor Design in Britain: An Ideological Battleground', in Tatiana C. String and Marcus Bull, eds, *Tudorism: Historical Imagination and the Appropriation of the Sixteenth Century* (Oxford, 2011), p.132.

167 Peter Mandler, 'Revisiting the Olden Time: Popular Tudorism in the Time of Victoria', in Tatiana C. String and Marcus Bull, eds, *Tudorism: Historical Imagination and the Appropriation of the Sixteenth Century* (Oxford, 2011), pp 14–35. Andrew Sanders, *In The Olden Time: Victorians and the British Past* (London, 2013), pp 62–3. Paul Readman, *Storied Ground: Landscape and the Shaping of English National Identity* (Cambridge, 2018), p.237.

168 Tom Brigden, *The Protected Vista: An Intellectual and Cultural History* (London, 2019), p.203.

169 Edward Mirzoeff, *Metro-land with John Betjeman* (BBC, 1973), Film, at 1min 22secs.

170 Mark Swenarton and Sandra Taylor, 'The Scale and Nature of the Growth in Owner Occupation in Britain between the Wars', *The Economic History Review*, vol.38, no.3, 1985, p.391.

171 Annette O'Carroll, 'Tenements to Bungalows: Class and the Growth of Home Ownership before World War II', *Urban History*, vol.24, no.2, 1997, pp 221–41. David Byrne, 'Working Class Owner Occupation and Social Differentiation on Interwar Tyneside', in William Lancaster, ed., *Working Class Housing on Tyneside 1850–1939* (Newcastle-upon-Tyne, 1994).

172 Speight, 'Who Bought the Inter-War Semi?', pp 30 and 7–9.

173 Stanley C. Ramsey, 'The Ready Built House', in Patrick Abercrombie, ed., *The Book of the Modern House: A Panoramic Survey of Contemporary Domestic Design* (London, 1939), p.131.

174 Speight, 'Who Bought the Inter-War Semi?', p.2.

175 RIBA, 'The Architect and Housing', p.651.

176 'Parliamentary and Political Notes', *The National Builder*, vol.13, no.6, January 1934, p.182.

177 Antoninus Samy, *The Building Society Promise* (Oxford, 2016), pp 103–6.

178 R. Graves and A. Hodge, *The Long Weekend: A Social History of Great Britain, 1918–39* (London, 1991 [1940]), pp 64–6.

179 Horsey, 'London Speculative Housing of the 1930s', p.149.

180 Simon Parker, Emma Uprichard and Roger Burrows, 'Class Places and Place Classes: Geodemographics and the Spatialization of Class', *Information, Communication and Society*, vol.10, no.6, 2007, pp 904–5.

181 Mike Savage et al., in Parker, Uprichard and Burrow, 'Class Places and Place Classes', p.904.

182 Deborah Sugg Ryan, 'Living in a "Half-Baked Pageant": The Tudorbethan Semi and Suburban Modernity', *Home Cultures*, vol.8, no.3, 2011, p.220.

183 Scott, *The Making of the Modern British Home*, p.16.

184 Scott, *The Making of the Modern British Home*, p.5.

185 Michael Young and Peter Wilmott, *Family and Kinship in East London* (Harmondsworth, 1965 [1957]), pp 132–3.

186 Scott, *The Making of the Modern British Home*, p.5.

187 James S. Duncan, 'Landscape and the Communication of Social Identity', in Amos Rapoport, ed., *The Mutual Interaction of People and Their Built Environment* (The Hague, 1976), p.399.

188 Lynsey Hanley, *Estates: An Intimate History* (London, 2012), p.19.

189 Harold Bellman, in 'Vote of Thanks and Discussion', *Journal of the Royal Institute of British Architects*, vol.45, no.11, 11 April 1938, p.536.

190 Barron, *The House Desirable*, p.2.

191 Sitwell, *British Architects and Craftsmen*, p.1.

CONCLUSION

1 Samuel Rogers, *The Pleasures of Memory* (London, 1806 [1796]), p.21.

2 Beresford Pite, 'Architects and the Architecture of Cottages', *The Architects' Journal*, vol.49, no.1262, 12 March 1919, p.150.

3 Charles Ruthen, 'The Architect and the State', *Journal of the Society of Architects*, vol.15, no.4, February 1922, p.88.

4 Evelyn Waugh, *Labels* (London 1985 [1930]), p.46.

5 Frederick Gibberd, 'The Architecture of New Towns', *Journal of the Royal Society of Arts*, vol.106, no.5021, April 1958, p.343.

6 Guy Ortolano, *Thatcher's Progress: From Social Democracy to Market Liberalism through an English Town* (Cambridge, 2019), pp 138–40.

7 'Small Houses and Architects: 1', *The Architects' Journal*, vol.93, no.2412, 17 April 1941, p.253.

8 Ruthen, 'The Architect and the State', p.86.

9 'Court Circular', *The Times*, 18 May 1920, p.17. Our Correspondent, 'New Council House at Nottingham', *The Times*, 21 May 1929, p.11.

10 'The Housing Bonds Scheme', *The Times*, 7 April 1920, p.11.

11 The British Newspaper Archive.

12 F.R.S. Yorke and Frederick Gibberd, 'Introduction', in *The Modern Flat* (London, 1937), p.16.

13 John Macarthur, *The Picturesque: Architecture, Disgust and Other Irregularities* (Abingdon, 2007), p.198.

14 Mathew Aitchison and John Macarthur, 'Pevsner's Townscape', in Nikolaus Pevsner, *Visual Planning and the Picturesque*, ed. Mathew Aitchison (Los Angeles, 2010), p.10.

15 Macarthur, *The Picturesque*, p.201.

16 Pevsner, *Visual Planning*, p.145.

17 William Whyte, 'The Englishness of English Architecture: Modernism and the Making of a National International Style, 1927–1957', *The Journal of British Studies*, vol.48, no.2, April 2009, p.452.

18 John Rex and Robert Moore, *Race, Community and Conflict* (London, 1967), pp 273–6.

19 Mark Pinney, *Little Palaces: House and Home in the Inter-War Suburbs* (London, 2003), pp 26–7. Miles Horsey, 'London Speculative Housing of the 1930s', *The London Journal*, vol.11, no.2, 1985, p.158.

20 Stuart Chapin, for Mass Observation, *An Enquiry into People's Homes* (London, 1943), p.192.

21 Mark Clapson, *Working-Class Suburb* (Manchester, 2012), pp 2–5.

22 Darrin Bayliss, 'Council Cottages and Community in Inter-War Britain', unpublished doctoral thesis, Queen Mary and Westfield College (London, 1998), pp 146–7. Andrzej Olechnowicz, *Working-Class Housing in England between the Wars* (Oxford, 1997), pp 123–4.

23 Raymond Unwin, 'Town Planning Institute', *The Builder*, vol.114, no.3922, 5 April 1918, p.209.

24 A.W. Hurst (HM Treasury), Memorandum to R.S. Meiklejohn (Deputy Controller, Supply, HM Treasury), cc. Sir Warren Fisher (Permanent Secretary, HM Treasury), 8 July 1921; The National Archives, T161/132.

25 Margaret Forster, *My Life in Houses* (London, 2014), p.22.

26 Forster, *My Life in Houses*, p.33.

27 Dame Henrietta Barnett, *Matters that Matter* (London, 1930), p.95.

28 Simon Pepper, 'John Laing's Sunnyfields Estate', in Boris Ford, ed., *Early 20th Century Britain*, The Cambridge Cultural History, Vol. 8 (Cambridge, 1992), p.295.

RECOMMENDED READING

PRE-1950

Adams, Maurice, *Modern Cottage Architecture*, B.T. Batsford, London, 1912

Addy, Sidney Oldall, *The Evolution of the English House*, ed. John Summerson, 4th impression, George Allen & Unwin, London, 1933 [1898]

Allingham, Helen, and Stewart Dick, *The Cottage Homes of England*, Edward Arnold, London, 1909

Ashbee, C.R., *A Book of Cottages and Little Houses*, Essex House Press and B.T. Batsford, London, 1906

Ashbee, C.R., *Where the Great City Stands*, Essex House Press, London, 1917

Barnett, Dame Henrietta, *Matters that Matter*, John Murray, London, 1930

Barron, P.A., *The House Desirable*, Methuen & Co., London, 1929

Batsford, Harry, and Charles Fry, *The English Cottage*, B.T. Batsford, London, 1938

Bertram, Anthony, *The House: A Machine for Living In*, A. & C. Black Ltd, London, 1935

Bertram, Anthony, *Design*, Penguin, Harmondsworth, 1938

Blomfield, Reginald, *The Mistress Art*, Edward Arnold, London, 1908

Blomfield, Reginald, *The Touchstone of Architecture*, Clarendon Press, Oxford, 1925

Blomfield, Reginald, *Modernismus*, Macmillan and Co. Ltd, London, 1934

Boumphrey, Geoffrey, *Your House and Mine*, George Allen & Unwin, London, 1938

Bourne, George, *Change in the Village*, Gerald Duckworth & Co., London, 1955 [1912]

Bowen, Elizabeth, 'Attractive Modern Homes', in *Collected Stories*, Everyman, London, 2019 [1923–1939]

Clarke, Kenneth, *The Gothic Revival*, Penguin, Harmondsworth, 1964 [1928]

Cobbett, William, *Cottage Economy*, C. Clement, London, 1822

Cohen-Portheim, Paul, *The Spirit of London*, B.T. Batsford, London, 1935

Conway of Allington, Lord, *Episodes in a Varied Life*, Country Life, London, 1932

Cran, Marion, *The Story of My Ruin*, Herbert Jenkins, London, 1924

Curtis Green, William, *Old Cottages & Farm-Houses in Surrey*, B.T. Batsford, London, 1908

Davison, T. Raffles, and William Axon, *Rambling Sketches*, British Architect, London, 1883

Dawber, E. Guy, *Old Cottages and Farmhouses in Kent and Sussex*, B.T. Batsford, London, 1900

Deeping, Warwick, *Sorrell and Son*, Cassell, London, 1964 [1925]

Ditchfield, Peter Hampson, *Picturesque English Cottages and their Doorway Gardens*, John C. Winston, Philadelphia, 1905

Ditchfield, Peter Hampson, *The Charm of the English Village*, B.T. Batsford, London, 1908

Ditchfield, Peter Hampson, *Vanishing England*, Methuen & Co., London, 1910

Durant, Ruth, *Watling: A Survey of Social Life on a New Housing Estate*, P.S. King, London, 1939

Edwards, A. Trystan, *The Things Which are Seen: A Revaluation of the Visual Arts*, Philip Allan & Co., London, 1921

Edwards, A. Trystan, *Good and Bad Manners in Architecture: An Essay on the Social Aspects of Civic Design*, Philip Allan & Co., London, 1924

Forster, E.M., *A Room with a View*, Penguin, Harmondsworth, 1983 [1908]

Forster, E.M., *Howards End*, Penguin, Harmondsworth, 1961 [1910]

Foster, Birket, *Birket Foster's Pictures of English Landscape*, with verses by Tom Taylor and Laura Taylor, Routledge, Warne and Routledge, London, 1863

Fry, Roger, 'A Possible Domestic Architecture', in *Vision & Design*, Penguin, Harmondsworth, 1937

Gilpin, William, *Observations relative chiefly to Picturesque Beauty . . .*, R. Blamire, London, 1786

Gilpin, William, *Remarks on Forest Scenery*, Vol. I, R. Blamire, London, 1791

Gilpin, William, *Remarks on Forest Scenery*, Vol. II, R. Blamire, London, 1791

Gilpin, William, *Three Essays: On Picturesque Beauty; On Picturesque Travel; and On Sketching Landscape*, R. Blamire, London, 1792

Gilpin, William, *Observations on the River Wye,* 3rd edition, R. Blamire, London, 1792

Ginsberg, Morris, *Sociology*, Thornton Butterworth, London, 1934

Gissing, George, *The Private Papers of Henry Ryecroft*, Archibald Constable & Co., London, 1903

Gloag, John, *Design in Modern Life,* George Allen & Unwin, London, 1946 [1934]

Gloag, John, *The Englishman's Castle*, Eyre & Spottiswoode, London, 1944

Graves, Robert, and Alan Hodge, *The Long Weekend: A Social History of Great Britain, 1918–39*, Cardinal, London, 1991 [1940]

Harvey, W. Alexander, *The Model Village and Its Cottages: Bournville*, B.T. Batsford, London, 1906

Hill, Octavia, 'Letter, 1879', 'Letter, 1886', and 'Letter, 1905', in Robert Whelan and Anne Hoole Anderson, eds, *Octavia Hill's Letters to Fellow Workers, 1872–1911*, Kyrle, London, 2005

Hitchcock, Henry-Russell, and Catherine Bauer, *Modern Architecture in England*, The Museum of Modern Art, New York, 1937

Hobhouse, L.T., *The Elements of Social Justice*, George Allen & Unwin, London, 1922

Hobhouse, L.T., *Social Development: Its Nature and Conditions*, Routledge, Oxford, 2010 [1924]

Holdenby, Christopher, *Folk of the Furrow*, Smith, Elder & Co., London, 1913

Holtby, Winifred, *South Riding*, Collins, London, 1936

Howitt, T. Cecil, *Nottingham Housing Schemes 1919–1928*, Nottingham, 1929

Hughes, Harold, and Herbert L. North, *The Old Cottages of Snowdonia*, Jarvis & Foster, Bangor, 1908

Hunt, T.F., *Half a Dozen Hints on Picturesque Domestic Architecture*, Henry G. Bohn, London, 1841 [1825]

Hunt, T.F., *Exemplars of Tudor Architecture Adapted to Modern Habitations*, Longman, Rees, Orme, Brown, and Green, London, 1830

Hussey, Christopher, *The Picturesque: Studies in a Point of View*, G.P. Putnam's Sons, London, 1927

Hussey, Christopher, *The Life of Sir Edwin Lutyens*, Country Life, London, 1950

Innocent, C.F., *The Development of English Building Construction*, Donhead Publishing, Donhead St Mary, 1999 [1916]

Jevons, Rosamond, and John Madge, *Housing Estates: A Study of Bristol Corporation Policy and Practice between the Wars*, J.W. Arrowsmith, Bristol, 1946

Jones, Sydney R., *The Village Homes of England*, The Studio, London, 1912

Jones, Sydney R., *English Village Homes*, B.T. Batsford, London, 1936

Kent, Nathaniel, *Hints to Gentlemen of Landed Property*, 1st edition, J. Dodsley, London, 1775

Kent, Nathaniel, *Hints to Gentlemen of Landed Property, to which are added Supplementary Hints*, 3rd edition, G. Nicol, J. Walker, London, 1799

Kerr, Robert, *The Gentleman's House, or How to Plan English Residences from the Parsonage to the Palace . . .* , Cambridge University Press, 2012 [1864]

Knight, Richard Payne, *The Landscape: A Didactic Poem*, W. Bulmer and Co., London, 1794

Knight, Richard Payne, *An Analytical Inquiry into the Principles of Taste*, 1st and 2nd editions, T. Payne and J. White, London, 1805

Lancaster, Osbert, *Progress at Pelvis Bay*, John Murray, London, 1936

Lancaster, Osbert, *Pillar to Post*, John Murray, London, 1938

Lancaster, Osbert, *Homes Sweet Homes*, John Murray, London, 1939

Lethaby, W.R., *Architecture: An Introduction to the History and Theory of the Art of Building*, Williams & Norgate, London, 1911

Lethaby, W.R., *Form in Civilisation: Collected Papers on Art & Labour*, Oxford University Press, London, 1922

Loudon, J.C., *An Encyclopaedia of Cottage, Farm and Villa Architecture*, Longman, Rees, Orme, Brown, Green & Longman, London, 1834

Malton, James, *An Essay on British Cottage Architecture*, Hookham and Carpenter, London, 1798

Massingham, H.J., *Country*, Cobden-Sanderson, London, 1934

Massingham, H.J., *English Downland*, B.T. Batsford, London, 1936

Massingham, H.J., 'Our Inheritance from the Past', in Clough Williams-Ellis, ed., *Britain and the Beast*, J.M. Dent and Sons, London, 1937

Masterman, C.F.G., *The Condition of England*, Methuen & Co. Ltd, London, 1960 [1909]

Masterman, C.F.G., *England after War*, Hodder & Stoughton, London, 1922

McGrath, Raymond, *Twentieth Century Houses*, Faber and Faber, London, 1934

Meason, Gilbert Laing, *On the Landscape Architecture of the Great Painters of Italy*, D. Jaques, London, 1828

Morton, H.V., *In Search of England*, Methuen, London, 1935

Muthesius, Hermann, *The English House*, Rizzoli/Wiley Blackwell, New York, 1987 [1904]

Nevill, Ralph, *Old Cottage and Domestic Architecture in South-West Surrey and Notes on the Early History of the Division*, Billing & Sons, Guildford, 1889

Nichols, Beverley, *Down the Garden Path*, Timber Press, Portland, 2005 [1932]

Nichols, Beverley, *A Thatched Roof,* Jonathan Cape, London, 1933

Oliver, Basil, *Old Houses and Village Buildings in East Anglia, Norfolk, Suffolk and Essex*, B.T. Batsford, London, 1912

Oliver, Basil, *The Cottages of England*, B.T. Batsford, London, 1929

Orwell, George, *Coming Up for Air,* Penguin, Harmondsworth, 1975 [1939]

Orwell, George, *The Lion and the Unicorn*, Penguin, Harmondsworth, 1982 [1941]

Parkinson, James, with E.A. Ould, *Old Cottages, Farmhouses and Other Half-Timbered Buildings in Shropshire, Herefordshire, and Cheshire*, B.T. Batsford, London, 1904

Percy, W.S., *Strolling Through Cottage England*, Collins, London, 1936

Pevsner, Nikolaus, *Pioneers of Modern Design: From William Morris to Walter Gropius*, Palazzo Editions, Bath, 2011 [1936]

Pevsner, Nikolaus, *Visual Planning and the Picturesque*, ed. Mathew Aitchison, Getty Research Institute, Los Angeles, 2010 [1940s–1950s]

Phillips, Randal, *Small Family Houses*, Country Life, London, 1924

Phillips, Randal, *The Modern English House*, Country Life, London, 1927

Phillips, Randal, *The £1000 House*, Country Life, London, 1928

Phillips, Randal, *Houses for Moderate Means*, Country Life, London, 1936

Pocock, W.F., *Architectural Designs for Rustic Cottages,* J. Taylor, London, 1807

Powys, A.R., *Repair of Ancient Buildings*, J.M. Dent & Sons, London, 1929

Price, Uvedale, *An Essay on the Picturesque*, J. Robson, London, 1796

Price, Uvedale, *A Letter to H. Repton, Esq. on the Application of the Practice as Well as the Principles of Landscape-Painting to Landscape-Gardening,* J. Robson, London, 1798

Pugin, Augustus Welby Northmore, *The True Principles of Pointed or Christian Architecture*, John Weale, London, 1841

Ramsey, Stanley C., 'The Ready Built House', in Patrick Abercrombie, ed., *The Book of the Modern House: A Panoramic Survey of Contemporary Domestic Design*, Hodder & Stoughton, London, 1939

Rasmussen, Steen Eiler, *London: The Unique City*, Jonathan Cape, London, 1937 [1934]

Reilly, Charles H., *Representative British Architects of the Present Day*, B.T. Batsford, London, 1931

Reilly, Charles H., *Scaffolding in the Sky: A Semi-Architectural Autobiography*, George Routledge & Sons, London, 1938

Reynolds, Joshua, 'Discourse Thirteen', in *Discourses on Art*, Collier-Macmillan, London, 1969 [1797]

Richards, J.M., *A Miniature History of the English House*, Architectural Press, London, 1960 [1938]

Richards, J.M., *The Castles on the Ground*, London, Architectural Press, 1946

Roberts, Cecil, *Pilgrim Cottage*, D. Appleton – Century Company Publishers, New York, 1933

Roberts, Henry, *The Dwellings of the Labouring Classes, Their Arrangement and Construction,* The Society for Improving the Condition of the Labouring Classes, London, 1850

Robinson, P.F., *Rural Architecture, or A Series of Designs for Ornamental Cottages*, Rodwell and Martin, London, 1823

Rogers, Samuel, *The Pleasures of Memory*, Cadell jun. and Davies, London, 1796

Ruskin, John, *The Works of John Ruskin*, Library Edition, 39 vols, ed. E.T. Cook and A. Wedderburn, George Allen, London, 1903–9

Ruskin, John, *Poetry of Architecture*, Vol. I

Ruskin, John, *The Seven Lamps of Architecture*, Vol. VIII

Ruskin, John, *The Stones of Venice*, Vol. XI

Ruskin, John, *Lectures on Architecture and Painting*, Vol. XII

Ruskin, John, 'The Eagle's Nest', in *Ten Lectures on the Relation of Natural Science to Art,* Vol. XXII

Ruskin, John, 'Lecture IV – Fairy Land: Mrs Allingham and Kate Greenaway', in *The Art of England*, Vol. XXXIII

Santayana, George, *Soliloquies in England*, C. Scribner's Sons, New York, 1923

Sayle, A., *The Houses of the Workers*, T. Fisher Unwin, London, 1924

Scott, Geoffrey, *The National Character of English Architecture*, B.H. Blackwell, Oxford, 1908

Scott, Geoffrey, *The Architecture of Humanism: A Study in the History of Taste*, Methuen, London, 1961 [1914]

Scott, George Gilbert, *Remarks on Secular & Domestic Architecture, Present & Future*, John Murray, London, 1857

Sharp, Thomas, *Town and Countryside*, Oxford University Press, London, 1932

Shaw, Richard Norman, *Architectural Sketches from the Continent*, Day & Son, London, 1858

Sherriff, R.C., *Greengates*, Persephone Books, London, 2015 [1936]

Silex, Karl, *John Bull at Home, [John Bull Zu Hause]*, trans., Huntley Paterson, George G. Harrap & Co., London, 1931

Smith, John T., *Remarks on Rural Scenery*, Nathaniel Smith, London, 1797

Spielmann, M.H., and G.S. Layard, *Kate Greenaway*, A. & C. Black Ltd, London, 1905

Stephen, Sir Leslie, *Hours in a Library, Vol. III*, Folio, London, 1991 [1892]

Stevens, Francis, *Views of Cottages and Farm-Houses in England and Wales*, R. Ackermann, London, 1815

Street, A.G., *Strawberry Roan*, Faber & Faber, London, 1932

Summerson, John, 'The Mischievous Analogy', in *Heavenly Mansions and Other Essays on Architecture*, The Cresset Press, London, 1949

Tawney, R.H., *The Acquisitive Society*, G. Bell & Sons Ltd, London, 1923

Tawney, R.H., 'Foreword', in Max Weber, *The Protestant Ethic and the Spirit of Capitalism*, George Allen & Unwin, London, 1930

Tawney, R.H., *Equality*, George Allen & Unwin, London, 1983 [1931]

Taylor, Tom, *Birket Foster's Pictures of English Landscape*, Routledge, Warne, and Routledge, London, 1863

Thompson, Flora, *Lark Rise to Candleford*, Penguin, Harmondsworth, 1982 [1939]

Thomson, James, *The Seasons*, London, 1730

Travers, Wilfrid, *Architectural Education*, Harrison, Jehring & Co., London, 1908

Unwin, Raymond, 'Cottage Plans and Common Sense', Tract No. 109, The Fabian Society, London, 1902

Unwin, Raymond, *Town Planning in Practice: An Introduction to the Art of Designing Cities and Suburbs*, T. Fisher Unwin, London, 1909

Unwin, Raymond, *Nothing Gained by Overcrowding*, London, 1918

Unwin, Raymond, ed., *The Nation's New Houses: Pictures and Plans*, The Daily News, London, 1919

Unwin, Raymond, and Barry Parker, *The Art of Building a Home,* Longmans, Green & Co., London, 1901

Unwin, Raymond, and M.H. Baillie Scott, *Town Planning and Modern Architecture at Hampstead Garden Suburb*, T. Fisher Unwin, London, 1909

Voysey, C.F.A., *Individuality*, Chapman and Hall, London, 1915

Waugh, Evelyn, *Decline and Fall*, Penguin, London, 2001 [1928]

Waugh, Evelyn, *Labels*, Penguin, London, 1985 [1930]

Waugh, Evelyn, *The Diaries of Evelyn Waugh*, Penguin, Harmondsworth, 1984

Weaver, Lawrence, 'Preface', in *The 'Country Life' Book of Cottages*, London, 1913

Webb, Mary, *The Golden Arrow*, Constable & Co., London, 1916

Webb, Mary, *Precious Bane*, Duckworth, London, 1978 [1924]

Webb, Maurice, and Herbert Wigglesworth, eds, *Raffles Davison: A Record of His Life and Work from 1870 to 1926*, B.T. Batsford, London, 1927

Wells, H.G., *Mr Britling Sees It Through*, Cassell and Co. Ltd, London, 1916

Williams-Ellis, Clough, *England and the Octopus*, Geoffrey Bles, London, 1996 [1928]

Williams-Ellis, Clough, ed., *Britain and the Beast*, J.M. Dent and Sons, London, 1937

Williams-Ellis, Clough, *Portmeirion: The Place and its Meaning*, Portmeirion, 2014 [1963]

Williams-Ellis, Clough, *Architect Errant*, Portmeirion Shops Ltd, Portmeirion, 1991

Wood, J., *A Series of Plans for Cottages or Habitations of the Labourer*, J. Taylor, London, 1806 [1781]

Yorke, F.R.S., and Frederick Gibberd, *The Modern Flat*, Architectural Press, London, 1937

SECONDARY

Aitchison, Mathew, and John Macarthur, 'Pevsner's Townscape', in Mathew Aitchison, ed., *Visual Planning and the Picturesque*, Getty Research Institute, Los Angeles, 2010

Allibone, Jill, *George Devey Architect, 1820–1886*, The Lutterworth Press, Cambridge, 1991

Angle, Helen, and Dr Sally Malam, *Kerb Appeal: The External Appearance and Site Layout of New Houses*, The Popular Housing Forum, London, 1998

Bainbridge, Simon, *British Poetry and the Revolutionary and Napoleonic Wars: Visions of Conflict*, Oxford University Press, Oxford, 2003

Ballantyne, Andrew, *Architecture, Landscape and Liberty: Richard Payne Knight and the Picturesque*, Cambridge University Press, Cambridge 1997

Ballantyne, Andrew, and Andrew Law, *Tudoresque*, Reaktion, London, 2011

Banham, Reyner, *Theory and Design in the First Machine Age*, Butterworth & Co., London, 1988 [1960]

Barrell, John, *The Spirit of Despotism: Invasions of Privacy in the 1790s*, Oxford University Press, Oxford, 2006

Barrett, Helena, and John Phillips, *Suburban Style*, Macdonald, London, 1988

Bennett, Tony, Lawrence Grossberg, and Meaghan Morris, eds *New Keywords: A Revised Vocabulary of Culture and Society*, Blackwell Publishing, Oxford, 2005

Bermingham, Ann, *Landscape and Ideology*, University of California Press, Berkeley, 1986

Bermingham, Ann, *Sensation and Sensibility*, Yale University Press, New Haven and London, 2005

Blakesley, Rosalind, *The Arts and Crafts Movement*, Phaidon, London, 2009

Boughton, John, *Municipal Dreams*, Verso, London, 2018

Boughton John, *A History of Council Housing in 100 Estates*, RIBA Publishing, London, 2022

Bourdieu, Pierre, *Distinction*, Routledge Classics, Abingdon, 2010 [1984]

Brigden, Tom, *The Protected Vista: An Intellectual and Cultural History*, Routledge, Abingdon, 2019

Brittain-Catlin, Timothy, *The Edwardians and their Houses*, Lund Humphries, London, 2020

Brodie, Allan, Jane Croom, and James O. Davies, *English Prisons: An Architectural History*, English Heritage, Swindon, 2002

Broom, John, *A History of Cigarette and Trade Cards*, Pen & Sword, Barnsley, 2018

Burnett, John, *A Social History of Housing 1815–1985*, Methuen, London, 1986

Campbell, Louise, *Studio Lives*, Lund Humphries, London, 2019

Cannadine, David, *The Rise and Fall of Class in Britain*, Columbia University Press, New York, 1999

Carey, John, *The Intellectuals and the Masses: Pride and Prejudice among the Literary Intelligentsia, 1880–1939*, Faber & Faber, London, 1992

Clapson, Mark, *Working-Class Suburb*, Manchester University Press, Manchester, 2012

Cockburn, Claud, *Bestseller*, Penguin, Harmondsworth, 1975

Conran, Terence, ed., *The House Book*, Mitchell Beazley, London, 1982 [1974]

Cook, Olive, *The English House through Seven Centuries*, Penguin, Harmondsworth, 1984

Copley, Stephen, and Peter Garside, eds, *The Politics of the Picturesque*, Cambridge University Press, Cambridge, 1994

Crawford, Alan, 'Englishness in Arts and Crafts Architecture', in *Architecture and Englishness 1880–1914*, Society of Architectural Historians of Great Britain, London, 2006

Creese, Walter, ed., *The Legacy of Raymond Unwin: A Human Pattern for Planning*, MIT Press, Cambridge, MA, 1967

Crouch, Christopher, *Design Culture in Liverpool, 1880–1914*, Liverpool University Press, Liverpool, 2002

Curl, James Stevens, *Victorian Architecture*, David & Charles, Newton Abbott, 1990

Darley, Gillian, *Villages of Vision*, Paladin Books, London, 1978

Darley, Gillian, *Octavia Hill: A Life*, Constable and Co. Ltd, London, 1990

Darley, Gillian, 'Octavia Hill: Lessons in Campaigning', in Elizabeth Baigent and Ben Cowell, eds, *Octavia Hill: Social Activism and the Remaking of British Society*, Institute of Historical Research, London, 2016

Darling, Elizabeth, *Re-forming Britain: Narratives of Modernity before Reconstruction*, Routledge, London, 2007

de Jong, Sigrid, *Rediscovering Architecture: Paestum in Eighteenth-Century Architectural Experience and Theory*, Yale University Press, New Haven and London, 2014

Dixon Hunt, John, 'The Cult of the Cottage', in *The Lake District: A Sort of National Property*, Victoria and Albert Museum, London, 1986

Durant, Stuart, *C.F.A. Voysey*, Academy Editions, London, 1992

Dyos, H.J., *Victorian Suburb: A Study of the Growth of Camberwell*, Leicester University Press, Leicester, 1961

Edwards, Arthur, *The Design of Suburbia: A Critical Study in Environmental History*, Pembridge Press, London, 1981

Evans, George Ewart, *Ask the Fellows Who Cut the Hay*, Faber & Faber, London, 2018 [1956]

Everett, Nigel, *The Tory View of Landscape*, Yale University Press, New Haven and London, 1994

Feiling, Keith, *The Life of Neville Chamberlain*, Macmillan, London, 1946

Forster, Margaret, *My Life in Houses*, Chatto & Windus, London, 2014

Forty, Adrian, *Words and Buildings*, Thames & Hudson, London, 2019

Fry, Roger, *Letters of Roger Fry*, ed. Denys Sutton, Chatto & Windus, London, 1972

Gaskell, S. Martin, *Model Housing: From the Great Exhibition to the Festival of Britain*, Mansell, London, 1986

Giddens, Anthony, *New Rules of Sociological Method: A Positive Critique of Interpretative Sociologies*, Hutchinson, London, 1976

Girouard, Mark, *Sweetness and Light: The Queen Anne Movement, 1860–1900*, Clarendon Press, Oxford, 1977

Girouard, Mark, *The Victorian Country House*, Yale University Press, New Haven and London, 1990

Girouard, Mark, *Town and Country*, Yale University Press, New Haven and London, 1992

Glendinning, Miles, *Mass Housing: Modern Architecture and State Power*, Bloomsbury, London, 2021

Goodhart-Rendel, H.S., *English Architecture Since the Regency: An Interpretation*, Constable, London, 1953

Gowrley, Freya, *Domestic Space in Britain, 1750–1840: Materiality, Sociability and Emotion*, Bloomsbury Publishing, London, 2022

Green, E.H.H., *Ideologies of Conservatism*, Oxford University Press, Oxford, 2008

Griffiths, Richard, *Fellow Travellers of the Right: British Enthusiasts for Nazi Germany, 1933–39*, Constable, London, 1980

Hall, Edith, and Henry Stead, *A People's History of Classics: Class and Greco-Roman Antiquity in Britain and Ireland 1689–1939*, Routledge, Abingdon, 2020

Hall, Melanie, 'Affirming Community Life: Preservation, National Identity and the State, 1900', in Chris Miele, ed., *From William Morris: Building Conservation and the Arts and Crafts Cult of Authenticity 1877–1939*, Yale University Press, New Haven and London, 2005

Hamilton, Alec, *Arts & Crafts Churches*, Lund Humphries, London, 2021

Hammond, J.L., and Barbara Hammond, *The Village Labourer*, Longman, London, 1978 [1911]

Hanley, Lynsey, *Estates: An Intimate History*, Granta, London, 2012

Hanley, Lynsey, *Respectable*, Allen Lane, London, 2016

Hanson, Brian, *Architects and the 'Building World' from Chambers to Ruskin: Constructing Authority*, Cambridge University Press, Cambridge, 2003

Hanson, Julienne, *Decoding Homes and Houses*, Cambridge University Press, Cambridge, 1998

Hardy, Dennis, and Colin Ward, *Arcadia for All: The Legacy of a Makeshift Landscape*, Five Leaves Publications, Nottingham, 2004

Helsinger, Elizabeth K., *Rural Scenes and National Representation: Britain, 1815–1850*, Princeton University Press, Princeton, NJ, 1996

Helsinger, Elizabeth K., *Ruskin and the Art of the Beholder*, Harvard University Press, Cambridge, MA, 1982

Hill, Rosemary, *God's Architect: Pugin and the Building of Romantic Britain*, Allen Lane, London, 2007

Hindle, Steve, *On the Parish? The Micro-Politics of Poor Relief in Rural England, c.1550–1750*, Oxford Studies in Social History, Clarendon Press, Oxford, 2004

Hitchcock, Henry-Russell, *Early Victorian Architecture in Britain*, The Architectural Press, London, 1954

Hitchcock, Henry-Russell, *Architecture: Nineteenth and Twentieth Centuries*, Yale University Press, New Haven, 1987 [1958]

Holder, Julian, *Arts and Crafts Architecture: 'Beauty's Awakening'*, The Crowood Press, Ramsbury, 2021

Holder, Julian, and Elizabeth McKellar, eds, *Neo-Georgian Architecture 1880–1970: A Reappraisal*, Historic England, Swindon, 2016

Horsey, Miles, 'London Speculative Housing of the 1930s: Official Control and Popular Taste', *The London Journal*, vol.11, no.2, 1985

Hoskins, W.G., *The Making of the English Landscape*, Penguin, Harmondsworth, 1985 [1955]

Hubbard, Edward, and Michael Shippobottom, *A Guide to Port Sunlight Village*, Liverpool University Press, Liverpool, 2009

Hynes, Samuel, *A War Imagined: The First World War and English Culture*, Pimlico, London, 1990

Jackson, Frank, *Raymond Unwin: Architect, Planner and Visionary*, A. Zwemmer Ltd, London, 1985

Jencks, Charles, *The Language of Post-Modern Architecture*, Rizzoli, New York, 1984

Johnson, Matthew, *English Houses 1300–1800*, Routledge, London, 2018

Jones, Ben, *The Working Class in Mid-Twentieth-Century England: Community, Identity and Social Memory*, Manchester University Press, Manchester, 2012

Joyce, Patrick, *Visions of the People: Industrial England and the Question of Class, 1848–1914*, Cambridge University Press, Cambridge, 1991

Kemeny, Jim, *The Myth of Home Ownership: Private versus Public Choices in Housing Tenure*, Routledge & Kegan Paul, London, 1981

King, Anthony, *The Bungalow: The Production of a Global Culture*, Routledge & Kegan Paul, London, 1984

Kumar, Krishan, *The Idea of Englishness: English Culture, National Identity and Social Thought*, Ashgate, Farnham, 2015

Lefebvre, Henri, *The Production of Space*, Blackwell, Oxford, 1991

Light, Alison, *Forever England: Femininity, Literature and Conservatism between the Wars*, Routledge, London, 1991

Lyall, Sutherland, *Dream Cottages: From Cottage Ornée to Stockbroker Tudor – 200 Years of the Cult of the Vernacular*, Robert Hale Ltd, London, 1988

Macarthur, John, *The Picturesque: Architecture, Disgust and Other Irregularities*, Routledge, London, 2007

MacCarthy, Fiona, *William Morris: A Life for Our Time*, Faber & Faber, London, 1994

Macleod, Robert, *Style and Society: Architectural Ideology in Britain 1835–1914*, RIBA, London, 1971

Mandler, Peter, *The Fall and Rise of the Stately Home*, Yale University Press, New Haven and London, 1997

Mandler, Peter, *The English National Character: The History of an Idea from Edmund Burke to Tony Blair*, Yale University Press, New Haven and London, 2006

Mandler, Peter, 'Revisiting the Olden Time: Popular Tudorism in the Time of Victoria', in Tatiana C. String and Marcus Bull, eds, *Tudorism: Historical Imagination and the Appropriation of the Sixteenth Century*, Oxford University Press, Oxford, 2011

Marsh, Jan, *William Morris and Red House*, National Trust, London, 2005

Matless, David, *Landscape and Englishness*, Reaktion, London, 1998

Matless, David, *About England*, Reaktion, London, 2023

Maudlin, Daniel, *The Idea of the Cottage in English Architecture, 1760–1860*, Routledge, London, 2015

McKellar, Elizabeth, 'All Roof, No Wall: Peter Boston, A-Frames and the Primitive Hut in Twentieth Century British Architecture, c.1890–1970', *Architectural History*, vol.62, 2019, pp 237–69

McKibbin, Ross, *The Ideologies of Class: Social Relations in Britain 1880–1950*, Oxford University Press, Oxford, 1991

McKibbin, Ross, *Classes and Cultures: England 1918–1951*, Oxford University Press, Oxford, 2000

McKibbin, Ross, *Parties and People: England 1914–1951*, Oxford University Press, Oxford, 2010

McKibbin, Ross, 'Reviews: "The People: The Rise and Fall of the Working Class 1910–2010". By Selina Todd', *Twentieth Century British History*, vol.25, no.4, 2014, pp 651–65

Mercer, Eric, *English Vernacular Houses: A Study of Traditional Farmhouses and Cottages*, Royal Commission on Historical Monuments (England), HMSO, London, 1975

Merrett, Stephen, *State Housing in Britain*, Routledge & Kegan Paul, London, 1979

Merrett, Stephen, *Owner Occupation in Britain*, Routledge & Kegan Paul, London, 1982

Miele, Chris, ed., *From William Morris: Building Conservation and the Arts and Crafts Cult of Authenticity, 1877–1939*, Studies in British Art, Yale University Press, New Haven and London, 2005

Miele, Chris, 'English Antiquity: Historic Buildings, Culture, and National Identity in the Nineteenth Century', in David Crellin and Ian Dungavell, eds, *Architecture and Englishness 1880–1914*, London, Society of Architectural Historians of Great Britain, 2006

Miller, Mervyn, *Raymond Unwin: Garden Cities and Town Planning*, Leicester University Press, Leicester, 1992

Miller, Mervyn, *English Garden Cities*, English Heritage, Swindon, 2010

Mingay, G.E., *Parliamentary Enclosure in England: An Introduction to its Causes, Incidence and Impact, 1750–1850*, Longman, London, 1997

Mordaunt Crook, J., *The Dilemma of Style: Architectural Ideas from the Picturesque to the Post-Modern*, John Murray, London, 1987

Mordaunt Crook, J., *The Rise of the Nouveaux Riches: Style and Status in Victorian and Edwardian Architecture*, John Murray, London, 1999

Mordaunt Crook, J., *William Burges and the High Victorian Dream*, Frances Lincoln, London, 2013

Mordaunt Crook, J., 'John Nash and the Genesis of Regent's Park', in Geoffrey Tyack, ed., *John Nash: Architect of the Picturesque*, English Heritage, Swindon, 2013

Morley, Ken, and Margaret Morley, *Wingrave: A Rothschild Village in the Vale,* The Book Castle, Dunstable, 1999

Morrison, Kathryn, *The Workhouse: A Study of Poor-Law Buildings in England*, English Heritage, Swindon, 1999

Mowat, Charles Loch, *Britain between the Wars 1918–1940*, Beacon Press, Boston, 1971

Mowl, Timothy, *Stylistic Cold Wars: Betjeman versus Pevsner*, John Murray, London, 2000

Mulvagh, Jane, *Madresfield: One Family, One Thousand Years*, Black Swan, London, 2009

Murray, Martin, *The Story of Cigarette Cards*, Murray Cards, London, 1987

O'Brien, Charles, *Houses: An Architectural Guide*, Pevsner Architectural Guides, Yale University Press, New Haven and London, 2016

Olechnowicz, Andrzej, *Working-Class Housing in England between the Wars: The Becontree Estate*, Oxford University Press, Oxford, 1997

Oliver, Paul, Ian Davis, and Ian Bentley, *Dunroamin: The Suburban Semi and its Enemies*, Barrie & Jenkins, London, 1981

Ortolano, Guy, *Thatcher's Progress: From Social Democracy to Market Liberalism through an English Town*, Cambridge University Press, Cambridge, 2019

Pepper, Simon, 'John Laing's Sunnyfields Estate, Mill Hill', in Boris Ford, ed., *Early 20th Century Britain*, Cambridge University Press, 1992

Pepper, Simon, and Peter Richmond, 'Upward or Outward? Politics, Planning, and Council Flats, 1919–1939', *The Journal of Architecture*, vol.13, no.1, 2008, pp 53–90

Pevsner, Nikolaus, *Studies in Art, Architecture and Design, Volume I: From Mannerism to Romanticism*, Thames & Hudson, London, 1968

Pevsner, Nikolaus, *South and West Somerset,* The Buildings of England, Yale University Press, London and New Haven, 2003 [1958]

Pevsner, Nikolaus, *Visual Planning and the Picturesque*, ed., Mathew Aitchison, Getty Research Institute, Los Angeles, 2010

Pevsner, Nikolaus, Ian Nairn, and Bridget Cherry, *Surrey*, The Buildings of England, Yale University Press, London and New Haven, 2002 [1962]

Pinney, Mark, *Little Palaces: House and Home in the Inter-War Suburbs*, Middlesex University Press, London, 2003

Powers, Alan, 'Edwardian Architectural Education: A Study of Three Schools', *AA Files*, vol.5, 1984, pp 48–59

Powers, Alan, *Modern: The Modern Movement in Britain*, Merrell Publishers Ltd, London, 2005

Priestley, Harold, *The English Home*, Frederick Muller, London, 1971

Rapoport, Amos, *House Form and Culture*, Prentice Hall, Englewood Cliffs, NJ, 1969

Ravetz, Alison, *Council Housing and Culture: The History of a Social Experiment*, Routledge, London, 2001

Readman, Paul, *Storied Ground: Landscape and the Shaping of English National Identity*, Cambridge University Press, Cambridge, 2018

Rex, John, and Robert Moore, *Race, Community and Conflict*, Institute of Race Relations and Oxford University Press, London, 1967

Robinson, Sidney K., *Inquiry into the Picturesque*, University of Chicago Press, Chicago, IL, 1991

Rose, Jonathan, *The Intellectual Life of the British Working Classes*, Yale University Press, New Haven and London, 2002

Saint, Andrew, 'The Quality of the London Suburbs', in Julian Honer, ed., *London Suburbs*, English Heritage, London, 1999

Saint, Andrew, *Richard Norman Shaw*, Studies in British Art, Yale University Press, New Haven and London, 2010

Samy, Antoninus, *The Building Society Promise*, Oxford University Press, Oxford, 2016

Sanders, Andrew, *In The Olden Time: Victorians and the British Past*, Yale University Press, New Haven and London, 2013

Savage, Mike, 'End Class Wars', *Nature*, vol.537, 2016, pp 475–9

Savage, Mike, Fiona Devine, and Niall Cunningham, 'A New Model of Social Class? Findings from the BBC's Great British Class Survey Experiment', *Sociology*, vol.47, no.2, 2013, pp 219–50

Sayer, Andrew, *The Moral Significance of Class*, Cambridge University Press, Cambridge, 2005

Sayer, Karen, *Country Cottages: A Cultural History*, Manchester University Press, Manchester, 2000

Scott, Peter, *The Making of the Modern British Home: The Suburban Semi and Family Life between the Wars*, Oxford University Press, Oxford, 2013

Scruton, Roger, 'David Watkin and the Classical Idea', in Frank Salmon, ed., *The Persistence of the Classical: Essays on Architecture Presented to David Watkin*, Philip Wilson, London, 2008

Scruton, Roger, *The Aesthetics of Architecture*, Princeton University Press, Princeton, NJ, 2013

Self, Robert, 'Introduction: Neville Chamberlain, 1921–1927', in *The Neville Chamberlain Diary Letters, Vol. 2: The Reform Years, 1921–27*, Ashgate, Aldershot, 2000

Self, Robert, *Neville Chamberlain: A Biography*, Ashgate, Aldershot, 2006

Sennett, Richard, *Building and Dwelling: Ethics for the City*, Penguin, London, 2019

Shasore, Neal, *Designs on Democracy: Architecture and the Public in Interwar London,* Oxford University Press, Oxford, 2022

Sillars, Stuart, *Picturing England Between the Wars: Word and Image 1918–1940*, Oxford University Press, Oxford, 2021

Speight, George, 'Who Bought the Inter-War Semi? The Socio-Economic Characteristics of New-House Buyers in the 1930s', *University of Oxford Discussion Papers in Economic and Social History*, vol.38, 2000

Spuybroek, Lars, *The Sympathy of Things: Ruskin and the Ecology of Design*, Bloomsbury, London, 2016

Stamp, Gavin, *The Great Perspectivists*, RIBA Drawings Series, Trefoil Publications, London, 1982

Stamp, Gavin, *Edwin Lutyens: Country Houses*, Aurum Press, London, 2001

Stamp, Gavin, 'Neo-Tudor and Its Enemies', *Architectural History*, vol.49, 2006, pp 1–33

Stamp, Gavin, 'Move over Merrie England . . . Shakespeare and Architecture', *Apollo: The International Art Magazine*, 20 July 2016

Sugg Ryan, Deborah, *Ideal Homes: Uncovering the History and Design of the Interwar House*, Manchester University Press, Manchester, 2020

Summerson, John, 'Introduction', in H.J. Dyos, *Victorian Suburb: A Study of the Growth of Camberwell*, Leicester University Press, Leicester, 1961

Summerson, John, ed., *Concerning Architecture: Essays on Architectural Writers and Writing Presented to Nikolaus Pevsner*, Allen Lane, London, 1968

Swenarton, Mark, *Homes Fit for Heroes: The Politics and Architecture of Early State Housing in Britain*, Heinemann, London, 1981

Swenarton, Mark, *Artisans and Architects: The Ruskinian Tradition in Architectural Thought*, Macmillan, Basingstoke, 1989

Swenarton, Mark, and Simon Pepper, *Building the New Jerusalem: Architecture, Housing and Politics 1900–1930*, IHS BRE Press, Bracknell, 2008

Swenarton, Mark, and Sandra Taylor, 'The Scale and Nature of the Growth in Owner Occupation in Britain between the Wars', *The Economic History Review*, vol.38, no.3, 1985, pp 373–92

Tankard, Danae, 'The Regulation of Cottage-Building in Seventeenth-Century Sussex', *Agricultural History Review*, vol.59, no.1, 2011, pp 18–35

Temple, Nigel, *John Nash and the Village Picturesque*, Alan Sutton, Gloucester, 1979

Thenhaus, Clark, *Unresolved Legibility in Residential Types*, ARD/ORO Editions, San Francisco, CA, 2019

Thomas, Geraint, *Popular Conservatism and the Culture of National Government in Inter-War Britain*, Cambridge University Press, Cambridge, 2020

Thompson, E.P., *The Making of the English Working Class*, Penguin, Harmondsworth, 1982

Tinniswood, Adrian, *Life in the English Country Cottage*, Phoenix, London, 1997

Tinniswood, Adrian, *The Long Weekend: Life in the English Country House Between the Wars*, Vintage, London, 2018

Todd, Selina, *The People: The Rise and Fall of the Working Class, 1910–2010*, John Murray, London, 2014

Tribe, Keith, 'Intellectual History as Begriffsgeschichte', in Richard Whatmore and Brian Young, eds, *A Companion to Intellectual History*, John Wiley & Sons, Chichester, 2016

Tyack, Geoffrey, 'Ruskin and the English House', in Rebecca Daniels and Geoff Brandwood, eds, *Ruskin and Architecture*, Spire Books, Reading, 2003

Tyack, Geoffrey, 'Architecture', in Francis O'Gorman, ed., *The Cambridge Companion to John Ruskin*, Cambridge University Press, Cambridge, 2015

Tyack, Geoffrey, *The Making of Our Urban Landscape*, Oxford University Press, Oxford, 2022

Umbach, Maiken, and Bernd Hüppauf, eds, 'Introduction', in *Vernacular Modernism: Heimat, Globalization and the Built Environment*, Stanford University Press, Stanford, CA, 2005

Urry, John, and Jonas Larsen, *The Tourist Gaze 3.0*, SAGE, London, 2011

Ward, Colin, *Cotters and Squatters: Housing's Hidden History*, Five Leaves Publications, Nottingham, 2005

Ward, Jan, *Raffles and Rupert Davison: The Ideal Home*, The Bourne Society, Caterham, 2016

Watkin, David, *The English Vision: The Picturesque in Architecture, Landscape and Garden Design*, John Murray, London, 1982

Watkin, David, *Morality and Architecture Revisited,* John Murray, London, 2001 [1977]

Webber, G.C., *The Ideology of the British Right, 1918–1939*, Croom Helm, London, 1986

Wellings, Fred, *Dictionary of British Housebuilders*, Fred Wellings, Beckenham, 2006

White, Roger, *Cottages Ornés: The Charms of the Simple Life*, Yale University Press, New Haven and London, 2017

Whyte, William, 'The Englishness of English Architecture: Modernism and the Making of a National International Style, 1927–1957', *The Journal of British Studies*, vol.48, no.2, 2009, pp 441–65

Whyte, William, 'Introduction', in *The Transactions of the Royal Institute of British Architects Town Planning Conference, London, 10–15 October 1910*, Oxford University Press, Oxford, 2011

Whyte, William, '"Beauty Is for All": Art in the Life and Work of Octavia Hill' [and] '"Some Dreadful Buildings in Southwark": A Tour of Nineteenth Century Social Housing', in Elizabeth Baigent and Ben Cowell, eds, *'Nobler Imaginings and Mightier Struggles': Octavia Hill, Social Activism and the Remaking of British Society*, London, Institute of Historial Research, University of London, 2016

Williams, Raymond, *Culture and Society*, Chatto & Windus, London, 1958

Williams, Raymond, *The Country and the City,* The Hogarth Press, London, 1985 [1973]

Williams, Raymond, *Keywords: A Vocabulary of Culture and Society*, Fontana Press, London, 1988

Williamson, Philip, *Stanley Baldwin*, Cambridge University Press, Cambridge, 1999

Woodforde, John, *The Truth about Cottages*, Routledge & Kegan Paul, London, 1969

Wright, Eric Olin, *Understanding Class*, Verso, London, 2015

Wright, Laura, *Sunnyside: A Sociolinguistic History of British Place Names*, Oxford University Press, Oxford, 2020

Wright, Patrick, *On Living in an Old Country: The National Past in Contemporary Britain*, Verso, London, 1985

Wright, Patrick, *The Village That Died for England: The Strange Story of Tyneham*, Jonathan Cape, London, 1995

Wrightson, Keith, *English Society 1580–1680*, Hutchinson, London, 1988

Young, Michael, and Peter Wilmott, *Family and Kinship in East London*, Penguin, Harmondsworth, 1962 [1957]

Zamarian, Patrick, *The Architectural Association in the Postwar Years*, Lund Humphries, London, 2020

INDEX

Note: *italic* page numbers indicate figures.

ACKNOWLEDGEMENTS

My research into interwar domestic architecture began in 2013, and there are many who have shaped and directed my journey since. Principal thanks go to my patient and generous doctoral supervisor Professor William Whyte, who did his best, over six years, to turn me into a historian. Any progress I may have made is a credit to his rigour, intellectual breadth, and resilient humour.

Doctors Geoffrey Tyack and Oliver Cox read my thesis with care and enthusiasm and gave invaluable advice on improvements and next steps. Dr Claire O'Mahony, who started me on my journey with her Design Master's course in 2013, has been an unfailing counsellor ever since. Dr Neal Shasore and Professor Mark Swenarton have been peerless sources of advice and stimulating conversation for years now. And Professors Christina de Bellaigue and Selina Todd provided constructive and stimulating formal engagement as I developed my research. My deepest thanks go to all those enumerated above. Likewise, to my colleagues at the Society of Architectural Historians of Great Britain, particularly Elizabeth Darling, Elizabeth McKellar and Max Sternberg, for their encouragement in the project's later stages.

The book would not have happened at all without the support of a number of crucial funders: Mike Day and Paul Abrey at Palma Pictures; the Marc Fitch Fund; the Scouloudi Foundation and Institute of Historical Research; the Voysey Society; Wates Group Ltd; and the Society of Architectural Historians of Great Britain. Absent the generosity of people and institutions like these, it is hard to believe that there would be much left of architectural history publishing.

At Worcester College, Oxford, I am particularly indebted to Mark Bainbridge, Renée Prud'homme, and Kamila Pecher in the library – for their guidance and good temper in retrieving endless Eland Collection books from the attic. And I want to pay tribute to a handful of archivists who went above and beyond in providing support, namely Helen Ellis-Smith for making me as welcome as she did at the Wates Archive; and Zoe Hendon and Claire Isherwood at the wonderful Middlesex University Museum of Domestic Design and Architecture (now sadly to close). Thanks in abundance must also go to the teams at Archives and Collections, the Library of Birmingham; the Cadbury Research Library at Birmingham University; the London Metropolitan Archives; the Modern Records Centre at Warwick University; the National Archives, Kew; Northampton Record Office; the Nottinghamshire Archives; Eve Watson and her colleagues at the Royal Society of Arts; the archivists at the Society for the Protection of Ancient Buildings; those at the Wandsworth Borough Council Heritage Service; and to Professor Simon Pepper for allowing me to use his Pointon Taylor ledger.

At Lund Humphries, I am very grateful indeed to my publisher Val Rose for her optimism, enthusiasm, and good guidance, and to Rebeccah Williams for her unending patience. Sarah Thorowgood and her production colleagues Pam Bertram and Jacqui Cornish have been a joy to work with. Any mistakes are mine alone.

Finally, to my children Tom and Freya, love and gratitude for putting up so affectionately with over two decades of architectural detours and specialist vocabulary. And – most deserving of all – the same to my wife Jane, who never expressed the least weariness at hearing (again) about outshots, bargeboards, or brick bonds. I would not have started and could not have finished my research without her.

PICTURE CREDITS